Readings in African Traditional Religion

Structure, Meaning, Relevance, Future

edited by
E.M. Uka

PETER LANG
Bern · Berlin · Frankfurt a.M. · New York · Paris · Wien

Die Deutsche Bibliothek – CIP-Einheitsaufnahme

Readings in African traditional religion : structure, meaning,
relevance, future / ed. by E. M. Uka. - Bern ; Berlin ;
Frankfurt a.M. ; New York ; Paris ; Wien : Lang, 1991
   ISBN 3-261-03911-6
NE: Uka, Emele Mba [Hrsg.]

© Peter Lang, Inc., European Academic Publishers, Bern, 1991

Printed in Germany

DEDICATION

This book is dedicated to:

The Presbyterian Church in Canada,
The Church of Scotland,
The Presbyterian Church in U.S.A.
and the Presbyterian Church in Nigeria
in deep appreciation of their contributions
to the World in manifesting the
Divine to the human.

TABLE OF CONTENTS

PART FOUR - IMPACT ON:

PART FIVE - ENCOUNTER WITH MODERN WORLD

EPILOGUE

INTRODUCTION AND OVERVIEW

The number of articles pouring out on African Traditional Religion (ATR) is now legion, the voice of scholars clamouring to be heard is babel. This volume, therefore, attempts to create some order out of what otherwise could lead to a veritable disorder.

To this end, six major sections have been carved out to cover the spectrum on the subject. The first section is on Definitions, and tells us about how the African perceives his world, the meaning and sources of his traditional religion and his conception of God and man.

The second section looks at ATR in terms of its academic and scholarly perspectives, such as historical, Western, academic and methodological perspectives.

The third section examines some vital elements like the theology, spirituality, ethics, and salvific value of African Traditional Religion. The section seeks to prove that ATR has all that it takes to be an authentic religion.

Section four reviews the impact of ATR on its environment as it bears on family life, nation building, education and health.

Section five deals with ATR and its encounter with world missionary religions like christianity and Islam.

The final section which ends with a selected bibliography on the subject considers the future and the way foreword for ATR.

It could be said that these sections provide the frame work within which materials on the subject could be placed.

PART ONE

TOWARDS A DEFINITION

PRECARIOUS VISION: THE AFRICAN'S PERCEPTION OF HIS WORLD

by

O.U. Kalu

Very often after arriving at a new place, the dominant feeling is one of being hemmed in. This is quickly followed
by attempts to establish familiarity with the new location and,
in common parlance, "get to know the place". As soon as familiarity is established, a sense of security is ensured as the mind
automatically arranges the new reality in an orderly fashion. One
gets to know the survival modes (political and cultural) in the
new environment. It is, therefore, a very natural approach to
the study of any culture to describe the way people perceive
their world.

In fact, communities very assiduously preserve their
myths of origin as an explanation of why things are the way
they are. There is nothing peculiarly African about this trait.
The Jewish version is amply illustrated in the Genesis saga. Old
Testament scholars agree that the story of Creation in the Book
of Genesis is not the beginning of the history of Israel; that
history started when the Jews were already settled in Palestine.
Naturally, they wanted to establish who they were and how they
came to be there. The story was that their founding ancestor
was an Aramean, named Abraham. The saga moves through the
sojourn in Egypt, a miraculous rescue, untold years of wandering
in the wilderness (symbolically expressed as forty years) and the
settlement in Palestine. The climax of the story, of course, is
the miraculous way in which they conquered and settled the land.
The explanation was a convenant made with Yahweh who sup-
planted other gods (both Jewish and Palestinian) and became the
ONE and TRUE GOD, the source of Jewish uniqueness. The story
did not end there. One step backwards, the origin was stretched
to the foundation of the whole inhabited earth and the cosmos
by the powerful word of mouth of that ONE and TRUE GOD.

The evidence that the story was developed and perpetuated is clear in Deuteronomy 26:5ff. which gives a record
of a response to be made in a festival liturgy:

> And you shall make response before the Lord Your
> God, "A wandering Aramean was my father; and he

went into Egypt and sojourned there, few in number;
and there he became a nation, great, mighty, and
populous".

And so the myth of origin ran to conclusions which were drawn
from it. The basic conclusion was a perception of the world in
which God was Supreme and in which the relationships between
man and nature and between man to man were governed by the
sovereignty of god and His Convenant with men. The conclusions
are spelled out in Joshua 24.

    If we move nearer home, we find similar accounts.
For the Yoruba, it was the enterprising god, Obatala, who first
thought of creating a habitable world out of the watering
domain of Olokun. Olodumare permitted it and Obatala sojourned
to earth by a chain, landed at Ile-Ife and succeeded in creating
a world. However, while on a return trip to the abode of the
gods to report his success, jealously enraged, Olokun flooded the
new earth. The destitute first men had to bargain with shrewd
Eshu to carry their message to the Olodumare. Orumnila inter-
vened and the earth was saved. There are variations on the story
as details and twists are added as embellishments.

    The Igbo tell it a little differently but in an identically
incredible vein: the first man came down by a ladder to find
a watery, marshy earth. Somehow an Awka smith was sent to
use his fiery bellow to dry the earth. The problem was now how
to feed the new human beings. Their leader, Eri, was asked to
kill his eldest son and daughter and plant their heads. From the
head of the son sprouted yam and from the head of the daughter
sprouted coco-yam. Eri distributed the new products. Even today,
yam is the prince of agricultural products and the aym-growing
cycle dominates time reckoning and festivals. Just as an aside,
the custom was established that the progeny of Eri, the Nri
people, receive free food all over Igboland.

    One could multiply the stories from the rest of Africa.
The two variations range from myths when the earth and sky
were clearly demarcated to those when the sky was once-upon-
a-time near to the earth. It is said that a woman touched the
sky with her dirty hands and the sky abashedly retreated upwards.
Some less chauvinist accounts explain the separation by the evil
doings of men which scandalized the sky - the abode of the gods.

    It is palpable that as the myth spins out the outlines
of a cosmology (which is the impressive term for worldview)
emerges. Africa is vast in size, population and varieties of tribes.
Myths of origin abound and the varieties in ecology make it pos-

sible for different peoples to perceive their worlds differently. It is essential to stress that world-views are the intellectual or rational explanations of the order which undergird human lives and environments. The pattern of this underlying order could be derived from the myths, taboos, customs and proverbs of a community. The functions of world-views are that first they assist man to explain reality. The insecure feeling of being lost in an inexplicable, uncontrollable cosmos is thus taken care of. Secondly, such intellectual ordering of reality makes it possible to predict spacetime events and, finally, men can then exert control over these events. Thus, social order, various forms of divinations and the quest for survival and happiness are possible if men understand what makes the world tick and can control such forces. A world-view is the unified picture of the cosmos explained by a system of concepts which order the natural and social rhythms and the place of individuals and communities in them.

From the myriads of cosmologies a model can be constructed representing the basic and common features in Africa. If one must begin by reference to a white man, the German philosopher, Kant, observed that the two basic concepts which encapsulate most other experiences are those of Time and Space.

The concept of Time among Africans is currently a subject of debate among scholars. The argument is over the perception of distant Future, or lack of it, in the African mind. Some would, out of nationalistic fervor, wish to argue that Africans conceive of time just as Europeans do in a chronological fashion, moving from the past through the present to the future. Others maintain that the African does not really pay attention to chronometric reckoning of time. Thus, we have developed what is called "African Time" which often means showing up at a function many hours after the appointed time. This last is a moot point. More seriously, it is recognized that Africans conceive Time differently from Westerners. To Westerners time moves in a continuum or linear fashion thus:

Past   Present   Future

The Greek word for it is kronos, hence the English chronometric, chronology, chronometer which are all related to the linear measurement of Time.

Africans, on the contrary, reckon the movement of Time in a cyclical fashion. Perhaps this is derived from the cyclical agricultural seasons. Mircea Eliade has described a from of time-reckoning among non-complex societies as based on the Myth of Eternal Return. This myth suffused Greek and Roman thought: the fiery chariot, the Sun, goes down under the sea at the end of a day's journey and rises again bright in the morning. The seasons of the year repeat in an eternal cycle. Non-complex societies perceive in the movements of these natural phenomena the eternal order which governs the universe.

Time is reckoned differently by Africans who measure it in non-abstract terms. It is never nine o'clock in the morning; rather, it is that time when the sun begins to climb to her seat. Time is measured by events. The Greek word is Kairos. Time, is therefore, humanized and related to specific events. If an African went home to his village and some inquired as to when he returned, he would reply that he came home when the priests of Ifejioku first ate the new yam. The inquirer would recognize the time even though it is definitely non-specific, especially as the ceremony lasts for two native weeks. Time is peopled with events related to the movements of the sun, moon, important events in the lives of the family, clan and village-group and socio-economic events such as market days, etc. It is never abstract.

It is this fact which makes the conception of the future somewhat problematic precisely because events which form the point of reference have not occurred. The future is unreal because it does not contain events. Larger periods are counted by some in terms of successive age sets and are given the names of these age sets. Short-term future is obviously projected but the indefinite future is atrophied. There is a tendency to count backwards; hence the future is assimilated into the past. Christian scholars have explored the effect of this conception of Time on the important concept of Heaven. Scientists have wondered whether this materialistic conception of Time hinders development in theory and innovation in the physical sciences.

African conception of Space is just as problematic. In oral interviews the aged preservers of native wisdom may end up pointing to the sky, earth and underground as the abode of the gods. The implications are that there are three dimensions of Space. The Sky is the abode of the Supreme Being and major divinities. The Earth is inhabited by the Earth-Goddess, nature spirits, patron spirits of human activities and ecology and, of course, human beings. In the World Beneath are the ancestors and the guardian spirits of human beings, for instance, Chi the

14

daemon spirit of the individual. The Earth is invested like a besieged city by evil spirits. These spirits are those of men and women who (a) lived bad lives during their sojourn to Earth, (b) died "bad deaths" through smallpox, accidents, lightning or any others which are inexplicable, (c) did not receive proper burial rites. In obvious anger they would return to haunt their kin-groups for neglect. A fourth category refers to children who make pacts to visit the earth briefly. The Yoruba call them **Abiku** and the Igbo, **Ogbanje.** Worship and taboos are designed primarily to protect man from evil forces and to harness the good things of life.

The Supreme Being is the creator of all things, the protector of all beings, and the giver of all goodness. But he is, for the most part, not worshipped directly because other divinities and spirits perform this role. Confusion exists whether the African God is a remote god, minding his own business and leaving the earth to ancestral spirits and others. The words in prayers (liturgy) definitely refer to his presence but in few parts of Africa are altars erected for his worship.

In spite of the remarkable awareness of spiritual forces, the African places man at the centre of the universe. He is a noble, rational creature. Yet there is the Job-Like irony that his fate is determined by a personal god whom the Igbo call chi and the Tallensi, Yin. Nuor yin or BAD DESTINY spells failure in life. Man himself is made up of his body, personality soul, the motivating breath of life or spirit soul, and that important element, blood. The Akan of Ghana with a more precise language structure distinguish between sunsum (personality soul) and 'kra (spirit soul). One conjectures that it is the personality soul which reincarnates. The spirit-soul is the motivating force in life. The blood is like the distributor in a car. The blood also symbolizes the worth of the individual and his link to a kin group. Thus, pacts and expiatory rites are made with blood.

Reincarnation is crucial in understanding the African's perception of man and life. Life flows in a cycle from birth, naming ceremony through puberty rites, marriage, initiations into ascriptive societies, and non-ascriptive or achieved societies, adult roles to death. But death is not a terminus. The personality soul continues to live in the Spirit World until it reincarnates or acquires body again. A new life-sojourn begins. The Spirit World is a Mirror of the Human World with the same topography and similar social organization. Thus, the ancestors are often referred to as the living-dead. As an Ayio (Ghana) Prayer puts it:

Grandfather, do you see this water?
Please take it and give it to Toxla
that he may pour libation to those
who are asleep at Tagba.
This will keep them in the know of all
that we shall be doing,
so that whatever we do,
should bring us peace.

They still take active interest in the human kin-group. Among the Yoruba, the ancestors come back seasonally during the Egungun Festival to warn human beings of the fate which awaits immorality in the Other World. More important, it is believed that the wealthy man on the Earth will retain his social status in the Spirit World; the same holds true for people of inferior social status. This explains certain bizarre funeral rites such as burying slaves alive with their masters or burying treasures with people of high status. There are none of the egalitarian hopes which Christianity offers all the sojourners to the Life Hereafter.

The ethical implications of such a world-view are immense. For one, the African world-view is predominantly religious; both human life and nature are held sacred, intricately interwined and under the governance of the Supreme Being and His multifarious divinities. The predominant attitude is that human existence is precarious because of the machinations of evil spirits. In traditional African communities all forms of misfortunes - illness, death, failure - are explained by the activities of ubiquitous evil spirits, angry gods, revengeful ancestors and Destiny-Evil forces operating through man and nature. Thus, lightning, falling trees, animals and rivers could harm or kill the star-struck human. Witches are, in fact, unsuspecting and involuntary agents but sorcerers are more deliberate, voluntary, and ill-disposed.

In our traditional setting, men were faced with uncontrollable forces of nature; their reaction was to imbue these with spirits and to seek the aid of good gods, patron ancestors, magic, divination and elaborate propitiatory rituals as counters to the evil forces. Worship in such settings emphasized the wish of the client. A votary would variously plead with patron gods, placate evil spirits and end by threatening the god that if he failed to perform, his grove would be overgrown with grass. After all, what use could there be in a god or a charm which failed to yield dividends on the amount of energy and money spent on it? The typical attitude is expressed in a Ghanain prayer which asks the ancestors to:

Please make us all very fruitful
and give long life and prosperity to us all,
If anyone wishes death to this lineage
may he also suffer death.
The wicked people are like fire
which must be extinguished
before the good people enjoy a perfect peace.

This perception of human existence meant that the moral order must be maintained so that men can live in peace and have abundant life.

Our forebears, therefore, constructed a number of controls. The first was to emphasize character. Character was neither beauty nor wealth. Admittedly, beauty and success in farming, hunting and trading were regarded as a favourable nod from the gods and were rewarded with titles.

Character however, referred to moral uprightness, peace with gods and peace with men. Purity was essential in blocking the anger of gods or the ruin of evil spirits. Hence, seasonal festivals included purification rites and the onslaught of epidemics, a bad harvest, or incessant disasters were countered with divination and special purification rites. Secondly, they devised elaborate taboos which spelt out the bounds of acceptable behaviour in the economic, political and social lives of the community. A host of ritual officials underwent formal and informal training to mediate on behalf of the community because purity and proper ritual techniques were considered essential for their efficacy. Careless ritual or immoral behaviour nullified the action and endangered the life of the officiant. An inexplicable thunder could kill the offending priest.

In conclusion, the African perceived his world as a moral order, one in which his well-being or failure could be determined by the inscurtable will of the gods. He did not reject the gods by an asertion of humanity and thereby, as Prometheus, damning them. Rather, he evolved elaborate rituals and taboos with which he sought to manipulate the good gods for protection and abundant life. Human existence, in spite of occasional joys, was perceived as being precarious.

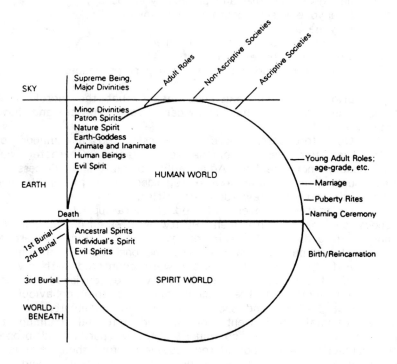

Diagrammatic representation of the African world-view.

TOWARDS UNDERSTANDING AFRICAN TRADITIONAL RELIGION

by

P.A. Dopamu

A. Introduction

Today, the term "African Traditional Religion" is a familiar one. The subject is studied in many African Universities, Colleges, Schols of Basic Studies, Seminaries and Colleges of Theology. In recent times, many European and American Universities have separate Institutes for the study of African Religion and Culture. In this way, we find that there is an increasing global interest in African Traditional Religion today.

But despite this global interest, and despite the volume of literature available on the subject, African Traditional Religion is still viewed or treated with disdain not by a few people, including educated Africans. This disdainful attitude stems not so much from the people's preconceived ideas about the religion, as from complete ignorance and faulty understanding of it. Preconceived erroneous notions can easily be corrected in the face of requisite understanding and realization of truth; so also can correct information remove abject ignorance on any given subject. The aim of this paper, therefore, is to present African Traditional Religion in its correct and true perspective.

The faulty understanding of African Traditional Religion has been inherited from the earlier writers on the subject. It is true that we owe a lot to these early writers for the wealth of information we gather from their writings, particularly on African ways of life and practices. Since Africans themselves had not written anything about their systems of thought, many of what we know of them today come to us through the arduos tasks of Ethnographers, Anthropologists, Missionaries, Explorers, Traders, and Travellers. These had put on record what they saw Africans do or practise, as well as what they heard Africans say. They had also interpreted these practices and sayings in their own way.

However, there are misinterpretations of African ways of life. Most early accounts by European Travellers, missionaries and colonial agents are generally unreliable in the sense that they are based on inaccurate information, cultural prejudice, and biased comparison. As Hassing has rightly observed:

> The study of African religion in the now somewhat remote past suffered partly because of lack of real knowledge and factual information, and also because of the often inadequate, notions of the earlier writers. The result was sometimes an inadequate, negative, or even false picture which saw little that was good in African religious life and thinking. (1)

We may quote a few examples by way of illustration. The explorer Sir Samuel Baker, writing in 1867 about the people of southern Sudan, said:

> Without any exception, they are without a belief in a Supreme Being, neither have they any form of worship or idolatry; nor is the darkness of their minds enlightened by even a ray of superstition. The mind is as stagnant as the morass which forms its puny world. (2)

Sir Richard Burton, the famous explorer, writing about West Africa said:

> The negro is still at that rude dawn of faith-fetishism and he has barely advanced to idolatry. He has never grasped the ideas of a personal Deity, a duty in life, a moral code, or a shame of lying. He rarely believes in a future state of rewards and punishments, which, whether true or not, are infallible indices of human progress. (3)

Burton thought that the African brain was too small for civilised development. In his own opinion, once an African had become adult, "his mental development is arrested, and thenceforth he grows backwards instead of forwards". (4)

The question may be asked: since much spade work has been done by scholars, Europeans and Africans, to correct the wrong impression people have about Africa, and since these old views have vanished from serious discussion, why do we need to recall them here? It is important to mention them here since, in the words of Davidson, "they still retain a kind of underground existence". (5) Thus many people today, Westerners as well as

20

Africans, still continue to regard African Traditional Religion as worthless and devoid of spiritual value.

In consonance with our previously stated aim, this paper will provide a framework for understanding African Traditional Religion, interpreting it in the light of its own Supreme worth to the people who profess it and, also, pin-pointing whatever is considered to be of lasting value in it. If we look at African Traditional Religion with blinkers, and from the standpoint of one who has a biased mind against the religion, we shall not see its value beyond our nose. But if we look at it with sympathy and reverence, humility and patience, and with a mind free of bias and prejudice, we may discover in the religion, a treasure of insights that could enable all other religions to come together, see together, learn together and indeed, converge more closely on fundamental issues.

B.   What is African Traditional Religion?

African Traditional Religion comprises the religious beliefs and practices of the Africans which had been in existence from time immemorial, and are still adhered to today by many Africans. It is the indigenous religion of the Africans which has been handed down by their forebears. That is why we agree with Awolalu when he says:

> When we speak of African Traditional Religion we mean the indigenous religion of the Africans. It is the religion that has been handed down from generation to generation by the forbears of the present generation of Africans. It is not a fossil religion (a thing of the past) but a religion that Africans today have made theirs by living it and practising it. (6)

In speaking of African Traditional Religion therefore, the following points should be made clear. First, African Traditional Religion is a revealed religion, but it has no historical founder like Christianity, Islam, Buddhism and Confucianism. The religion is revealed in the sense that it came into existence, like any other religion, as a result of human experience of the mystery of the universe. In an attempt to solve the riddle of the mystery of the universe, man everywhere has asked questions, searched for answers to

21

these questions, and come to the conclusion that this mystery must be a supernatural power, to whom belong both the visible and the invisible. This type of experience is equally true of the forebears of the Africans.

But it is the nature of man to respond to such human experience. Thus from the beginning, the forbears of the Africans had reflected upon their experience and responded rather intuitively, to the situations that encompassed their experiences. We must note that each African people must have responded independently to the experiences of their immediate environment. For this reason, we must expect to find both similarities and differences in African Traditional Religion. So also must we realise that ideas and practices which could not adequately provide the spiritual needs of man must have passed away in the process of intellectual, cultural and spiritual growth.

Secondly, African Traditional Religion is traditional. The word "traditional" may connote something that came into being long ago, something that belonged to the era of "primitivity". But African Traditional Religion is "traditional" not because it is fossil, static and incapable of adaptation to new situations and changes, but because it is a religion that originated from the peoples' environment and on their soil. It is neither preached to them nor imported by them. Africans are not converted into it. Each person is born into it, lives it, practises it, and is proud to make it his own. Thus the word "traditional" serves the purpose of distinguishing African Religion from any other religion that has been brought to the people through missionary zeal and by propagation.

Thirdly, African Traditional Religion has no written literature or sacred scriptures or credal forms. It is an essentially oral tradition. All we know of the religion, therefore, comes to us through oral traditions-myths and legends, stories and folktales, songs and dances, liturgies and rituals, proverbs and pithy-sayings, adages, and riddles. Some of these oral traditions are preserved for us in arts and crafts, symbols and emblems, names of people and places, shrines and sacred places. Works of art are not merely for entertainment or for pleasing the eye. But they usually convey religious feelings, sentiments, ideas or truths.

To the Africans, these oral traditions are veritable vehicles of transmission of knowledge. As Idowu points out, these oral traditions are our only means of knowing anything at all of the peoples' interpretation of the universe and the supersensible world, and what they think and believe about the relationship

22

between the two. (7) But oral traditions are sometimes subject to additions and substractions, modifications and distortions, exaggerations and confussions, to the effect that we find it difficult to separate truth from fiction. In this case, information passed on orally may not be a safe bet for accuracy. But despite the limitation of oral tradition, it is certain that the basic and relevant message of African Traditional Religion has been passed on unhampered from one generation to another by words of mouth.

One other question we must ask is whether we can speak of a unified African Religion, or whether it would be more appropriate to speak of African Traditional Religions. We are aware of the fact that there is a diversity of beliefs and practices among the various ethnic groups in Africa. Even, within an ethnic group, we have significant differences. For example, divinities among the Akan of Ghana are not as pronounced as among the Yoruba of Nigeria. And among the Yoruba, the divinities prominent in one area may be given little or no attention in another area.

But despite these differences, there is an underlying identity in the traditional religion of the Africans that enables us to say with conviction that African Traditional Religion is a unified religion. There is a regular rhythm in the general pattern of the people's beliefs and practices. This regular rhythm is the universal belief in the Supreme Being as an integral part of African world view and practical religion. In the words of Idowu:

> We find that in Africa, the real cohesive factor of religion is the living God and that without this one factor, all things would fall to pieces. And it is on this ground especially - this identical concept that we can speak of the religion of Africa in the singular. (8)

So far, we have shown that the Africans have their own living religion. Whatever might have been the various attitudes of foreign investigators therefore, and whatever might have been their errors of identity, we know to the contrary that Africans have a concept of God and that this is expressed in their religion. Those who have approached the study of African peoples with caution, reverence, imaginative sympathy, appreciative understanding, and perhaps, experienced some of what they studied, have come to realize that Africans are "incurably religious". It does not need any apologetics to prove that religion permeates African life and activity. From the womb to the grave, religion governs everything.

What Idowu says of the Yoruba is equally true of the whole of Africa:

> The real Keynote of the life of the Yoruba is neither in their noble ancestry nor in the past deeds of their heroes. The Keynote of their life is their religion.
> In all things, they are religious. Religion forms the foundation and the all governing principle of life for them. As far as they are concerned, the full responsibility of all the affairs of life belongs to the Deity ... Through all the circumstances of life, through all its changing scenes, its joys and troubles, it is Deity who is in control. (9)

Mbiti also emphasises this point when he says:

> Wherever the Africa is, there is his religion: he carries it to the fields where he is sowing seeds or harvesting a new crop; he takes it with him to the beer party or to attend a funeral ceremony; and if he is educated, he takes religion with him to the examination room at school or in the University; if he is a politician, he takes it to the house of parliament. (10)

Every member of each locality is inescapably bound up with the religious systems of the community. And it is hard to think of any African community where we have irreligious people. This is why, when Christianity and Islam were brought to the African peoples, the two world religions were readily accommodated and integrated into their pattern of life. The Africans needed no "sermon" to establish the fact of the existence of God.

C. The Salient beliefs of the Africans

The detailed description of African Traditional Religion is beyond the scope of this short paper. However, we are in a position to give, succinctly, the fundamental beliefs of the Africans.

a. God

1. His names and attributes

Throughout Africa, there is the belief in One Supreme Being. Each ethnic group has a name for the Supreme Deity. We have **Olorun** among the Yoruba, **Chukwu** among the Igbo, **Soko** among the Nupe, **Nyame** among the Akan, **Osanobwa** among the Edo, **Mawu** among the Ewe, **Ngewo** among the Mende, **Yataa** among the Kono, **Kwoth** among the Nuer, **Unkulunkulu** among the Zulu, **Kalunga** among the Ovambo, **Akongo** among the Ngombe, and **Mulungu** among the Akamba, to name a few.

The fact that Africans have names for God according to their locality indicates that God is not merely an abstract concept, a vague entity, but a veritable reality. Such names of God are pregnant with meaning. They tell us something about the people's concept of God. They describe the nature and character of God. In them, many of what we know about God - His attributes, His works, His purpose, His relationship to man and to divinities - are found. For example, the Igbo name of God, Chineke, means "the Source Being Who creates all things", while the Edo name for God, Osanobwa, means "the Source of all things Who carries and sustains the world or universe".

There are also attributes of God which show, unmistakably, that God is a reality to the Africans. These attributes are words or phrases ascribing traits, properties, qualities, or characteristics to the Supreme Being. Such attributes are necessarily anthropomorphic. These appendages and appelations tell what the people really think God is, what they consider to be His nature, and what they believe to be His role and position in relation to the world and the supersensible realm. Thus, Africans believe that God is unique, Supreme, King, Creator, Judge, Omnipotent, Immortal and Holy.

2. The Worship of God

Many foreign investigators gave the impression that God is not worshipped by the Africans. A.B. Ellis, D. Westermann, P. Baudin (11) and many others thought that God, as known to the Africans is not an object of practical religion.

Certain aspects of African beliefs and practices apparently lead to this view. Firstly, there are stories telling of God's withdrawal from the affairs of the world. Secondly, the divinities feature prominently in African Traditional Religion. Everywhere we have their temples and shrines, images and emblems, priests and priestesses. People pray to them from time to time and they receive regular sacrifices.

But this is almost not the case with regard to the Supreme Deity. Many African societies neither have images of God nor dedicate temples to Him, and priests of God are hard to come by in many localities. In consequence of this, organized worship of the Supreme Being is not common.

But Africans have reasons for these apparent testimonies. Firstly, the Supreme Being is not represented by an image because He is unique and incomparable. In the African thought, we cannot liken Him to anything.

Secondly, people do not build temples for God's worship because they think of God as omnipresent. And since He is everywhere, He cannot be localized. That is why the Yoruba describe God as **A te rere kaye** "He who spreads over the whole extent of the earth." This means that Deity is so great, and so majestic that He cannot be confined within space.

Thirdly, the divinities who receive the day-to-day sacrifices are only approached as intermediaries. As we shall see later, they are only ministers of the Supreme Being, and they have no absolute existence, power or authority. That is why every act of worship or ritual before any of the divinities, has an ultimate reference to the Supreme God Who must sanction it. The Yoruba, for example, say **A se A se** means "May it be sanctioned by God" or, "May it receive approval".

However, it is wrong to say that God is not worshipped by Africans. By worship, we do not only mean the act of adoration which is restricted to a particular location like the temple or shrine. We also mean the act of communicating with the divine. Prayers and offerings are two essential elements of African worship. People take the advantage of God's omnipresence and pray to Him everywhere. For example, among the Yoruba, there are ejaculatory praises of God. If a Yoruba is asked the question: "Do you wake up well?", he will say: **Mo dupe lowo Olorun** - "Thank God" or "Praise God". Among the Kono, the site of a new farm is selected with a prayer first to God, and then to the ancestral spirits. (12) The Mende end prayers with the formula: **Ngewo jahu** - "God grant it". There are also ejaculatory prayers to Ngewo, and these are usually for deliverance or blessings. (13) All these show that Africans believe that God is everywhere, and that He is close to hear, and ready to help.

Beside these short, spontaneous, ejaculatory prayers to God, there are societies where people worship God directly and make regular prayers to Him. These notable exceptions can be illustrated in the beliefs and practices of the Ashanti in West Africa, and also of East Africa.

Nearly every Ashanti compound has an altar dedicated to God. It is a particular tree, called **Nyame dua** - "God's tree". The **Nyame dua** is planted in front of the house. On its forked branches, there is usually a basin in which are placed God's offerings. hardly a day goes-by without offerings being placed in the pot for Nyame. (14) Nyame also has His priests, temples and festival. The festival usually takes place on a Saturday, which is the sacred day of Nyame.

The Nandi pray daily to Assista, the Supreme God, often in the morning and the evening. An early morning prayer uttered by the old men is as follows:

> Assista, in this way have I made my prayer to you. Keep watch over my children and my cattle. I have come near to you morning and evening. Assista, I have made my prayer to you. Do not now say, I am tired. O our spirits, keep watch over us who are living on the earth, and do not say: We are put to death by men. (15)

The Nandi also pray directly to God at birth, four months after birth, at planting and harvesting times, when building a new house, when making things, and when the men are away fighting. (16)

Thus, to say that Africans do not worship God is to ignore the fact that African worship is a varied and complex affair through which an act of communication and communion between man and the supersensible world is achieved. Africans communicate with God, both in times of stress and material well-being, and they believe that God is the Disposer Supreme.

b. Divinities and Ancestors

The divinities are spiritual beings. They share aspects of the Supreme Being in consequence of which they become gods with small letter "g". That is why it is not correct to say that they are created. It will be correct to say that they emanated from the Supreme Deity, or that they were engendered by Him, brought forth by Him, or came into being in consequence of Him.

In other words, the divinities have the attributes, qualities or characteristics of the Supreme Being, and they are in consequence, off-springs of God. Thus the Edo say that Olokun, the arch-divinity, is the son of Osanobwa; the Akan say that **Abosom** (divinities) are the sons or children of Nyame; the Ewe say that the **vodu** (divinities) are the children of Mawu-Lisa who is also the twin of Nana Buluku; and the Yoruba usually describe Orisa-nla as the son or deputy of Olodumare.

The divinities were brought into being to serve the will of God in the theocratic government of the world. One important truth about African Traditional Religion is that the divinities are the objective phenomena of the religion. The divinities being real to the people, are believed to exist with definite functions or duties. That is why they are described as ministers or functionaries with portfolio in the theocratic government of the world. Thus Songo (Yoruba), Amadioha (Igbo), Sokogba (Nupe), and Xevioso (Ewe) are divinities associated with thunder.

The divinities also serve as intermediaries between God and man. God is frequently worshipped through them and they receive day-to-day sacrifices. In point of fact, people regard them as the convenient and appropriate channels through which they can reverence the exaltedness of the Almighty. But they are usually regarded as means to an end and not ends in themselves.

However, we must not blink the fact that there are times when people regard a divinity as an end in himself. This may happen in a situation where a divinity is credited with miraculous powers. And those who benefit from him may so much adore him that they forget that God is the Ultimate - Fountain of all benefits from whom the divinities receive their power and authority. But, whatever power may be attributed to the divinities, whatever benefits people may have received from them, people ultimately turn to God in times of difficulties and troubles, when all else has failed, and when the divinities themselves cannot offer any help. That is why we agree with Idowu when he says about the Yoruba:

> Olodumare is the Fountain of all benefits. He is the Author and Giver of all the good things that man can possess - children, wealth, possessions, good living, good character, everything that exists for the benefits of man. It is a strong belief of the Yoruba that both divinities and men draw from His inexhaustible providence. (17)

28

The ancestors are regarded as spirits in the sense that they are no longer visible. But they are not spirits in the sense that they are like divinities or God. Africans distinguish between ancestors, divinities and God. "Deity and the divinities are distinctly, out-and-out, of the supersensible world while the ancestors are related to the living community in a way that cannot be claimed for Deity or the divinities who are definitely of a different order". (18) In other words, the ancestors are still regarded as heads and members of their earthly families. They are regarded as ever-present among the families to which they belonged while they were living human beings. Thus "a cardinal fact of African life and thought is that the living and dead together form one community whose members are mutually dependent upon each other". (19) That is why Mbiti (20) has described the ancestors as the "living-dead".

Africans think of the ancestors as having the same emotions as the living members of the community. They can bless their folk or affect them adversely, they can be jealous or fickle, they can bring peace or disaster. It is for this reason that the living take care not to offend them. To neglect the ancestors is to court disaster. Africans therefore, believe that communion and communication between those who are alive here on earth and those who have passed to the great beyond must be made in their quest for well-being. Africans approach the ancestors as intermediaries between men and God or divinities. They are remembered from time to time. Oaths are taken in their names. And when they are offended, they usually demonstrate their feelings by some vindictive action. They are only placated with abundant offerings.

c. The moral order

So far, we have seen that God is the Creator of the universe, according to African belief. We have also seen that God brought the divinities into being to help Him in the theocratic government of the world. Africans, however, believe that for the orderly maintenance of the world, the divinities and ancestors have laid down norms and set patterns or codes of conduct. They know that in order to sustain the well-being of human society, certain things which are morally disapproved by the Deity must not be done. These are what the Yoruba call **EEwo** - "Things forbidden, things not done." (21) It is realised that the action or conduct of any member of the community can affect the other members for good or for evil.

These norms and codes of conduct can be seen as moral values. From the beginning, God has put His law in man's heart, and has endowed man with the sense of right and wrong. Man's conscience has always instructed him on this. Such things which are forbidden and must not be done are taboos.

Taboos can be interpreted as prohibited actions, the breaking of which is followed by the supernatural penalty. The breaking of taboos is regarded as sin.

Some investigators thought that either Africans have no concept of sin or they only have an imperfect notion of it. For example, J.K. Parratt discussing the sense of sin and morality among the Yoruba, said:

> The sense of sin among the Yoruba, if any, is nothing comparable with the developed ethical conception of sin which is to be found in both the Old Testament and the New Testament. (22)

This statement is neither true of the Yoruba nor other African peoples. Africans have always had the sense of sin. This may even be seen in the various stories of creation we have in Africa. These stories give us the impression that there was once a kind of "Golden Age", something of a "Garden-of-Eden" when, in the Yoruba tradition, (23) everybody could make a journey to the spiritual world and back as he liked, having immediate, direct contact with God; when, according to the Mende, man could ask God for anything and have it. (24) This is saying that from the beginning, God maintained communion and fellowship with man.

However, all African stories of creation are universally agreed that something happened which disrupted the existing peace of the created order, and put a barrier between the Supreme Being and man. What happened is variously told in the traditions of the Africans. The Yoruba will say that "a greedy person helped himself to too much food from heaven", or, that "a woman with a dirty hand soiled the face of heaven." (25) In Northern Nyasaland, (26) it is believed that man's habit of quarrelling, with ungrateful cries, eventually drove God to seek peace and quiet above. The Mende (27) believe that God withdrew because man and woman came to Him so frequently that He thought they would wear Him out with their requests. The Yao (28) believe that God withdrew to heaven because man set the grasslands alight.

30

The motif of all these stories is all one. As Idowu puts it, "man sinned against the Lord of Heaven and there was immediately a barrier which cut him off from the unrestricted bliss of heaven. The privilege of free intercourse, of man taking the bounty of heaven as he liked, disappeared". (29) In other words, things went well between God and man in the beginning, but man ruined it all by his perversity. It was man's sin which provoked God's departure.

Sin is fundamentally the performance of acts of which God disapproves. It is man's spontaneous act of disobedience to God. The sanctions and norms (or taboos) are recognised as the approved standard of social and religious conduct on the part of individuals in society. "A breach of, or failure to adhere to, the sanctions is sin, and this incurs the displeasure of Deity and His functionaries. Sin is, therefore, doing that which is contrary to the will and directions of Deity. It includes any immoral behaviour, ritual mistakes, and offences against God or man, breach of covenant, breaking of taboos and doing anything regarded as abominable and polluting. We cannot speak of sin in isolation - it has got to be related to God and man". (30)

Among the Yoruba, it is believed that an evil doer is ultimately punished by God. Gos is regardes as **A–da–ke–da–jo** - "He who executes judgment in silence". And the Yoruba say: **A mookun jale, bi oba aye ko ri o, Oba toke n wo o** - "You who steal in the cover of the night, know you assuredly that if the earthly king does not see you, the heavenly king (i.e. God) does". In other words, whatever man does, whether openly or secretly, God sees and passes judgment.

In general, African people believe that morality and sin go together. Morality enhances God's fellowship and maintains the well-being of the society. But sin isolates man from God and disrupts his well-being as well as that of the society in which he lives.

Furthermore, people believe that it is God who ultimately punishes sin, though He may use other agents in the execution of His purpose. God is believed to be the impartial Judge. His judgement is regarded as absolute, sure and inescapable. And that is because He is ever-present, all-knowing and all-seeing.

We must, however, know that God's reaction to sin is not just to punish it. He has given room for reparation and the removal of sin. That is why when people know that they have committed some sin or violated any of the norms, they do all things possible to remove the stain in order to avert the attendant doom or remove the existing suffering.

What is actually done depends on the nature of the sin or suffering. The sinner may be purified by a diviner or priest, by undertaking a ritual washing in a river; he may confess his faults and make amends - for example, it is believed that a woman that commits adultery may suffer in childbirth, and if she finds the pains of labour grievous, she will immediately confess to the midwife any adulterous acts she may have committed. The sin and its consequences become less by being confessed.

The sinner may also employ propitiatory sacrifice to restore his well-being, especially if the offended divinity is known. In addition to any of the fore-going exercises, the sinner may use magic and medicine to restore his well-being, especially if a fault is attended by sickness. This is why among the Nuer, "medicine, aspersions, fumigations and other modes of expulsion and cleaning are used in addition to the atoning act of sacrifice." (31) Even when people do not have a sense of guilt, they still use magic and medicine to ensure total well-being. That is why medicine is not only therapeutic (curative) but also prophylactic (preventive).

Magic, on the other hand, is used to avert unseen dangers and all untoward happenings. For example, among the Yoruba, we have **arobi** (magic that removes evil things from one's way), **isora** (magic that protects the body against harm), or **Owo** (magic that protects one against all untoward happenings). In fact, magic and medicine are closely related to religion, and they form an element of African Traditional Religion. But their full discussion is beyond the scope of this paper.

d. The here-after

Africans believe that life here on earth is not interminable. They know that the inevitable phenomenon called death will come upon man, who only is a sojourner on God's earth. No matter how long a person lives, death must come as a necessary end.

But the people believe that death is only a transition. It is only a means of passing from the world of the living to the world of the spirits. The people hold the view that when death occurs, the soul of a man who had lived well to a ripe old age, and died a good death, will return to the Supreme Being and continue existence in the abode of the ancestors.

There are good and bad deaths. Bad death includes those who are killed by thunder or small-pox, those who die in water and those who die during pregnancy. Usually these are not given full funeral rites.

As to what happens to the deceased in the afterlife, we have different concepts among African peoples. Some consider that the afterlife itself is not as important as the present life. Some believe that the good people will reincarnate while the bad will be banished or become ghosts that haunt desolate places. In most cases, the notion of the afterlife has meaning only in concrete terms in relation to the present life of the community. That is why the ancestors are usually referred to as "father" or "mother", such titles as they bore while still human beings.

However, there are notable exceptions to the foregoing concept. For example among the Yoruba ofNigeria, and the Dogon of Mali, speculation about the meaning of human existence is projected forward to a distant and transcendent future. In other words, we have eschatological systems which tell of immortality of the soul or final judgement.

The Yoruba eschatology consists of three major phases: separation of the deceased, transformation of the soul, and incorporation of it into the spirit world. The funeral ceremony separates the soul of the deceased from the family and enables it to get into the spirit world. The soul goes before the Supreme Deity and receives judgement in accordance with the belief that "all we do on earth, we shall account for kneeling in heaven". If the deceased had led a good life on earth, his soul will go to **orun rere** (good heaven), where there is no sorrow or suffering. He can choose to reincarnate in his family. But if he had led a bad life, the soul will go to **orun apaadi** (bad heaven; heaven of postsherds) where everything is unpleasantly hot and dry, and where he will remain for ever, because he cannot reincarnate. (32)

On the whole, it appears that many African peoples think of the hereafter as having similar features to those of the present life. They believe that for the good people the quality of the afterlife is an enlarged copy of the life we live here on earth without its labour, sorrows and toils. The community of the ancestors is organised in a fashion similar to earthly society, but with amenities for peaceful enjoyment and happiness considerably enhanced. The real picture of the life after death is therefore, a life of an unending fellowship in the community of one's kith and kin who had gone before into the world beyond.

33

D. Conclusion

In conclusion, let us examine the place of African Traditional Religion in the contemporary world. African Traditional Religion has become the religion of the minority in many parts of Africa, and rapid decline is in the cults in consequence of social advancement, cultural contact with the outside world and the adoption of Christianity and Islam. The religion is today practised mostly by the people in villages and illiterate elements in the urban areas.

Although it is not possible to say with certainty that the religion is practised by enlightened men and women, we strongly believe that there are still highly educated Africans who still derive benefits from the religion in one way or another. There are enlightened people who still remember their ancestors or "pacify" the spirits by going to their home towns to perform the ceremony, although with the pretext that they are "throwing a party" for their people. Also, we still have many educated people that use magic and medicine, though secretly.

In point of fact this is one area of African Traditional Relgion which will persist for a long time to come. This is because, by their nature, Africans usually seek supernatural aids and interventions in all things - they want protection against sorcery, withchcraft, motor accident, misfortune and evil of all kinds; they want success in all undertakings; they want to overcome sterility and barrenness; they want protection against robbers and legal matters. For all these and others, many Africans still resort to the use of magic and traditional medicine, and more often than not, they either really or psychologically derive maximum satisfaction from this art. That is why today, we still have many traditional medicine-men and magicians making their services available to the increasing clientelle.

It is, indeed, high time we made scientific study of the art and found ways and means of improving it so as to suit modern times and meet modern needs.

We are not advocating a return to African Traditional Religion. Indeed, there is no denying the fact that Christianity and Islam are now the dominating religions, particularly in Nigeria and generally in Africa. These are great religions of spiritual value with which African Traditional Religion can no longer compete. But we must point out immediately that these religions originated from particular cultures and developed within particular settings. Not only that, they are heavily tainted with the cultures of those who propagated them so much so that in adopting them, Africans also adopted the cultures of the propagators.

Such acculturation has not helped Àfricans so much, especially where everything African is now seen by Africans themselves as an element of backwardness or primitivity. One is flabbergasted at the rate at which things are going out of order. There is a startling relaxing of traditions, of restraints, and of established law and order. Ideas which, until yesterday, were regarded as inseparable from social decency and justice, which were able to direct and discipline conduct, are increasingly being eroded and swept aside. The good-will of one's neighbour is no longer given due consideration and the emphasis is on the ego.

Self-centredness looms large in the mind of everybody. The rich are feeling the elation of wealth, while the poor are groaning under the consequences of poverty. The priviledged are riding the "docile horses" of the underpriviledged. Those who have power are using it with no moderation. In some corners of Africa, people are subjected to different species of oppression and, indeed, reduced to a state of vassalage. Man has come to regard himself as "coming of age", with the attendant implication that he has less to do with the Source Being, if not altogether to do without Him. And the expression of many people in society is that of good-humoured social indulgence, emboldened by sexual magnetism, insobriety, wickedness, material greed and all vices indescribable.

We can blame all these partly on acculturation and partly on misguided enlightenment. Africans have their own culture which is greatly enshrined in their religion. There is much we can learn from African Traditional Religion, and this will be of supreme value in interpreting the adopted religions. Within the African cultural setting, respect for elders and constituted authority, obedience to law and order, love of one's neighbour and society, living together in harmony and helping one another, are some of the things which African Traditional Religion teaches, emphasises and enjoins on all people to the effect that those who go outside these accepted norms stand the risk of isolation, retribution or divine punishment.

Islam and Christianity also teach all these but with less emphasis on the repercussions or violation, both here on earth and in the world beyond. Thus today, a man may swear rather falsely on the Bible or the Qur'an with the belief that these do not kill; rather than swear falsely on the emblem of Ogun, the god of iron, because he knows that he stands the risk of being hurt by iron implements which are in use in his everyday business.

Not only that, people who belong to the same trade, cult or association usually enter into mutual compact not to do anything detrimental, not only to members but also to members' relations. For example, adultery and cheating were not so rampant as of now, and those guilty of these offences were punished by the society. But today, a man can seduce his friend's wife with impunity.

The more we look at African Traditional Religion with blinkers, the further we are led away from the richness of reality it offers. Though we do not recommend that we should worship the various divinities, we strongly believe that there is no harm in teaching our children that these are real spiritual beings, and that anti-wickedness divinities such as **Songo, Ayelala, Sopono, Buruku, Ogun, Amadioha, Sokogba, Gu** and **Xevioso,** are all out to punish moral offenders such as thieves, robbers (armed or unarmed), cheats, adulterers, exploiters, corrupt and dishonest persons, perpetrators of all vices, and violators of law and order in the society. If children grow to know the repercussions of disobedience, they will always be guided by their conscience whether to do right or wrong. And this may go a long way to eradicate corruption, material greed and lawlessness which are all visible results of immorality in the African society of today.

Footnotes

1   Per Hassing, in the Preface to: McVeigh, M.J., **God in Africa: Conceptions of God in African Traditional Religion and Christianity** Claude Stark, Vermont, 1974, pp. xviif
2   Baker, Samuel, "the Races of the Nile Basin", **Transactions of the Ethnological Society of London,** h.s., 5 (1867), p. 231, as quoted in E.E. Evans-Pritchard, **Theories of Primitive Religion,** The Clarendon Press, Oxford, 1965, p. 7.
3   Burton, R.F., **A Mission To Gelele, King of Dahome,** 2nd ed., (2 vols) Tinsley Brothers, London, 1864, vol. 2, p. 199.
4   Davidson, Basil, **The African Genius,** Little Brown Company, Boston-Toronto, 1969, p. 24.
5   **Ibid.** p. 25.
6   Awolalu, J.O. "Sin and Its Removal in African Traditional Religion", **Journal of the American Academy of Religion,** 44/2 (1976), p. 275.

7   Idowu, E.B. **Olodumare: God in Yoruba Belief,** Longmans, London, 1962, pp. 6ff.
8   Idowu, E.B. **African Traditional Religion, op.cit.** p. 104.
9   Idowu, E.B. **Olodumare, op.cit.** p. 5.
10 Mbiti, J.S., **African Religions and Philosophy,** Heinemann, London, 1969, p. 2.
11 (a) Ellis, A.B., **The Yoruba speaking Peoples,** Chapman and Hall, 1869, p. 2.
    (b) P. Baudin, **Fetishism and Fetish Worshippers,** Benziger Brothers, 1885, pp. 9ff.
    (c) D. Westermann, **African and Christianity,** O.U.P. London, 1973, pp. 65ff.
12 Smith, E.W. (ed): **African Ideas of God,** Edinburgh House Press, London, p. 266.
13 **Ibid.** pp. 280ff.
14 **Ibid.** p. 252f.
15 Smith, E.W.: **African Beliefs and Christians Faith,** Lutterworth Press London, 1936, p. 70.
16 **Ibid.** pp. 71-73.
17 Idowu, E.B.: **Olodumare, op.cit.** p. 53.
18 Idowu, E.B.: **African Traditional Religion, op.cit.** p. 184.
19 Mc Veigh, M.J.: **God in Africa, op.cit.** p. 29
20 Mbiti, J.S.: **Concepts of God in Africa,** S.P.C.K. London, 1970, p. 179.
21 Idowu, E.B.: **Olodumare, op.cit.** p. 146.
22 Parratt, J.K.: "Religious Change in Yoruba Society," **Journal of Religion in Africa,** Vol. 2, 1969, p. 118.
23 Idowu, E.B.: **Olodumare, op.cit.** p. 21.
24 Smith, E.W.: **African Ideas of God, op.cit.** pp. 278f.
25 Idowu, E.B.: **Olodumare, op.cit.** p. 22.
26 Smith E.W.: **African Ideas of God, op.cit.** p. 54.
27 **Ibid.** pp. 278f.
28 Young, T.C.: **Contemporary Ancestors,** London 1940, pp. 144f.
29 Idowu, E.B.: **Olodumare, op.cit.** p. 22.
30 Awolalu, J.O.: "Sin and Its Removal in African Traditional Religion", **op.cit.** p. 279.
31 Evans-Pritchard, E.E.: **Nuer Religion, op.cit.** pp. 192f.
32 Idowu, E.B.: **Olodumare, op.cit.** Chap. 14.

SOURCE: RELIGIOUS UNDERSTANDING AND CO-OPERATION IN NIGERIA
Proceedings of a Seminar Organized by the Department of Religions, University of Ilorin, Ilorin, Nigeria 7th-11th August, 1978 (Edited by I.A.B. Balogun, B.A., Ph.D., (London) Professor and Head of Department.

THE CONCEPT OF GOD IN AFRICAN TRADITIONAL RELIGION

by

E.M. Uka

All African peoples believe in God
They take this belief for granted.
It is at the center of African
Traditional Religion and dominates
all its other beliefs. (1)

The age-long question in African's encounter with the "Christian" West has been; "Is there an African concept of God? If Africans' know God, what God or which God do they know? Their own God or the real God"? (2)

In order to answer this question, Western Missionary scholars according to Professor Bolaji Idowu, invented the title of 'high god' or a Supreme God, any term except that which would identify God in African belief with the Christian God. A.C. Bouquet expressed the Western mind when he observed that it was absurd to equate the African High God with the Deity of the Lord's prayer. (3) So the research on the African concept of God continues, no longer with the onus of proving that the High God or Supreme God is the real Supreme God of the Lord's Prayer but with the fresh demand of having the result of the research published, preached, disseminated, and taught especially in Western schools and sunday schools so that others may discover as Andrew Lang, a Western scholar had discovered that African traditional religion is a "monotheistic religion in which God is believed to be eternal, omniscient, beneficient, moral, omnipotent, creative and satisfying all man's needs - rational, social, moral and ethical." (4)

Granted there is a concept of God in African traditional religion, this paper will proceed to describe the nature and character of this God and the rest of the supernatural world. It will also examine the links between the supernatural world of God and the natural world of men, the media through which the supernatural world is revealed to the African and how they respond to it. The paper will conclude on a strong note that the nature of God as the Supreme Being is the most minimal and fundamental idea about God found in all African societies.

The Controversy on the African Concept of God

Even though Africans believe in God and have a notion of Him as the Supreme Being, Western missionaries and anthropologists who came in contact with Africans doubted if they had any concept of God. For example, the discussion between Edwin Smith (5) (a Missionary in Africa) and Emil Ludwig (an eminent Anthropologist) centered around the claim of Edwin Smith that he was teaching Africans about God Ludwig, according to this report was so perplexed that he wondered "how can untutored African conceive of God?" "Deity he claimed was a philosophical concept, which savages were incapable of framing".

Ludwig was not being unfair to Africans by asking if they were capable of comprehending God. He was merely acting his age, and culture. The 18th - 19th Century Christian West was concerned with clarifying the concept of God in non-European world. The God who was the subject of their concept was the God worshipped by Jews, Christians and Mohammedans, not the God worshipped by Buddhists, Hindus, Parsis and possibly by Africans. Their concern was to find out in what ways this God can be characterised and the arguments to prove His Existence. (6)

In order to clarify the meaning of God, they asked, "what attitudes do human beings have towards the entity which they refer to as God?" They observed that people are awed by their God, they fear Him, worship Him, love Him, feel indebted to Him. He is their ultimate concern, they feel a sense of awe beside Him, they stand in dread of Him. So, the term God could only be used and understood with reference to these God-attitudes. It is only by virtue of these attitudes that the word God is empoyed.

Knowledge of God

How could God be known? The 'Christian' West denies that knowledge of God could be acquired either from the sciences or by studying the Bible as one would do to any other historical document. It was St. Anselm, a medieval Christian philosopher and theologian who preferred to defend his faith by intellectual reasoning rather than by arguments based on the Bible. He asked himself what would an entity be like which was worthy to be called God? His answer consisted in a simple formula for revealing God's character. He said "God is a being than which none greater can be thought." He then argued that what is involved in this formula is that God necessarily exists. This argument is referred to as the ontological argument for God's existence.

Teleological Argument

Many 'Christian' philosophers have claimed that both the character of God and the fact that He exists will be revealed to anyone who considers how the world is ordered and acts law-like, and is not choatic. Why do natural objects such as the rain and trees behave in a goal-oriented manner even though they posses no consciouness nor thought and therefore cannot willfully reach their goals? The world they perceive is created and governed by God and displays to all who would regard it with wonder and awe, the existence and the character of its creator. Both the cosmological and teleological arguments for God's existence fall within this category. (7)

A Western missionary with the preceding background was more likely to think about God in philosophical categories - (ontological, cosmological, teleological, metaphysical) than an African who took his belief in God for granted.

Equipped with a Western philosophical, intellectual, ideological and scientific background the "Western" missionary to Africa could hardly comprehend African beliefs and responses to God. Hence many funny names such as animism, idolatry, paganism, heathenism, fetishism, witchcraft magic, juju etc. were used to describe African traditional religion. (8)

African response to Christian Mission

As soon as African university trained clergymen appeared on the intellectual scene in the field of religious studies, their first concern was to prove that African people are not religiously illiterate and to refute the Western conception of African traditional Religion, particularly their concept of African God, as a God they got on loan from the West. In Nigeria, for example, Professor Idowu, a Methodist Minister and Theologian wrote his Ph.D. Thesis for University of London on **Olodumare - God in Yoruba Belief.** (9)

In Ghana Dr. Danqua wrote on the **Akan Doctrine of God** and in Kenya, East Africa, Professor John S. Mbiti, one of the foremost African theologians produced a magnificient book on the **Concepts of God in Africa.** He also wrote **African Religions** and **Philosophy** and **Introduction to African Traditional Religion.**

All these and other works were written in order to clarify and to refute Western misconceptions and misinterpretations of African traditional religion and their concept of God (See article on "ATR in African Scholarship"). Infact, western criticism of African traditional religion had a salutary and tonic effect on Africans who had not begun to clarify their belief in God for non-Africans to understand. Now the issues about African traditional religion and their concept of God are clear following the amount of literature on the subject (see section on Bibliography). For our purpose, we shall refer to most of these works.

Concept of God in African Traditional Religion

We shall consider the structure, nature, attributes and worship of the African God.

The African thinks of God within the framework of his religion. African traditional religion, if we want to be more specific should bear the name of the particular African Community in question, such as Dinka Religion, Yoruba Religion, Mende Religion, Nupe Religion, Nuer Religion, Lugbara Religion, Igbo Religion etc. (10) African Religion is regarded as traditional, in the sense that it is native, indigenous, handed down from generation to generation; and as that which continues to be practised by living men and women today as the religion of their forebears. (11)

In other words, the religion is traditional not as something that belongs to the past, to the archives, but as something that is undergirded by a fundamentally indigenous value system that has its own pattern, its own historical inheritance and traditions from the past. As A.C. Bouquet has put it "... traditional religion as used for indigenous religion in Africa is religion as it actually is today. But religion as it is today is meaningless unless its basic past is related to the present." (12) So in discussing

42

the African traditional concept of God, we are indeed dealing with its present realities.

The Structure of God in African Traditional Religion

To talk of the concept of God in Africa is to examine the nature of the supernatural as composed of the High or Supreme God, together with the divinities, spirits, ancestral spirits, totemic spirits and the processes of their relationship with the world of men. We shall consider each of these in turn, together with the means through which the gods or spirits reveal themselves to men and how men respond to them.

The One Supreme God (13)

In many parts of Africa, many people traditionally believe in one single, Supreme God who is the creator of the world and of man. He is believed to be all knowing, all powerful, all wise. The names given to the Supreme God in different African societies reflect these intrinsic attributes. For example, among the Mende people of Sierra Leone, **Leve** is the Supreme Creator God, the one who is high-up. According to K. Little: **Leve** or **Ngewo** is directly translated as Supreme God. All life and activity, in both a material and non-material sense derive from him.

"Ngewo created the world and everything in it, including not only human beings, animals, plants and so on, but spirits also. In addition, he invested the whole universe with a certain non-material kind of power or influence which manifests itself in various ways and on specific occasions in human beings and animals and even in natural phenomena, such as lightning, waterfalls and mountains. He is the ultimate-source and symbol of that power and influence ..." (14) In Ghana, the Akan people call God - **Onyame** - the Supreme Being, God the creator of all things, the Deity. In Nigeria; the Bini people call God - **Osanobua** - i.e., Creator of the world, sky, earth, and of life and death. The Igbo called God **Chineke** - the creator God, **Chi-ukwu** - the Great Spirit. Among the Yorubas God is referred to as **Olodumare** - the

Almighty, the Supreme God; as **Olorun** -owner or Lord of Heaven. In Kenya God is given such names as **Akuj, Mungu, Ngai** etc. (15)

From these few sample names given to God by some selected African societies with a bit of an elaboration on the Mende conception of God, we have a clear picture of God as the Lord and creator of the world and all that there is in it. This assertion is fundamental to traditional religious beliefs in Africa. Mbiti (16) has also shown from his research into the nature of God in Africa, that apart from this intrinsic attributes, God in Africa also has eternal attributes such as being self-existent, the first and the last, invisible, incomprehensible, mysterious and immutable. Mbiti has also described the moral attributes of the Supreme God to include pity, kindness, love, comfort of God, faithfulness of God, goodness of God, the anger, the Will, the justice and the holiness of God. It is the notion of the moral attributes of God that strengthens the African traditional ethical sanctions and this in turn upholds the community solidarity. The African believes in God's providence. It is God who provides sunshine, moonshine, rain, fertility, health and plenty. Africans also believe that God not only provides, He also protects, guards, controls and saves His people. In short, Africans see God as King, Ruler, Lord and Master of the world. They see Him also as Judge, their conqueror who delivers His people from their enemies. In addition to these attributes, Africans interpret afflictions as mysteries which only God can solve. Hence they think of God as capable of causing his people to suffer great afflictions through disease, misfortunes, poverty, draught, famine, flood and death. Africans believe that these afflictions come to them because God allowed it to happen. Quite often, they attribute it to a failure on their part, hence they seek to make ammendments in prayers and sacrifices.

One would expect the Supreme God to be the center of worship and life of the people. But usually, more attention is paid to the lesser divinities and spirits. The Supreme God usually has no temples, no priests, no organised regular worship or sacrifices. This is why it is easy for a stranger to misunderstand this aspect of the African religion. Sometimes, the Supreme God is thought of being too far away or too remote to have any dealings with men. This notwithstanding, it is remarkable how spontaneously individuals in distress could turn to the Supreme God with informal prayers of the greatest intimacy and simplicity without resorting to any shrines or diviners. (17) In all, as W. Schmidt said: "the belief in, and worship of one Supreme deity is universal among all 'primitive' peoples. ... The 'high God' is

44

found among them all ... prominently enough to make his dominant position indubitable ..." (18)

Spirits - An Ubiquitous phenomena in African belief (19)

It is a common feature among traditional African people to believe in a host of spirits who inhabit all sorts of places such as trees, hills, rivers and sometimes plants and animals. For this reason, African traditional religion was variously described as animism or even as 'nature religion.'

Divinities: Derivatives From Deity with no absolute existence at all(20)

The general belief about divinities is that they are created by God to perform specific roles. They did not come into existence on their own volition. Their status is mediatorial, they are believed to be intermediaries between God and man, a means to an end, not ends in themselves. As emanations of God, they share the limitation of all other creatures. Their powers are limited to the performance of specific functions assigned to them by God. None of them enjoys the unlimited powers ascribed to God. Thus there are special divinities concerned with matters of war, of hunting, fishing, farming, metal-work etc. Each divinity has his own local name in the local language which is believed to be a manifestation or an emblem of His being. For example, among the Yorubas of Nigeria, **Ogun** is the divinity both for war and of iron. Hence it is worshipped by warriors and hunters, by blacksmith and all who work with machinery under modern conditions. For the Igbo of Nigeria, **Ala** is the earth divinity or mother goodess who gives fertility both to the earth and to women. This means that the earth is sacred and respected and is known to be the guardian and superivisor of morality. Elaborate sacrifices are offered to **Ala** for appeasement, especially during the festivals when the people need special favours or when they break **Chukwu's** taboos. The people also have an obligation to thank **Ala** for her bounties during the New Yam Festival.

Major divinities sometimes have temples or shrines set up for them with special priesthood, rituals and festivals. The divinities occupy a much more important place than the spirits.

Ancestral Spirit (21)

An ancestor is a departed spirit who stands in particular close relation to the tribe or family. Among Africans, there is the belief that communication and communion is possible between the living and the dead. This belief upholds that the dead has the power to influence, help or molest the living. So it could be said that there is a continuing interdependence between the living and the dead or the living-dead, as Mbiti calls them. This living-dead are the closest link we have with the spirit world, infact they also act as intermediaries between God and men. They know the needs of men from whose company they had withdrawn bodily. For the African, their dead are never really gone. Diop, a Senegalese poet, hit the nail at the head concerning the general attitude of Africans to their dead ones when he wrote thus:

> Those who are dead are never gone:
> they are there in the thickening shadow.
> The dead are not under the earth;
> they are in the tree that matter,
> they are in the wood that groans,
> they are in the water that runs
> they are in the hut, they are in
> the crowd, the dead are not dead
>
> . . . . . .
>
> The dead are not under the earth:
> they are in the fire that is dying
> they are in the grasses that weep
> they are in the whimpering rocks,
> they are in the forest, they are in the
> house, the dead are not dead. (22)

Since they are considered as living-dead, they depend on those still in the world for their care and sustenance. That is why they are usually offered libation with food and drink and **'kola.'** If they

46

are neglected, they would go hungry and in anger could send misfortunes as a reprisal for being neglected. This means that they are bound to have special shrines where they could be served with food offerings and also venerated.

In these circumstances it is not surprising that early missionaries often interpreted African traditional religion as 'ancestor worship.' It is the African's strong sense of continuing communion with their living-dead, and the honour and service they still give them that deceived the western missionaries into thinking that the dead were being worshipped, when in actual fact they were being venerated. Professor Farmer argues this case thus - "The ancestor is a departed spirit who stands in close relation to the tribe or the family ... by natural affection and filial piety. The commonly used phrase-ancestor-worship must not mislead us here, nor be allowed to suggest a distinctly religious significance in the cult of ancestor which it does not necessarily possess". (23)

To qualify as an ancestor, in the spirit world, one must fulfil certain conditions namely: the conduct of the person while he lived must be above board. He must attain a reasonable old age; he must have been married with children. He must not die a bad death - i.e., death through accident, lunacy, epilepsy, suicide or through any form of violence. (24)

Totemic Spirits

There are some African people who traditionally believe they have a special spiritual relationship with certain animal species, plants, objects or places. Such objects constitute the totem of the tribe or clan and as such is treated with great respect as something set apart, holy unto the people. If it is an animal, it must never be killed except in certain ritual circumstances.

The totem species provide sources to establish the identity of a tribe and to explain its history. It also helps to maintain a strong link, a kind of mystical spiritual kinship between the people, the world of the spiritual powers and the world of nature. In this context, it is gross misunderstanding to describe African traditional religion as "animal worship, or tree worship or even idol worship. The phenomenon of totemism is not only common among Africans, it is also reported to be found among North American, Indians and the Australian Aborigines. (26) Having looked at the world of the spirits let us now consider how they relate and reveal themselves to the world of men and matter.

Religious Leaders: Helpers in relating the gods to men

In traditional African religion, the world of men and the unseen world of the spirits maintain something like a symbiotic relationship which however requires people to serve as the link between their fellow men on the one hand and God, spirits and divinities on the other. In African traditional societies, any man who is the leader of a family, or the eldest person in a home or the leader of a clan can conduct the dealings with the gods for himself, his family or the clan.

Apart from these "lay-priests", there are those who are trained and skilled, some are said to be specifically called by the gods to act as priests to the people. Such professionals include diviners, medium, seers, priests, ritual leaders, rainmakers and medicine men. (27) These religious leaders are the custodians of the religious treasures and religious knowledge of the people. They embody the presence of God to the people as well as their moral values. But sometimes the priests tend to invent spurious objects of worship and thereby largely making divinities ends in themselves, rather than as means to an end.

Revelation from God and the divinities to men

God and the spirit world as we have described belong totally to the useen realm. They cannot be seen with the naked eye. Inspite of this, they are known to influence the fortunes of men on earth. Efforts are made therefore to determine where the gods could reveal themselves so that they could be worshipped and consulted.

One of the avenues through which the gods reveal themselves or their wishes to the traditional African is through dreams and the objects in created world.

Other forms through which the gods reveal themselves are in men's conceptions in symbols and in objects, like an extraordinary stone, or tree, an earthen pot, a wooden pole, an empty seat or a carved wood or stone image representing the likeness of a god. Missionaries lumped all these materials together as 'idols', and they used to say 'The heathen in his blindness bows down to woods and stone.' But it is the missionary not the traditional African who is blind here. The African bows down to the indwelling spirit and knows quite well that the image and symbol can never be identified with the divinity. They are merely representations of divine presence and power.

One of the features of African traditional religion is that it has no sacred book or scriptures. Rather, the religion depends on oral tradition that is embodied in a series of myths. These myths are sacred stories. They are not mere fairy tales nor inventions of ignorant men trying to give scientific or historial accounts of earliest times. On the contrary, they represent a re-activation of the very powers of the gods that are being narrated in the myths. Those who recite and those who hear them become so merged and so personally involved in what is being narrated that they feel caught up in what is being done by the gods. So they share in those great events as much as the first men who performed it. In so doing, the men respond to the gods by affirming once again their relations with the gods upon whom they depend. Myths therefore, constitute a kind of revelation of the intents and purposes of gods for men.

All in all, the gods therefore, reveal themselves to their votaries through special experiences like dreams, through sacred places or shrines and through symbols, images and myths. (28)

Response of men to the gods (29)

The gods do not only reveal themselves to men, men also respond to the gods, through festivals and the rituals that go with them. For the traditional African, with his cyclical conception of life, the world is seen as constantly being used up, decaying and being destroyed by evil forces. It therefore needs periodic renewal which can come only from the sources of all life and power, the gods themselves. This is what the periodic rituals and festivals seek to do - to secure from the gods, a fresh influx of vital power for the whole of life. And since the life of the traditional African is very closely linked to process of nature, the main festivals are tied to the agricultural seasons

- these are the seasons when the gods are guests to their votaries. (30)

Response through prayers, offerings and sacrifice (31)

As we have noted, the traditional African is very much aware of the existence and the power of the spirit world and their impingment on them. So they perform acts of worship - prayers, offerings and sacrifices - to keep alive their contact with them. When trouble comes and there is crisis, people instinctively and automatically turn to God in prayers. Such prayers are intentional prayers, they are not prayers read from a prayer book. They are prayers in which the people express concrete needs for good health, for protection from danger, for safety in travelling and for security, prosperity and preservation of life both for the individual and for the community. For the community at large, prayers may be asked for rain, cessation of epidemics, for victory in war and the acceptance of sacrifices and offerings. These prayers, offerings and sacrifices are made to draw the attention of the gods or God to their needs.

Response through obedience and moral conduct

Another vital way by which a traditional African responds to the gods is by the observance of the traditional codes of conduct. The Africans have a deep sense of right and wrong. They believe that their morals - customs, rules, laws, traditions and taboos are given to them by God. They also believe that the departed spirits and some of the divinities are guardians or custodians of these moral lawas. They punish those who break the taboos and moral laws.

So the people know that wrong doings are serious offences. When however serious offences are committed, they are expected to be confessed to the gods through the priests in order to avert divine punishment that could inevitably occur. Because of this, great emphasis is laid on morals in order to keep the society from disintegrating. Without the observance of the moral conduct there would be chaos and confusion. So morals guide the people in doing what is right and good, both for their own sake and that of their community.

Conclusion

In this paper, we have tried to describe what Africans traditionally know, actually believe and actually think about God and the supersensible world. We have noted the nature and structure of the supersensible world as made up of the creator God, the spirits, the divinities, the ancestor spirits and the totemic spirits. The role of religious leaders and other functionaries who link up the people with spirit world is noted, together with the various ways in which the gods reveal themselves to the people. We have also seen how the people respond to the gods and the Creator God. In all, we may conclude that the concept of God as the Supreme God is fundamental to African traditional religion.

Footnotes

1 J.S. Mbiti, **Introduction to African Religion.** (London: Heinemann 1975) pp. 40.
2 E.B. Idowu, **African Traditional Religion: A Definition.** (New York: ORBIS Books 1975) pp. 92.
3 **Ibid.,** cited by Idowu.
4 **Ibid.,** Andrew Lang cited by Idowu.
5 E. Smith ed. **African Ideas of God,** (London: Edinburgh Press, 1950) p. 1.
6 Leon Pearl, **Four Philosophical Problems: God, Freedom, Mind and Perception.** (New York: Harper and Row 1963) pp. 3-16.
7 **Ibid.,** p. 14.
8 B.H. Kato, **Theological Pitfalls in Africa** (Kenya: Evangelical Publishing House, 1975) pp. 18-24.
9 E.B. Idowu, **Olodumare: God In Yoruba Belief,** (London: Longman, 1962)
10 G. Lienhardt, **Divinity and Experience: the Religion of Dinka,** (Oxford: Clarendon Press, 1961).

S.E. Nadel, **Nupe Religion,** (Oxford: Clarendon Press (1954).

E.E. Evans-Pritchard, **Nuer Religion,** (Oxford: Clarendon Press, 1956).

J. Middleton, **Lugbara Religion** (Oxford: Clarendon Press 1960).

11 E.B. Idowu, **African Traditional Religion: A Definition.** (New York. ORBIS Books 1975) pp. 105-106.

12 **Ibid.,** A.C. Bouquet cited by idowu, p. 106.

13 J. S. Mbiti, **Concepts of God in Africa,** (London: SPCK. 1979).

14 K. Little, **The Mende of Sierra Leone;** Routledge and Kegan Paul, 1951) p. 217.

15 J.S. Mbiti, **Introduction to African Religion,** (London: Heinemann 1975) pp. 42-44.

K.A. Opoku, **West African Traditional Religion,** (Accra: FEP. 1978) pp. 15-18.

J.S. Mbiti, **Concepts of God in Africa, pp. 19-29.**

Ibid., pp. 31-41.

16 **Ibid.,** pp. 56-59, 80-85.

17 H.W. Turner, **Living Tribal Religions,** (London: Ward Lock Educaton 1971) pp. 14-15. See also

E. Ikenga-Metuh, **God and man in African Religion,** (London: G. Chapman 1981).

18 Cited by Idowu, **African Traditional Religion: A Definition,** p. 89.

19 J.S. Mbiti, **Introduction to African Religion,** pp. 65-76.

See alo E.B. Idowu, **op.cit.,** pp. 173-178.

20 **Ibid.**

21 **Ibid.,** Idowu, pp. 178-188. See also

Turner, **Living Tribal Religions,** pp. 15-16.

22 See K.A. Opoku - p. 35, p. 54-60.

23 Cited by Idowu, p. 179.

24 K.A. Opoku - **West African Traditional Religion,** p. 36.

25 Turner, p. 16.

26 Turner, pp. 17-23.

27 Mbiti, **Introduction to African Religion,** p. 150.

28 E.P. Modum, 'God as Guests: Music and Festival in African Traditional societies' in O.U. Kolu ed. **Readings in African Humanities,** (Enugu: Fourth Dimension Publication 1978) pp. 45-57.

29 Turner, pp. 27-32; See also

Mbiti, **Introduction to African Religion,** pp. 54-62.

30 E.P. Modum, "God as Guests," p. 53.

31 Mbiti, pp. 175-179.

THE CONCEPT OF MAN IN AFRICAN TRADITIONAL RELIGION: WITH PARTICULAR REFERENCE TO THE IGBO OF NIGERIA

by

Emefie Ikenga-Metuh

Man, Ancestors and the After-Life

'Until recently,' writes Benjamin Ray, 'Western scholars have failed to appreciate the extent to which African religions are founded upon a systematic anthropology and ethics'. (1) However, writers are becoming increasingly aware that African religions are in fact anthropocentric. According to Mbiti, 'man is at the very centre of existence and African peoples see everything else in its relation to this central position of man. ... it is as if God exists for the sake of man'. (2) Both expresses a similar view: "African Religion is centred more in man than in God or in nature." (3) Everything else in African world-view therefore seems to get its bearing and significance from the position, meaning and end of man in African thought. Here we shall examine the place and destiny of man in Igbo thought.

Man in Igbo thought can be viewed from different perspectives. Viewed from the standpoint of his origin and final destiny, man is best understood in relationship to Chukwu, God his creator. Man comes from God. He has a definite mission to fulfil in God's plan and he will eventually go back to God. Viewed ontologically, man is a force in the universe full of forces. Socially, the Igbo doctrine of man strikes a balance between his personal identity as a unique individual person and his collective identity as a member of his society. We shall now elaborate on each of these aspects as they are understood in Igbo thought.

The Igbo word for man is 'mmadu'. Arazu claims that he learnt from an Igbo sage that the etymological meaning of the word is 'mma' (goodness) du (exists). This word, says the sage, was first pronounced by God when he looked at the world he had made and said 'mmadu', 'Let goodness exist.' This may well be, but this meaning has no appreciable influence on the Igbo understanding of the nature and significance of man. (4)

The word mmadu refers to a human being irrespective of his age, sex, or status. Thus the term mmadu distinguishes the human species from other beings - plants, animals, and spirits.

It is often used as an antonym of 'mmuo', spirit, with the sense that spirits are the invisible counterparts of humans. Hence the Igbo often speak of 'Ndi mmadu na ndi mmuo' - human persons (ndi, Singular = onye) and Spirit persons. Spirits and humans are both persons. Spirits are distinguished from humans in that they are invisible and are exceedingly more powerful. Religion for the Igbo is an interplay between mmadu and mmuo, humans and spirits.

Man in Igbo beliefs is seen primarily as a creature of God. Igbo myths do not emphasise the direct creation of man by God. (5) However, many Igbo names and proverbs see man as a direct creature of God. For example the following common personal names reflect Igbo ideas of man as God's creature: Madueke, man does not create, Onyeneke, who creates except God?, Chukwukere, God created, Ekechukwu, the creature of God. One of the proper names of God is Chineke, The Spirit that creates. So also some proverbs affirm that man is God's creature - Eke kere onye bu Chi ya', the creator who creates one is his God. Chukwu kere ya kegburu ya ekegbu'. The God created him, very poorly endowed him. 'Ofu nne n'amu, ma ofu Chi adighieke', you may indeed come from the same mother, but you are not created by God in the same way.

These names and proverbs show among other things that God is both the creator of the human race as a whole as well as the creator of each individual person. Impregnation by itself is not enough to bring a human being into existence. A special intervention of God is necessary. The effects of this intervention vary in different people. God's direct intervention and personal concern for man is further illustrated by the Igbo beliefs about 'Chi', personal destiny, said to be a part of God himself in each individual person, as will be demonstrated below.

Igbo Anthropology

In Igbo thought it is necessary to distinguish between the notion of man and the self. Paradoxically, man is one, but the self is multiple. Man is not subject to the body and soul dichotomy as in Western thought. Man can exist in his material body or out of it without being split. When out of the material body, man can be described as a spiritual body. A dead person is always visualized in a bodily form, as a sort of unquantified

54

body, imagined to be like the shadow of a man on a sunny day. Man is the individual person created by God. A living person is called 'Onye mmadu', a dead person is called 'onye mmuo'. Hence it is the full individual person not a part of him or his soul which survives after death. Similarly, at conception, a new individual person is created by God. This is so inspite of beliefs about re-incarnation. What reincarnates as we shall see is not the person-hood of the ancestor but an aspect of his self.

The Igbo believe that man is endowed with three different principles or selves. Man can operate in one or more of these selves in different contexts. These three principles are: **Obi**, Heart or Breath, **Chi**, Destiny, and **Eke** or **Agu**, Ancestral Guard-ian. Obi, Heart, is a man's life-force, the animating principle which links man with other life-forces in the universe. **Chi**, is the Destiny-spirit believed to be an emanation of the Creator which is in man, and the **Eke** is the ancestral-guardian which links man with his family and clan. (6)

The Heart, **Obi**, is man's animation principle, and the seat of affection and volition. For example, a good and kindly man is called 'Onye obi oma', and a courageous man is called 'Onye obi Ike'. **Obi**, Breath, resides in the biological heart which is also alled 'Obi', but the 'breath' is an immaterial spiritual substance which sometimes leaves the body - in dreams and under the influence of witchcraft. Of the fright or sensation one feels in the face of sudden danger, the Igbo says, 'Obi'm efepu'. My heart has flown away. The breath is a life-force which links man with other cosmic forces. It may be attached through witchcraft or sorcery and may be weakened or die. It can be strenthened by magic or by eating another human heart through witchcraft. At death, the heart leaves the body but it does not survive. (7) Nowadays, one hears of **mkpulobi**, seed of the heart. It is becom-ing customary to translate **mkpulobi** as 'soul' and identify it with the Christian soul, but this is a concept completely alien to tradi-tional Igbo beliefs. Traditionally, **mkpulobi** is the same as obi, breath, as defined above.

About **Chi**, Meek writes 'One of the most striking doctrines of the Ibo is that every human being has associated with his personality, a genuis, or spirit-double known as Chi'. (8) He then compares **Chi** to the Egyptian notion of Ka, which was the double or genius, of a man, an ancestral emanation, apparently which guided and protected him during his lifetime, and to which he returned after death. **Chi** is associated with a child from the moment of its conception. Igbo beliefs say that at conception, God assigns a Chi to each person, and places before the **Chi** several parcels of fortunes. Whichever the **Chi** chooses, becomes the destiny of the child entrusted to his care. This parcel of destiny which is also referred to as **Chi,** contains the total luck or misfortunes the child will have in life. **Chi** has, therefore, two ambivalent conceptions - the parcel of destiny, and the guardian spirit who chooses the destiny parcel. Thus a lucky man is called, 'onye chi oma', someone who has a good **Chi,** and the unfortunate man is called, 'onye chi ojoo', someone who has a bad **Chi.** The role of Chi as a guardian spirit is brought out by the Igbo proverb, 'Nwata n'amu iri enu, Chi ya achiri uche n'aka', when a child is learning how to climb a tree, his Chi is breathless with anxiety'. When a person dies, his Chi goes back to God to give account of his work on earth. When a person reincarnates, he is given a different **Chi** by God. Hence, a rich person at reincarnation could be born a poor person. A man's abilities, faults, or misfortunes are ascribed to his Chi.

The idea of Destiny so pervades Igbo life and thought that it is reasonable to assume that it is an ancient and basic concept in Igbo religious system. Every event in a man's life whether it is success or failure is 'onatara Chi', a gift of destiny. The goal of a man's life is to achieve his 'akara Chi', the destiny imprinted on his palms.

Although the **Chi** comes into association with a person immediately on conception, the person does not usually establish a formal **Chi** cult until he or she becomes a parent. Before this time, his **Chi** shares in the sacrifices which his father or uncle offers to his own Chi. The shrine of a man's **Chi** consists of an 'Oha' or 'Ebo' tree, at the base of which is placed a round flat stone picked from a river bed, and a clay dish which serves as a receptacle for food offerings. A woman also sets up her Chi shrine at her husbands house after the birth of her first child. The shrine is set up with some relics (sand or branch), taken from her mother's shrine; and consists of a tree, an earthen mound - ever which is built a thatched roof. In the shrine is kept a wooden bowl 'okwa Chi', to give offerings to Chi. Sacrifices are usually made at planting and harvest seasons. Outsides these periods, offerings are made whenever the owner feels inclined.

Eke, Ancestral guardian, is believed to be an ancestral shade incarnate in each newly born baby. Eke is therefore connected with Igbo concept of reincarnation. A person's Eke, is usually referred to as 'Onye noro ya uwa', the person who brought him to the world, and is usually an ancestor, a deity or an Arusi. The child is believed to take after the **Eke** in appearance or character or both. In cases of doubt, the parents consult a dibia or diviner and perform the rites of 'Igba Agu'. If this is not done, the child may fall sick and die because the parents cannot identify the person who has been reincarnated nor be certain of the taboos and cults he must observe. **Eke** links the individual with life-force of his clans. The belief in **Eke** makes it possible for the dead to reincarnate in the living from generation to generation. Each person makes sacrifices to his Eke for good fortune. As soon as the diviner identifies the Eke, the parents arrange to perform the rites of bringing the Eke to their home. This is done by the eldest male. He takes kola nuts to the grave of the appropriate deceased relatives and in a simple prayer asks the Eke to follow him home. He touches the grave with a knotted palm frond, carries it home and places it in the family 'Onu Okike', or the shrine of Eke. After a sacrifice, the Eke is believed to have come home. (9)

Man In The Universe

Man, 'Mmadu', is best seen as life-force interacting with the life-forces in the universe. He is endowed with different principles or selves which link and allow him to interact with other beings in the world. **Chi** links man with God, Eke links him with the ancestors, while Obi or Breath links him with the entire universe of life-forces.

Obi, as a life-force, is capable of growth, diminution and death. By maintaining harmonous relationship through rituals, man contributes to the strengthening of his life-force. Man can further strengthen himself with charms and medicines. The strength of a man's life-force is made manifest in his general well-being - good health, large family, prosperity and good status in society. A person's life-force may be the object of attack by witches, sorcerers, unappeased deities or evil spirits, and thus weaken or even die.

Man is at the centre of this universe of forces. Above all beings or forces is Chukwu, God, Spirit or Creator. He gives existence power of survival and increase to all the other forces. After him come the deities, and then the founding ancestors of the different clans. These, though one time human beings, dispose of great powers and influence because they were the first to whom God communicated his vital force, with the power of exercising influence on posterity. They constitute the most important chain binding men to God. (10) After them come the ancestors and other living-dead of the family and tribe. Then come the living in the order of prime-geniture. Under man and subordinate to him are the physical forces in the universe - animals, plants, minerals. The universe is like a spider's web in which all beings are linked together by a network of relationships and interact upon one another. Harmonious interaction leads to the strengthening of beings. While pernicious influences lead to the diminution of beings. This belief is illustrated by an incident which happened at Ozubulu, a town at the central part of Igboland some four years ago. The catechist of a christian group, who had cut and sawed up an 'iroko' tree to get some money to pay the dowry for a wife for his son, suddenly died one morning while working in his barn. While his church prayed for the repose of his soul in the church, his relatives in the village consulted an oracle which attributed his death to his failure to placate the spirit in the tree. (11) The oracle ordered a series of rituals to restore the harmony thus disrupted to avoid more of such mysterious deaths. Thus, all life-forces can influence one another for good or for evil. Harmonious relationships ensure increase of the life-force of man. Much of Igbo religion consists of rituals to maintain or restore this harmony.

Man, Family and Community

Igbo, like most African peoples, tend to define a person in terms of the group to which he belongs. A person is thought of first of all as a member of a particular family, kindred, clan or tribe. Even today in an Igbo village one is rarely asked; who are you?; but rather 'whose son are you?; and what lineage or clan do you belong to?' Thus one learns from an early age, that 'I am because I belong'. An individual without a family is an abnormality. The family makes the man. The family is made up of not only one's living relatives at the widest possible scope, but also the dead members and those yet to be born.

The bond which links the family community is not only a socio-biological bond but also ontologico-spiritual. The **Eke,** ancestral guardian, assigned by God, is usually, though not exclusively, a member of the family or a spirit related to the family. The Eke is said to be reborn in the new member of the family to whom he is assigned and thus gives him his form, character or personality. The Eke thus maintains the unbroken ontological bond between a person, his family, lineage, clan and tribe. A son's life is the prolongation of the life of his father, his grandfather, his ancestors and the life of the whole lineage. As its numerical strength increases, so does its life-force become stronger. Hence the greatest tragedy that can befall a man and his lineage is for him to die childless. (12)

Every segment of the Igbo society is regarded as and functions as a family - the Umunna (kindred), Ebo (Lineage), Ogbe (Village), Obodo (Town or village-group). The head of each segment, the Okpara (first born), is, by virtue of the right of primo-geniture, the spiritual as well as the administrative head. He inherits the Ofo, the ancestral staff of authority, with which he performs the rites at the ancestral shrines on behalf of the entire group. Through his acts and words communion is renewed, discord is healed and the advice and aid of the ancestors are enlisted. The lineage head settles disputes and organises rituals for maintaining harmony with the invisible forces. He sometimes rallies members and organises the cultivation of the common land, building of new homesteads, rituals for betrothal and marriages of members, naming ceremonies, rites for cures of prolonged childlessness, cases of illness, or death in the family. Similarly, the Okpara, rallies the lineage or clan for rituals connected with matters of widers concern like the rites at the beginning of the planting season, initiation rites, annual festivals, prolonged draughts, widespread epidemics, the new yam festivals, and so forth.

Man And His Divinely Ordained Destiny

For the Igbo, life is communion. Communion is not limited to the relationship with the created order - the universe, the spirits, ancestors, his family, and community, but also relationship with the Creator himself, Chukwu. Man is indeed bound to God by ties of creation and by his divine providence over the world of which man is part. But even more, Igbo beliefs suggest that man is ontologically linked to God through the Chi, 'the spark or emanation of God in each person'. This spirit of God in man guards and administers the contents of his destiny, which is received from God. So God's providence is not limited to the general world plan for the guidance of the universe. He has a worked out plan for each individual person and his own spirit remains with each person to direct its implementation. God's plan for man, once sealed, is unalterable. The deities, ancestors and some agents of evil may temporarily interfer with it, but the performance of appropriate rituals rectifies it.

Man's mission on earth is to work to realise the contents of his destiny amidst the threats from mystical forces beyond the visible realm and evil men from within his own community. To achieve this, he seeks the aid of the good spiritual beings - his Chi, the ancestors, and deities through making the appropriate rituals. From the visible world, he can count on the support of his family, lineage, the clan, and other social institutions. His success depends on how he marshals the favourable forces through rituals, sacrifices, prayers, vows, offerings, making of good medicines, charms, and so forth, to neutralise the machination of evil forces. Divination reveals to him the snares of his enemies and the correct ritual remedy to apply. What one gets after exhausting all these means of realising his destiny, is his destiny. For says an Igbo proverb 'Ebe onye dara, ka Chi ya kwaturu ya', where a person falls, there his Destiny pushed him down.

This raises the whole problem of predestination and human responsibility. In Igbo thought, predestination and human responsibility are conflicting but they are not diametrically opposed concepts. It is true that what one may hope to get out of life is only what has been predestined by God. But what one actually gets is his own responsibility. He only gets what he has worked for. In other words, where a person is not resourceful, a particular fortune in his destiny package may be lost. Since no one knows the contents of his destiny, he must keep trying as if what he wants is there. The Igbo proverb, which says 'whoever says yes, his Chi says yes' expresses this dialectic appropriately. Thus Igbo view of predestination unlike the Western concept of predestination does not imply that what is predestined by God must come to pass irrespective of whatever the individual does. Rather, it is like an award by God to the individual and held in trust for him by his Chi. The responsibility of obtaining the benefits of the award rests on him. He can get all the award or may loose a good part ot it, depending on how hard he worked and how skilfully he managed his affairs under the guidance of his Chi. But try as he would, he cannot get anything that is not included in the award.

Fortes explains this dialectic of fate and responsibility implicit in the African concept of man with the stories of Oedipus

60

and Job drawn from Greek mythology and the Bible respectively. One vision of predestination as illustrated by the story of Oedipus (who killed his father and married his mother because it was predestined), presents it as fatalistic and amoral. Another view of predestination illustrated by the story of Job (who through his devotion and patience achieved God's designs for him) presents it as moral, responsible and free. But whereas in Western thought these two visions of predestination are irreconcilably opposed, in African thought, they are combined in a dynamic vision of man. He is both subject to fate and free. He is at the same time a victim of restriction imposed by destiny and the architect of his own future. He is both innocent and responsible both Oedipus and Job. (13) In other words, human destiny in African thought is both unalterable and alterable. Viewed as package sealed by God and given to man, it is unalterable. Viewed as a resource to be exploited, it is alterable.

The Final Destiny of Man – Eschatology

Igbo belief in the survival of the human person after death, in ancestors as the 'living dead', and in reincarnation, suggest that there is a strong belief in the after-life. Generally, the after-life is viewed from the point of view of the continuing relationship of the dead with the living, and not as the final end of man or of the world. There is very little speculation about 'the last things'. Eschatology either in the sense of the culmination of individual lives, or of human history in general, is of marginal interest in traditional religion. This is understandable, given the African conception of life as a cyclic process of concern is the eternal now; since the past and the fulfilment of man is sought in the present. Consequently, the after-life is conceived in terms of the present life. The environment and social structure of each society are each projected into the invisible world and form the framework of its conceptions of the after-life. In this context, ideas about immortality, judgement, and retribution play very little part.

Man In The After-life

Death is not the final end of man in Igbo thought. All men continue to live in some form or the other after their death. Those who lived a good life and died a good death (Onwu Chi' = natural death at ripe old age), and received funeral rites appropriate to their status, go to the Spirit-land, 'Ala Mmuo' where they continue a life similar to their earthly life and are eventually allowed to reincarnate 'into uwa'. While those who lived bad lives, or died evil deaths, 'Onwu Ojoo', (e.g. violent deaths, or deaths by horrible diseases) are banished to 'Ama nri mmuo na mmadu', an intermediate state between the spirit-land and the land of the living. This latter place, is the Igbo concept of hell. Its occupants are visualized as frustrated wandering and restless evil spirits.

The abode of the good spirits of the dead, ala mmuo, is a carbon copy of the abode of the living. The two differ only in that one is visible and the other invisible. A geographical map of the land of the living would represent the spirit-land in every particular: every town, village and homestead would be situated exactly where it is in the land of the living. However, the land of the spirit is imagined to be underneath the land of the living, probably because the bodies of thedead are buried in the ground. Arthur Leonard succinctly described this:

> In the spirit-land, every country or locality is marked out or defined just as it is in this world, so that each town, community, or household has its own alloted portion to which, as people die, they go. (14)

The layout of a village in the spirit-land is patterned on the normal Igbo village: there is the Obi Uno or Okpuno, residential area; there is the Agu, reserved farmland, and immediately on the outsirts of the village is the Ajo Ohia, bad bush, where rubbish and all decaying matter is dumped. The bodies of the dead whose lives or deaths are utterly repugnant to the accepted religious standards are also unceremoniously dumped in the Ajo Ohia to symbolise total rejection and excommunication by both the living and the dead. All these are believed to exist in the Ala Mmuo. The Ndichie, ancestors, are believed to reside in the Obi Uno, and go out to do farmwork in their own Agu, or farmland. The Ama nri mmuo na mmadu, the intermediate place between the living and the spirits where the Akalogeli, or restless spirits of the damned are restricted, presumably corresponds to the Ajo Ohia or bad bush of the village of the living. Sacrificial victims of the Ichu aja sacrifices to evil spirits, are usually deposited at roadjunctions at the outskirts of the town to prevent the evil spirits from entering the village. The idea behind this is that at the roadjunction, the evil spirits will stop to eat their sacrificial food and then go back to the bad bush, or wander off along a route away from the village. Wandering aimlessly is part of their punishment.

In the same way, the social life of the spirit-land is patterned on Igbo social life. The ancestors, enjoy the social life of the normal Igbo village. They have their homes, their wives, livestock, farms and their slaves. This is the reason why the dead are buried with their domestic and professional equipment. In the olden days a man was even buried with his youngest wife and his strongest slaves, but their stay in the spirit-land is believed to be temporary, lasting until they reincarnate.

This belief not only puts a limit on the amount of property he may take to the spirit-land, but also explains why the ancestors are venerated, and literally fed for only one or two generation after their death. They are believed to have reincarnated by the end of this time. An informant told me that prayers at funeral rites do not request increased happiness for the deceased in the spirit-land but for his safe arrival there and his quick reincarnation with even greater prosperity and success. For the Akalogeli, there is very little joy and no hope. Their confusion, frusration and isolation are symbolized by the gloom, stench, disorder, and darkness of the bad bush where they are dumped.

The social organization of the spirit-land is also patterned on the Igbo. The population is organized in lineages, clans and families and the community retains its class structure with chiefs, elders, lineages clan heads rich and poor. Life is led as in this world. Women assume their roles in the home and society and each person occupies the same status and pursues the same profession as during his earthly life. The rich stay rich, the poor remain poor; farmers, traders, wine-tappers, smiths, continue their trade, hence professionals are buried with their tools. This is clearly illustrated by an incident reported in the life of the great Christian missionary Bishop Shanahan. In a conversation, he tried to convince a chief of the joys of heaven which could be achieved in the next life by those who became Christians in this life. The chief listened attentively and then asked: 'That is Heaven you say, but tell me, will all the other chiefs be there too? Or ... 'when he was told that they would not if they continued in this life as pagans, he answered: 'you see... If I go to Heaven and they go off somewhere else. ... I'd be up there in Heaven all by myself ... while all my brother chiefs would be down in the other place you speak of ... No! I'd rather be with my own'. (15)

The Igbo conceive of the spirit-land in materialistic terms. Their heaven is a clan heaven. Fulfilment in the next life is achieved when one reaches to occupy one's proper place among one's own in the next life. Damnation is viewed as an excommunication and a perpetual exclusion from clan life and from the cycle of life, and reincarnation. This is not necessarily a defect or an imperfection, nor should it be interpreted to mean that the Igbo concept of life after death is a rudimentary or primitive stage in the evolutionary process. The full significance of the Igbo conception of the after-life cannot be appreciated if we simply compare it with Christian beliefs. A more critical evaluation would view the problem in the broader perspective of the limitation universally found in all human attempts to conceive of the invisible in terms of the visible, the unknown in terms of the known.

Both Christianity and Igbo Religion seek answers to the basic questions concerning man's destiny, and their answers are basically the same but cast in different imagery: both the good and the bad continue to live in the next life; there is retribution in the next life based on one's conduct in this life; purificatory rites obtain forgiveness of sins and remission of punishment in the next life. However, there is an essential disagreement on what consistitutes a reward or punishment. While Christianity emphasises estrangement from God and physical discomfort, or hell fire as punishment and the pleasure of a heaven of bliss and union with God as reward, Igbo traditions emphasise intergration or exclusion from one's community as constituting adequate reward or punishment. Besides, the idea of a place of eternal reward or punishment which is central to the Christian concept of the after-life is completely absent from the Igbo beliefs. Igbo beliefs view life as a continuing cyclic process. After a brief stay in the spirit-land one is allowed by God to reincarnate to continue the joyous cycle of life. The wicked are deprived of the joy of reincarnation. This again shows the Igbo priority of values: Life and its increase, and the sense of community, are the values most prized by the Igbo and these are what they look forward to having in the after-life.

God an Man in The After-Life

God plays a very important role in the after-life of every human being, just as he is involved in the process by which man comes into being and the various vicissitudes he passes through during his earthly sojourn. Most of what have already been said can be summarized with special emphasis on the role God plays.

Death alone does not make a person an ancestor. Much depends on how a person lived and how he died. Although how a person lives or dies are to large extent his responsibility, in the final analysis, it is tied up with his Chi, destiny. For example, that a person dies at a ripe old age ('onwu Chi') or suffers a bad death, is beyond his control. This derives from his Chi received from God. So, somehow, God determines who may or may not become an ancestor.

This again raises the thorny question of predestination. The Igbo try to get around this in many ways. First, they would argue that God did not choose the Chi, but offered the choice to one's Chi, the guardian-spirit. They would further reason that the choice of a bad destiny must be as a result of one's bad life in his previous existence, for which the present life is a retribution. Thus the Igbo phrase 'Chukwu ga ekpe', (God will judge), means much more to the Igbo than anybody with a Western European background could ever imagine. To Igbo, it means that God will judge and suitably reward or punish every deed, not only in this life or in the after-life, but also in one's subsequent terms of life after reincarnation. God may even extend such a punishment to one's family.

Moreover, God influences man's after-life in other ways. There is a general belief for example, that 'When men have run their course on earth, they return to their master the Supreme Being, Chukwu, and live with him in the spirit world.' (16) Details as to how and when the dead reach the Creator vary from one locality to another and are not generally very clear, but it is commonly believed that when a person dies, his spirit remains in this world for some time, wandering restlessly in the vicinity of his home and the other places he used to frequent during his lifetime. After the completion of the funeral rites, the spirit enters the **Ndichie,** ancestral shrine. Meanwhile, his Chi goes before **Chukwu** for an interview, which has some aspects of a judgement. This is borne out by numerous Igbo sayings which imply that God will judge each individual after death and mete out punishment or reward. For example, a person who is wronged but cannot get redress, may say 'Iga ahu, Chukwu mu anya', 'God will judge', 'Ikpe di na be mmuo', 'Justice is in the spirit-land', certainly refer to the intervention of God to demand an account of one's term of life in this world. God then decides whether one reincarnates at once or remains for some time in the spirit-land.

About this interview between the departed spirit and the Creator, Leonard writes:

> When the burial rites are concluded, the soul then goes in the presence of the Creator, and after it has been conculted or interviewed by Him, it is permitted according to the wishes it expresses, either to remain forever in the land of the spirits or to return once more to the world. (17)

After this interview, the spirit settles in the spirit-land as a full fledged **ndichie.** On earth, this is symbolically celebrated after the funeral rites by the installation of the **Ndichie,** ancestral shrine, inside the **Obi,** reception hall. The new **Ndichie** may now be venerated inside his house by his descendants. Before the ceremony, 'no food can be offered to the homeless spirit inside the hut, **Obi** or compound'. (18)

The Ancestral Cult

Put simply, the final end of and the aspiration of every Igbo is to reach the spirit-land of his ancestors, to be venerated by his descendants as an ancestor, and eventually to reincarnate. Ancestors are therefore people who have made it to the spirit-land and are being venerated by their descendants. This veneration is often referred to as 'Ancestral Cult' or 'Ancestor Worship'. Whether, it could be appropriately called worship or not is a topic of lively debate among scholars which is beyond the scope of our discussion here.

However, offerings made to the ancestors are called by the Igbo 'inye fa nni', feeding them. Sometimes, this is taken literally, and ancestors may be persuaded to grant a request by promises of a more generous offering or by a threat of starving them should they fail. On the whole the relationship with the ancestors is governed by the principle of reciprocity. The Igbo say, 'Aga na achu aja, ka ikpe n'ama ndi mmuo', 'We shall continue to make offering so that the fault will lie with the ancestors'.

The ancestors are the elder members of the family. As spirits, they have enhanced powers which they are believed to use mainly to protect the interests of their families in which they will eventually reincarnate. They act as intermediaries between God and members of their families. They jealously maintain discipline in their families, and may inflict severe punishment on those members whose behaviour threaten the existence and progress of the family.

This notwithstanding the Igbo are very close to their ancestors. They receive more attention in daily and annual acts of worship than the Supreme Being or the deities. As members of the family, they are invited to be present and participate in most family activities; they are invoked to share in the kola communion, whether it is blessed at public gatherings or split at home to entertain guests. They are invoked to participate at naming ceremonies, marriages and funeral rites of other members of their family.

The annual festival of 'Ilo Mmo' (feasting the spirits) is a time of family reunion and the strengthening of family ties with the ancestors. The 'Umu Ada' (daughters of the lineage who have been married out) bring with them offerings which the 'Okpara' (the family head) who is also the living representative of the ancestors, will offer to the ancestors on their behalf. Quarrels between members of the family are settled and the festival ends with great feasting and rejoicing. The ancestors are thus symbols of peace, unity and prosperity in the family. (19)

Hence the conception of life and time for the Igbo as for many Africans is one of a cyclic process. What happens after death is not the terminal, definitive stage of man's life, is only a phase in the continuing round of human existence. The Igbo wants to live and continue to live with a strengthened life-force with each cycle of life. The living are happy that they are alive. The visible world is preferable to the spirit-land, even though the ancestors who live there are believed to be more powerful. Their enhanced powers are used to obtain better living conditions for their living kinsmen in anticipation of when they themselves will reincarnate to enjoy the prosperity thus given to their families. In this sense, African Religion is said to be this worldly and life-affirming. (20)

Footnotes

1   Ray Benjamin, **African Religions,** Prentice Hall, Inc. New Jersey, 1976, p. 132.
2   Mbiti, J.S. **African Religions and Philosophy,** Frederick A. Prager, New York, 1969, p. 92.
3   Booth, Newel, Jr. **African Religions: A Symposium,** NOK. Publishers, New York, p. 23.
4   Arazu, R. 'A Cultural Model For a Christian Prayer' In African Christian Spirituality, Ed. by Alyward Shorter, Orbis Books, New York, 1978, p. 114. Incidentally, masquerades are called Mmanwu. This would then mean 'Let goodness die.' This is improbable. In Udi area, the deities are called Mmaa'. It appears that 'mma' is an archaic word whose original meaning is now obscure.
5   Ikenga-Metuh, E. **God and Man In African Religion,** Geoffrey Chapman, London, 1981, p. 3ff.
6   Ezekwugo, C. 'Chi, The True God In Igbo Religion; Unpublished Thesis, University of Insbruck, 1978, p. 234.
7   Meek, C.K. **Law and Authority In a Nigerian Tribe,** Oxford University Press, 1937, p. 55.
8   Meek, C.K. **Law and Authority In Nigerian Tribe,** p. 57.
9   Metuh-Ikenga, E. **God and Man In African Religion,** p. 88.
10 Temples, Placide, **Bantu Philosophy,** Presence Africaine, Paris, 1969, p. 61.
11 This incident happened in 1979. I heard that his wife died later in a similar mysterious way.
12 Shelton, J. Austine, **The Igbo-Igala Borderland Religion and Social Control in Indigenous African Colonialism.** State University of New York Press Albany, 1971, p. 53.
13 Meyer Fortes, **Oedipus and Job In West African Religion,** Cambridge University Press, 1959, p. 25-81.
14 Leonard Arthur, G. **Lower Niger and Its Tribes,** Macmillan, and Co. New York, 1906, p. 186.
15 Jordan, J.P. **Bishop Shanahan of Southern Nigeria,** Dublin, 1971 (ed), p. 30.
16 Leonard, Arthur G. **Opus Cit.** 1906, p. 141.
17 Leonard Arthur, G. **Opus Cit.** p. 150.
18 Metuh-Ikenga, E. **God And Man in African Religion,** p. 153.
19 Metuh-Ikenga, E. **Opus Cit.** p. 96.
20 Parrinder, Geoffrey, **Religion In Africa,** Penguin African Library, 1969, p. 85.

WHERE AFRICAN RELIGION IS FOUND

by

J.S. Mbiti

Sources of African Traditional Religion

African traditional Religion has been described in various ways mostly by Western scholars or missionaries as animism, idolatory paganism and heathenism , fetishism, witchcraft magic, and juju.

One of the main reasons why the religion has been variously described and distorted by outsiders is due to the absence of authentic written sacred records like the Christian Bible or the Muslim Quran, where beliefs about God, spirits, man, the world, and life beyond this world are well defined and described.

So, for all of such people whose religions are not documented in a written form, a lot of speculations have attended the description of their religion.

Mbiti argues that African Traditional Religion has a well defined sources and a well defined mass of religious tradition, ritual and ceremonies which are transmitted orally and by practices from age to age. These sources include inter alia shrines, sacred places, religious objects, arts and symbols, music and dance, proverbs, riddles and wise sayings, myths and legends, beliefs and customs. Each of these sources will now be commented upon in brief.

African Religion is Found in the Rituals, Ceremonies and Festivals of the People

Africans like to celebrate life. They celebrate events in the life of the individual and the community. These include occasions like the birth of a child, the giving of names, circumcision and other initiation ceremonies, marriage, funerals, harvest festivals, praying for rain, and many others. Some of these rituals and ceremonies are done on a family basis, but others are observed by the whole community. They have a lot of religious meaning, and through their observation religious ideas are perpetuated and passed on to the next generations.

African Religion is Found in Shrines, Sacred Places and Religious Objects

There are many of these. Some shrines belong to a family, such as those connected with departed members of the family or their graves. Others belong to the community and these are often in groves, rocks, caves, hills, mountains, under certain trees and similar places. People respect such places and in some societies no bird, animal or human being may be killed if it or he or she is hiding in such places.

At the shrines and sacred places, people make or bring sacrifices and offerings, such as animals, fowls, food, utensils, tools, and coins. They also make prayers there. They regard such places as holy and sacred places where people meet with God.

Some of these religious places are man-made, and may be large enough to look like a big house (which is called a temple). Others are simply natural places which are secluded or situated away from people's homes and fields. Often there are people (priests) who look after communal places of worship, keep them clean, receive people who come to pray or make offerings and sacrifices, and protect them from desecration or misuse by unauthorized individuals.

Religious articles and objects are many, and we find them in all African societies. Some of them are tied round people's necks, arms, legs and waists. Some are kept in pockets, bags, on house roofs, or gates leading into the homesteads. Other religious objects are swallowed and thought to remain in the stomach; or they are dug into the ground in the houses and fields. There are other religious objects which people hide secretly wherever they may think most convenient. In shrines and sacred places, one finds many religious objects of different kinds, sizes and colours.

Shrines, sacred places and religious objects are outward and material expressions of religious ideas and beliefs. They help people in practising and handling down their religion.

70

African Religion is Found in Art and Symbols

Arts and crafts are part of the African heritage. Often African art expresses religious ideas. We find it on wood, stools, calabashes, stones, sticks, pots, handicrafts, domestic animals and human bodies. It is also expressed in the form of masks and carvings on wood, ivory and stone.

There are many kinds of symbols. They are found often where art is found, since they are a part of art. Some are represented by insects, birds, animals, certain trees, figures, shapes and colours of all kinds, masks and carvings. For example, among some people the colour of white is the symbol of death, and when a person has died, relatives smear themselves with white chalk or other substane; and in some areas the chameleon is a symbol of protection and security. In many parts of Africa, the sound of the owl is a symbol of bad omen or death.

Each people has its own symbols, whose meaning are generally known to almost everyone. But there are other symbols which can only be interpreted by a few individuals, as, for example, the symbols used in initiation, divination and secret societies. Religious ideas have created many of the symbols; and in turn the symbols themselves help to communicate and strengthen the religious ideas.

African Religion is Found in Music and Dance

A lot of African music and songs deal with religious ideas and practices. The religious rituals, ceremonies and festivals are always accompanied by music singing and sometimes dancing. Music gives outlet to the emotional expression of the religious life, and it is a powerful means of communication in African traditional life. It helps to unite the singing or dancing group and to express its fellowship and participation in life. Many musical instruments are used by African peoples, as we mentioned in the previous chapter, such as the drum, flute, rattle, whistle and others.

Where African peoples have migrated from one part of the continent to another or to overseas countries, they have often taken their music and dance with them. Through these many religious ideas are also retained and celebrated. This is the case among peoples of African descent now living in North America, South America and the West Indies. Some of them still observe religious festivals with dance and songs whose African words they do not understand, since they were taken there by their slave forefathers from West Africa two or three hundred years ago. That shows how powerful music and dance are in retaining and spreading religious ideas over wide areas and for a long period.

African Religion is Found in Proverbs, Riddles and Wise Sayings

We have said that proverbs provide us with a rich source of African wisdom. Some of these proverbs are religious. They contain religious beliefs, ideas, morals and warnings. They speak about God, the world, man, human relationships, the nature of things and so on. They are set withing a cultural and social environment of the people who have produced them ans use them. Because proverbs are short, it is easy to remember them. Many people know a lot of proverbs and are skilful in using them at the right moment for the right purpose. Since proverbs are easily passed on from one person to another, we find that many of them go back several generations.

Riddles are used mainly for entertainment and stimulating people's thinking. Some of them also contain religious ideas. Wise sayings are often about the world in general, viewed from the religious and moral perspectives.

African Religion is Found in Names of People and Places

Many African names of people and places have meanings. These meanings are often religious. They are given to mark religious ideas and experiences. For example, in Nigeria the name Babatunde means 'father returns'. It is given to a male child born immediately after the death of his grandfather. For a girl it is Yetunde, 'mother returns'. The meaning of these names shows the belief that death is not the end of life, and that the departed return to be 'born' in their family although in fact only some of their features are reborn, and not the entire departed person as such). In Uganda the name Byamuhangi means 'they are of (or

72

for) the Creator'. It is given to a male child by the parents as an indication of their belief that the child belongs to God the Creator. Also in Uganda the name Muwanga means 'the one who puts things in order'. It comes from the legend that one day the sun and moon were fighting and when darkness came over the land the people cried to God for help. Then God sent the divinity Muwanga (won of Wanga) to separate the fighting 'brothers', and put each in its place. This is a religious legend, and there is now a divinity known as Muwanga who symbolizes the idea of order and harmony.

There are many names all over Africa which have religious meanings. Therefore wen can say that African Religion is found in people's and place's names. This shows the influence of religion in the life of the people. It also shows that people with such names are in effect religious carriers.

African Religion is Found in Myths and Legends

Stories myths, legends an biographies of people are another area where we find African Religion. We said in the first chapter that since there was no writing among African peoples, traditional wisdom and experiences and history were passed down through the word of mouth. Therefore, stories, legends and myths became a very important source of information and means of communication. Many religious ideas are found in these oral ways of communication, and every African people has plenty of such stories and myths. For that reason, when people listen to them, or read about them they are listening to the African religious ideas which may be found in them, and many religious ideas are readily taught and spread through the form of stories, legends and myths.

African Religion is Found in Beliefs and Customs

Every African people has a set of beliefs and customs. Beliefs are an essential part of religion. Customs are not always religious, but many contain religious ideas. Religion helps to strengthen and perpetuate some of the customs; and in turn the customs do the same to religion.

Beliefs and customs often go together. They cover all areas of life. Beliefs generally deal with religious ideas; customs deal with what people normally approave of and do.

This book will talk about many religious beliefs of African peoples. They cover topics like God, spirits, birth, death, the hereafter, magic, witchcraft, and so on. When we come across African beliefs, we are in fact dealing with African Religion, although religion is much more than its beliefs. The beliefs are handed down from generation to generation, sometimes with modifications. Without them no religion can inspire its followers. Even when people are converted from African Religion to another religion, they retain many of their former beliefs since it is hard to destroy beliefs. Some of the beliefs in African Religion are like beliefs in other religions, but some are completely different.

Beliefs have a lot of influence on people. But some beliefs can be and often are false; yet people stick to them firmly and act accordingly. Therefore, it is good to understand people's beliefs well, because it is these beliefs which influence their behaviour. In addition to religious beliefs there are beliefs in other areas of life like politics, economics, science, and so on. Everyone holds certain beliefs, because we all need one or other kind of belief in our daily life. For example, if a woman did not believe that fire (or heat) would cook her food she might not be able to provide food for the family everyday. If you did not believe that your letter would reach your friend or parents, you would not write it.

Thus, beliefs are very important and essential for every day. African Religion has many beliefs, and by studying them we are able to understand not only the religion but the people who follow it.

African Religion is Found in All Aspects of Life

We have shown the many areas of African life where we find traditional Religion. They lead us to conclude that it is seen in all aspects of life. Therefore, it influences all areas of life. African Religion has been largely responsible for shaping the character and culture of African peoples throughout the centuries. Even if it has no sacred books, it is written everywhere in the life of the people. To be an African in the Traditional setting is to be truly religious. It has been rightly said that 'Africans are notoriously religious'. In each African society, religion is embedded in the local language, so that to understand the religious life of the people properly, one needs to know their language. In each society there are also individual men and women who have a good knowledge of the religion of their people, and others who are responsible for the performance of religious ceremonies and rituals. These pass on their knowledge to people in general and through training others to carry out the religious life of their community.

PART TWO

PERSPECTIVES IN AFRICAN TRADITIONAL RELIGION

THE STUDY OF AFRICAN TRADITIONAL RELIGION IN HISTORICAL PERSPECTIVE

by

Udobata Onunwa

Introduction

Until recently, the history of African Traditionl Religion has not been of interest to many scholars. Some have consistently maintained that the religion has no history while others held that the study of its history is not possible. Consequently, the presentation of the religion which had been made by several scholars (European or African) in the past four hundred years or so had been tilted towards serving specific goals and interests.

Any study on African Traditional Religion which will focus attention on its historical past would certainly be involving and exacting in its demands of intellectual resources, time, patience and objectivity. This is because this aspect of the religion is an entirely virgin ground. Besides, the prejudices of the past studies have tremendously influenced many who would like to embark on the project.

Yet the relevance of a historical study of African Traditional Religion in recent times can no longer be ignored. In spite of the previous attempts to deny the possibility or relevance of such project, it is now widely accepted by scholars that a comprehensive study of the religion is expedient. In pre-colonial African religion, its theology, rituals, organizations, symbols and rhetoric intimately suffused the whole structure of society. The traditional religion was indeed **Society** itself as there was no clearly defined distinction between the **Sacred** and the **Profane.** Consequently, any systematic study of the traditional religion in any African Society must as a matter of fact (if it is not going to be a peripheral, academic and irrelevant exercise) be carried out in this all-embracing context.

Harold W. Turner has identified two complementary aspects of this comprehensive approach. He sees the historical study of African Religion in two phases: first, professional historians showing interest and in the second place, history of religions' scholars bringing a specialist knowledge of the characistic dynamics and internal processes of religions ... forms of decay and revival, degeneration and reformation, fresh revolution, transposition and conservation. (1) This underlines the belief that to penetrate the core (i.e. the structure, working and meaning) of any aspect of society, one must needs to understand its development, its history.

Inhibitions to a Historical Study of African Traditional Religion

Those conversant with the study of African Traditional Religion know that it was a project pioneered by non-votaries of the faith. Two groups of writers who pioneered the study were the anthropologists and the Christian theologians. Both had their biases and interests and consequently projected those traits in their works. The anthropologists, who thus far, have dominated the study have a standard approach which is **synchronic** rather than **diachronic**. In effect, they continued to describe the religion in a timeless ethnographic present. This synchronic approach was in the past fully accepted when it was erroneously believed that precolonial Africa was by and large static until impacted upon from about the middle of the last century by European economic and political imperialism. (2) The social anthropologists, (with the exception of a few like E.E. Evans-Pritchard and Robin Horton (3) who were concerned with the problem of change over the centuries) portrayed the religion of a petrified society that was alive until it was destroyed by the colonial administration. Two outstanding African historians, Professors J.F.A. Ajayi and E.A. Ayandele have jointly inferred that the notion of a static precolonial traditional religion is only a measure of our ignorance. (4) Yet the old prejudices are hard to eradicate.

Indeed, some other defects and pitfulls which had long term implications are observed in the anthropologist's interpretation of African Traditional Religion. For instance, he works with a preconceived hypothesis and model. He therefore selects his evidence to fit and prove the viability of his model. He thus does not tell the full story nor does he study a religious phenomenon in its entirety.

Probably, a more serious defect of the anthropological interpretation of African Traditional Religion is its inability to investigate the capacity of Africans for abstract philosophical thought. One who, therefore, sees the religion in purely functional terms would miss a good deal of the philosophical and moral wisdom embedded in the system. (5)

The Christian trained theologian has on the other hand hardly touched the task facing the historians of African Traditional Religion. He has, nonetheless, produced a spate of literature on the religion. His problem is that although he is a history of religion's scholar, he is never concerned with the origins, growth and development of the systems in the past. His contributions have predominantly taken a descriptive stance. He has approached the study methodically and seen the religion as a living religious system.

This descriptive survey of African Traditional Religion has been popularized by Professor E.G. Parrinder, an eminent scholar whose contributions in the field of African religious studies have been immense. Yet most of the descriptive surveys tend to concentrate on "beliefs" without giving due recognition to the socio-cultural and ritual fabeic within which they are embedded. They thus reduce African Traditional Religion to a set of "doctrines" analogous in structure to Western Faiths: God at the top, followed by a graded order of divinities, then the ancestor-spirit and lastly the forest-spirits and fetish objects. (6)

This defect is traceable to the neglect of the historical background of the religious phenomena. Obviously, a purely phenomenological stance adopted by many theologians tends to lose cognisance of the social dynamics which influence beliefs and practices.

Newell S. Booth Jr. has succintly summarized the defect in both the anthropological and theological studies of African Traditional Religion. In his own words, "in anthropological writings, that which is **religious** may be "lost" in the larger social context while in writings by historians of religion, the essential "Africanness" tends to be obscurred by the concern for **religion** as such". (7)

Professor E.G. Parrinder's problem is that he is pessimistic about the possibility of a historical study of African Traditional Religion. He believes that African Traditional Religion has a long history but in view of the absence of written documents from within the religion, it is difficult to know that history. He therefore concluded that:

> The history of traditional religion is unknown and few foreign descriptions were made before this century that merit close study, though there are a few hints in some of the more careful explorers' writing. This means

that the development of religion can rarely be guess-
ed ... (8)

Having rejected the idea of a historical study of African Traditional Religion, Parrinder decides to adopt Sir James G. Frazer's
enumerative approach. This approach has been castigated by a
good number or schlars for being either too exhaustive and covering too many religious phenomena or tending towards an abstraction and lacking in interpretative depth.

Unfortunately, Professor J.S. Mbiti, an outstanding
indigenous African Scholar of the traditional religion has equally
denied the possibility of a historical study of the religion. He has
not only denied the possibility of such a project but indirectly
inferred that African Traditional Religion has no history, no
founders, no missionaries, no converts and no prophets. In his
view, it is impossible to describe its history. (9)

A Historical Study of African Traditional Religion: A Ciritique

Although there have been several handicaps to a
meaningful attempt to the study of African Traditional Religion in
historical perspective, the pioneer effort of Professors T.O. Ranger
and I.N. Kimambo is a welcome and encouraging breakthrough
in the discipline. This new development is a result of the ongoing
quest for adequate methodology for the study of traditional religion. The work has shown that it is now possible for one to
reconstruct the African religious past. This new work might
probably be a follow up to the works of Jan Vansina, Daniel
F. McCall among others who have demonstrated the values of
oral traditions in modern historiography. (10) T.O. Ranger and
I.N. Kimambo published **Historical Study of African Religion** in
1972. Both men are professional "secular" historians who felt that
the absence of their colleagues in the field of religion has created
a big vaccum in interpretating African Traditional Religion. The
book has argued that it is impossible to understand the traditional
religion without proper understanding of the historical dimensions
which shaped the religion. This is in effect suggesting a reintegration of religious history into African historiography as a whole.
This will give a 'holistic' approach to the study.

The book has tried to show the various methods of
reconstructing the early religious history of African Societies.

Although the case studies were made in East and Central Africa, the methodology of data collection and analysis would nonetheless fit into other parts of Africa. They therefore serve as a paradigm for any historical reconstruction of the religious experience of any other part of Africa. The specific case studies in the book clearly demonstrate the values of the historical study if adequate historical questions are asked about African religious ideas and institutions. If no other credit is recognized in this book, it has successfully dismissed the misconception of the cultural and racial bias of the scholars which made them refer any "higher" element of negro civilization to the exaggerated diffusionist "Hamitic Theory". Through the analysis of archeological data and oral information, it is now obvious that there was a high degree of interaction between different ethnic groups. This effort should not be seen as "a historians' take over-bid" in the study of an important aspect of African Society where historians had been conspicuously absent for a long time. It is rather a valuable contribution to supplement the ongoing attempt in the field to reconstruct the religious past of Africa.

A Projected Scheme for a Historical Study of African Traditional Religion

To probe into the rich cultural legacies of a "pre-literate African Society," a few important aspects of the religion should be identified. (11) This will help to suggest a scheme for an indepth and comprehensive historical study of the religion.

The first aspect of the religion worth discussing is that of its concepts, ideas and theology. This has to do with a philosophy which man creates to enable him to explain the origin of 'spatio-temporal' phenomena - (his universe, his relationship with that origin and place in the created universe). This embraces such issues like the origin and destiny of man, the nature and qualities of the creator of the universe, the "lesser deities," interaction of the created beings and the distribution of powers among them.

Because the Society is a preliterate one, the ideas are embedded in those myths and legends which deal with origins of things. A careful sifting of myths and legends about gods, should bring out meaning and relevance to the time when African societies began to have a clear perception of the supreme God.

The next aspect would be an assessment of the priests and other cultic personnel. This would involve their lineage, special rights and responsibilities, the method of selection (call) and installation, their transformation into a high spiritual plane soon after they are initiated, etc.

Thirdly, there is need for a critical investigation into the symbols and language which go with organized religions. The music and art of African societies are included in the investigation - this involves the incantations and secret formulae found in the liturgy of the traditional religious worship. Much of African music and art are invariably part of the traditional life and expression.

The fourth aspect may be seen as a census of recognied beings - primarily to identify the nature of their distribution and characteristics. For instance we would like to know how the ecology of a community has affected the religious expression. In some places where there are big rivers, forests, hills, stones or other natural phenomena which are recognized as objects of religious worship, one would like to know how and why attitudes to such object vary from one place to the other, or from one ecological zone to the other. In Nigeria, the Igbo people are conveniently zoned into five different identifiable subculture areas which indlude:

i. The North subculture area made up of Nsukka, Udi, Awgu and Nkanu.
ii. The North West Area including Umunri, Awka, Anam, Onitsha and Nnewi areas.
iii. The North-East incorporating Izzi, Abakaliki, Ezzamgbo, Ikwo, Uburu, Okposi, Afikpo and Ohaozara.
iv. The South Igbo area include the Ngwa Owerri and Ohuhu people. Others are Isu-Item and the Isu-ama subunit of Okigwe, Orlu, Mbano.
v. Finally the Cross-River Igbo subculture area of Abam, Abiriba, Ohafia and Arochukwu and other neighbouring communities. (12)

One would like to know whether "river beings" or "hill beings" were seen as essentially of the same kind or of different kinds or could it be the same being that inhabited all the streams in a subculture area even if those streams were known by different names in different villages. The Imo River, for instance, is known by different names in the various towns it flows past in Eastern Nigeria.

84

The pragmatic manipulation of the four above aspects by religious experts to obtain or attain perceived social and "beyond-earthly" objectives of man in his temporal existence, is the fifth aspect that may engage the interest of the scholar. The sixth and possibly the final aspect is the response of the above five aspects to the influence of internal and external change-agents.

The above scheme may look difficult to accomplish in the face of lack of written documents by votaries of the faith dating far back into the early periods of African history. The task is however not entirely impossible. One can optimistically conclude thet the contributions of Professor Merrick Posnansky along this line is an evidence that African's ancient religion could be restructured. (13) In the same vein, D.D. Hartle and Thurston Shaw have carefully shown that in Eastern Nigeria, such a reconstruction of the past through archeological discoveries is possible. (14) Archeology will therefore help to throw more light on the early religious practices of the Africans. Comparative linguistic study has much to say about the migration of divinities and ideas. Armed with such data, a scholar would be able to discuss themes such as the evolution of the panthean of any given African society with some measure of confidence and certainty.

Specific Application of the Above Scheme

As a humble contribution to the on going quest for an adequate methodology to a comprehensive study of African Traditional Religion, the present writer has used the above scheme in an indepth study of the theme of God and gods in Igbo traditional religion. (15) In the said study, the writer examined such items as "The Igbo and their perception of the World" which is a historical profile of the people and an assessment of their world views as their scales expand and they imbibe new ideas. In the various subculture areas, these items are examined in relation to their historical experience, contact with neighbours etc. Other items examined include the "belief in God," "names and titles of God," "attributes of God," "Worship of God." His methodology which he christened **Culture-area and Phenomenological Approach** is a "multi-dimensional one" which incorporated a quest into the history of the people. In addition it took cognizance of the previsous recommendations of some scholars who had called for a "multi-dimensional" or "poly-methodic perspective" in the study of African Traditional Religion. He thus applied a broad-based interdisciplinary method thereby combined as many perspectives as possible in order to reveal the full semantic, existential and social meanings of African religious systems. This has enabled him to attempt a systematic study of the manifestation or forms of the religion and their associated meanings from the morphological, typological and comparative viewpoints or in other words the vocabulary, grammar and syntax of the religious system. (16)

The analysis of Igbo concept of time helped to identify the significance of the various Igbo names of God in the different subculture areas. For instance, the analysis of the semantics as well as the migration theories gave valuable hints on the different manifestations of the religion in the areas. The analysis of oral information revealed a high degree of interaction between people of one subculture area and the other, some cross-cultural similarities between some Igbo communities on the periphery of Igbo territory and their non-Igbo neighbours. In addition, some communities within the "core-Igbo area" or "the Igbo heartland" manifest some similar cultural traits with other distant non-Igbo societies. Some of the interactions have been traced to gradual filtering movements of small groups of people into some areas rather than to great conquests and migrations of large number of people.

Similar investigations could be carried into the religious systems of any other given people. Recognising that no one single theoretical framework could fully provide such an indepth analysis of the religion of a people, the need for an interdisciplinary co-operation obviously involves a historical study and perspective. The inclusion of the historical method in the study has revealed that the Igbo traditional religious heritage has shown remarkable versatility in its history and development; absorbing, rejecting coalescing with and reforming different types of materials on its way.

Conclusion

In the foregoing discussions, we have suggested that the curent and future study of African Traditional Religion be given a **diachronic** perspective, unlike the apparent neglect of history in the previous studies. This can be done by fitting the study into the scheme outlined above. Such an effort will no doubt show that although we believe that the traditional religion (and in fact religion in general) is one of the most conservative aspects of human life and society, it has been responsive to the continuous political, economic, ecological and institutional changes which have characterized man's life on earth.

Indeed, it should be noted that although we speak of the traditional African religion as "traditional" it has been changing not only in the broad space of African continent but also over all historical time. It was not only the rise of empires and the pressures of Christianity, Islam and colonial administration that have characterized the changes. Several other factors were involved. Religious change is inherently a gradual and unobstrusive phenomenon - the use of iron, conquest of new stretches of forests for agriculture, long distance trade, mastery of seas and hunting for games in big forests all have their implications for African Traditional Religion. Whether it is realized or not, the changes have been going on all through the years.

Several elements which would prove helpful in the reconstruction of African religious history include archeology, myths and legends as well as a comparative linguistic study. No one particular element nor discipline could therefore provide a balanced and elaborate data for such a gigantic project. The use of these elements - myth, archeology, legend, linguistics, etc. to reconstruct African religious history would undoubtedly help to bring out a systematic presentation of African religion. That will be meaningful in the context of every community's peculiar experience and perception of its world and of its place and destiny in it, instead of what would win the applause of Western rationalism.

Okot P'Bitek, the Ugandan-born radical scholar had earlier on castigated fellow African scholars who did not have such aim in their writings on African Religion. They rather wrote to impress their Western audience by tilting their descriptions of African deities towards Western theological pattern. It has to be emphasized that African Societies were not patterned on Cartesian rationalism. Far from that, we appreciate the fact that scriptures of African people are written in the corpus of the oral accounts known as myths, legends and folklores, which attempt to explain the origin of things. Some of the myths and legends do not even show logical coherence, yet they serve the purposes.

Recent attempts by some scholars on the reconstruction of African Traditional Religion through the use of oral information have debunked the prejudices and biases of some earlier writers who ignored oral information as a viable tool of historical reconstruction. The new attempts are not only encouraging but also refreshing. The study of Traditional Religion must be an all-embracing project (including among other perspective, the historical) if we shall understand how the religious beliefs, practices, institutions, etc. have been adjusting to the continuously moving and changing rythms of life.

Footnotes

1 H.W. Turner, "The Way Forward in the Religious Study of African Primal Religions" **Journal of Religion in Africa,** 12, 1 (1981) 5.
2 See Adiele E. Afigbo "Religion in Nsukka: A Historical Prolegomeon." (Unpub. Seminar Paper, University of Nigeria, Nsukka, March 15-16 1983), p. 2.
3 Robin Horton, "Ritual man in Africa," **AFRICA,** 34,2 (1964) 85-104; "African Traditional Thought and Western Science", **AFRICA,** 37, 2, (1967) 50-71; "The High God: A comment on Father O'connell's **AFRICA,** 2 (1971); "On the rationality of Conversion, Part I", **AFRICA,** 45, 4 (1975) 292-306; Caroline Ifeka-Moller, "White-Power: Social Structural Factors in Conversion to Christianity in Eastern Nigeria 1921-1966" **Canadian Journal of African Studies,** 8 1 (1974) 55-72. J.D.Y. Peel and Robin Horton, "Conversion and Confusion: A Rejoinder on Christianity in Eastern Nigeria," **Canadian Journal of African Studies,** 10, 3 (1976) 481-498.
4 J.F. Ade-Ajayi and E.A. Ayandele, "Emerging Themes in Nigerian and West African Religious History." **Journal of African Studies,** 1, 1 (1974) 32.
5 U.R. Onunwa "The Study of West African Traditional Religion in Time-Perspective" (Unpublished Ph.D. Thesis, University of Nigeria, 1984), p. 80.
6 B.C. Ray "Recent Studies of African Religion." **History of Religions** 12, 1 (August, 1972), 82.
7 Newell S. Bouth Jr. (Ed) **African Religions: A Symposium** (New York: NOK Publishers, Ltd.) 3
8 E.G. Parrinder, **Africa's Three Religions** (London: Sheldon Press Ltd. 1976) p. 9 (First Published as Religion in Africa, 1969) p. 9.

9   See J.S. Mbiti **African Religions and Philosophy** (London: Heine-
     mann, 1969) pp. 4, 5, 190, 191.

10 Jan Vansina **Oral Traditions** (Chicago, 1965) Daniel F. McCall,
     Africa in Time Perspective (N.Y. O.U.P. 1969). First
     published by Boston University Press 1964. C.F. David
     Henige, **Oral Historiography** (London: Longmann, 1982).

11 See U.R. Onunwa Ibid; 140-141.

12 See Adiele E. Afigbo Ibid; p. 611.

13 Merrick Posnansky "Archeology, Ritual and Religion" in T.O.
     Ranger and I.O. Kimambo (eds). **The Historical Study
     of African Religion.** (London: Heinemann, 1972) 29-30.

14 D.D. Hartle, "Archeology in Eastern Nigeria." **Nigeria Maga-
     zine** No. 93 (June 1967) pp. 136-7.
     Thurston Shaw, **Igboukwu: An Account of Archeological
     Discoveries in Eastern Nigeria.** (London: Faber and
     Farber, 1970).

15 Udobata R. Onunwa **Studies in African Traditional Religion:
     A Quest for Methodology.** (Enugu: Fourth Dimension
     Publishers) Forthcoming 1986.

16 See H.W. Turner, "The Way Forward, Ibid." 1-2.

AFRICAN TRADITIONAL RELIGION IN WESTERN SCHOLARSHIP

by

Ogbu U. Kalu

I. The Problem

Okot P'Bitek died a few years ago. He was a maverick, articulate, Ugandan scholar. During his years in Oxford studying anthropology, he came face to face with racism in an intellectual citadel. He recoiled into the beauty of African culture especially as recorded in its oral tradition such as the **Song of Lawino** and the **Song of Ocol.** He broke out from these to examine how Europeans have wrongly portrayed African culture and traditional religion in their writings. (1) That was in 1970.

A couple of years later, when E.B. Idowu, a Yoruba scholar, whose doctoral dissertation was on the Yoruba God, Olodumare (later published as a book in 1962), documented European terms and notions of African religion, a reviewer quipped that Idowu was quarrelling with dead men. Most of the authors of the reviewed perceptions were as dead as the door nail. (2) Idowu's **African Traditional Religion: A Definition** was an effort to define the nature of African religions as an academic discipline.

The reviewer wasEuropean and preferred a good quip to the reality. Both P'Bitek and Idowu drew attention to one of the ironies in academics, namely, that in the reconstruction of some of the aspects of the world we have lost, the surviving portrait may be fully erroneous and more representative of the biases of the scholar than the reality. Indeed, the emendations or excretions created by the scholar may distort the true portrait. African Traditional Religion has suffered this. It has, therefore, been argued that the study of African Traditional Religion schould now begin to lay emphasis on methodology. The clearing of the under-brush should begin by examining the goals, undergirding ideologies, methods and conclusions of earlier scholars.

Some years ago, Professor C.C. Ifemesia observed that if scholars succeeded in recovering the authentic religious beliefs and rituals of practitioners without analysis, much would have been achieved because the analyses, garnished with erudite theories and models, had fully joined natural forces to ruin the vitality of indigenous religions. This is the rationale and power in Christian Gaba's **Scriptures of an African People: The Sacred Utterances of the Anlo** (3) containing the prayers without the analyses which formed the second part in the original University of London doctoral dissertation. This book came out in 1973 and was followed in 1975 by Aylward Shorter's **African Christian Theology** in which the first section was devoted to the study of methodology. (4) The same concern for a review of how African traditional religion has been studied informed H.W. Turner's seminal article, "The Way Forward in the Religious Study of African Primal Religions." (5)

These authors were interested in mapping out the path for the future. But first, the past must be understood and, for the most part, that past was dominated by Western scholars. So, their prejudices, ideologies and methodologies must be firstly understood.

One must hasten to add that such a review is neither an inverted racism no a constriction of the resources available for a proper and comparative study of primal religions. H.W. Turner had, in 1981, raised the spectre when he observed that:

> There has been a widespread tendency, often appearing at conferences, for African scholars to reject all studies of African primal religions made by non-Africans and using what are labelled "merely Western" categories and methods. This rejection has been supported by some Westerners anxious to atone for attitudes which have depreciated, despised or distorted African religions in the past. (6)

Okot PBitek pointed to the core of the problem when he noted that African scholars themselves were now perceiving and interpreting their indigenous religions through Western binoculars while Hellenistic and Christian categories provide the view-finders. Okot P'Bitek characterized such studies as a betrayal and the evidence of the colonization of the African's mind.

Besides, comparative studies cannot be meaningfully done when one of the component parts has not been properly studied. The study of African Traditional Religion in Western scholarship is, therefore germaine to the definition of an academic discipline.

II. Variegated Images I: Early Colonial

The image of African traditional religions in Western scholarship has changed in time and without this time perspective, the impression of quarrelling with dead men might persist. Western scholarship has an in-built corrective and vibrant character and, thus, images painted by certain groups at some points in time are usually corrected by others as interests and ideologies change.

The outline of the changing perspectives begins with the first commentators on African cultures and religions who were not Europeans but itinerant Arab scholars. But as the trans-Sahara trade contacts were supplemented with voyages of discovery by Europeans, new sets of information reached Europe. Shipmasters and curious traders and explorers fuelled the output. The exigencies of European politics forced deliberate processes of colonization. Colonial officials of various hues added to the pool of commentaries either as amateur ethnographers or official documenters of ethnographic information. Social Sciences developed in Europe and produced a cadre of anthropologists. Here, it must be pointed out that sociology referred to the study of civilised European societies while **anthropology** referred to the study of primitive societies. Some anthropologists were of the arm-chair variety who wrote profusely and propounded racist social theories based on the reports and diaries of explorers such as Hakluyt. Others did field work. Various schools of anthropology sharpened the methodology and the effects of the changing goals and methods showed in the image of African religions in Western scholarship. Indeed, modern commentators such as H.W. Turner, Robin Horton, Aylward Shorter, Benjamin Ray, Newell Booth and such-like reveal similar concerns as those of the Africans while others, coming from comparative religion perspective, are more concerned with issues of theories and comparisms.

An enduring or resilient group of commentators is the christian missionary group. From the Portuguese Missionaries, from various orders, through the varieties of Protestant denominations who have operated in the continent came books, articles and conference records suffused with images of African religions.

Let us look at these variegated images in greater detail: Ibn Battuta's account of his trans-Saharan crossing into black Africa and sojourn in Western Sudan is revealing of the attitude of itinerant Arab scholars and geographers. (7) Their accounts cover the period from the eighth through the 15th Century

93

when Europeans had virtually no knowledge of and no contact with West Africa. Ibn Battuta dismissed the religion of his host as pagan, wrote many anecdote of their crude civilization and cannibalism and ridiculed their ignorant efforts at muslim practices. An aspect to the account is the nature of islamic presence in Western Sudan: moslems were more interested in commerce, contact with the royal court and enjoyed a quarrantined residence. Naturally islamic influence was more crucial in diplomatic and administrative services provided for the kings by the Arabs. **The Kano Chronicle** has detailed much of these and Al-Maghili's treatise which has been compared to Machiavelli's **The Prince** epitomized the character of islamic presence. They were too insulated from the real lives of the people. Besides, accounts in this period tended to be romantic, emphasising the esoteric and designed to excite imagination than as accurate portraiture. An interesting aspect to this early islamic attitude to African religion is the irony: on the one hand, a perjorative tradition was developed which flourished both in the **quarrantine** and **jihadist** phases but in the **mixing stage,** traditional religiosity was so deeply assimilated that her influence could not be wiped out even in the midst of orthodoxy. Doi and Abdul have illustrated the assimilation of Yoruba traditional religion into islam, for instance, **ifa** divinatory system has influenced divination in islam.

The predominantly romantic and racist ideology became even more pronounced in the period which J.H. Parry dubbed as the **Age of Reconnaissance,** when "voyages of discovery", expeditions sponsored by philanthropists and trading companies became the order of the day. The building of European hegemony with wide contact with other races and cultures was a romanticized affair. Imagination was fired with lurid accounts which boosted morale and encouraged funding agencies.

Two attitudes prevailed in their accounts: some took the position that the level of religiosity was too low to be honoured with mention in a book. A certain Duarte Pecheo Pereira (1505-1520) is quoted to have brushed the issue aside by observing that "The Negroes are idolatrous. We shall avoid mentioning them". (8) The Portuguese deviced the word **fetiche** (fetish) as a summary, in one word, of African religion. This explains the absence of information on religion in the works of some respected voyagers of the 15th and 16th Centuries.

As the resources of the Renaissance period improved scientific knowledge in Europe, as the commercial contact in gold and slave widened, European hubris, confidence and ethnocentrism bloomed. A second attitude emerged as a number of commentators

94

came to the scene who gave fuller accounts, however pejorative. Shipmasters such as John Barbot and Captain Theodore Canot, for an example, left more detailed accounts of the terrain.

John Barbot observed that the religion of the negroes of the Coasts of North and South Guinea

> is a gross superstitious paganism, though most ... acknowledge a Supreme Being but in a very erroneous manner ... being thus prepossessed they turn their thoughts and practice to those absurd inferior gods in whom they put all their confidence. (9)

Barbot's description of Upper Guinea which appeared in 1732 typifies the position of various shipmasters of the period: Flammond D'Olfart Dapper, Captain J. Welsh who visited Benin, William Bossman who served as a factor of the Dutch Company in El Mina and described the coast of Guinea in 1705, Herbert Thomas who travelled through Southern Africa and de Brosses who observed the religious culture at Whydah and wrote about the **Cult of the Fetish Gods** in 1760.

However, the work of de Brosses is a point of departure. He started the scientific speculations on the origin of religion, the comparative analyses of various religions, thus linking the Guinea Coast with Egypt. This was a pursuit which later characterized the Age at Enlightenment and formed the background to the speculations in J.G. Frazer's **The Golden Bough.**

Frazer used the questionnaire method without field work. In 1877 he sent a booklet entitled **Questions on the Manners, Customs etc. of Uncivilized or Semi-Civilized Peoples** to administrators, missionaries and others in remote parts of the world. Beyond speculations on **origin** of religion, Frazer's conclusions supported a comparative religious approach:

> The idea of regarding the religions of the world not dogmatically but historically in other words not as systems of truth or falsehood to be demonstrated or refuted, but as phenomena of consciousness to be studied like any other aspect of human nature - is one which seems hardly to have suggested itself before the 19th Century. Now when, laying aside as irrelevant to the purpose in hand the question of the truth or folly of religious practices, we examine side by side the religious of different races and ages, we find that, while they differ from each other in many particulars,

the resemblances between them are numerous and fundamental, and that they mutually illustrate and explain each other, the distinctly stated faith and practice of other races. Thus, the comparative study of religion soon forces on us the conclusion that the course of religious evolution has been, at all events in its earlier stages, can be fully understood without a comparison of it with many others. (10)

. It is not only the methodological problem which raises Frazer's work to a great concern, it is rather the ideology, either African religion was at a primitive level or it was a degraded form. As P.D. Curtin put the matter:

Travellers to West Africa continued to turn up evidence, both spurious and genuine, indicating an earlier contact with the east. In the light of culture theories suggesting possible "degeneration" from an earlier, higher stage of development, it was natural to interpret West African Religion as a "corrupted" version of Zoroastrianism or a degraded form of the religion of ancient Egypt. (11)

Others along the route to the unilinear theory of evolution of religion include Sir R.F. Burton. Burton deserves a whistle stop because he was quite an interestingly acerbic character. At one level, he was a brilliant linguist, relentless collector of anthropological fact and a wit. At another level, he earned much wealth and fame. Yet there was a cantakerous streak in his nature; he was constantly plagued by unhappiness. Above all, he hated negroes - so much that he refused to accept a posting as Vice-Consul in 1861 if he was to reside in Fernando Po. He ridiculed the Creoles of Sierra Leone with as much savagery as he attacked the inhabitants of Dahomey. His portrayal of African Religion was precise in its application of Darwin's theory of evolution onto social and cultural contexts:

The negro is still at that rude dawn of faith - fetishism and has rarely advanced to idolatory ... He has never grasped ideas of personal deity, a duty in life, a moral code or a shame of lying. He rarely believes in a future state of rewards and punishment which whether true or not, are infallible indices of human progress. (12)

96

T.J. Hutchinson's two accounts of his **Impressions of West Africa** (1858) and **Ten Years' Wandering among the Ethiopians From Senegal to Gabon** (1861) amplify these views. Indeed, Robert Rotberg's study of **Africa and Its Explorers** (1970) (13) has provided further documentation from East and Central Africa to show that social darwinism influenced much of the commentary of african traditional religion in this age and later blossomed into a golden bough.

E.E. Evans-Pritchard's lecture series which were published as **Theories of Primitive Religion** (14) castigated the quest for origins of religion by arm-chair theorists such as Frazer as "unscientific". This is a curious castigation for those who were basking in the sunshine of the hey days of scienticism. It, however, misses the point: the theorists were children of their day. The 19th century was suffused with speculative, philosophical anthropology. Besides, Gobineau was spawning his scientific theories of race across the channel. The image of African Traditional Religion was only one of the many casualties.

Meanwhile, informal relationship with "primitive" peoples soon gave way to crown colonies and deeper involvement into full-bloosomed colonies under the pressure of competition and scramble. Perhaps, as Adam Kuper's study of **Anthropologists and Anthropology 1922-1972,** would suggest, the science of anthropology emerged into a full discipline. The exigencies of governance nudged maters. Two works by women are indices of the change of perception. Mary Kingsley's **West African Studies** (1899) urged a more careful study of indigenous cultures so as to avoid

> the false and exaggerated views given of them by stray-travellers, missionaries and officials who for their aggrandisement ... made the stay-at-home statesmen think that Africans are still awful savages or silly children. (15)

Lady Lugard's **A Tropical Dependency** (1906) was in the same vein partially because the rich heritage of Northern Nigeria had impressed and partially because it had become clear that exaggerations by commentators were deliberate attempts to wear the mantles and accolades of either Livingstone or Stanley, who went in search of Livingstone. Perhaps, it needs to be stressed that the image of African Traditional Religion changed with the attitude towards Africa and her culture.

III. Variegated Images II: Data for Governance

Mary H. Kingsley went further to conclude that:

> It is our duty to know the true nature of those people with whom we are now dealing in tens of thousands, so that by this knowledge we may be enabled to rule them, wisely. (16)

This plea or realization of the necessity to base administrative and political policy on a definite knowledge of the peoples and societies of the region was a reflection of new conditions. Firstly, in the scramble for colonies, Europeans came into contact with large numbers of people with myriads of culture. Secondly, the newly-acquired territories were too large for easy domination. As Rotberg and Mazrui showed in **Protest in Black Africa,** many forms of protest arose and threatened the installation of new administrative structures, new legal systems, courts, enforcement agencies, new financial policies, especially taxation, a new economic order based on legitimate trade and generally a new civilization. Thirdly, colonization was followed by rumours of war and soon the First World War. The inter-war years witnessed a massive economic depression followed by a second World War and a battered Europe. T.S. Eliot's **Wasteland Poems** and Spengler's **The Decline of the West** betrayed the collapse of hubris and the notion of Age of Progress. The West could not muster the material and human resources for a truly imperial rule. Baffled officers, therefore, sought ethnographic data for governance.

Admittedly, Western colonizers anticipated much of this need. The British, for instance, at first encouraged administrative officials to engage in amateur study of cultures. This lies at the root of Charles Patridge's acclaimed **Cross River Natives** and A.G. Leonard's **The Lower Niger and the Tribes.** Soon, the government appointed official anthropologists from among the administrative ranks before resorting to the employment of trained anthropologists. It was discovered that these professionals, like typical academics quickly veered to broad theoretical pursuits. Thus Northcote W. Thomas, Charles H. Meek, S. Leith Ross, Talbot, Jeffreys and a host of others in Southern Nigeria pursued detailed studies of a variety of tribes from the 1920's to the 1940's. In the 1930's, the government also sponsored **Intelligence Reports** on smaller units written by colonial officials. R.S. Rattray did the same for the Ashanti of the Gold Coast while a number of studies appeared for East and Central Africa.

G.I. Jones, a colonial official, who started amateurely, took his furlough in Oxford and developed into a seasoned anthropologist, has observed that some of the early studies were very descriptive. But, at least, the methodology changed significantly. Field work, interviews, use of native clerks and so on became paramount in the collection of data. Even if some interpretations were inaccurate, wild theorization petered down, though not off. Taking Igbo religion for an example, H. Palmer, M.D.W. Jeffreys and others still conjectured broadly off the mark, concerned as they were with Hamitic and Junkun origins of Igbo religious structures and symbols.

The study of African religions benefitted from these descriptive data because the "magico-religious system" of the people was found to be central to establishing order. For instance, oracles, secret societies, sacralized social and political structures constituted either opposition or possible support to the new order. This aspect needs further explanation: the depleted resources of the colonizers forced the use of **indirect rule** system in British colonies. This involved the grafting of indigenous systems into the new order. It was necessary to sift through the old order for viable agencies for domesticating the new. Moreover, it was discovered that the African world-view was predominantly religious. Therefore, the religion which underpropped the world view must be understood.

The stress is the significant change in attitude between the romantic period and the middle period of the colonial. At the turn of the century, Europeans still laid emphasis on trade and commented with an eye to matters of commercial importance. Knowledge of political and social structure was elementary. Religion was for the most part ignored. Travellers wrote to please their audience as well as to inform. Religion was mere pagan error. But spectacular festivals, human sacrifice, judicial ordeals, polygny, were curiosities and were recounted at length. The literature was characterized by attention to the repellent aspects, love of the extraordinary, the exotic and the blending of genuine intellectual curiosity with a libidinous fascination for descriptions of other people who break with impunity the taboos of one's own society. Accounts were generally unsystematic and there was the tendency to blame African Traditional Religion for the failings of the society. Paganism, they argued, fuelled reptilian passions.

With J. Beecham's **Ashantee and the Gold Coast** fresh air seeped in with an effort to understand indigenous religious structures. (17) This trend bloosomed in the colonial period with the constraints of data for governance.

A good example of how the new approach to African culture influenced the study of African religions is the career of R.S. Rattray. He is best known for his two works on **Ashanti Law and Constitution** and **Religion and Art in Ashanti.** As he wrote in 1928, he was hired as an official anthropologist to provide data on governance. He started with the legal structure of the most powerful and independent tribe of the Gold Coast. In his own words,

> I soon found myself, in pursuance of my earlier intentions, constantly confronted with words in the Ashanti language, which, while primarily associated with religion, were nevertheless continuously found in connexion with legal and constitutional procedure. (18)

He discovered that Ashanti law and religion were so intimately associated that he had to study the religious structure before continuing with the previous task. Rattray's importance is that he reflected on the ideology undergirding the study of religion. He rejected the older school which would relegate all that curious spiritual past to shelves and glass cases, the fate of a dying culture. He believed that African religion was co-extensive with other ingredients of culture and that the soul, the inner dynamics should be recovered as those of a living religion capable of producing as much as the foreign religions. Rattray's problems were firstly, the tendency among the progressives, within the colonial establishment, who wished to "retain all that is best" and secondly, the christians who wished to civilize and convert. The first group would have a hard task to pick and choose and, thus, truncate a living religion. Besides, their agents, the educated Africans, had lost touch with the authentic religion. The second group could not be abandoned with the result of leaving the Africans unchristianized and yet Rattray knew that Christianity was destructive of the inner core of African religion. He battled with his dilemma with an empathic study of African religion and with the firm conviction that

> before our civilization began to break down pure native customs, (Ashanti religion) guaranteed very similar standards to these set by the higher form of Christian ethical teachings. (19)

100

With the years came the development of scientific, independent professional studies. The volume of studies on African religion and culture increased rapidly. But professional anthropologists are often like combatants from various army formations each wearing the colours of their formation. Varied perceptions on how to study cultural ingredients grew with increased level of field work and horning of methodology. Some sought to analyse the function, others the **structure,** others the **meaning** shrounded by symbolism while some were more interested in the **conflicts, dynamics,** and "contradictions" which would catalyse change in societies. Since African world-view is predominantly religious, the increased wave of anthropological studies benefitted the study of religion.

The early works were predominantly **functionalist** in approach: E. Evans-Pritchard on the Nuer, Linehardt on the Dinka, Nadel on the Nupe, Rattray on the Ashanti, Daryll-Forde on the Ekoi, Kenneth Little on the Mende, John Goody on the Lo-Daga, M.M. Green on Mbano, R. Smith on the Mbembe of the Upper Cross-River and R.E. Bradbury on the Edo, Paul Bohannon worked on the Tiv but Downes concentrated on **Tiv Religion,** David Gamble on the Wolof of Senegambia and Merra MeCulloch on **The Peoples of Sierra Lenoe.**

In latter years, scholars shifted from broad ethnographic studies to specfic analyses of religion and religious ideas, for instance, Fortes on inscrutable fate, **Oedipus and Job in West African Religion,** R.T. Parson's **Religion in an African Society** based on the Kono people of Sierra Leone, Robin Horton's intellectualist hypothesis on the relationship between the enlargement of scale and religious ideas, Victor Turner's seminal studies on ritual, symbolism and religion among the Ndembu. Others such as N. Paden's **Religion and Politics in Kano** examined the role of religion in politics and state formation. One of themost interesting anthropologists in this area is Simon Ottenberg whose series of books and articles on Afikpo is a mine of information and the application of analytical methods.

The two decades of 1970's and 1980's have witnessed a different set of approaches. Much water has flowed under the bridge: African Traditional Religion has emerged into an academic discipline. J.S. Mbiti's **African Religion and Philosophy** heralded the birth. Secondly, African scholars started to study their own culture with nationalist fervour, from first-hand experience. The resilience or persistence of African religiosity which S.N. Ezeanya dubbed as "endurance of conviction" ensured that one was not studying a dead religion but an alive force. Thirdly, the need for

101

text books became urgent; fourthly, the problems of defining the discipline and the quest for viable methodology became increasingly crucial. These concerns produced **The Journal of Religion in Africa** first edited by Andrew Walls and later by Adrian Hastings and published by E.J. Brill, Leiden. These concerns have also determined the spate of new works by H.W. Turner, Newell Booth, Marion Kilson, Benjamin Ray and others. For East and Central Africa, Ranger and Kimambo's **The Historical Study of African Religion** reveals a crop of new scholars and approaches. The historical approach emphasizes the effect of moving time frame on religious ideas. African Traditional Religion was never static. (20)

Typical of the new trend are two sets of studies. The first is the West European approach typified by the French and the Germans. In 1912, Leo Frobenius enthused,

> I have gone to the Atlantic again and again... But I have failed to find it governed by the 'insensible fetish'... I discovered the souls of these peoples and found that they were more than humanity's burnt out husks. (21)

This set the stage for the Kulturkreis approach which fits with Magraet Mead's emphasis in **Patterns of Culture** that each ingredient of culture makes meaning within the total context of that culture. It became possible to study African religious traditions within their cultural context. Many German scholars including Placide Temple's study of **Bantu Philosophy** were influenced by Frobenius' positive attitude.

The French, with their interest in symbols and ideas went further to probe the **soul** of the African. Marcel Griaule's **Conversations with Ogotemmeli,** a priest of Dogon, Mali, further underscored the realization that behind African religiosity was a world-view which was explained by and underpropped religion. As Dominique Zahan said, it was possible to study ironically the animating principle of life of the African or **The Religion, Spirituality and Thought of Traditional Africa.** Myth was not the other word for error but a means or vehicle of expressing experience.

The second notable fact is the work of E.G. Parrinder who brought out the first text-book on African Traditional Religion in 1949 and followed this with two others, by the grace of Sheldon Press in 1954 and 1969.

He attempted a systematic portraiture of African Traditional Religion which has her authenticity, inner structure and dynamics and was worthy of study. Parrinder did field work and for many years encouraged the study of African religiosity and supervised many theses in this area. It could be said that before J.S. Mbiti, Parrinder was the most prominent pioneer in the field.

IV. Variegated Images III: Christian Crusaders

The hostility of Christianity to African religions is a truism and has been the cause of much commentary. On the one hand, it is realized that this attitude applied to all other non-christian religions because of an affirmation of the uniqueness of christian belief. On the other hand, it has been explained by the differing world-views. Christians recognized that they could not induce the Africans to abandon a covenant with the gods of their fathers without destroying the religion which underpropped the world-view and culture. A power-encounter and conflict were inevitable. Persecutions followed: the missionaries used the powerful clouts of the government and traders to persecute traditionalists. However, the relationship with the colonial officers was always fraught with ambiguities. The traditionalists were not passive, they used every available means to regroup and attack converts.

The main contention here is that the Western christian contribution to the study of African religions has been influenced by two factors: her self-understanding and perception of other religions. Both factors have not been shifting with the changing contours of European theology. Admittedly secular factors affect theological reflection but this paper will sidestep a fuller discussion of these.

Suffice it to say that initially, Western christian self-perception was characterized by two facts: the uniqueness of christianity and the church as the only receptacle of truth and vehicle of salvation. Secondly, Western Christians shared the racist ideology which suffused their cultural milieux. Both Protestant and Catholic theologies blanketed out other religions with the sound of the gavel which pronounced: **extra ecclesiam nulla salus est**: there is no salvation outside the church. A combined force of this assertion and racism caused the conflict with traditional African religion. It ensured that early missionary writings were prejorative as the fearful titles of the books indicated.

Curiously too, cross-cultural mission was underpropped by a heavy dose of propaganda. There was need to boost morale, material resources and volunteers. Missionary bodies established magazines, held open air services, rallies, deputations, door-to-door campaigns, used women and children, broke into clubs and organizations of various types to raise funds and personnel. They had to convey a derogatory image of a benighted African awaiting to be saved with the light of gospel, an image of communities held in captivity by witch doctors who were agents of fearful Satan. The exotic, the romantic aspects of African culture and religion were collected to impress donors and volunteers. Fired with poems of Ruyard Kipling and the stirring novels of G.A. Henty, christians posed as soldiers marching on to war against African religiosity. The image in the literature was derived from this crusading ideology.

As times and perception changed, the Western churches began to recognize that though other religions are human constructs, they do, in God's providential pedagogy, provide a "preparation for the gospel". This **Areopagus** attitude ameliorated the degree of hostility to African religions. It boiled down to an acknowledgment that other religions as such are not outside but within the history of salvation. In some ways an individual can be saved not despite but in one's community of faith, because in some way these religion incarnate sufficient "religious beginnings" (incepta religiosa) of a supernatural response to the revelation in Christ.

In recent years, the epoch-making Vatican II took a very radical posture. Some documents are very pertinent:

i. Decree on the Church's Missionary Activity (**AdGentes,** Dec. 7, (1965)
ii. **Evangelii Nuntiandi,** Dec. 8, 1975
iii. Declaration on the Relation of the Church to Non-Christian Religions (**Nostra Actate,** Paul VI, Oct. 28, 1965).
iv. The Attitude of the Church towards the Followers Of Other Religions (Secretariat for Non-Christian Religions, march 3, 1984).

A thorough analysis of these documents would reveal the radical proposition of the church's stance on dialogue with other religions. It involves a re-understanding of certain key theological points: ecumenism, the universality of God's creation of the oiukemene, the fact of Israel's election, the uniqueness of Christ, the Jewishness of Christ, the universality of Christ, the theological basis for dialogue, and the Salvation of peoples of non christian religions. Admittedly, the Protestants had focussed on this important missiological problem and this produced H. Kraemer's seminal study. Vatican II in **Lumen Gentium** came with a refreshing verdict:

> Those also can attain to everlasting salvation who through no fault of their own do not know the Gospel of Christ or his Church. (22)

Nostra Actate affirmed that other religions often "reflect a ray of that Truth which enlightens all" (Jn. 1:9) and that "the Catholic Church rejects nothing that is true and holy in these religions" (no. 2, cf. **Lumen Gentium**, No. 17) for there are "treasures that a bountiful God has distributed among the nations of the earth", that Roman Catholics should converse with followers of religions in order to "recognize, preserve and foster the good things, spiritual and moral, as well as the sociocultural values found among the followers of other religions."

This set the stage for a concerted study of African traditional religion designed to identify those elements which could be baptized and used in evangelization. A number of studies by Aylward Shorter and other christian scholars fell within this category. Behind this ideology was a fundamental theological basis: firstly, to indicate which elements fell under the judgement of the gospel; two, to identify which elements could serve as the **vehicle** for spreading the gospel. The sole aim of the church was to mission according to Christ's mandate.

In conclusion, christian crusaders have been forced by the exigencies of the mission field to turn into empathetic scholars. Much of the ideologies in Europe have changed with the upturns in socio-political and economic changes. The study of African Traditional Religion has benefitted. Many curricula in higher education include the study. It is gradually coming of age.

Footnotes

1 Okot P'Bitek, **African Religions in Western Scholarship** (Nairobi: East African Publishing Bureau, 1970).

2 E.B. Idowu, **African Traditional Religion: A Definition** (London: SCM Press, 1973); **Olodumare: God in Yoruba Belief** (London: Longman, 1962).

3 Christian Gaba, **Scriptures of an African People: The Sacred Utterances of the Anlo** (New York: NOK Publishers Ltd., 1973).

4 Aylward Shorter, **African Christian Theology** (London: Geoffrey Chapman, 1975).

5 H.W. Turner, "The Way Forward in the Religious Study of African Primal Religions", **Journal of Religion in Africa**, 12, 1 (1981), 1-15.

6 **Ibid.**, p. 2.

7 Noel King and Said Hamdum (eds.) **Ibn Battuta in Black Africa** (Oxford University Press, 1971).

8 Cit. R.U. Onunwa, "The Study of West African Traditional Religion in Time Perspective", Ph.D, University of Nigeria, Nsukka, 1984, p. 44.

9 John Barbot, "A Description of the Coasts of North and South Guinea, 1732" in **A Collection of Voyages and Travels** Vol. V, (London, 1746); Theodore Canot, **Memories of a Slave Trader** (London, 1835).

10 Cit. L.M. Angus-Butterworth, "Sir James Frazer (1854-1941) and the Golden Bough", **Contemporary Review** Vol. 230 no. 1335 (April, 1977), 196-200.

11 P.D. Curtin, **The Image of Africa: British Ideas and Action, 1780-1850** (University of Wisconsin Press, 1964), p. 400.

12 R.F. Burton, **A Mission to Gelele, King of Dahome** (London, 1864), p. 199.

13 Robert I. Rotberg (ed.), **Africa and Its Explorers: Motive, Methods and Impact** (Cambridge, Mass. 1970).

14 E.E. Evans-Pritchard, **Theories of Primitive Religion** (Oxford: Clarendon Press, 1965).

15 Adam Kuper, **Anthropologists and Anthropology: The British School, 1922-1972** (London: Penguin Books, 1973); Mary Kingsley, **West African Studies** (London, Macmillan & Co, 1899); Lady Flora Lugard, **A Tropical Dependency** (London: Nesbit & Co, 1906).

16 Mary Kingsley, **West African Studies,** p. 414.

17 J. Beecham, **Ashantee and the Gold Goast** (London, 1841).
    For the bibliography and details on this section of the
    paper, see, O.U. Kalu, "The Formulation of Cultural
    Policy in Colonial Nigeria" in E. Ihekweazu (ed.),
    Modern and Traditional Culture (Enugu: Fourth Dimen-
    sion Publishers, 1985) ch. 9.
18 R.S. Rattray, "Anthropology and Christian Missions", **Africa,** 1
    (1928), p. 99.
19 **Ibid.,** p. 106.
20   i   R.M. **Downes, Tiv Religion** (Ibadan: University Press,
          1970);
     ii   E.E. **Evans Pritchard, Nuer Religion** (Oxford, University
          Press, 1956);
    iii   D. **Forde, Yako Studies** (Oxford, University Press 1964);
     iv   Mayer **Fortes, Oedipus and Job in West African Reli-
          gion** (Cambridge, University Press, 1959);
      v   Max Gluckman, **Customs and Conflict in Africa** (Oxford,
          Blackwell & Mott, 1960);
     vi   J.R. Goody, **Death, Property and the Unconscious** (Stan-
          ford, University press, 1962);
    vii   M.M. Green, **Ibo Village Affairs** (London, Sidgwick &
          Johnson, 1947);
   viii   Sylvia Leith-Ross, **African Women: A Study of the Ibo
          of Nigeria,** (London: Routledge & Kegan Paul, 1939);
     ix   Keneth Little, **The Mende of Sierra-Leone** (London,
          Routledge & Kegan Paul, 1951);
      x   S.F. Nadel, **Nupe Religion,** (London, Routledge & Kegan
          Paul, 1954).
     xi   Simon Ottenberg, **Leadership and Authority in an Afri-
          can Tribe** (University of Washington Press, 1971);
    xii   R.T. Parsons, **Religion in an African Society** (Leiden:
          E.J. Bril, 1964);
   xiii   E.G. Parrinder, **West African Religion** (London: Epworth
          Press, 1949); **African Traditional Religion** (London,
          Sheldon Press, 1954); **Africa's Three Religions** (London:
          Sheldon Press, 1969);
    xiv   Benjamin C. Ray, **African Religions: Symbols, Rituals
          and Community** (New Jersey, Prentice-Hall, 1976);
     xv   Aylward Shorter, **Prayer in Religious Traditions** of
          Africa, (Nairobi, OUP, 1975);
    xvi   Placide Temples, **Bantu Philosophy** (Paris: **Presence Afri-
          caines,** 1959), etc. For the rest, see, the bibliography!

21 Leo Frobenius, **The Voice of Africa,** Vol. 1 (London: OUP, 1902).

    ii   Marcel Griaule, **Conversations with Ogotomelli** (London, OUP, 1951).

    iii   Dominique Zahan, **The Religion, Spirituality and Thought of Traditional Africa,** (Chicago; University Press, 1970).

22 **Lumen Gentium,** no. 16.

AFRICAN TRADITIONAL RELIGION IN AFRICAN SCHOLARSHIP: AN HISTORICAL ANALYSIS

by

Udobata R. Onunwa

Introduction

One of the greatest difficulties that beset the study of African Traditional Religion is that it was pioneered by those who did not belong to the faith nor wanted to do so. It was a project embarked upon by early European travellers, missionaries, colonial administrators and anthropologists. Indigenous African scholars who joined later were also not votaries of the religion but mostly wards of the early missionaries. Unfortunately, the votaries of the faith have scarcely done anything. Consequently, it was never been a study from "faith to faith" - a votary expressing the tenets of his religion.

The study thus far, has moved from one stage to the other: beginning with random picking of materials to functionalist stage through that of evangelist-strategist stance to the nationalist-apologetic posture. More recently, a new approach (the culture-area approach) has developed in the hands of some indigenous scholars as a way out to remedy the pitfalls that had characterised the earlier studies.

The fate of those earlier studies were worsened by a welter of other contingent factors - paucity of reference written sources from within the religion, the nature of the religion itself with its combination of unity and extreme diversity. Consequently, those who came out with religious and racial prejudices had no other alternative than to resort to bizarre tales and lurid speculations in the presentation of facts about the religion. In terms of scholarship, this class of work was quite subjective and most unreliable because they were intended to titilate the sit-at-home popular minds in Europe who were eager for exotic or on the part of the missionaries, intended to stimulate financial subscriptions to aid those in mission lands.

This paper will address itself to a critical reappraisal of the contributions of indigenous Africans to the study of the Traditional Religion. It will adopt a systematic chronological order of the various approaches adopted by the scholars in order to assist the reader to understand the factors (aims, goals and interests) that conditioned the writings. We shall, however, pick a few prominent writers from each indentifiable group of scholars.

Different Categories of African Scholars of the Traditional Religion

Harris W. Mobley has classified writings from the indigenous scholars (particularly those from Ghana in West African subregion) into two broad categories. The first has been described as the "Literature of Tutelage" in which the indigenous African writers presented the views that pleased their European mentors. The other is "the Critique" written by those Africans who were considered representatives of responsible leadership in both Church and State. In addition, those writers demonstrated their concern for both the faults and the achievements of the Europeans. (1) It is this later group that presented a more balanced view of the European concept and treatment of African Religion and Culture.

However, a more comprehensive classification of African scholars of the Traditional Religion and Culture could be made. The first is the "nationalist writers" who reacted against the European attitudes to Africans and theirway of life. They thus became the poneers of the "nationalist struggles" for political independence which came much later.

The second group of scholars includes the "secular agitators" for political and cultural independence of their people. They were inspired by the legacies of the first group of "nationalists" whom they admired greatly. It was at the dawn of the political struggle for national independence that most of the scholars and writers in this group did their job. Most of them were products of schools managed by the Christian missions but later turned against those missions in their desire to defend their indigenous culture and religion.

The third group is made up of ordained men of their various Christian missions who like their European counterparts and mentors used their brilliant knowledge of African Traditional Religion and culture to interpret the Christian Gospel to their fellow African people. Some of them rejected the derogatory terms which the Western scholars had persistently used for African Tradtional Religion. We see them as "nationalists" in the sense that they sought the identity of the African personality through

110

their struggle for the indigenization of Christianity. They may also be called "Confessional Scholars" because they diligently professed their Christian faith while remaining Africans and valued some aspects of their traditional religion and culture which they wanted to use as a means to interpret the Christian faith.

As an overview to the various categories of works identified above, we may also recognise some more recent works which point to a new direction in understanding and interpreting African Traditional beliefs and practices. This has been taking different forms - for instance, the new "culture-area" approach which hasnot been fully explored and utilized by scholars. The gauntlet is yet to be fully picked up in the current search for adequate methodology. (2)

Early African Nationalist Writers

The earliest group of nationalist writers who used African Tradtional Religion as a means of defending "African personality" included among others, Edward Wilmot Elyden, J.E. Casely Hayford, John M. Sarbah, Samuel Lewis, J.B. Horton, J. Abayomi Cole, P.J. Meffre and Mojola Agbebi.

E.W. Blyden was an outstanding and brilliant West-Indian born Liberian statesman. Born in 1832, he was known to have emigrated to settle in Liberia at a tender age of eighteen. He attended the Alexandrian High School, Monrovia and trained as a teacher under its principal Rev. D.A. Wilson, who was a graduate of Princeton Theological College. Under such strict Presbyterian influence, Blyden grew up a puritanical Christian minister who hated double standard of morality. Consequently, he fell out with missionaries whose preachings could not agree with their life style. He studied theology, classics, geography and mathematics. After his ordination as a Presbyterian minister in 1858, Blyden had the singular privilege to succeed his former Principal, Rev. D.A. Wilson at the Alexandrian High School. Thereafter, he became a well-known author and preacher (had over fifteen books, seventy-five articles to his credit) and later died in SierraLeone where he spent his later years. (3)

Blyden's primary concern as a teacher and pastor was to grapple with the lingering myth of European people's idea of the inferiority of the negroes. He therefore relentlessly sought to present Black Africa a respected and important participant in the World Community of nations - devoting his life to full-time enlightenment of the Black. He later saw the pastoral ministry as an impediment to the achievement of his life ambition - therefore abandoned the office.

In 1872, Blyden founded the weekly newspaper, **The Negro** while he was living in Freetown and in 1874, he founded another newspaper, **The West African Reporter.** He used these media as powerful instruments to disseminate information about the admirable qualities of the negro race. His writings therefore became both critical and constructive.

In 1887, Blyden published **Christianity, Islam and the Negro Race.** In it, he argued that Islam had an elevating and unifying influence which did not disrupt the African social fabric. He went on to argue that Islam had brought the Africans the benefits of a major world civilization without necessarily creating in them a sense of inferiority. In 1908, he published **The African Life and Customs** in which he showed that there had been an African social and economic system which isnot 'inferior' to   any system.

Although Blyden did not write a systematic and comprehensive description of the features of the Traditional Religion, he, nonetheless, tried to show that the religion and culture are essential features of African life. In all, he tried to show that African life style, religion and culture have been authentic aspects of life comparable to those of any Western society and should not be described as inferior by any standard.

One other popular figure of the period was John Mensah Sarbah. Born in 1864, Sarbah became the first Ghanaian to be called to the English Bar. He died at a tender age of forty-six on November 28, 1910. (4)

His research among his Fante people began with the collecton of their oral traditions, proverbs and customary laws. Eventually, this culminated in the production of his **Fante Customary Laws** (1897) and **Fante National Constitution** (1906). In both books, Sarbah not only tried to explain the authentic values of African traditional ways of life and belief but also critically exposed the weaknesses of the missionary attempts to misrepresent African Religion. Besides, he did not spare other secular European writers' views on African culture and religion which he described as biased, prejudiced and misinforming.

Although Sarbah's criticisms of the European ideas of African religion and culture were not as radical as those of Blyden before him or Casely Hayford after him, he was, nonethe-

112

less consistent and articulate in his views. For instance, we hear him often say:

> one must admit that missionary methods were not perfect - the attempts to turn the African into spurious European, has been deservedly unsuccessful. (5)

He like his contemporaries, wrote against the persistent mis-representation of African culture and religion by European writers. He was, however, optimistic that, sometime, blanket condemnation of the traditional cultures by white writers who were either not informed, or biased and prejudiced, would cease.

J.E. Casely Hayford was born in Ghana to a clergyman, Rev. Joseph de Graft Hayford. His was a privileged boy yet content to identify with his fellow Africans. On his return from Fourah Bay College where he studied, he took up teaching appontment. After a short stay in the classroom, Hayford did not find it exciting enough as a viable means to put his views across to the people. He therefore left for England to study Law.

On his return from England, Hayford did not practise law but rather took up journalism. He thus became one of the earliest African journalists and used his privilege as a member of the Gold Coast Legislature in 1910 to project what he understood as "African Personality".

In his **Ethiopia Unbound: Studies in Race Emancipation** (1911), Casely Hayford explained the values of African traditional institutions which he defended vigorously. He advocated that African Religion should be studied diligently before any reliable and dependable assessment of its tenets and practices could be made. He described Fante religion (the traditional religion of his people) as an authentic faith that had enriched his people's spiritual aspirations.

We would like to include the works of Dr. J.B. Danquah within this group. This is because his early publications took the same "nationalist stance" though they came much later than those already discussed above.

Danquah had no formal secondary school education but was a hardworking youngman who improved on himself through private studies. He took up a job as a law clerk on completing his primary education at the age of seventeen. He enlisted in the Gold Coast Volunteer Corps when the First World War broke out. Soon after the end of the War, Danquah met Casely Hayford who had a tremendous influence of him. He later took up a job as a reporter and writer for the Congress newspaper, **The Gold Coast Leader** for a period of three years.

He left for London in 1921 through the help of a brother. After a period of six years of hard work Danquah was able to obtain a doctorate degree in philosophy and law and returned to the then Gold Coast to emark on the interpretation of the traditional customs of his people. In 1928, he published **Akan Laws and Customs** in which he claimed he had made a simple presentation of the customs as the people knew them.

When in the mid 1940's, the theme of the Supreme Being dominated European discussions on African Religion, Danquah wrote to dismiss the erroneous views that the African High God was a remote or an absentee God. He in 1944, published **Akan Doctrine of God** in which he violently reacted against the missionary teaching about the African concept of God. He insisted that Akan belief was monotheistic. In an attempt to put his ideas across to his Western colleagues whom he wanted to impress, Danquah degenerated into weak polemics and apologetics which almost marred his work. The attempt to relate Akan names and concepts of God to those of the Ancient Near East had no strong convincing evidence.

His involvement in the politics of Ghana made Danquah form his own political party in 1949. In the process, he fell out with the political philosophy of the late Dr. Kwame Nkrumah who ordered his detention in prison custody where he died in 1964.

Pre-Independence "Secular" Writers on African Traditional Religion

A new breed of nationalist writers whose interest was not on the Religion per se but on the political emancipation of their people emerged in the late 1930's and early 1940's. Although their predecessors and they themselves did not set out to study African Traditional Religion in a systematic way, they nevertheless, saw the religion as an important aspect of African life and a weapon that could be used to project the personality of the African. Some of the men in this group like their predecessors, received Western education overseas but their experiences abroad challenged them to struggle for the emancipation of their people from all forms of foreign domination. Inspired by the efforts of their predecessors like Blyden, the new group of learned Africans

114

started to publish challenging and stimulating articles and books, soliciting for their people's right to self-determination.

Among this group of African humanists were men like Nigeria's Dr. Nnamdi Azikiwe, Mazi Mbonu Ojike, Ghana's Kwame Nkrumah, Kenya's Jomo Kenyatta etc. They were vigorous and uncompromising in their criticisms of Western attitude to African culture. They didnot only set out to criticise the Europeans but also encouraged their fellow Black Africans to recapture the beauty and meaning of their age-long traditions. In Dr. Nnamdi Azikiwe's pungent **Renascent Africa** (1937) and Kenyatta's **Facing Mount Kenya** (1938) and Mazi Mbonu Ojike's **My Africa** (1946) we see a systematic and consistent nationalist effort to defend the African noble past. This could be illustrated with Kenyatta's work.

Although Kenyatta did not show in **Facing Mount Kenya** any sign of hot resentment of warped judgment, he clearly brought out his critical views and laid them as it were, at the bar of public opinion. (6) He graphically discussed the traditional pattern of land ownership and tenure in comparison with the European manner of control, the principles of traditional religion and education. Besides, he laments how the traditional order had been thwarted by foreign system which "valued material knowledge and left personal relationships out in the cold". Consequently, he castigated what he described as the "denurturing effect of missionary teaching" and glorified what the Africans understood to be the "spiritual assumptions of the past". (7)

A group of learned academics in universities who combined within their interest, a concern for culture and the church may be considered along this group. Some of them struggled to introduce and develop the study of African Traditional Religion in the older universities in the former British colonies e.g. University College, Legon (Ghana), University College Ibadan, (Nigeria) and the University College Makerere (Uganda). For instance, Professors C.G. Baeta and S.G. Williamson introduced the study of African Traditional Religion in the University College Legon after a hectic struggle as an alternative special paper for African students taking the degree of the University of London as an external degree.

One whose works stand out conspicously within this group is the late Dr. K.A. Busia, a learned academic and teacher who combined love for academics with politics as well as love for the church. An Ashanti, born in 1913 and educated at Oxford, Busia obtained a doctorate degree in Social Anthropology at the end of the Second World War. He headed the Department of

Sociology in the University College Legon till 1958 when he opted for active politics. He was critical of the type of Christianity introduced to the Africans by some illiterate missionaries who didnot understand the fundamental meaning of the traditional religion in African life. He saw the model of Christianity introduced in Africa as a system that had tried to destroy the basic African modes of thought and life. He came out with the conclusion that Christian churches were still alien institutions which were only intruding upon but not integrated with the traditional social institutions in areas of marriage, birth, death and widowhood. (8) He later in 1955 recommended to the Methodist Church in Ghana that for "conversion to the Christian faith to be more than superficial, the Christian Church must come to grips with traditional beliefs and practices. (9)

Indigenous Christian Scholars of African Religion

This group of scholars has sought to present the values of the traditional religion as objectively as possible but their mission-oriented background had extensively influenced their writings which tilted towards evangelism. They could be described as "functionalists" as well as "nationalists" in the sense that they sought to make the traditional religion a tool for evangelization of the Africans just as the colonial administrators wanted to use some elements of the religion and traditional culture as useful data for governance. The "nationalist" tendency in their works is revealed in their attempt to reject the derogatory terms used by the European writers for the traditional religion. Many of the scholars in this group were ordained ministers of their various Churches and had studied the Traditional Religion with a subtle motive of using it as a form of "preparatio-evangelica". For instance in the mid 1950's many Roman Catholic priests in the former Eastern Region of Nigeria had embarked on studies on how the Igbo Traditional Religion could be used as a stepping stone to a meaningful interpretation of the Christian ritual of the Mass to the illiterate converts to Christianity. (10) This was in compliance with the suggestion of Bishop J. Shanahan (an outstanding missionary to Igboland) who had earlier advised that what the Traditional Religion needed was transformation and not destruction. On this basis, therefore, many indigenous Roman Catholic priests did doctoral theses in Rome on the various aspects of the traditional religion and culture as a way to enhance their evangelical strategy.

In Nigeria, other indigenous scholars who have done systematic study on traditional religion include E.B. Idowu, F.A. Arinze, E.C.O. Ilogu and J.O. Awolalu among others. Their works were not only based on extensive field work data but also had an interpretative depth.

Professor E.B. Idowu, a Methodist minister and theologian is one of the Africans to pioneer the study of African Traditional Religion (with the help of Professor E.G. Parrinder) as an academic discipline at the University College, Ibadan in the 1950's. He published in 1962, his **Olodumare: God in Yoruba Belief.** This was a product of his original research conducted in the 1950's as a part of the doctoral thesis he submitted to the University of London in 1955. The Yoruba scholar, like Danquah before him, projects the basic Yoruba belief in the Supreme Being and struggles to make his readers see Yoruba religion as monotheistic or at worst as a "diffused monotheism". He explores the relationship between the Supreme Being and the other subordinate deities in the Yoruba pantheon. He dismissed the idea that the **Olodumare** is a **deus remotus** or deus **absconditus.** In an extreme nationalistic tone, Idowu dismissed the derogatory terminologies which Western scholars had consistently used for African Traditional Religion. To him, such terms as "paganism", "fetishism", "idolatry," "heathenism", "primitive" etc, should not be used for African Religion, however value-free they might be (see his **African Traditional Religion: A Definition** (1973).

Bishop F.A. Arinze's **Sacrifice in Ibo Religion** (1970) is a revised version of his doctoral thesis presented to the Urban University Rome, in 1960 with the title "Ibo Sacrifice as an Introduction to the Catechesis of the Holy Mass". In spite of the author's attempt to be objective, the title of the work tilted towards evangelism and his bias for Christianity is not hidden.

Professor Edmund C.O. Ilogu is interested in the interaction of Christianity with the traditional religion and culture, particularly that of the Igbo. His **Christianity and Igbo Culture** (1974) is a revised version of his doctoral thesis "Christian Ethics in an African background". In it, Canon Ilogu (an Anglican priest) tries to work out a modality for the Church to take in making use of some valuable elements in the traditional culture to make Christianity incarnate in Igbo society.

In Ghana, a number of scholars had produced works of similar value and interest. They include C.G. Baeta's **The Challenge of African Culture** (1955), J.H. Nketia, **Funeral Dirges of**

the Akan People (1955); W.E. Abraham, **The Mind of Africa** (1962); S.G. Williamson, **Akan Religion and the Christian Faith** among others whom we have earlier on discussed.

In Nketiah's study of music, he saw values in the indigenous drumming and introduced it at the University College Legon when he joined the staff in 1952. He had earlier done an advanced study in music at the London School of Oriental and African Studies which he continued at the Juillard and North Western Universities in the United States. His study of indigenous music and religion made him emphasize their importance in understanding Christian religion by Africans. Consequently, we hear him say:

> if Churches in Africa are to grow as African Churches not as extensions of parishes and bishoprics ... they must be allowed to take root in the soil of the African culture in which they are planted ... (11)

This evangelical interest has overshadowed any other contributions of such eminent scholars like Professor Harry Sawyer. Canon Sawyer is a veteran theologian, teacher and university administrator whose fundamental interest is the indigenization of Christianity through the study of African Traditional Religion. He has pointed out that his primary concern in the study of the traditional religion is to provide a prolegomenon which later theologians would expand and improve within the framework of Christian evangelism. He provides in his **God, Ancestor or Creator?** (1970) a new approach (the Thematic approach) in the study of God in three West African societies: the Akan, Mende and Yoruba using materials in the language, literature, social life and institutions of each of the three ethnic groups. Earlier in 1968, he had jointly published **The Springs of Mende Belief and Conduct** with W.T. Harris in which he makes a description of the traditional concern of the Mende with special emphasis on morality and stability of society.

We would identify in this group, the works of Professor John S. Mbiti. He is one of the foremost African indigenous theologians to look at the traditional religion of Africa on continental level. His **African Religions and Philosophy** (1969) is a general descriptive survey of African religion based on wide reading and personal contact. The information given on the concept of time is stimulating but has been questioned by many authorities. In **Concepts of God in Africa,** Canon Mbiti gives a wide range of information presented in somewhat a "catalogue" style.

118

He tries to respond to the European emphasis upon the remoteness of the African High God by explaining his importance in African cosmology, ritual and ethics. This book falls in line with Danquah's **Akan Doctrine of God** (1944) and Idowu's **Olodumare: God in Yoruba Belief** (1962) which have expounded the African High God in such a way as to make it comparable to the Western philosophical systems. Mbiti's works have been taken to task by a good number of scholars especially those with strong sociological training and orientation. In the first instance, the works try to be exhaustive, covering too many societies and too many types of religious phenomena. Often they tend towards abstractions, lacking both every 'feel' for African religious ideas and behaviour and any interpretative depth. (12) They also rely much on outdated anthropological theories and ethnographic data and at times reveal a noticeably Western theological orientation. The traces of Western theological influence in Mbiti's works have also been criticised by Professor A.J. Shelton who has noticed constant emphasis upon the superiority of Christianity thereby putting African religion in second place. (13)

An Overview

As an overview to the various categories of work produced by indigenous Africans in the field of African Religious Studies, one may identify some more recent works which point to a new direction. One such new approaches is the one taken by the Ugandan scholar Okot P'Bitek who has criticised many other indigenous African scholars of African Religion including Danquah, Busia, Abraham, Idowu and Mbiti for not presenting the Traditional Religion in such a systematic way that the votaries of the faith might understand it. He accused them of dressing the African deities in an awkward Hellenistic garb in order to impress the European audience whom they set out to convince of the viability of African Religion. (14) Okot is particularly caustic in some sense. Even when he agrees that wrong terminologies like heathenism, paganism, idolatry, fetishism etc used by Western writers should not be used for African Religion, he hardly admitted that some of the African writers before him had made the same corrections.

Professor C. Gaba has shown some keen understanding in his explanation of the Anlo-Ewe Traditional Religion. He has

119

done this while collecting and interpreting the Anlo traditional believer's conception and communication with the "Holy" - thus showing a considerable understanding of the phenomenological methods in the study of primal religions. He does not write to please any interest group but has given a balanced view to satisfy the spiritual and the intellectual aspects of man.

The same insight is shown by Dr. Ikenga-Metuh among other indigenous scholars in the recent past in his attempt to elucidate the Igbo understanding of the relationship between God and man in man's temporal and eternal dimensions of his existence. The data are collected from oral history, language and ethnography and the facts are explained from the point of view of theology rather than that of anthropology or sociology but however, incorporating both. (15)

Similarly, Professor Adiele E. Afigbo has through an analysis of oral information and archeological data attempted a reconstruction of loose pieces of Igbo cultural history in his **Ropes of Sand** (1981). The effect is not only intellectually rewarding but also points to the need for a reexamination of systems that had in the past been dismissed as unreliable and given warped judgment.

Summary and Conclusion

From the foregoing, one can see that the contributions of Africans in the study of African Religion have been immense. No matter the pitfalls of each methodology, the spate of literature existing on the subject can no longer be ignored. The 'nationalists' presence has been felt. Thus from the above analysis of the contributions of the indigenous Africans to the study of African religion one may discover that two principal factors have influenced the works of the Africans: "nationalism" and "indigenization". The 'secular' scholars were extremely nationalistic. Theirs was the danger of attempting to explain African religion on alien standards and consequently many nationalist writers over-reacted in the face of the arrogance and insults of the Western writers. The 'Confessional scholars' who are Christian theologians have on their part been verymuch interested in "indigenization" of Christianity as an African Religion.

Most debates, conferences and polemics of the mid-1950's and early 1960's on "indigenization", "Africanization", "Theo-

120

logia Africana" or "Black Theology" were concerned with the practical methods of making Christianity an authentic "African Religion" with the materials gleaned from some elements of the traditional religion. When a collection of highly qualified African theologians met in Ibadan Nigeria in 1966 to discuss African Traditional Religion in the light of Biblical theology, they were unanimous in their decision to make Christianity relevant to the traditional situation. This according to them would be achieved by interpreting Christianity to Africans in the context of their tradtional religious experience, language and culture. Consequently, the discussions and the academic papers presented at the conference have resulted in a book edited by Kwesi Dickson and Paul Ellingworth. (16)

It is distressing to note that educated African Christian theologians who studied African Traditional Religion with this evangelical bias did not realize that they had indirectly subscribed to the superiority of Christianity to the traditional religion despite their efforts to show the Traditional Religion as a people's search for the Ultimate Reality. Regrettably, any attempt to study the Traditional Religion as a means to an end (to explain any other form of religion) and not and end in itself is bound to be academically unsound and spiritually deficient. More recent studies on African Religion have not only realized this pitfall but have also embarked on serious quest for adequate methodology for the future study of the Traditional Religion as an academic discipline.

Footnotes

1 Harris W. Mobley, **The Ghanaian Image of the Missionary.** (Leiden: E.J. Brill, 1970) pp. 2 & 7.

2 See U.R. Onunwa, "The study of West African Traditional Religion in Time - perspective" (Unpub. Ph.D. Thesis, University of Nigeria 1984) 129.

3 M.Y. Frankel, "Edward Blyden and the concept of African Personality", **AFRICAN AFFAIRS, 72, 292** (July 1974) 277.

4 H.W. Mobley, **Ibid.,** 32.

5 J.M. Sarbah, **Fante National Constitution** (1906) p. xiv. Quoted from H.W. Mobley, **Ibid.,** 35.

6   U.R. Onunwa, **Ibid.,** 107.

7   T.O. Ranger, "The Churches, the Nationalist State and African Religion", in Fashole-Luke, Gray, et.al. (eds.) **Christianity in Independent Africa** (Ibadan: Ibadan University Press, 1976) 479.

8   K.A. Busia, **Report on a Social Survey of Sekondi-Takoradi** (London: Crown Agents for Colonies, 1950) 79.

9   K.A. Busia, **Christianity and African Culture** (1955) p. iii of the Introduction.

10 S.N. Ezeanya and M. Maduka, "From Igbo sacrifice to the Mass" **LUX** 2 (1952-53) 43-44.

11 J.H. Nketia, "The Contributions of African Culture to Christian Worship" **International Review of Mission** XLVII (1958) 268.

12 B.C. Ray, "Recent Studies of African Religions" **History of Religions** 12, 1 (August 1972) 82.

13 A.J. Shelton, "Strange Syncretism: The Interpretation of African Religions Via Christ and Europe", **The Conch** 2, 1 (1970) 36.

14 Okot P'Bitek, **African Religions in Western Scholarship** (Nairob: East African Publishing House, 1971) 47.

15 See C.R. Gaba, **Scriptures of an African People: The Sacred Utterance of the Anlo** (New York: NOK Publishers, 1973). Cf. E. Ikenga-Metuh, **God and Man in African Religion.** (London: Geoffrey Chapman, 1981) 10-12.

16 Kwesi Dickson and P. Ellingworth (eds.) **Biblical Revelations and African Beliefs** (New York: Mary Knoll Orbis Books, 1969).

AFRICAN TRADITIONAL RELIGION AS AN ACADEMIC DISCIPLINE

by

J.O. Awolalu

Introduction

In order that theremay be intelligibility (and thus avoid 'Babel'), we need to spell out what we want the word academic to connote. This word can be used in two senses - one good and the other bad or derogatory. In the good sense, academic means 'belonging to or having to do with an academy or a college or university.' In the derogatory sense, it means too much concerned with rules and theories, without practical value or importance'.

To be academic in the good sense is to be scientific, to be down to earth, to be able to make a thorough study. To be asked to examine the study of African Traditional Religion as an academic discipline, therefore, is to spell out how African Traditional Religion can be studied in a scientific, well-planned and directed manner in an institution of learning.

We need to explain what we mean by African Traditional Religion. This is the indigenous religion of Africa handed down from generation to generation. It is the religion that resulted from the sustaining faith held by the forebears of the present Africans which is being practised today in various forms and intensities by a very largenumber of Africans, including some who claim to be Muslims and Christians.

I deliberately speak of African Religion (and not religions) even though Africa is a large continent with multitudes of nations, complex cultures, innumerable languages and myriads of dialects. In spite of all these differences, there are many basic similarities in the religious systems of the Africans. Everywhere, there is the concept of God (called by different names); there is also the concept of divinities and/or spirits as well as belief in life after death which leads to the veneration of the ancestors. Every locality may and does have its own local deities, its own festivals, its own name or names for the Supreme Being, but in essence, the pattern is the same. There is that noticeable "Africanness" in the whole pattern. This is where we disagree with John Mbiti who chooses to speak of the religion in the plural "because", according to him, "there are about thousand" African peoples (tribes), and each has its own religious system ... (1)

The fundamental beliefs of Africans in general consist of the following:

(i)   that this world was brought into being by the Source of all beings known as theSupreme Being;

(ii) that the Supreme Being brought into being a number of divinities and spirits to act as His functionaries in the orderly maintenance of the world;

(iii) that death does not write 'the end' to human life but opens the gate to the hereafter - hence prominence is given to belief in the continuation of life after death;

(iv) that divinities and spirits together with the ancestral spirits are in the supersensible world but are interested in what goes on in theworld of men;

(v)   that there are mysterious powers or forces in the world and that their presence makes man live in fear;

(vi) that if men and women are to enjoy peace, they should live according to the laid-down directives of the Supreme Being and His agents.

This religion has its own peculiarities: it has no written literature but yet 'written' everywhere for those who care to see and read (we shall examine this later under sources of African Traditional Religion); it has no historical founders or reformers like Jesus Christ, Mohammed, Asoka, or Gautama the Buddha. Yet, the adherents of the religion are loyal and conservative worshippers.

A study of the religious systems is ultimately a study of these people and their philosophy. Their religion and their philosophy go side by side and they are to be studied together.

The study of African Traditional Religion is fairly new, and not long ago it might have been doubted whether there was an African Religion to talk about. But much research into the people's religion has been done in the last and present centuries and African Universities have come to include courses in African Traditional Religion in their studies. In fact, is was the inclusion of courses in African Traditional Religion that made the various governments in Africa (in the wake of national consciousness) allow the old Departments of Divinity to continue to exist but under different names and different contents of teaching. The old Departments of Divinity were mainly (if not solely) Christian and these did not meet the aspiration of the present Africans.

For a long time African Traditional Religion was misunderstood, misrepresented and misinterpreted. Written literature that was made available on the subject was highly unreliable. This was so because the writers were non-specialists; but were administrators, sociologists, anthropologists who were strangers and were hostile to African cults. They condemned African beliefs and practices and daubed them as undesirable superstitions, paganism, heathenism, idolatry, fetishism and the like. These writers neither knew the language of the people whose religion they were describing, nor did they bother to get the truth from African elders who had the facts about their religion. We shall now examine a few of these writers as a means of illustrating the misconception and misinterpretation of the African culture.

Leo Frobenius in his book, **The Voice of Africa,** tells us that before he visited Africa he had read a Berlin Journal where it was asserted that:

> Before the introduction of a genuine faith and a higher standard of culture by the Arabs, the natives had no political organisation, nor, strictly speaking, any religion ...
> Therefore, it is necessary, in examining the pre-Muhammedan conditions of the negro races, to confine ourselves to the description of their crude fetishism, their brutal and often cannibal customs, their vulgar and repulsive idols.
> None but the most primitive instincts determine the lives and conduct of the negroes, who lack every kind of ethical inspiration. (2)

Here the unknown writer in the Berlin Journal gave a wrong information, alleging that Africans had no religion before the advent of Islam.

We have a further illustration of this kind of misconception of the Africans and their beliefs in the discussion which took place between Edwin Smith (a missionary in Africa) and Emil Ludwig (an eminent biographer). Edwin Smith had told Ludwig what the missionaries were doing in Africa, teaching Africans about God. Ludwig, according to this account, was perplexed. In his perplexity, he remarked, "How can the untutored African conceive God? ... How can this be? Deity is a philosophical concept which savages are incapable of framing." (3)

These two quotations show the ignorance, prejudice and pride of theEuropean theorists who sat at home and imagined what life looked like in Africa. They neither knew nor confessed their ignorance about Africa and the Africans. This is why Professor Idowu aptly described this period as "the period of ignorance and false certainty" in the study of African Traditional Religion.

In 1867, the explorer Sir Samuel Baker presented the following report to the Ethnological Society of London on the Nilotes of the Southern Sudan:

> Without any exception, they are without a belief in a Supreme Being, neither have they any form of worship or idolatry; nor is the darkness of their mind enlightened by even a ray of superstition. (4)

Here we see that "Baker was far more interested in reinforcing popular prejudices than in reporting ethnographic fact." (5) From what we gathered from other sources relating to the Nilotes, we know that Baker was quite wrong. He neither understood the people's language nor did he make a thorough study of the peoples' religion.

While Baker denied that Africans had any belief or a form of worship, R. Burton, a famous explorer credited them with fetishism and idolatry.

> The negro is still at that rude dawn of faith - fetishism - and he has barely advanced to idolatry. ... He has never grasped the ideas of a personal Deity, a duty in life, a moral code, or a shame of lying. He rarely believes in a future state of rewards and punishments, which, true or not, are infallible indices of human progress." (6)

According to Burton, the negroes had no belief in God and no sense of morality. This idea was confirmed by T. Cullen Young who attempted to distinguish between God of the animists and God of Christians.

"It is quite easy to credit the African with a knowledge of God, but I wish to suggest that we will find it wise to accept these statements with the greatest reserve. The God of the animist is very hard to find, and when we do glimpse Him it is to recognize a being so remote from any human contacts, and therefore, so removed from the God and Father of Jesus Christ, that one almost feels as if the God of the African had to be put wholly out of sight before the other can come in ..." (7)

But, as a contrast to the speculators, we have genuine seekers after truth who doubted if there could be a people anywhere in the world who were totally devoid of culture and religion, particularly the knowledge of the living God. Prominent among such truth-seekers were Andrew Lang, Archishop Soderblom, and Father Schmidt of Vienna. Father Schmidt, for example, said:

> ... the belief in, and worship of, one supreme deity is universal among all really primitive peoples - the high God is found among all, not indeed everywhere in the same form or with the same vigour, but still everywhere prominently enough to make his dominant position indubitable. He is by no means a late development or traceable to Christian missionary influences. (8)

And, in 1857, T.J. Bowen writing about the Yoruba declared:

> In Yoruba, many of the notions which the people entertain of God are remarkably correct. They make him the efficient, though not always the instrumental, Creator. Theyhave some notion of His justice and holiness, and they talk much of his goodness, knowledge, power and providence. ... They may extol the power and defend the worship of their idols, whom they regard as mighty beings, but they will not compare the greatest idol to God. (9)

Statements, such as were made by Father Schmidt and T.J. Bowen above, raised doubts in the minds of those who might earlier have accepted the statements of the stay-at-home-investigators and curid collectors. Thus while there were some casual observers attempting to write off Africa as a spiritual desert, "there were undoubtedly, a few who had the uneasy feeling that the story of a spiritual vacuum for a whole continent of peoples could not be entirely true." (10)

From the beginning of the present century a large number of serious-minded investigators wrote on African Traditional Religon. Among them could be mentioned R.S. Rattray, P.A. Talbot, A.B. Ellis, S.S. Farrow, S.F. Nadel and E.G. Parrinder. Africans ought to give credit to these scholars who were able to conduct their researches under difficult conditions and were able to commit them into writing which African scholars could read, criticise and improve upon. "In actual fact, some of these early investigators were more careful than some modern ones who appear to know too much theoretical off-the-spot anthropology and sociology, and who just pick from the researches of other people or rush to Africa during the summer, interview one or two people and then rush back to produce volumes on the subject." (11)

In recent years, Africans came on the scene. Prominent among these scholars are J.B. Danquah who wrote **The Akan Doctrine of God.** In the book, Danquah attempted to prove to the Western writers that African Religion is not polytheism but that the religion knows one God - and that the one God is not remote. Danquah, however went to the other extreme of calling God an Ancestor. (12)

E. Bolaji Idowu argued for a monotheistic interpretation of Yoruba Religion and claimed that the concept of the supreme deity is the "one essential factor by which the life and belief of the Yoruba cohere and have sustenance ... since He is so urgently real". (13) In Idowu's view the divinities that are prominent in Yoruba religion are functionaries of God and they have no existence apart from Him. In this way, Idowu sees Yoruba system of belief as diffused monotheism.

John Mbiti presented a good survey of African Religion and Philosophy and attempted a synopsis of African concepts of God. He emphasised the position of eminence accorded the Supreme Being everywhere in Africa.

But Okot p'Bitek in his **African Religions in Western Scholarship** criticised every African philosopher and theologian on the ground that those African scholars "instead of carrying out systematic studies of the beliefs of their peoples and presenting them as the African peoples actually know them ... claimed that African peoples knew the Christian God long before the missionary told them about it. African deities were selected and robed with awkward hellenic garments by Jomo Kenyatta, J.B. Danquah, K.A. Busia, W. Abraham, E.B. Idowu and others. (14)

I do not think that Okot p'Bitek is fair in his criticism; there is a world of difference between saying that a people know God and saying that they know the Christian God. I am sure that none of these African theologians criticised by p'Bitek will say the latter. All that these scholars will say is that there is one God and that the concept had been there in Africa before the advent of Islam and Christianity. To speak of Christian God or African God is detestable, for example, to Idowu. He maintains that indulging in this kind of statement is heretical.

128

Moreover, p'Bitek cannot imagine Africans crediting the Supreme Being with attributes such as have been given to Him by Christians. I do not know of any African scholars who have described divinities as "eternal, omnipresent, omnipotent, omniscient" as p'Bitek has alleged. There is a world of difference between the Supreme Being and the divinities. It is, therefore, unfortunate that p'Bitek claimed that "the African deities of the books clothed with the attributes of the Christian God are, in the main, creation of the students of African religions; they are all beyond recognition to the ordinary Africans in the country-side." (15)

I found p'Bitek to be particularly caustic. Even when he agrees that wrong terminologies (e.g. heathenism, paganism, idolatry etc.) which were coined by Western writers in their imaginary speculations are meaningless and should be dropped, he hardly acknowledged the fact that some of these African scholars before him had made this correction.

But the joy of it all is that we are having more and more of the African scholars discussing and writing on the religion of their people. It makes for sound scholarship when writers criticise one another. Such criticisms will encourage African writers to intensify their researches.

Justifiable Reasons for its Inclusion in the School Curriculum

Religion in its bewildering variety of expression is perhaps the most elusive, intriguing and difficult subject for scientific treatment. African Traditional Religion has its own peculiarities and it is by making a systematic and scientific study of these peculiarities that we can place the religion in its proper perspective.

Students of African Traditional Religion know that other continents make a scholarly study of their religions - for example, the Asians study Islam, Hinduism and Buddhism; and the study of these religions has gained prominence all over the world. In the U.S.A. these Asian Religions draw more scholars than Christianity or Judaism can boast of. These Asian Religions have long history behind them and they have a lare number of literature to boast of. African Traditional Religion has nothing comparable to this.

In Harvard University, Cambridge Mass., U.S.A., there is a Centre for the Study of World Religions where I stayed and studied for one year in 1973-74. Of all the religions in the world, only African Tradtional Religion is NOT studied regularly. The Centre started studying A.T.R. four years ago on and off when it had Professor Mbiti, followed by Dr. Gaba and my poor self. I was followed by Dr. Lawal of the Institute of African Studies, University of Ife. It took some time before the authorities of the Harvard Divinity School could send out Preston Williams and John Carman on the recruitment tour of African Scholars to teach A.T.R. in the School. And when they came it was Okot p'Bitek (who disagrees with all African scholars) that has the greatest fascination for the recruitment panel. Whatever happens, people all over the world are getting to know that Africans have indigenous religion worth studying.

For the first time, at the International Association for the History of Religions (XIIIth Congress) held in Lancaster in 1975, African Traditional Religion was constituted into a Group where African scholars presented papers. It was at that Congress that the Secretary General (Professor Werblowsky) met me and requested me to inaugurate a West African Association of the I.A.H.R. He has since written to me again about this. Until we form an Association in West Africa, we cannot serve on the Committees of the I.A.H.R. This is another reason why I think we ought to intensify our academic study of A.T.R.

Furthermore, A.T.R. is now being offered at the Grammar School level, and it is a paper being examined at the H.S.C. (or G.C.E.A. level). For effective teaching at that level, we need to equip men/women at the University level who will then go to teach young ones at the High School level.

My observation as a teacher of A.T.R. in the University is that when students first came to the University, they find it strange to learn that the indigenous religion could be taught as a discipline. But as they go on with the course, they are awakened to things of value in their traditional culture. They now see that which they have hitherto not been seeing. Indeed the scale falls off their eyes and their sense of value is changed. They become the richer, not the poorer, for the inclusion of such a discipline.

Literate Africans themselves use wrong terminologies in describing their people's religion. Thus Paganism, Heathenism, Idolatry and such like are freely used. By academic training, people will know what appropriate words are to be used in referring to this religion.

In Nigeria, we have three religions which influence the people. For mutual understanding, the three religions ought to be studied. Such a study will bring out the cross-fertilization that is there between one religion and another. It will be wrong to close our eyes to what is given prominence by the people. We see lucky charms worn by men and women; we have symbols of divinities and spirits all around us; we cannot deny seeing libations of water and wine poured or a bit of food cast out ceremonially; there are many traditional festivals in which we have been active participants or passive observers. All that this is telling us is that the majority of Africans, no matter how educated, still hold to the traditional religion of their fathers. It seems that this idea will not disappear for very many years to come. That which the people hold dear, ought to be examined by a University which stands for Culture and learning and for a search for truth. To make an academic study of the peoples' religion is also to understand their world-view. To ignore these traditional beliefs, attitudes and practices can only lead to lack of understanding of the peoples' behaviour and problems.

Sources of African Traditional Religion

African Traditional Religion has no written scriptures or records, yet we can say that it is written every where for those who have eyes to see.

This religion permeates every aspect of the peoples' lives and can be found in their riddles and proverbs, songs and dancing, rites and ceremonies, myths and folk-tales, shrines and sacred places, and in their artistic designs. The old people and the cultic functionaries are the repositories of essential information.

Riddles and Proverbs

The people's riddles and proverbs are full of wisdom and a large number of them reflect their religious beliefs. We have expressions such as "If men were God". "God never sleeps", "The tailless cow has the flies driven off on his behalf by God", etc. All these pithy sayings portray the dependence of Africans upon God.

Songs and Dancing

The Africans are a singing race. A lot of their music is of a religious nature. In these songs, they portray their joy and sorrow, their hopes and fears. In each song there is a wealth of material for the student who will patiently sift and collate. Ritual songs and dancing follow prescribed patterns and a study of them will reveal a lot of the people's beliefs.

Rites and Ceremonies

Words are uttered and actions are performed during worship - there are invocations and prayers, there is the offering of sacrifice or pouring of libations.

Shrines and Sacred Places

These are scattered all over the place but can be located only by those who are looking for them. They may be accommodated in a room in a house, or a corridor of a house or they may be separate buildings. In some cases, they are found in groves or at the foot of a tree or on top of a hill.

In these shrines are found sacred objects and the remains of sacrificed animals or birds.

Artistic Designs

Many of the African traditional arts are expressions of the people's beliefs - There are terracotas and bronzes (e.g. at Ife) and Nok in Northern Nigeria. There are mud sculptures - divinities, men and animals are represented in clay e.g. Olokun, Elegba, Ala, etc. There are also wood carvings - masks, twins etc.

Problems besetting the Study

The study is fairly new and there is not much of reliable literature.

The continent is large and there is a great variety and multiplicity of peoples. A casual observer will say that there is no central tradition.

As we have variety of peoples so also do we have a variety of languages and myriads of languages. To study the religion of a people effectively, one has got to understand the language.

Oral traditions have their limitation:

a) It is only in careful listening to elders and interpreting facts that something useful can result.

b) Elders and priests who are custodians keep secrets and some die without handing over to the subsequent generation.

c) Some elders give half-truth.

d) There are duplications and in some cases triplications in the traditions, myths or legends. The investigator finds it difficult to know which is which.

Social and political changes take place in Africa and these changes affect culture and religion of the people. These changes require scientific and academic studies.

Because of those problems, can we give up the attempt as almost, if not altogether, impossible? No! For this can only be the attitude of the unlettered, the result of a puerile mind. But if we are to study the subject what should be the right approach or our guiding principles?

Right Approach to the Study of Traditional Religion

In our approach to the study of African Tradional Religion we should bear in mind the 'Highway Codes' as Professor Idowu put it:

133

Caution

We must be objective and broad-minded. In other words, we should not be prejudiced or have pre-conceived notion. This is where the foreign investigators went wrong. They had the wrong notion that African had nothing of enduring or spiritual value to offer to the world, hence they (the investigators) coined such ir-ritating and nauseating terminologies as heathenism, fetishism, idolatry, and the like. Unfortunately, they passed on the same wrong notion from generation to generation. We should bear in mind that we do not know it all. Therefore, our attitude should be, "Let's find out". If we presume that we know it all, we will simply be defeating our purpose. We should also heed the warning of A.C. Bouquet that scholars should not study religion as if it were fossils, for such an exercise will be both meaningless and valueless. African Traditional Religion is a living religion practised by living men and women. In fact the study of it is the study of the people who practise it. Therefore, we should study it from anthropological, psychological and sociological point of view.

Study from Within

We should be involved and take part in all they do. For example, we might find it necessary to remove shoes or hats, clap hands or sing and dance as the occasion may demand. No doubt it might cause us some inconveniences but it is worth it all. We will be the better for it because they will not be able to hide anything from us. We should have a first hand knowledge. This axiom might well be applied to the student of African Tradi-tional Religion: "What I see I remember, what I hear I forget, but what I do, I know". It is only by doing this that we would gain a worthwhile knowledge.

But this cannot be achieved without a considerable knowledge or mastery of the native language of the people practising the religion. So it is imperative that we understand the language. An interpreter might distort the whole issue.

Rattray showed a good example when he studied the Akan religion. He said "I made it known to them (the Ashanti) that I asked access to their religious rites. For this reason, I at-tended all their ceremonies with all the respect and reverence I could well accord to that which I know could have been very old before the religion of my country had yet been born as an entirely new thought but that its roots stretched back and were fed by the streams which still flows from Ashanti today". (16)

It is very important for the student not to be blind to some obnoxious practices of theAfrican Traditional Religion. We are not attempting to sing the praises of the past. It is very tempting for the student to be inclined to hail and praise all the practices with the spirit of 'vigorous nationalism' or merely to project a favourable image of Africa. That would be morally and spiritually wrong. The student must not be prejudiced.

Reverence

We must study the religion with reverence. We should realise that it deals with the Transcendent Being, sacred, mysterious and dear to the adherents of that particular religion. (Every religion deals with the soul). Therefore, the study of African Traditional Religion is a delicate thing. And it should be handled critically and with sound judgement.

The materials collected must be carefully handled. Since most of them are from oral sources, we must sift the facts carefully.

We must do area studies to avoid generalisation. Africa is large, therefore, any study of African Traditional Religion to be profitable should be regional.

It is the ideal thing to make the 'on the spot' study rather than depend upon secondary sources.

African scholars must make materials available by publishing research materials. We have here the problem of getting publishers. The tendency now is for African publishers to prefer a general study of Africa to an area study. For scholarship, the latter should be preferred.

Scholars must adopt modern approach to their study. There is the need to take photographs (possibly using colour films) and to tape-record information collected from informants. We must atempt to film important rites and ceremonies which figure prominently during important festivals.

I saw something of this type of Professor Daniel of Syracuse University U.S.A. who gave the American public the films 'Bathing the face of god" and "The Hajj."

Content of the Study

Our study must include:

a) The people's world view - creation, organisation and maintenance of the world.
b) The structure of African Traditional Religion.
c) Belief in God.
d) Belief in divinities and spirits.
e) Belief in mysterious powers.
f) Belief in life after death.
g) The relationship between God and the divinities.
h) Worship - Rites and Ceremonies -
   Cultic functionaries
   Prayer and sacrifice
   Sacred Seasons
   Sacred Places.
i) God and Society including social morality.

Future of African Traditional Religion

This is difficult to predict. There is the impingement of two major religions (Islam and Christianity) on A.T.R. The Western culture which is imbibed by many of the elites minimises the influence of A.T.R.

What is more? Traditional Religion lacks written literature and only the priests and the elders remember the essentials of the Religion. Children have drifted away from home in thirst for education and so it isnot easy for a father to hand over to his children.

But we must not lose sight of the force of nationalism which urges Africans to look into their glorious past and which in recent years has encouraged scholars to research into African culture, art and religion. Some books are already produced, and many more will be produced.

The urban centres still keep shrines and observe traditional festivals.

Across the seas, the traditional Yoruba Religion, for example, is having its grip on the Afro-Americans. In Brazil and Cuba the divinities have been associated with saints.

136

In Brazil

Ogun	-	St. Anthony
Sopona	-	St. Lazarus
Sango	-	St. Jerome
Yemoja	-	Lady of Conception
Oshun	-	Lady of Candlemas

In Cuba

Ifa	-	St. Francis of Assissi
Oshun	-	Virgin of Cobre
Oya	-	St. Teresita
Obatala	-	Lady of Mercy
Yemoja	-	Virgin of Regla
Osanyin	-	St. Raphael

We also haveAfro-Americans now living and worshipping the Yoruba way in South Carolina. All this gives one the impression that African Traditional Religion in one form or another will continue to be practised.

Footnotes

1 John Mbiti, **African Religions and Philosophy,** (London Heinemann, 1969), p. 1.
2 Leo Frobenius, **The Voice of Africa,** Vol. I. (London, O.U.P., 1913) pp. xiif.
3 E. Smith (ed.)**African Ideas of God,** (London Edinburth House Press, 1950) p. 1.
4 Quoted by B. Ray, **African Religions,** (Prentice Hall, 1976) p. 3.
5 B.C. Ray, op.cit., p. 3.
6 R. Burton, **A Mission to Gelele, King of Dahome,** (London, Tinsley Brothers, 1964) Vols. 2, p. 199 (Quoted by Ray, pp. 3 & 4.
7 T. Cullen Young, **African Ways and Wisdom,** (London 1937) p. 44.
8 See Evans-Pritchard, **Theories of Primitive Religion,** London 1965) pp. 103f.

9   T.J. Bowen, **Adventures and Missionary Labours,** 1857; (re-
      printed, London Frank and Cass 1968)
10 E.B. Idowu, **African Traditional Religion,** p. 92.
11 J.O. Awolalu, "What is African Traditional Religion?" **Studies
      in Comparative Religion,** vol. 9 No. 1 (Winter 1975)
      p. 56.
12 J.B. Danquah, **The Akan Doctrine of God** (London 1968, 2nd
      edition)
13 E.B. Idowu, **Olodumare, God in Yoruba Belief,** (London Long-
      man 1962) p. 202.
14 Okot p'Bitek, **African Religions in Western Scholarship,** Nairobi
      East African Publishing House, 1974), p. 47.
15 Okot p'Bitek, op.cit., p. 88.
16 R.S. Rattray, **Ashanti** (O.U.P., 1923) (Revised 1969) p. 11.

METHODOLOGY FOR THE STUDY OF AFRICAN RELIGION

by

E. Ikenga - Metuh

The purpose of this article is to determine the methodologies of the different studies of African religion, and to show that though distinct the methodologies are interrelated.

The Problems of African Religion

There are a number of problems which any study of African Religions mus contend with. Firstly, traditional African societies are pre-literate societies. African Religions therefore have no written documented source. There are no sacred scriptures. Rather, the religion is written in the hearts, minds, spoken language, beliefs and practices of the people. Religion pervades and permeates every aspect of life, and is so knitted to life that one would have to study the whole life of the people in order to get an objective view of these religion. 'Where the African is, there is his religion. (1)

Secondly, African religion is ethnic religion. It is folk religion which has grown out of the experience and practices of the people and therefore tailored to suit the particular needs and situations of each ethnic group.

Methodology of Anthropological Study

In view of these problems, the first step in the study of African religion is to make an anthropological study of the religious system of individual African societies. This is necessary in order to get a true image of African religion in its various social contexts. Any viable methodology of the anthropology of African religions would have to adopt a number of approaches in order to do justice to the various dimensions of African religion; namely Limited Comparative and Historical Approaches.

Limited Comparative Approach

Shorter has accused the first generation anthropological studies of African religion and society of being 'fiercely particularist.'

Insisting on a thorough going studies of each of every ethnic group and professing on almost total agnosticism in respect of any similarities or links between them. (2)

He acknowledged the insights and contributions made by anthropological studies, but warned that all these should not be allowed to rest there. The anthropological studies of individual societies must usher in comparative studies.

A move within the anthropologist camp initiated by Evans-Pritchard sought to counter balance particularism with a comparative approach, and functionalism with quest for meaning. On particularism/comparison, he suggests

'A number of systematic studies of primitive philosophies has to be made. When that has been done, a classification can be made on the basis of which comparative studies can be undertaken which possibly may lead to some general conclusions'. (3)

The comparative approach which Evans-Pritchard is proposing here presumes the study of the religion of each group as 'a systems of the ideas and practice in its own right' (4) religious beliefs and practices of the individual societies. So that particularist approach is a necessary prerequisite for the comparative approach.

Limitation of Scope of Comparison

It is only common sense that for any comparison to be effective, the range of the things compared should be limited. This is the weakness of the 'Enumerative Approach' in Shorter's classificaton.

In Parrinders own words, it tries 'to treat African Religion on a comparative basis (by) gathering material from various parts of the continent'. (5) Thus, its attempt to cover too many societies and too many phenomena weighs on the effectiveness of its comparisons and it often ends up in only making an enumeration of different items of beliefs and traditions from a large collection of societies. Further more, because of the large area covered it often ignores the socio-cultural contexts and the historical dimensions of African Religion. Consequently, its analysis is often lacking in dept and paints a larger-than life picture of African Religion. The delimitation of the scope of the comparison should be along geo-cultural lines. This should among other things throw some light on the significance of environmental and cultural factors in determining the similarities and differences in religious beliefs; and may lead to historical conclusion about cultural link between the societies compared. (6)

African Religion as a cultural phenomenon has a history. Thus no study of African Religion which ignores the historical dimension can be said to be objective. The historical study transcends every aspect and every stage of the study of African religion. It is as much important in the anthropological study as it is in the phenomenological and theological study. It is necessary for the study of particular societies as well as for the comparative studies.

Anthropologists and writers on African religion have never doubted the importance and value of the historical study of African Religion, but their efforts in this direction have been hampered by the pre-literate nature of African societies and paucity of information form archeology. According to Evans-Pritchard:

> Nuer religion, like any other, has of course, a history, but we can only trace it in so far as it survives in the memories of the Nuer themselves for reports by travellers, which start barely a century ago, are on this matter, slight and unreliable. Ethnological research, can only supply indirect evidences, archeological research were it to be undertaken, probalby with none at all. (7)

The scepticism about the possibility of a scientific study of the history of African religion was dispelled by the results of the research of a team of scholars drawn from some American and East African universities now published in the book **"The Historical study of African Religion"**, edited by T.O. Ranger, and I.N. Kimambo. By combining the use of oral history more recent political history, and contemporary socioreligious analysis, they were

able to show that there has been a high degree of cultural interaction between different African ethnic groups and how this has
resulted in the introduction of new cults and the modification
of existing one. In the words, of H.W. Turner.

> We now see something of the dynamics of African reli-
> gions, their capacity for change, and innovation, and
> their influence upon other forces at work in history. (8)

Methodology of the Phenomenological Study

The phenomenological study of African religion to a
certain extent, pressuposes the anthropological study. The phenomenological study, as it were, begins where the anthropological
studies stop. This is partly due to the nature of African religion
and partly due to the scope of phenomenological studies. African
religion is ethnic religion. In the small scale societies in which
it is so interlinked and interlaced with other aspects of social
life the study of African religion necessarily involves the study
of the society in which it is found.

The phenomenological study of religion is defined by
Turner, as the 'systematic study of the manifestations, or form
of religion and their associated meanings from morphological,
typological and comparative view-ponts'. (9) Husserl repeatedly
states that phenomenology is a 'descriptive science'. It describes
and distinguishes the phenomena given in consciousness without
introducing doubtful presuppositions or infallible deductions. (10)
In other words, it examines and describes the religious facts, the
beliefs and practices as they present themselves but refrains from
making judgements regarding the truths and truth-values of the
various religious manifestations. In view of its scope and objectives, the phenomenological studies, requires the anthropological
studies of African religion and builds on its results. With the aid
of anthropological studies it seeks to understand the full significance of beliefs and practices in their socio-cultural contexts,
and then proceeds with its own peculiar methods which are
descriptive, comparative and historical approaches. Where necessary, it also uses the thematic approach.

Descriptive Approach

The main thrust of the phenomenological studies is descriptive. Since religious phenomena cannot be divorced from their socio-cultural contexts, it requires the assistance of anthropological studies to lay bare the full significance of religious phenomena as found in their socio-cultural contexts. For Booth has compared beliefs and practices considered outside their contexts to 'the way in which a collection of African masks in a museum gives us very little understanding of the significance of any particular mask in the context of a wholeoutfit worn in a dance celebrating some even of a communal significance'. (11) However, phenomenology goes beyong the social and cultural dimension. It considers the religious as a value 'sui generis'. So it considers and describes religious phenomena specifically as experiences, and concentrates on their religious significance. Its analytical tools are concepts, categories and terms drawn from the study of comparative religions. Huserl has praised Rudolf Otto's description of the religious consciousness, in his famous book **'The idea of the Holy as** of masterly piece of phenomenological analysis. (12) Otto's analysis of the structure of the religious consciousness is based on an elucidation of the key-word 'the Holy.' He was able to show that this word includes in its meanings two sets of contrasting but complimentary notions. On the one hand there are rational notions like purity, moral goodness, attraction etc., and on the other, irrational notions like 'numinous' fearful, mysterious, etc. By the skilful use of these notions, one is, as it were, led to see the structure and processes of religious consciousness.

The phenomenological study of African religion would apply this model in the analysis of different facts and phenomena in African religion. It could be applied to the study of different traditional beliefs and practices like concepts of God, the deities or ancestors. It could more easily and with more predictable results be applied to the study of more overt phenomena like annual rituals, shrines, sacred symbols, and masks. Such an analysis would lead to a deeper understanding of the religious significance and functions of these phenomena.

Comparative Historical Approach

The methodogy of the phenomenology of religion is not only descriptive and explanatory, but also comparative. However, unlike anthropological studies, what are compared are not whole religious systems in their socio-cultural contexts. Rather, it takes out and compares similar facts and phenomena which it encounters in different religions. The purpose is not to grade them accordingly as they are thought to be more developed or less developed on the evolutionary scale. Rather, the purpose is to gain a deeper and more accurate insight of concepts or beliefs, so compared.

In view of this for the phenomenology of religion, the differences between religions are as important as the similarities. Most religions as expression of the encounter of the human mind with the 'Divine', have striking similarities. Yet each religious tradition claims to be unique, and different. The differences are further explained by the perculiar socio-cultural and historical conditions which have conditioned it. The phenomenon of religion doesnot concern itself with the absolute character of different faiths. However, through careful comparison of similarities and disimilarities found in many religions, it seeks to get a deeper understanding of some of their beliefs and practices.

The History of Religions Approach

The phenomenon of religion makes use of the history of religions in its comparative approach. The history of religions is not only the study of religious phenomena in their historical contexts but also their structural connections. Hence historical phenomenology of religion must be distinguished from the history of one particular. Put simply, the latter is the history of one religion e.g. Church History, History of Islam, or History of Hinduism, while the former is the History of Religions. The history of religions therefore does not limit itself to the study of the history of one religion, but studies at least a few religions in order to be able to compare them. The scope is to arrive at a deeper understanding of the characteristics of different religious concepts, practices and institution through the study of their various manifestations. So that, the history of religions presupposes the history of individual religions and deserves its data from them.

The scope of historical phenomenology thus, goes beyond the 'comparative culture-history' approach of contributions to the Ranger and Kimambo edited volume. (13) It is not limited to determining the developments in religious thoughts and practices in responses to some socio-cultural, political changes in the history of a given society. It goes beyond this conclusion reached by Shorter after the study of the impact of the culture contacts resulting from spread of the conus-shell discemblem in East Tanzania:

> We thus detect in African Traditional Religion a development of ideas and enrichment in theology, going hand in hand with processes or organisational change brought by external Contacts and the interaction between African peoples. (14)

On the theme of the concept of God in African Religion which was Shorter's concern in the article under reference, the response of historical phenomenology would not stop at determining belief in God in its various historical stages of origin and development in African Religion. Rather, it would compare the African ideas of God drawn from its own history with those of other religious tradition in order to get a better understanding of the characteristics and significance of the concepts of God generally and its African type in particular.

Methodology of Theology of African Religion

Every religion and religion-based culture can be said to have a theology, because, argues Shorter, theology is no more than 'theo-logia' 'a speaking about God or god'. (15) However, theology is more than 'God talk.' Every theology is God talk' but not every 'God talk' is theology. A mere profession of faith in God is not theology, even though 'faith' is a datum or raw material for theology. The classical three worded definition of theology given by St. Anslem says that theology is 'Fides Quaerens intellectum' faith seeking clarification. In other words, theology is a methodical reflection of faith with the scope of presenting it as a coherent system. (16)

145

Faith, which is the object of theology is not faith in the abstract, but the faith of a believing community. This has wide ranging implications for the methodology of the theology of African religions. Since believing communities in Africa is a plurality, there should be a corresponding plurality of African traditional theologies. Thus declares Shorter.

> a methodology which treats African religious systems as a single, unified phenomenon is simply not faithful to facts

But continues Shorter:

> In saying this, we are not denying the fact that in African tradition many elements, such as the idea of the Supreme being religious concepts of authority, rituals and so on, may transcend basic ethnic and cultural allegiances, but such facts must be demonstrated before they can be made the basic for general theological statement.(17)

Thus the search for the theology of African religions would centre primarily around the different ethnic groups. It is here that one would expect to find coherent systems of beliefs. This means that a theology of African religion would benefit a great deal from the anthropological study of African religions, and infact presupposes it. Anthropological study of African religion is necessary both in its particularist and comparative dimensions, to determine both the significance of different beliefs in their social contexts, and the spread of any item of belief within any culture area or region. Welbourn in his tribute to Mary Douglas refers to her opposition to theologians and students of comparative religion who compare religious features out of their place in the total culture; they sometimes compare incomparables and often obscure the essential human character of religious behaviour. /18) Any viable theology of African religion must therefore take into account the findings of anthropological studies.

The theology of African religion also benefits from, and presupposes the phenomenological study of African religions to obtain a deeper understanding of the characteristics of the different religious concepts, practices, and institutions; so that theological studies actually begin where the anthropological and phenomenological studies stop.

The next strand in the methodology of the theology of African religions is interpretation. The different beliefs and practices of religion may have been accepted on faith by the adherents, but they are yet meaningless. Those who accept them must have seen some reasonableness in accepting them, and some compatibility and coherence between the different items of belief. Interpretation or what in effect is the act of theologizing, seeks to make this implicit reasonableness and coherence of the faith, explicit. This is done through hermeneutics, or the science of interpretation. One of its elementary rules of precedure is to move from the known to the unknown, to use known principles to clarify unknown facts.

In this connection, it has often been asked whether concepts and categories drawn from Western philosophy and theology could be useful in the theological study of African religion. Of course, it would be reductionism to force elements of African religious beliefs into Western theological moulds, or to use Western concepts to evaluate African beliefs as if the validity of these concepts depends on their conforming to Western models.

However, it must be pointed out that African religious beliefs are 'like' and 'unlike' Western concepts. Since comparison is a legitimate scientific method, it is not only legitimate but also beneficial to compare the religious concepts and beliefs of both religions. This will clarify the theological thought implicit in the beliefs and concepts.

There have been various attempts to use some European categories, concepts and logic to explain African beliefs. An attempt which has provoked both criticism and compliment, is Placide Tempel's use of the Bergsonian concept of 'Vital Force' (which he claims to be an authentic Bantu concept) to explain every aspect of Bantu life and beliefs, their psychology, epistemology, ethics, as well as their religious beliefs. (19) His theory, which is in the nature of a hypothesis, is so well argued and so well illustrated that some writers who may have some reservations about his conclusion would still agree that overall, his theory is 'on the right lines'. (20) Other less successful attempts, like Alexis Kagame's attempt to use Aristotelian categories to classify African concepts of being, or attempts by some African beliefs, can hardly escape the charge of reductionism. (21)

Evans-Pritchard has pointed out the risks of reductionism implicit in the use of comparative categorical approach in the theological study of African religion. According to him, African religious concepts and categories need not fit into the well known Western scheme-monotheism, polytheism, pantheism, animism. They are best understood, he says, as involving elements of these schemes at different levels and in different contexts of experience. (22) It is precisely because of this that they should be compared so that the peculiar characteristics of African religious concepts could be seen. Very significant in the comparative categorical studies are certain pairs of categories drawn from Comparative Religion which stand at the extremities of different continuums within which certain God/Man relationships necessarily fall e.g., Deism and Theism, Divine Transcendence and Immanence; Divine Grace and Human Responsibility and so forth. Relevant African concepts could be weighted with these theological categories, in order to determine where they fall in the continuum.

Conclusion

The search for the methodology of African religion has been hampered by the assumption that African religion is so radically different from the major world religions that it requires a different type of study and a completely different methodology. Infact, the assumption seems to be that African religion can only be studied anthropologically because it is ethnic and preliterate and therefore 'primitive religion'.

Thus, in the writings on African religion, one finds that some authors inadvertently drift from anthropological accounts to the phenomenological and on to the theological presentation, without distinguishing them. This has made it difficult to determine which methodology to use.

African religion, like other religions, can be studied from different perspectives. There could be an anthropological, psychological, phenomenological or theological study of African religion. The type of study one wants to do will determine the methodology one needs to use. The methods used in anthropological studies are not identical with the methods of phenomenological or theological studies. From this point of view, the study of African religions is polymethodical.

However, because all of these studies of religion (anthropological, phenomenological and theological) have a common object of study, (African religion) there is a certain interdependence and hierarchy among them and their corresponding methodologies. Or, as Turner put it, 'there is a dialectical interaction between the various methods as well as hierarchical arrangement among them'. (23) The anthropological study of African religion which studies religious belief in their socio-cultural contexts is a prerequisite for any deeper study of African religion. Any other type of study of African religion presupposes it because it studies the effect of the milieu on religious beliefs and practices, and thus clarifies them. Results of anthropological studies provide data for phenomenological and theological studies provide very useful data for theological studies.

Similarly, the methods of these three types of studies are distinct but show a marked similarity. The anthropological method begins with the study of individual societies and then proceeds through historical and limited comparative approaches. The method of phenomenological studies is mainly descriptive. It makes use of history of religious and comparative religious beliefs uses logic as well as comparative categorical approach.

The methodology of African religion being sought for therefore is not one but many. African religion is polymethodical. The anthropological studies has its own methodology different from the methodologies of the phenomenological and theological studies. Writers on African religion should therefore first determine from what perspective they want to study African religion, for they will determine the appropriate methodology to use.

Footnotes

1   Mbiti, J.S., **African Religions and Philosophy** (London, 1969),
        p. 1.
2   Shorter, **African Christian Theology,** 39.
3   Evans-Pritchard, E. **Nuer Religion** (Oxford, Clarendon Press
        1956), p. 3 15.
4   Ibid.
5   Parrinder G.E. **African Traditional Religion,** (London)
6   Shorter, Aylward, Opus Cit. p. 52, quoting Evans-Pritchard,
        Essays In Social Anthropology, (London, 1962, p. 46-65.)
7   Evans-Pritschard, E. **Nuer Religion** (Oxford 1958), p. 311,
        C.f Mbiti, J.S. **African Religions and Philosophy,** p. 23.
8   Turner, J.R.A. 12, 1 (1981), p. 5.
9   Ibid.
10 Macquarrie, J. **20th Century Religious Thought** (London SCM
        Press, 1963), p. 218.

11 Booth, N.S. (Jr.) (ed) African Religion (New York: Nok Pub.
        1977), p. 23.
12 Macquarrie, **Twentieth Century Religious Thought,** 213.
13 Ranger, T.O. and Kimambo, I.N. **The Historical Study of Afri-
        can Religions** (London, 1972).
14 Shorter, **African Christian Theology,** 26.
15 Ibid., 27.
16 Macquarrie John, **Principles of Christian Theology,** (London:
        SCM Press; 1966), p. 1-3.
17 Shorter, African Christian Theology, 27.
18 Welbourn, F.S. Mary Douglas and the Study of Religion.
        Journal of Religions in African, Vol. III. (1970).
19 Temples, P. **Bantu, Philosophy** (Paris Presence Africaine, 1959).
20 Smith, E.W. **African Ideas of God** (London, Edinburgh House
        Press, 1950).
21 Kagame, A. **La Philosophie Bantu Rwandaire De L'Etre**
        (Braussels, 1956).
22 Evans-Pritchard, **Nuer Religion,** p. 316.
23 Turner, J.R.A., 12, 1 p. 2.

PART THREE

THE THEOLOGY OF AFRICAN TRADITIONAL RELIGION

THEOLOGY OF AFRICAN TRADITIONAL RELIGION:
A REVIEW

by

E.M. Uka

> Can there be an indigenous African theology? ... if
> by African theology we mean any new principles ap-
> plicable only to Africa or any special additions to, or
> substraction from, theological science for the sake of
> Africa. The data of christian theology, the Biblical
> Revelation is fixed: theological method, concerned with
> the scrutiny, interpretation and application of this will
> not ultimately be determined by local factors ...
> Theological integrity will resist even the temptation
> to develop certain forms of doctrine simply because
> they are readily assimilable in Africa. These doctrinal
> forms must be tested on general Biblical and theolog-
> ical principles. (1)

Even though this observation was made by Andrew F.
Walls over two decades ago, the premise of his observation is
still extant i.e. the Western christian and ecclessiastical mentality
of taking the Biblical revelation (or religion) as fixed and final,
while other forms of revelation and religion are faulty and
foolish. This impression that African theology has to be rooted
in the Bible and the view that there cannot be a valid theology
of African Traditional religion unless such a theology finds expression or validity within the context of christian theology is what
this paper has set out to re-examine. The need to re-examine
this assumption is more urgent now than ever before when African
theologians would dare to say

> ... there is need to translate christianity into genuine
> African categories. This is what we call African Theolo-
> gy. It is an attempt to couch essential Christianity
> into African categories and thought forms. Such an
> exercise is not to be confused with an exercise in
> couching African world-view in christian form. (2)

In the light of Pobee's view, for example, we argue that theology
cannot be said to be theology only when it is christian theology

153

or imported theology. I do not think it is blasphemous to say African theology, which implies an inquiry into the indigenous religious beliefs and practices of the African people. African theology is not even "the fourth dimension to christianity," (3) as Setiloane would claim, nor is it the contextualization or indigenisation of christianity into the African culture and tradition, as Idowu and Mbiti and others would persuade us to believe. (4) What they have tried to do is to interprete Christianity in African terms in order to make it intelligible to Africans and thereby persuade them to become Christians.

The upshot of this development has been that "mission churches" have tended to become more African and more meaningful to the Africans as they could now use African music, idioms, parables, symbols, robes and liturgical forms in worship. This cultural accommodation of christianity to African customs seems to be what has generally been referred to as African Theology. (5)

In the light of the above review, this paper argues that what should rightly be called African Theology is the theology of African Traditional or indigenous religion not the African Theology that tries to solve the problems of indigenisation of a new and foreign religion.

In order to clarify what we mean by the theology of African Traditional Religion, this paper will aim at freeing "Theology" from those Western concepts which have for a long time restricted and imprisoned it, so that conceptualizing may be done in a fresh way. The form of theologising which has substantially prevailed during recent centuries can fairly be accused of being arid and limited in its imagery. It has been intellectual and abstract, stamped by Western or North Atlantic modes of thought. Moreover, it was developed by professionals and strongly influenced by their particular interests. It was marked by jargons whose use restricted much of the work to an artificially limited language group, fed by books rather than by being immersed in life. It is expected that as people recover their own histories and selfhood from colonial dominated histories, they would begin to establish bases for indigenous theologies, since theologies are not mere combinations of ritualism and moralism, but an intellectual effort concerned with the potential release of men from any kind of bondage they are in.

Theology arises wherever there is a **Theos**, a god, and wherever there are believers who try to work out the implications of their belief in a **theos**, a god. So, some scholars consider theology as a form of thinking that seeks to explain and systematise beliefs of a people about their god. By this token, there are bound to be theologies for 'Muslims, for Jews, for Hindus, for Christians and therefore for African's too. In effect, through theology, a religious faith or belief brings itself into a certain kind of expression. When a belief or a faith expresses itself in theology, it implies that what is being expressed is not faith or belief in general, but the faith of an historic community, i.e. of a distinct group of people. In this context, theology functions to express the content of a particular faith in the clearest and most coherent language available. In sum, it could be said that theology is rooted in the religion or belief system of a community. It aims at giving a faith, a religion, a coherent verbal expression. As an intellectual enterprise, it aims at attaining the highest possible degree of intelligibility, clarity and consistency in its attempt to investigate, explain, and systematise the understanding of a particular religion of a people. It is in this vein that we shall speak of African theology, as the specific faith or religion of Africa or of an African historic community like the Igbo or the Yoruba of Nigeria, or the Ga of Ghana or the Dinka of Sudan.

What is clear from the above attempts to explain what theology is, is the fact that theology, as a systematised investigation has not only its own formal and material objective, it has also its methods and approaches as well as its sources. According to Macquarrie, (6) theology, particularly the christian theology has six formative elements that call for special consideration. They include: experience, relevation, scripture, tradition, culture and reason. (7) It is the contention of this paper that the Theology of African Traditional Religion contains more or less, these vital elements of theology. So, if theology as Paul Tillich would say, forces a relgion to make careful description of its concepts, even so can the theology of ATR compel Africans to make a careful description of the concepts of ATR and how they could be aplied with logical consistency. (8) In this case, a theology of ATR would seek to express and articulate the faith in such a way that old members of the community will get fresh insight and the young ones understand what their parents believed. So the task of theology goes beyond the mere expression of a religious faith to that of finding explanations that really fit a phenomenon even if they are paradoxical. (9)

By applying Macquarrie's six-point criteria to African Traditional/indigenous Religion, we come up with the following clarifications:

Experience

The word experience, according to the Concise Oxford Dictionary means the process of personally observing or encountering something as they occur in time. With regard to a religious faith, experience therefore implies encountering "the wholly other", the mysterious dimension of life which is felt to be other than ourselves. It is what Rudolf Otto describes as having an awareness of the Holy, the mysterious tremendum, that inspires fear and at the same time attracts.

According to Macquarrie, experience appears first on the list because theology implies participation in a religious faith, so that some experience of the life of faith precedes theology which seeks to make sense of such experience and in process brings the content of the faith-experience to clear expression in words. The African, as "homo Africanus", i.e. an African human being, experiences, (encounters) the mysterious dimension of life. He does not have to be "a Western christian African" to undergo this experience. He undergoes the experience essentially as "homo Africanus" who lives in community with his fellow Africans and shares a common life of faith with them, as proven by their cosmogonic myths such as that of the Igbo of Nigeria. (11)

Revelation (12)

Macquarrie considers Revelation as the primary sources of theology, and a basic category of theological thinking. If in general terms, we say that what is disclosed in revelation is the dimension of the holy, then in the revelatory experience, it is as if the holy, the other than ourselves, the mysterious dimension of reality, "breaks in", and "reveals itself from beyond man towards man".

In African traditional religion as well as in other traditional religions, "the holy" is believed to manifest itself in nature. Hence natural phenomena tend to take on the dimensions of a

156

revelatory situation. It is in this sense that we speak of African traditional religion as revealed religion that is, its revelation came into existence as in other religions, as the product of a special experience of the mystery in the universe or of the Holy. In indigenous African religion, revelation comes not only through special experience but also through special places, through symbols and idols and through myths. In all, revelation is seen or encountered as a different order or reality from the reality of the ordinary mundane world and it speaks to situations past, present and future.

Since theology expresses the faith or beliefs of a community, call in the African community, it means that the community's revelation cannot be founded on private revelations. As Macquarrie puts it: "A community of faith within which a theology arises, usually traces its history back to what may be called a 'classic' or primordial revelations." (Macq. p.7) It is a revelation that has the power to found a community of faith, a revelation which therefore becomes fruitful and important to the life of the community and is re-enacted from time to time until it becomes normative for the experience of the community.

Scripture (13)

If revelation is primordial, and was given at the origin of a community, how can modern people have access to it?

It is in this regard that scripture, i.e., the sacred writings of the community of faith, plays an important role of providing a storage, a kind of memory bank by which the community can recall its past. It is not in all cases that scripture is written. For example, in African traditional religion, the basis for interpreting reality, i.e., its scripture, is not written. Its sources include songs, arts and symbols, wise-sayings, myths, legends, beliefs and customs, names of people and places etc. Scripture, (written or unwritten) is a major instrument in maintaining stability and a sense of continuing identity in a community itself. It is the norm in the theology of a community, that is, the intellectual effort to express the content of a particular religion of a community in the clearest and most coherent language available.

Tradition (14)

Tradition in ordinary parlance means the handing down of statements, beliefs, legends and customs from generation to teneration. Speaking from a religious point of view, e.g., from the Jewish religious view, tradition refers to the unwritten body of laws and doctrines or any one of them which is said to have been received from Moses and handed down orally from generation to generation. In the christian sense, tradition refers to a body of teachings or doctrines or any one of them which is believed to have been delivered by Christ or His apostles but were not committed to writing. In church history, traditions refer to the practices and policies adopted by the church in order to solve some of its administrative and socio-cultural exigencies. Whereas the Roman Catholics hold that the revelation in Christ has been transmitted to them both in scripture and tradition, the Protestants believe that the revelation of Christ is through the scripture alone.

With reference to tradition, as one of the formative factors in theology, Macquarrie contends that it functions like scripture, and as a bulwark against individualism or privatisation in interpreting norms and values. In other words, tradition complements scripture in ensuring, for example, that christian theologians have their minds enlightened and their thoughts directed by the communal wisdom and experience of the church not by their egoistic or private considerations.

In the case of African Traditional Religion, the absence of a written scripture has been noted. So what we have as the tradition is the collective and shared world-views, practices, morals and the generally accepted way of life of the people. In the context of Igbo indigenous religion, tradition is the **Omenala**, i.e., the complex concept embodying the traditional norms and customs of the people; (15) the body of answers to fundamental existential problems.

As tradition in christian theology helps to guard against private interpretations of beliefs and practices, so also does it act as a bulwark against rank, individualism and egotism in interpreting the beliefs and practices contained in indigenous African religion.

In order to keep tradition (and scripture) alive and relevant, each generation appropriates the tradition and reinterpretes it in its own categories of thought. Such reinterpretation is needed if the tradition is to survive as a living and growing tradition.

158

Culture (16)

So far, we have dealt with the factors in Macquarrie's definition of theology which refers to theology's character as an intellectual discipline. We shall now consider the cultural setting which theology seeks to give expression in the clearest and most coherent language available. If theology is to make sense and be made intelligible to the people it applies to, it has to employ the language or thought forms of the culture within which it is undertaken. This means that theology must be pertinent to a culture which it seeks to address. So a theologian should explicitly recognise the cultural constraints as a factor to reckon with. As Macquarrie would say - "recognition of the cultural factor is equivalent to acknowledging that there is no final theology". In other words, theology should be an ongoing exercise, since its formulations are culturally conditioned and, therefore, need re-interpretation as cultural forms change.

With reference to Theology of African Traditional Religion, the cultural factor is an important element in view of the changing scenes of the culture due to Arabic (Islamic) and Western (Christian) cultural impact on indigenous Africa. The element of culture renders the task of Theology for African indegenous (Traditional) Religion important and urgent since it would seek to clarify and render intelligible, indigenous African beliefs and traditions which have tended to be distorted, discredited or even destroyed due to the pervading impact of christian and moslem religions.

Reason (17)

Reason constitutes another factor that has to do with theology's character as an intellectual discipline. It provides tools for the analysis of reality. According to Macquarrie, reason may broadly be divided into speculative and critical reason. In its speculative exercise, reason endeavours to construct a theory of reality such as Anselem's ontological proof of the existence of God. This was based on pure reason alone. In critical reason, both elucidatory and corrective functions are fulfilled. In its elucidatory functon, reason sifts, analyses, expounds and generally speaking brings to light the content of revelation. This use of reason on the one hand would not be an autonomous exercise, but would always be subject to the divine revelation itself, and on the other hand it would be used as a tool to interpret revelation according

159

to the same canons and hermeneutic principles that is used for the guidance of interpretation in general.

The corrective use of reason assigns much larger role to the rational factor in theology. It is directed upon the revelation or alleged revelation itself - questioning its credentials, submits it to scrutiny and criticism, removes from its content whatever may be regarded as irreconcilable conflicts with other well-founded convictions that are held. In this respect the role of reason in African theology is not quite the same as in Christian theology. According to Sarpong, the African believes in God and spirits but he is not interested in rationally defining these realities, and most of the theological terms used in such an exercise mean nothing to him. The ordinary African is not "logical" in the Western sense of being a sophisticated philosopher, a type of Western Cartesian rationalist. He does not reason along strict syllogistic lines. (18) This, however, does not mean that he is hot a thinker or that he does not reason. In fact, he reasons in a pragmatic way, philosophises in his own right. To his way of thinking, behaviour must be related to his needs, to what he considers good, useful and helpful. In short, his way of thinking is utilitarian.

Defining the theology of African Indigenous Religion

So far, we have tried to establish the fact that the intention of theology is to give verbal and rational expression to a religious faith or a belief system in such a way as to attain the highest possible degree of clarity, and intelligibility.

Granted the unique status of African Theology therefore, one can regard books such as **Akan Doctrine of God,** by J.B. Danqua, **Olodumare - God in Yoruba Belief** by Bolaji Idowu; **Concepts of God in Africa** by J.S. Mbiti and many others like that as attempts to articulate aspects of African theology. Through these books African theologians have given verbal expression to the indigenous religious faith of Africans.

At this juncture, it is pertinent to briefly review some of the theological works on African traditional religion. The aim here is to determine the context, the content and the methodology of African theology in contemporary times.

The Context of African Theology (18)

The relationship of God to man and man to God is the subject and the context of theology. This relationship calls for constant review and re-thinking in the light of all available data.

In the light of this explanation, the context of African theology could broadly be seen through the precolonial, colonial, post colonial and contemporary periods. During the precolonial period the written theological task was performed mostly by non-Africans who wondered if Africans believed in God and had a religion. The picture painted by one western missionary concerning the Africans as heathen is worthy of mention. He portrayed the African as "a heathen who was spiritually lost, wicked, a willful sinner, without Christ, having no hope and without God in the world." In other words, the African could not conceive of God and therefore had no religion. What the African called his religion was variously described as Juju, ancestor-worship, animism, idolatry, fetishism, paganism, polytheism and the like.

Given the temporal conditions of the Africa which was variously described as marked by "dire poverty, wretched homes, unremitting toil, gross intellectual ignorance," and the moral condition which was described as "recking with filthy and degrading habits, abominable practices, unmentionable cruelties and crimes, the Western missionary theologian wondered if there could ever be an indigenous African Theology and Ethics. (19)

The precolonial, colonial and post colonial periods presented a religious situation that cried out for explanation, for a theology. Theologies emerged to demonstrate that the African had a religion, believed in a supreme God and had a life that was regulated by a system of morals. But a fundamental weakness in these theologies as articulated both by Africans and Europeans was their over dependence on Western christian and ecclesiastical categories in describing and evaluating African religious beliefs and practices. The upshot from this was the emergence of what is termed "African Christian Theology". This situation leaves the contemporary African theologian with the task of freeing 'African Theology' from those dominating concepts and categories which have long restricted and imprisoned it. As a matter of fact, theologising in past centuries had been intellectualistic and abstract, stamped by western or North Atlantic modes of thought. This style of theologising must now give way to "theologies of the people, by the people and for the people", implying theologies in context, theologies that have the capacity to respond meaningfully and creatively to live-issues of cultural importance. Theologies that can explain, intelligibly and coherently African religious moods and modes.

The Content of African Theology

The content of African theologies have largely dealt with clarifying and systematising the concepts of God among Africans. Arising from these studies or theologies, are helpful attempts to explore and explain the concept of God, the divine origin of the earth, the belief in man as the custodian of the earth, and of man as fully human only in the context of his community. Since African traditional religion recognises the power of evil spirits in the world, this presents a call for a theology of evil spirits too.

Other beliefs, practices and institutions that call for a serious theological rethinking are issues connected with authority, death, life after death, the living-dead (Ancestors), widowhood, mourning and funeral rites. Other items include: marriage, title taking, poverty, chastity, human sexuality, secret societies, naming ceremonies, rain making, magic, rituals and festivals, tabus, sacrifices and the concept of wealth. Theological endeavours in this direction will enhance the independence, authenticity and identity of African theological categories, beliefs and practices.

Methodology of African Theology

We have noted that theology is a methodical and systematic reflection of faith with the aim of presenting an intelligible and coherent system. Writing about the Biblical Basis or Present Trends in African Theology, Mbiti drew our attention to three main areas of African Theology - "Theologia Africana". They are oral Theology, and symbolic theology, and written theology. (20)

He argued that oral theology is produced by the masses through songs, sermons, teaching, prayer, conversations. This is the stage of theology before it is committed to writing. It is infact the earliest form of Theology. Speaking strictly within the context of indigenous African religion, oral theology found expression in music and dances, in proverbs, riddles and wise sayings. It was found in names of people and places; in myths and legends, in beliefs and customs which were verbally and freely used by the people. Mbiti described oral theology "as theology in the open air, unrecorded theology, generally lost to libraries."

Symbolic theology is expressed through art, sculpture, drama, symbols, rituals, dance, colours and numbers. These symbolic elements constituted a veritable means of communicating and clarifying ideas about what Africans believed about God, the spirits and the world. So the use of symbols could be seen as a method used by Africans for performing a theological task.

Written theology could be seen as one of the most important developments and communicate by indigenous Africans to clarify record the beliefs and practices of their indigenous religious faith. The votaries of the faith do not make as much use of the written theology as they make of the oral and the symbolic.

Given the plurality of African traditional religions, and their corresponding theologies, it could be said that historically they passed through the oral, symbolic and written stages. Presently they retain all the features. So in terms of methods of doing theology, the oral, symbolic and written could be treated as sound and acceptable.

Ikenga Metuh, in his article on methodology for the study of African Religion, has something to say on methodology of Theoloy of African Religion. (21) Since theology by itself is a method of clarifying teaching, beliefs and practices either orally symbolically or in written form, anthropological study of African religion could equally enhance African theological effort. According to Metuh, the touch of anthropology will help to determine both the significance of different beliefs in their social context and the spread of any item of belief within any culture area or region. Indigenous African theology can also benefit from the phenomenological study of African traditional religion; as it would enable it to obtain a deeper understanding of the characteristics of the different religious concepts, practices and institutions.

Conclusion

In sum, it could be said, that the African traditional religion has a distinctive theology of its own as other religions. Its theology is authentic, with identity, character, content, context and a methodology. It is valid, both as an academic discipline and as an intellectual quest for the fulfilment of spiritual and felt needs of the African.

Footnotes

1 A.F. Walls, in Harry Sawyerr (ed)., **Christian Theology in Independent Africa,** (Freetown, 1961).

2 John S. Pobee, **Towards an African Theology,** (Abingdon-Nashville, 1979) pp. 17-22. See also Harry Sawyerr, "What is African Theology?" in **African Theological Journal** No. 4 (1971) pp. 7-24.

   Gabriel M. Setiloane, "Where Are We in African Theology?" **Africa Theological Journal** Vol. 8 No. 1 p. 12 n.d.

3 Ibid. Gabriel M. Setiloane p. 8.

4 E. Bolaji Idowu, **Towards An Indigenous Church** (Oxford, 1965); J.S. Mbiti, **Concepts of God in Africa,** (London, 1970). A.M. Lugira, "African Christian Theology" in **African Theological Journal** Vol. 6 No. 1 n.d.

   Mustete, Ngindu "The History of Theology in Africa: From Polimis to Critical Ironics", in **African Theology En Route** ed. Appia-Kubi & S. Torres, Orbis Books: NY 1979 p. 27.

   J.S. Mbiti, **African Religions and Philosophy,** (London 1969).

   Ikenga-Metuh, Theological Basis for christianising African Forms of Worship of God" in **The Nigerian Journal of Theology** (vol. 1 No. 1 1985) pp. 70-88.

5 Gunther J. Hermann, "Contextualization of Christian Theology in Africa" TCNN Research Bulletin No. 2 Dec. 1978, pp. 12-31. See Aylward Shorter, **African Christian Theology,** (London, 1975). See also a host of articles in **African Theology En Route** edited by Appia-Kubi and S. Torres NY: Orbis Books 1979, pp. 23-73.

6 John Macquarrie, **Principles of Christian Theology,** (New York: Charles Scribner's 1966) pp. 1-17.

7   Ibid. p. 4-6.
8   Paul Tillich **Systematic Theology.** Vol 1 (Chicago: University of Chicago, Press 1951) p. 1-8.
9   Seward Miltner, **Theological Dynamics,** (New York: Abingdon Press, 1972 pp. 182-192.
10 J. Macquarrie, pp. 5-8.
        It is to be noted however, that an individual's experience of Revelation could have an essential relevance to a community situation.
11 Ikenga-Metuh, "The Religious Dimension of African Cosmogonies" **West African Religion** (vol. 17 No. 2, 1978) pp. 9-20.
12 J. Macquarie, pp. 10-12.
13 Ibid. pp. 8-10.
14 Ibid. pp. 10-13.
15 Edmond Ilogu, **Christianity and Igbo Culture** (London: E.J. Brill, 1974) pp. 22-24.
16 Ibid. pp. 12-13.
17 Ibid. pp. 13-17.
18 Peter K. Sarpong, "Christianity meets Traditional African Cultures" in **Mission Trends** (5): **Faith meets Faith,** G.H. Anderson and Thomas F. Stransky ed. (New York: Paulist Press 1981) pp. 238-241. See Evans-Pritchards: "Reinterpretation of Levy Bruhl's la Mentalite Primitive" in **Theories of Primitive Religion,** Oxford: 1965) pp. 78-99.
        J.S. Mbiti **African Religions and Philosophy,** (London: Heinemann 1969) pp. 209-210.
        Byang Kato, **Theological Pitfalls in Africa** (Kenya, 1975) pp. 18-24.
19 Robert Hall Glover, **The Progress of World wide Mission** revised and Enlarged by Herbert Kane (New York: Harper and Brothers 1960) pp. 4-5.
20 John S. Mbiti, "... Towards an appreciation of African Oral Theology" **African Theological Journal** Vol. 8 No. 1 pp. 15-25.
21 Ibid; 15; Ikenga-Metuh, "Search for Methodology of African Religion", in **West African Religion** vol. xx, 1983, pp. 76-88.

SPIRITUALITY IN AFRICAN TRADITIONAL RELIGION

by

E.M. Uka

Introduction

This paper seeks to identify some of the distinctive marks of African spirituality in the context of African Traditional Religion.

In order to accomplish this, we shall first of all review some of the views of scholars on the subject of spirituality. We shall examine spirituality in the context of indigenous African religon in order to show its distinctive marks and authenticity. The lesson to be learnt from African spirituality will go a long way to arrest the demise of the spiritual in contemporary African societies.

Concept of Spirituality in non-African Traditional Religion

According to Aylward Shorter, (1) spirituality is Christian in origin. Like many other words in the Christian vocabulary it has been devalued and taken to mean a religion characterised by inward or interior emphasis. This is what spirituality is not meant to be; because according to Shorter, spirituality is a dynamic concept which derives its meaning from **spiritus,** which means life-giving force which stems from God and quickens baptised Christians. There is nothing esoteric about spirituality. Rather, it is a new mode of living. It implies a new dimension; a new birth to a believer's life.

In his book **African Christian Spirituality,** Shorter identifies 'Christian Spirituality' from the writings of some African scholars. From a study of these writings he characterised African spirituality as revolutionary. It is revolutionary in the sense that it is a revolt against materialism on the one hand and shallow religiousity on the other. Secondly, it is a revolt against a world that dehumanises ... the blackman. Thirdly, it is a revolt aginst cultural passivity, a call to renew creativity that has its roots in African past. Fourthly and finally, it is a revolt against a religion that is inward looking and oblivious of the community. Shorter arrived at these elements of African Christian spirituality by drawing attention to the fact that christianity in modern Africa is extremely shallow. It is a mere form of escapism bred by underdevelopment.

Kofi Appia-Kubi, (2) in his paper on "Indigenous African Christian Churches: signs of authenticity", argues that spiritual hunger is the main cause of the emergence of the indigenous African Christian Churches and not political, social, economic and racial factors. In these churches, the religious need for healing, divining, prophesying and visioning are fulfilled by Christian means. These spiritual experiences according to Appia-Kubi are the pivot of most African religions.

In his article on "Spirituality: The search for the transcendent", James Calahan, observed, that the search for the Divine is not a phenomenon which is peculiar to the modern age. The search, he asserts is as old as the human race and constitutes the basis of many world religions that have developed down the ages. This search differed according to the different situations in which man found himself. For example, a farmer, a tiller of the soil saw the deity as the one who provides fertility to the ground. For the Hindu, spirituality is "a tireless quest for the Truth". In Hinduism God is Truth, and man's relation with the Truth is developed through a kind of asceticism or Yoga which detaches him from himself and absorbs him into the All, where the problems of human existence cease to exist. Budhism, (4) a missionary religion of the East, founded by Siddharta Gautama, the enlightened one sees life as pain and this pain arises from sense perception and life. The belief is that the body and sense life in general constitute a kind of prison for the soul. So as "a religion" its aim is to free the soul from the prison of the body and the senses. Hence its "religion" is "a spirituality of liberation", a longing of the spirit to be free from the bondage of the material body. Islam as a religion also, is a form of human yearning for the transcendence. At the heart of Islam is the doctrine of submission to the will of Allah. Prayer in Islam is meant to illuminate the heart and polish the soul. The prayer act implants in the worshipper something of the mystery of God and His greatness. It directs the believer to pray towards Allah alone. In addition to the prayer act is the obligation to fast. Fasting reminds muslims of their duty to God. These practices constitute his quest for the transcendence - his spirituality is the search for a kind of union or absorption with their deity.

Another author on spirituality is Michael Collins Reilley. (5) He is the author of an outstanding book: **Spirituality For Mission.** According to him, spirituality refers to the life of the spirit, that is a life characterised by an interior or inward emphasis. Reilly argues persuasively that man is an embodied spirit. He is spirit because he can transcend the material, and biological limitations of his being. Because he is a self transcending being, man possesses motives and can express himself creatively as a poet, musician, builder and a scientist. Poetry, music, technology and science are the result of the life of the spirit.

Reilley's second proposition about spirituality is the fact that man is religious. He takes a theological stance and describes man's relationship with any kind of transcendent deity, real or supposed as religious. Religion, therefore concerns man's total conception of the meaning of reality; his world view as it is determined by his relationship with a deity. Flowing from this world-view are definite ways of living and acting. This basic, practical existential attitude of man by which he understands his existence and the meaning of reality, constitutes his spirituality. In other words, spirituality is the way a man acts and reacts habitually to ultimate objectives which flow from his world view. In this context, an African life which is determined by ultimate concerns and ethical demands, possess spirituality i.e. a variety of modes for expressing his needs, and awareness of God. (6)

The Basis of African Traditional Spirituality

Having reviewed some of the meanings and import of spirituality in other religions, we shall now examine the basis of spirituality in African traditional religion, the ways and means by which it is expressed and its merits.

The traditional African is known to be "deifocal" (7) that is he believes everything comes from God and all happenings and events are ultimately traceable to God. He thinks of God as the power that creates and controls all natural processes and all human destinies. God is believed to be the Supreme Being, pre-eminent in all things, the giver of life, light and sufficiency. As **Ikenga Metuh** aptly puts it:

God preceds everything in existence
He depends on nothing for His existence ...

He exists of himself
He is creator of verything, Lord of everything.
He continues to preserve everything in existence,
which therefore depend on Him for its
continued existence.
He is the Great Providence, Chukwu.
God is all powerful; He knows everything; He is
all good; He is in no way evil and cannot will
evil. Death and the evil in the world cannot be
traced to Him. He is kind and merciful.
He is a person, and listens and understands and
often grants our requests ... God's transcendence
does not contradict his immanence. (8)

When man is compared with God, man is seen to be a creature of God, dependent on God, controlled by God; he is limited, transistory and powerless. He is however, bound to God by ties of creation and by God's divine providence over the world of which man is a part.

According to Mbiti, (9) almost every African society has its own myths concerning the origin of man. It is generally acknowledged that God created man and placed him in a state of happiness in the world. And made provision for him, giving him food, knowledge of fundamental skills, domestic animals, light and fire, weapons and tools, children, doctors, medicine. God gave man certain rules to keep in order to sustain their relationship with Him.

Different peoples tell different stories of how the original state of bliss between God and man, and man and his environment was disrupted because man violated the rules.

This resulted in tragic consequences for man in that God separated Himself from man and man lost happiness, peace and free food supply. As Mbiti further observed, it would seem that the African image of the happy life is one in which God is among the people. His presence supplies all their needs for food, shelter, peace and the gift of life. Because of this, the majority of African peoples attempt to go after God in acts of worship for the goodies they can get from Him, not for God's own sake. So, it could be said that African acts of worship are basically utilitarian, a searching primarily for a lost paradise, a kind of humanism, rather than a search for God Himself. (10)

Another version of God and man relation is based on the fact that man is indeed at the center of the universe. According to this account given by Ikenga-Metuh, (11) man has above him the Supreme Being and other very powerful heavenly deities while below him is **Ala,** the Earth Deity, the Queen of the under world presiding over hundreds of local spirits and ancestors. In the ontological order of beings man is in the center of the universe with God, the deities, the spirits and the ancestors above him, and the nature forces like witchcraft, **Ogwu,** medicine, below. Man looks at superior divine forces for help and protection against evil spirits and the forces of evil.

E.P. Modum, (12) in his article "God as Guests ... in African Traditional Societies", noted that the traditional African visualises life and the world as a whole in the context of his relationship with the sacred realm or the invisible world. According to him, the traditional African is basically a religious being. He believes strongly in the existence of a Being or beings whose wishes he must conform with. In other words, he accepts that his existence in the world is determined by some kind of force which he cannot afford to ignore. So he seeks to relate totally and intimately to Him.

So at all levels, (mythologically, ontologically and religiously) there is a strong evidence to show that life on earth for the traditional African is precarious (13) without the aid or intervention of the Supreme Being, the deities and the ancestors. In consequence, the African believes that the key to his existence lies in his relationship with these invisible and "numinal" world, without whose co-operation life will be hallow, nasty and meaningless.

Ways and Means of Experiencing and Expressing Spirituality

Given the fact that the traditional African seeks to live in harmony with his God and the other deities and ancestors from where he derives peace, prosperity, procreation, protection from danger, healing, justice and the like, it follows that as of necessity he develops ways and means by which he continually experiences and expresses them. Through works of arts and crafts and symbols, we see how the African conceives and comprehends the Supreme Being and the deities in the invisible world. Proverbs, riddles, myths, wise sayings and names of peoples and places reflect the depth of what the African thinks and believes about men in relation to the "numinous"; also by means of charms, divination, sorcery, witchcraft, magic and the like, we see the

171

negative ways and means by which the traditional African attempts to contact, control and commission some agents of the spirit world". (14)

Having noted some of the negative and debit side of African spirituality, we shall however, concentrate more on the positive and helpful aspects of spirituality which are attained through periodic festivals, acts of worship (including prayers, sacrifices) and oath-taking. These basic practices, existential acts by which the African acts and reacts habitually to the Supreme Being, the deities and the ancestors; these means by which he expresses his need, his dependence and his dedication to the gods constitute the pith of African spirituality. We shall now describe elements of these spirituality through which the African celeberates and affirms life. (15).

Festivals

One of the ways by which this quest for God and dependence on God finds expression is through traditional (agricultural) festivals. Through festivals, we discover the strong desire by a traditional African society to have the gods participate directly in the material, moral and spiritual life of the community. Apart from the recreational aspect, festivals also afford the people a means of social interaction. In terms of moral, and ethical orientation of the society the festivals constitute the best expression of the African's desire to communicate with his God and ancestors in order to ensure the moral values and the peace and prosperity of the society are maintained.

A good example of a traditional African festival is the Ekpe festival of Ngwa people of South Eastern Igbo land. This particular festival is the culmination of a series of seven other religious festivals ranged along the agricultural cycle. They are **Akpa Unwu,** celebrated after the planting season in April. It is dedicated to the patron deity who protected the people from famine in the absence of yams which had been planted. The next one is **Ira Ugu.** This one marks the harvesting of vegetables especially pumpkins and corn which succour the people while they wait for the new yam. **Iwa ji** festival is the next one. It marks the beginning of the new yam festival in July, when the first fruits of yam harvest are presented to the patron deity of yam **Ifejioku.** The people rejoice greatly at this festival for being alive to reap what they had sown. The rest of the festivals include **Igba Ogbom,** which takes place between August and September. It is followed by **Ifu Aka** which is marked by thanksgiving and prayer ceremonies. **Ize mmuo** comes up in November and finally the Ekpe festivals crowns it all in December.

In sum, it is to be noted that during these festivals of the Ekpe cycle, the society truly celebrates herself, her institutions her solidarity and belief systems. Since the festivals include dances, musical performances, prayer incantations, sacrifices, they are performed as evidence of the desire of the people to associate with the persons of their gods, the spirit of the ancestors and with the life of the community. Through these periodic festivals, the people's desire to have the gods participate directly in the material, moral and spiritual life of the community all the year round are made manifest. In so doing, the spiritual and moral tone of the people are uplifted. So we could say that the celebration of religious festivals by traditional African societies is an index of their spirituality.

Prayers, Sacrifices, Oath-Taking

Apart from traditional religious festivals, the other media through which the spirituality of the traditional African finds expression include, prayers, sacrifices, oath-taking etc.

Prayer

This is not only a veritable expression of a people's religious belief but also on index of their spirituality. Prayer is a universal religious phenomenon which stems from the natural human yearning to give verbal expression to thought and emotion which a person feels towards God. Prayers for Africans have concrete intentions. They do not pray for praying sake. Given their knowledge of God as the great providence, the all powerful, the supplier of all good things, the kind and merciful God, they ask for good health, for healing in times of sickness, for protection from danger, for safety in travelling, for children in marriage, for safe delivery for pregnant women, for long life, and prosperity for many children, for rains during drought, for food during famine, for cessation of epidemics, for victory in war, for security of the village, prosperity of the land and for the preservation of both plant, animal and human life.

Apart from petitions for help and for protection, African prayers also give expressions of joy, thanksgiving, confidence and hope in God. Other forms of prayer are confessions of sin or profession of innocence. A person wrongly accused almost spontenously appeals to God to vindicate him. Prayer, therefore, is a true symbol of African spirituality as it demonstrates the Africa's appreciation, longing, and cultivation of values, which express his desire to respond to divine promptings. Ikenga-Metuh (17) has ably shown through his study of a variety of Igbo prayers that traditional African prayers contain ethical and moral values and provide occasions of re-affirming the ethical and moral principles on which their religion is founded. Such belief includes the idea that God punishes the wicked and blesses the righteous. Because of this belief, African spirituality has a strong ethical orientation. In all, the prayers of traditional Africans who have no strong technological or scientific powers to rely on for the solution of their problems, fall back almost completely on God, the Supreme Being who they believe is capable of solving all their problems either material or moral.

In this connection, it is to be noted that the satisfaction of material needs continue to hold very strong attraction in their prayers. So while Christian spirituality glories in withdrawing into the desert and in mortifying the flesh and in fasting for days, denying themselves material and sensual pleasures, African spirituality seems to be engaged solely in affirming life, enjoying life, promoting life, and like the Calvinists they tend to consider material prosperity as an evidence of God's favour on their labours.

Sacrifice (18)

This is another means by which the traditional African seeks to relate to God. It is a deeper level of prayer involving the offering of gifts to God or gods as a means of expressing the intensity of one's desire to communicate with God or the invisible world. According to Kristenson, the primary religious meaning of sacrifice involves a confession of faith, a participation and co-operation in the divine life. Here, the person or community offering the sacrifice steps out of the world of men into the world of the gods. He achieves this through the mediation of the offering.

Types of Sacrifice

Ikenga-Metuh, in his study of sacrifice among the Igbos identifies **Igo Mmuo** as consecretory sacrifice and **Ilo mmuo** as expiatory sacrifices. These sacrifices are of positive effect since they offer a prayerful act of participation in divine life. They make the profane sacred. There are also sacrifices of negative effect such as **Ichu Aja** - the exorcist sacrifice, and **Ikpu Alu**, purificatory sacrifice. These have as their primary purpose, not a quest for communion with God, but an attempt to cleanse the pollution arising from a violation of sacred prohibition which threatens the moral order of the community as a whole.

In offering sacrifices therefore, a ritual act is performed to show that something (offering) has been removed from human use and given over to God. By that ritual act, the person or community offering the sacrifice passes from the human to the divine realm to achieve communion with God, the source and fulness of life. In effect, the offering of sacrifices denote deeper expressions of prayer and indeed constitute a forceful index of spirituality among traditional Africans as they offer opportunities for votaries to dedicate, consecrate, cleanse and celebrate their relationship with their God.

Oath Taking (19)

One final expression of spirituality, i.e. a form of existential attitude by which a traditional African habitually acts or reacts to false accusation or seeks to establish the veracity, of his claim or accept responsibility for a particular high office of trust is by oath taking.

An oath according to Oxford English Dictionary is a solemn and formal appeal to God or to a deity in witness of the truth of a statement or the binding character of a promise. So an oath is an invocation of (God) or a deity to witness to the truth of a statement or to a promise. For example, if a person is suspected of theft or murder or of sexual misconduct etc., he or she could clear himself or herself by taking a solemn oath.

An oath involves (God) or a deity to bear testimony on the truth of what is being said, be it a promise to be honoured, or a statement which is claimed to be authentic. In either case God, a deity or the ancestors is invoked as a witness. Any of them is expcted to visit with vengence the party or person who violates a promise, a claim or an agreement in which a god's name is invoked.

God (or the appropriate divinity) is invoked because of the peoples belief in His truthfulness, righteousness, impartiality, sound judgement and power to reward the innocent and punish the liar, the unjust and the wicked.

In other words, God or the gods are regarded as the executors of the terms of the oath. They justify the Innocent and punish the liar.

Objects of oath taking include symbols that are respected and feared in a society such as: the shrine of earth goddess "Ala" or f the thunder god - "Amadioha" (among the Igbo of Nigeria), objects with magical power such as guns, matchets, womens' cooking utensils in the home (like pestles and mortar) tombstones, a sacred staff authority and justice, i.e. "Ofo", or corpses.

The strongest oath is that in which the sacred objects or medium on which an oath is taken, is licked with the tongue or the water in which the object is emersed is meant to be drunk.

In Ghana, a person taking an oath eats or drinks something which has some connections with a deity who is invoked to punish him if he forswears himself.

Oaths arise in situation of uncertainty, strong suspicions and fear. A father before he dies may require a son to swear an oath, to keep his instructions. Friends could swear not to cause each other any harm or not to break an agreement over a piece of property or not to seduce each other's wife. Oaths are also administered when sorting out criminals, especially when unknown thieves break into a house all suspectected persons are caught and compelled under oath to swear to their innocence. Oath taking therefore, is a factor in social relationship. It is a manifestation of belief in the power of a divinity to utilize any object to effect justice. In this context, it is an index of traditional African spirituality since it demonstrates how the traditional African without a well developed legal system sought the aid of God, or of the deities and ancestors to vindicate the innocent and to directly punish the guilty.

Summarily, an evidence of the conscience-factor in man i.e. the instinct to pass judgement upon oneself in accordance with moral law of the land, the regards, respect and fear of the power of a deity, the belief in the ability of the "spirits" to inflict harm or nullify human actions and the utter dependence of the human on the divine are all brought out in a dramatic episode of Oath Taking, albeit, in a subtle way.

Conclusion

This paper has considered traditional African spirituality to mean that the African believes the key to his existence lies in his relationship with the 'numinous'. This relationship finds expression in various habitual acts of devotion by which the African existentially (and occasionally mystically), relates to the Supreme Being and the deities. These acts involve inter alia: agricultural festivals, prayers, sacrifices, and oath-taking. By them, one could easily, understand and identify how the African sought for divine assistance, and how he expressed his dependence, his belief, his worship and obedience to the Supreme Being and the deitis.

In this way we approach African spirituality not in terms of looking for a corpus of doctrines to analyse but by identifying and describing modes of expression and of relationship between man and the invisible world. The traditional -African, it is observed, conveys his spirituality through a conception of himself and his relationship to the invisible, and how in process he sets in motion his most genuine values and the consciousness of his lack of power. In this way his spirituality, among other things, gives coherence and meaning to his social and religious experience and makes explicit the relationship between the Supreme Being and man by showing that the sacred is a dimension of the whole of life. Spirituality, therefore involves interaction and participation between the divine and the human. It provides an expression for the search and the experience for a deeper meaning to life and existence. As Zahan would say "the essence of African spirituality lies in the feeling he has of being ... an integral part of the world in whose cyclical life he sees himself deeply and necessarily engaged". (20)

In sum, African spirituality, in the way it has been presented in this paper, could be seen as an explanatory device which could be of help in understanding the habit and behaviour of the African. It could be used as a guide to determine who he is and what he can do and what he can avoid. In all, his spirituality could be seen as the spring of his "action system" as manifested in his overt and covert behaviour.

Footnotes

1   Aylward Shorter, **African Christian Spirituality,** (London: Geoffrey Chapman 1978) p. 3-8.
2   Kofi Appiah-Kubi "Indigenous African Christian Churches: Signs of authenticity" in **Bulletin of African Theology,** (Vol. 1 No. 2 Juillet-Decembre, 1979) pp. 241-249.

3   James Cahalan, "Spirituality"; The Search for the Transcendent" in **LUCERNA**, Vol. 1 No. 1 (Enugu: Bigard Memorial Seminary July-December 1978) pp. 43-55.

4   David A. Brown, **A Guide to Religions,** (London: SPCK 1975) pp. 123-153.

5   Michael C. Reilly: **Spirituality for Mission,** (New York: Orbis Books, 1978) pp. 22-45.

6   Louis Bouyer, **A History of Christian Spirituality,** (London: Burns & Sales, 1963-9). I am making reference to Bouyers work (as reviewed by Robert M. Yale - under the title "Christian Spirituality" in **Evangelical Review of Theology,** Vol. 2 No. 1 April 1978) pp. 103-112), in order to draw attention to a major work on Christian Spirituality. Here Spirituality for example, has nothing to do with justification by works. It seeks to bring the whole of one's life in the world into progressive conformity with the will of God through desert and monastic asceticism.

This were the hall marks of spirituality during the Middle Ages. On the contrary, the African affirms and celebrates life in terms of what he can enjoy and achieve through the help of the Gods.

7   E. Elochukwu Uzukwu, "Igbo World and Ultimate Reality and meaning" in **LUCERNA,** Vol. c. No. 1. June 1983, pp. 9-24, cf. Emefie Ikenga-Metuh **God & Man in African Religion,** (London: Geoffrey Chapman, 1981). This Book is extremely useful in any study of God-man relation in African context.

8   Emefie Ikenga-Metuh, **God and Man in African Religion,** p. 16.

9   John S. Mbiti, **Concepts of God in Africa,** (London SPCK 1971) pp. 171-177.
    John S. Mbiti, **African Religions and Philosophy,** (London: Heinemann 1965) pp. 95-99.

10 Dominique Zahan, **The Religion, Spirituality And Thought of Traditional Africa,** trans Kate Ezra and Lawrence M. Martin. (Chicago: The Univ. of Chicago Press 1970) p. 5. Mbiti has also made similar remarks in his books cited above.

11 Emefie Ikenga-Metuh, **God and Man in African Religion,** p. 103.

12 E.P. Modum, "God as Guests: Music and Festivals in Africa Traditional Societies" in **Readings in African Humanities,** edited by O.U. Kalu (Enugu: Fourth Dimension 1978) pp. 45-54.

13 O.U. Kalu, Ibid., p. 37-43.

14 J.S. Mbiti, **Introduction to African Religion,** (London: Heine-
    mann, 1975) pp. 164-167). E.G. Parrinder, **African
    Mythology,** (London: Paul Hamlyn 1967).
15 Mbiti, Ibid., p. 19.
16 J.N. Amankulor, "Epke Festivals as Religious Ritual and Dance
    Drama" in **Ikenga** (July, 1972) pp. 35-47. This work is
    cited by E.P. Modum in "God as Guests".
17 Emefie Ikenga-Metuh, **African Religions in Western Conceptual
    Schemes: Studies in Igbo Religion** (Ibadan: Claverium
    Press, 1985) pp. 127-199.
    cf. J.S. Mbiti, **The Prayers of African Religion,** (New York:
    Orbis Books 1975).
18 Ibid. E.I. Metuh, p. 59-70, cf. Francis A. Arinze, **Sacrifice
    in Igbo Religion,** (Ibadan: Univ. Press 1970).
19 R.C. Mortimer "Oaths" in **Dictionary of Christian Ethics,**
    edited by J. Macquarrie (Philadelphia: The Westminster
    Press 1967) p. 234. See also Kofi A. Opoku,, **West Afri-
    can Traditional Religion,** (Accra: FEP 1978) pp. 152-158.
    J.S. Mbiti, **African Religions and Philosophy,** pp. 210-212.
20 Dominique Zahan, p. 4.

ETHICS OF AFRICAN TRADITIONAL RELIGION

by

E.M. Uka

What is Ethics?

Ethics is the science which enquires into the meaning and purpose of life and conduct. It represents a systematic attempt to consider the purposeful actions of mankind, to determine their rightness or wrongness, their tendency to good or evil. (1)

"Wehen a man asks "What ought I to do about it?" he is raising an ethical problem which assumes that there is a right and a wrong mode of action. In this regard, conduct is defined as conscious or purposeful action or action that is directed to an end. Ethics therefore could be described as the science of moral duty, designed to determine ideal human character and the ideal human action. Ethics relates to the inner motivation as well as to outward manner of life. (2)

Ethics therefore in a traditional African society seeks to determine the sources of purposeful action, its rightness or wrongness, their tendency to good or evil. So in this paper we shall consider, not only the sources but also the basis for ethics in African traditional society. Since African Traditional religion permeates every aspect of the life of an African, and whereas any religon worthy of consideration has ethical content and implication, therefore we shall consider African traditional religion as the source of the African mode of conduct while the customs, rules, traditions and taboos constitute the basis or the regulators of moral action in African traditional societies.

Basic Ethical Principles in Traditional Societies

According to John Lewis (3) if a society is to survive, there must be some regulations with regard to conduct among its members. These codes of conduct reflect the following fundamental principles:

(1) No human society can exist without some regulations in sexual affairs. This control is supplied by the kinship regulations and certain rules regarding marital fidelity which are supported by penal sanctions. Invariably, specific rules and customs are established to secure the stability of the marriage relationship and to provide adequate care for infants.

(2) Every society must in some ways place a curb on violence.

(3) In every society theft is prohibited and, the sanctity of contracts and bargains enforced.

(4) Respect for human life is upheld. So the saving of life and the caring for the sick reflects the idea and underlines a very wide range of attitudes and norms of human behaviour in every society.

These principles underscore the need for proper relationships among members of any given society. This fact seems to be basic with human societies and distinguishes them sharply and radically from animal groups. That is, human societies are normative societies; they are moral societies, they observe moral norms. That is, the welfare and solidarity of a people can not be separated from the moral actions of the individuals. So actions which contribute to the welfare of the community are said to be good while those that do not enhance the welfare of the community are said to be bad. Mbiti expresses it succintly thus:

> What strenghtens the life of the community is held to be good and right. What weakens the life of the community is held to be evil and wrong. (4)

This fact needs to be driven home from the point of view of the Hobbesian thesis which argues that civilization, progress and development derive from a society which enforces morality. (5) But enforced morality is not genuine morality. It is law. There is a fundamental difference between law and morality. Law comes from external authority, while morality is internal, coming from our rational and social nature and does not depend on external authoritative enforcement for its observance. That is, morality conforms men to virtuous principles of conduct.

Kant (6) however talks about his categorical imperatives - that is the moral law which binds all men unconditionally and whose observance is a precondition for progress, peace or development in any society.

There was no progress, no development, no industry in Hobbes' **State of Nature** because there was no morality. The

181

moral law was not observed, so there was according to Hobbes "a state of war of all against all". That is, every man was against his fellowman and that resulted in making human life solitary, poor, nasty, brutish and short.

Morality i.e. the acquisition of respect for the rules and institutions of society, therefore is indispensable to social solidarity, to peace and progress especially in a traditional society with no police force and no prison yards to confine persons with deviant behaviour. Consequently, moral laxity, egoism, individualism, lack of sense of duty, disregard for the institutions of society were frowned at and strictly discouraged in traditional societies.

Morality in Traditional African Society - The Nigerian Example

The view that morality and religion in a traditional society cannot be separated is strongly affirmed by Opoku when he said:

> Generally morality originates from religious considerations and is so pervasive in African culture that the two cannot be separated from each other. Thus we find that what constitutes the moral code of any particular African society - the laws, taboos, customs and set forms of behaviour - all derive their compelling power from religion. This morality flows out of religion and through this the conduct of individuals is regulated and any break of the moral code is regarded as evil and punishable ... And this system has one desirable ideal - social harmony and pears for the good of any man and society!!! (7)

The implication of the above assertion is that morality in African traditional society was not introduced by christianity, nor was it invented by society, to preserve itself as some scholars would argue. For example Durkheim (8) is of the view that society invented morality when it was faced with the problems of peace and of living together. In order to meet these ends, it evolved a system of self preservation which people call morality. According to Durkheim what religious people call "the voice of God(s) is nothing but the voice of the people." It is the will of the community codified for the well being of the society. It is furhter

182

argued that what people call conscience is just the notions which the society has planted in man by providing a body of approved behaviours. And because of the hope of reward or punishment, these notions called conscience are intensified in man.

Contrary to this Durkheim's view of morality, the traditional African views morality as given to them by God from the beginning. He also believes that the ancestors and the spirits keep watch over the people to make sure that they observe the moral laws and are punished when they break them. According to Mbiti (9) most African peoples acknowledge God as the final guardian of law and order and of moral and ethical codes. Therefore, the breaking of such order either by the individual or by a group is ultimately an offence against God. Idowu (10) also persuasively argues that for the Yorubas of Nigeria, their moral values derive from the nature of God Himself whom they consider to be the "pure and Perfect King". In order to aid man in ethical living, **Olodumare** puts in him **Ifa-aya,** the oracle of the heart or the oracle which is in the heart. It is this oracle of the heart that guides man and determines his ethical life. Ikenga Metuh (11) writing on the Igbo of Nigeria says that the Igbos believe that God is the author and upholder of the moral order. According to their sacred stories, their myths of creation, God is recognised as creator of the whole world. He is all good. He requires moral goodness. This according to Metuh is a fundamental dogma in African ethical belief. Just as the Yorubas believe in **Ifa aya,** its oracle of the heart which determines their ethical life, so the Igbos believe in a small voice from the heart which directs them to good deeds and warns them of evil. Hence the Igbo word for conscience i **Obi** i.e. heart. A good conscience is **Obi oma** or **Obi ocha** and bad conscience is **Obi ojo** a bad heart. So the normal state of a man's conscience affects his character.

In sum, God as creator of the world is believed to be the ultimate source of moral law and the final guardian of the moral order. In principle, He cannot commit evil against His creation. He is not the source of evil in the world. When people suffer from misfortune or calamity, they interpret it as the result of their misdoing.

Hence every form of pain, misfortune, sorrow, or suffering and sickness, every death whether of an infant or an adult every failure of the crop on the farms, of hunting in the woods or of fishing in the water: every bad omen or dream, these and all manifestations of evil that man experiences are blamed on somebody in the corporate society. Though rational explanations may be found yet mystical explanations are also given. (12)

God as the upholder of the moral order, punishes those who violate His will and rewards those who do His will. The violation of divine will includes: theft, murder, adultery, incest, robbery, rape, cruelty, coveteousness, violence, greed, selfishness, breaking of promises, disrespect for parents and elders, patricide, falsehood, hypocrisy, wickedness, cheating, treachery, dishonesty, destroying yam tendrils on other people's farm, alteration of land boundaries, setting fire on another person's house or crop, disclosing secrets or sacred information, and violation of taboos and violation of menstrual prohibitions etc. These acts which disrupt human relationships and endanger societal peace and harmony are considered as offences against God. (13) They are punished in various ways and at times the entire community are punished by the tutelary spirits who act as God's agents in this regard. The punishments for individual culprits include affliction with terrible and sometimes incurable diseases, deaths, bad luck in activities such as hunting, fishing, travelling, courtship, business transactions, childlessness, bad dreams, suicide, snake bite and deformities. For serious violations such as murder or incest or patricide punishment could come to the entire community in the form of famine, drought, flood, earth quake, thunder and lightning, epidemic, locust, invasion or enemy attack. (14)

God, using His agents, not only punishes evil, but also rewards virtuous and good life in both private and public affairs. Reasonable and social virtues approved of God include moral values such as love, honesty, truthfulness, justice, obedience, loyalty, compassion, chastity before marriage and faithfulness during marriage, friendliness, helpfulness, self control, courage, bravery, respectfulness, hospitality, humility, patience, wisdom, sincerity, kindness, forgiveness, and the like. (15) All these virtues are regarded as manifstations of a good character which according to the Yorubas are implanted by God in man as **Iwa**. (16)

Enforcement of Morals: Metaphysical Means

The African believes not only in the Supreme God as the author and upholder of morality but also in the ancestors, divinities, or spirits as the messengers of God through which He enforces His will among men and in the world that He created. As Opoku puts it:

184

God is generally held to be the source of morality and it is the responsibility of the gods acting on His behalf to see that the laws are upheld, and to punish those who infringe them. Besides these however, the gods have their own individual taboos which their devotees are expected to uphold. (17)

Awolalu and Dopamu have also given credence to the role of the divinities as the agents of God in maintaining the moral order in society. They said:

... in maintaining the society, God has brought the divinities into being. They act both as His ministers in the theocratic government of the world and as intermediaries between Him and man. Through these functionaries, God gives society cohesion and persistence. (18)

So we find that among the Igbos, for example, the need to promote the moral order and health of the society and to punish offenders who cause disorder and chaos are enforced by the minor divinities such as: **Agwu, Amadioha, Ekwensu, Ala, Ndichie** (19) etc. These divinities are employed by the Supreme God both as agents of His will power and authority to act as guardians of social morality, and as instruments of punishment against those who threaten moral order and social stability.

For example, **Agwu** (20) the patron deity of medicine men, grants the power of healing to those threatened by illness. **Agwu** knows the herbs and all the antidotes against illness and "bad medicine". **Agwu** chooses the votary on whom to invest the power of healing. In so doing, he ensures that medicine men do not exploit the sick through high charges. If they do, **Agwu** withdraws his healing power from such medicine men. In this way the deity ensures that good health is not only the preserve of the rich but also the privilege of ordinary members of the society. The fact that **Agwu** can withdraw his healing power from a medicine man or can punish him, acts as a check on the abuse of professional ethics by the medicine men.

Amadioha (21) - the god of thunder, represents the righteous anger of God over the violation of certain traditional norms. When crimes appear to escape the notice of other guardians of morality, the supreme God (Chukwu) may warn from heaven through His thunder. When lightning kills, it is often believed to be the result of **Chukwu's** retributive justice. Alteration of land boundaries, wrongful seizure of other persons property, maltreatment of a widow or an orphan, burial of dangerous objects to hurt an innocent person are the likely offences that cause the god of thunder to strike. When it strikes, it could either provide the right boundary lines or unearth and destroy hidden dangerous objects. **Amadioha** specialises in punishing moral offenders.

Ekwensu (22) is translated in missionary catechism as the Devil. G.T. Basden describes **Ekwensu** as the ruler of all agents of wickedness. Elizabeth Isichei refers to it as the spirit of violence, patron god of warriors. Since all divinities are the agents of the Supreme God, so is **Ekwensu** God's agent for inflicting punishment on offenders.

Ala: (23) The earth goddess

Ala is the most important divinety in Igbo social and moral life. She is the guardian of morality, the source of fertility in women, in vegetation and agricultural products. She ensures health and wellbeing to the community by preventing the incidence of plagues, famine, droughts and barrenness among women. The moral code sanctioned by **Ala** is spoken of as **Nso-Ala** i.e. abominations against the earth deity.

Among the moral prohibitions regarded as **Nso-Ala** (abominations) are serious, personal and moral crimes such as incest among close relatives, murder, suicide by hanging, fighting with a masquerade, stealing yams from the farm or barns, wilful abortion, pregnancy within a year of husband's death. Abnormal and unnatural behaviour by human beings are also considered as **Nso-ala.** These include giving birth to more than one child at a time, conception before a girl's first menstruation, death resulting from leprosy or small pox, a child which cuts the upper teeth first. Abominations also include abnormal and unnatural acts of animals: e.g. fowl that lays one egg, a tettered goat brings its young one unattended, a dog that brings forth only one welp.

Apart from these abominations (**Nso-Ala**) there are minor prohibitions and pollutions of the earth deity. These include **sex prohibitions** such as having sexual relation with certain categories of one's kin; adultery with non-relative, having sex in the bush even with one's wife or on the ground; having sex with a menstruating woman, adultery with a woman in her husband's house. There are also death prohibitions: e.g. to bury a woman with an unborn child in her womb, to mourn those who die of infectious diseases especially small pox, leprosy or elephantiasis of

186

the scrotum, violent death by accident, a woman going outside the compound during the mourning period after her husband's death or to visit the shrine of **Ala** before the completion of the funeral rites of her husband.

Breaches of any of the abominations, whether minor or major pollute the community and strain the relationship between the earth goddess and the people. They evoke social horror and terror which pose a great threat to the cosmic and social order. The argument is that by the breach, the culprit antagonises the Earth goddess "on whose ground he stands, whose products he eats and in whose bosom he will be buried". He alienates the ancestors who then withdraw their protection and expose him as an easy prey to evil spirits. If he dies, he dies in a state of defilement, and cannot be honoured as an ancestor.

Ancestors (24)

The earth goddess is believed to work in close conjunction with the ancestors to produce the moral code by which the community lives and regulates its affairs. In this regard, they are believed to act as agents of the Supreme God from who they derive their power and authority.

The ancestors act as the guardians of traditional ethics. Since they had lived examplary lives on earth, they are concerned with the preservation of these moral virtues whose foundation they laid when they were still alive. For example, the existing norms, ethos, customs and traditions constitute the sayings and deeds of "Our Fathers" the ancestors. A deviation from what they said and what they did constitute a violation of what "Our Fathers" preserved for our contemporary wellbeing. The founding fathers of a village or a clan for example are said to give them their laws sanctions and taboos. So Awolalu says:

> While here on earth, the ancestors were the custodians and guardians of morality in the society. They set the norms of conduct which the society must follow as given to them by their own ancestros ... (25)

Shrine: The Abode of the Gods, Priests, Medicine Men; Custodians of Sacred Places (26)

Another powerful agency for enforcing societal norms and values are the shrines with their priests or medicine men. In a traditional African society, the shrine served both as the visible tribunal for justice and public order and as the focus of the people's belief system where norms are enforced. For instance, in charges of incest or witchcraft or theft or murder, the suspect is meant to clear himself at the shrine by swearing to his innocence. The fact that the shrines represent the abode of the gods and whereas the gods are believed to be concerned with issues of justice, morality and public order, therefore anyone swearing falsely exposes himself to the wrath of the gods. In like manner, the shrines and their attendant priest provide the people not only with avenues for clearing themselves from false charges but also with avenues for offering purification, and pollution rites when found guilty of wrong doing. In this way the shrines enforce the norms and values of the society and provides avenues for offenders to atone for their errors.

Enforcement of morals through social Institutions

According to John Beattie,

> To maintain an orderly system of social relations people have to be subjected to some degree of compulsion. They cannot all the time do exactly as they like. For often self interest may incite behaviour incompatible with the common good and so it is that every society some rules some kind of constraint on people's behaviour are acknowledged and on the whole adhered to. (27)

This view in effect summarises the need to enforce morality in traditional societies. We shall therefore consider some of the social institutions through which conformity to societal norms and values are ensured.

The Family (28)

This primary unit of society is an agency in socializa-tion process. It provides the medium for the internalization of a given culture. Through this process the parents of a child (who represent the legislative, executive and judiciary arms of a society all roled into one) inculcate in a child, the norms and values of the larger society. This is done through teaching the child the good habits of honesty, hardwork, punctuality, cleanliness, respect for elders and reverence for the gods. The child also learns by induction from the parents the virtues of living at peace with neighbours and in harmony with members of the extended family. Through a process of reward for good conduct and punishment for bad conduct, societal norms are enforced through the parents.

Age Grade and Secret Societies (29)

Functionally, these are powerful agents of socialization in traditional African societies. As groups, these bodies uphold and transmit vital societal and group norms and values. They evolve a number of ways designed to prevent or restrict members from spurning acceptable societal or group values with impurity. For example joking relationship among the groups could serve as an oblique manner of expressing disapproval to non-acceptable behaviour and as a constraint. Gossips among the groups also operate as a deterrent factor on the behaviour of members. People avoid being the object of gossip. Satire and ridicule are even more overt than gossips and tend towards the punitive. The dread of being used in satirical songs and dances serve to restrain members from bad conduct.

Informal methods of Moral Education (30)

Morality is also enforced by informed methods of moral education such as stories told in myths, fables, folktales and by riddles, proverbs and songs. These are various kinds of ways in which virtues are explained, extolled and discussed while vices are exposed, explained and condemned.

For example in folktales or fables (i.e. short stories in which familiar animals are actors but their speeches, attitudes, tastes and judgments are those of human beings) relevant lessons on human experiences are taught. Vices like disobedience, pride, arrogance, boastfulness and insincerity are shown to place those engaged in them at a disadvantage; while virtues such as sincerity, loyalty, obedience, honesty, humility, perseverance, respect for elders and parents, kindness and faithfulness are said to bring honour and prosperity to those who practise them.

Most of the folktales and fables are put in songs in which virtuous persons are honoured with praises and commendations and with rights and privileges, while persons of mean character are condemned without reservations. These methods of communicating moral values equally assist in enforcing them in traditional African societies.

Conclusion

It is obvious from the preceding discourse that ethics in an African traditional society is communal ethic not an individualistic ethic. It is an ethic concerned with the welfare and moral tone of the community. It is as a result of this that the Yoruba have a saying that:

> If a member of one's household is eating poisonous insects and we fail to warn him, (to desist) the effect of his action will rob neighbours of their sleep. (31)

So arising from the communal nature of the ethics is the fact that whatever strengthens the life, the prosperity, the solidarity, the success of the community is held to be good and right while the things that weaken or threaten the welfare, the peace and solidarity of the community is said to be evil and wrong. The things we have noted to be morally wrong and evil include robbery, murder, incest, stealing, being cruel, etc.

To safeguard the welfare and solidarity of the community there are taboos or prohibitions which indicate the things that are forbidden, offensive and dangerous to the norms and values of the society. There are also codes of ethics, morals, customs, laws and traditions which constitute the main pillars for the welfare of society. Some of the actions that are held to be

190

morally right and good include among other things practising
justice in public life, keeping the traditions and customs of the
society. The good and bad codes of conduct are not written. They
are embedded in the society's customs, traditions, rituals, beliefs
and practices. People assimilate them, become socialised in them
as they grow and become participant members of their community
and society. (32)

The people believe that God is the author of their
morality and its ultimate guardian. The spirit and divinities are
His agents for blessing the good and for punishing the evil. In
cases of national calamities, the people interpret evil phenomena
as signs of God's punishment on them for their violation of some
moral principles or the product of their falling moral standards.

Essentially, therefore the ethical or moral observances
or regulations we have looked at are directed towards relationship between man and his fellow man in society and between man
and the ancestors, the divinities or spirits. So what we find as
the content of traditional African ethics are social regulations
which govern conduct in society.

Any breach of the right conduct amounts to a moral
evil. Therefore what lies behind the idea of what is morally
"good" or "bad" is ultimately in the nature of the relationship
between individuals in a particular community. So there is no
"secret sin" as Mbiti would say. Something or someone is "good"
or "bad" depending on his actions. If one's actions conform to
the norms and mores of the community, he is a good person, if
they don't he is a bad person. In effect it is an ethics of shame
not of guilt. That is, if relationships are not hurt or damaged
and if there is no discovery of a breach of custom or regulation
then an act is not "evil" or "wicked" or "bad" since no shame
is involved. (33)

In view of this Mbiti argues convincingly that the essence of African morality is more "societary" than spiritual, it
is a morality of conduct rather than a morality of being. (34)

Apart from being a morality of conduct, African (Igbo
of Nigeria) traditional ethics is teleological in the sense that the
community believes that social actions and relationships are guided
by moral considerations. (35) So taboos are observed because to
contravene them would upset the moral and harmonious relationships between man and the cosmos. African (Igbo) traditional
morality lays emphasis on what works, what gives happiness and
enhances the survival of the individual or the community. In this
sense it could be described as utilitarian. (36) Also traditional
African morality is communitarian. That is, an evil act by member

of the community tarnishes not only the personality of that member but also that of his father, mother, brothers, sisters, uncles, cousins, aunts and even that of the entire community. Finally African Traditional Morality could be described as legalistic (not in the western legal sense but in the sense of a communal opinion poll). It punishes wrong doers with physical ordeals or with financial and material fines. Often, public opinions in the form of shame, ridicule disapproval or isolation and the withdrawal of communal supports are aimed at discouraging wrong doing while praises, commendations, rights and privileges are accorded to the just, the innocent and the law-abiding.

African traditional morality therefore, could be described as prescriptive, societary, teleological, communitarian and 'legalistic'. Indeed it is a morality of conduct rather than a morality of being. It defines what a person does rather than what he is.

Footnotes

1 Gilbert Kirby, **Understanding Christian Ethics.** (London: St. Paul's Press 1973) p. 1.
2 Ibid. pp. 1-2.
3 John Lewis, **Anthropology Made Simple,** (London: W.H. Allen 1969) pp. 147-148.
4 J.S. Mbiti, **Introduction to African Religion,** (London: Heinemann, 1975) p. 177.
5 Thomas Hobbes, **LEVIATHAN,** ed. with introduction by M. Oakeshott (Oxford: 1946) p. 32.
6 I. Kant, **Groundwork of the Metaphysics of Morals,** Trans for H.J. Parton and Published under the title **The Moral Law** (by Hutchison University Library, 1969) p. 67.
7 Kofi, A. Opoku, **West African Traditional Religion,** (Accra: FEP. 1978) pp. 152-153.
8 Emil Durkheim, **The Elementary Forms of the Religious Life** (N.Y.: The Free Press 1965) pp. 37-45.
9 J.S. Mbiti, **African Religions and Philosophy,** (London: Heinemann, 1965) pp. 207-208.
10 E.B. Idowu, **Olodumare: God In Yoruba Belief,** (London: Longman 1962) p. 154.
11 E. Ikenga-Metuh, **God and Man in African Religion,** (London: Geoffrey Chapman 1981) pp. 12-15.

12   J.S. Mbiti, **African Religions and Philosophy,** p. 209.
13   Akpenpuun Drugba, **The Relevance of Christian Ethics in the Search for Political Values in Nigeria.** Unpublished Ph.D. Thesis - UNN, 1984, p. 120.
14   Mbiti, **Introduction to African Religion,** p. 181; A.B. Jacobbs **A Textbook on West African Traditional Religion,** (Ibadan: Aromolaran Pub. Co. 1977) pp. 245-247.
15   Mbiti, **African Religions and Philosophy,** p. 212.
16   Idowu, **Olodumare,** pp. 144-168.
17   K.A. Opoku, p. 156.
18   J.O. Awolalu, and P.A. Dopamu, **West African Traditional Religion,** (Ibadan Onibonoje Press, 1972) p. 156.
19   E. Ikenga Metuh, **African Religions In Western Conceptual Schemes: The Problems of Interpretation,** (Ibadan: Claverianum Press, 1985) pp. 40-45.
     See also Victor C. Uchendu, **The Igbo of Southeast Nigeria,** (New York; 1965) p. 97.
     C.K. Meek, **Law and Authority in a Nigerian Tribe,** London 1937, pp. 21-24; Elechi Amadi, **Ethics in Nigerian Culture,** (Ibadan: Heinemann 1982) pp. 15-29.
20   E.M. Uka, **Moratorium: Ideology or Utopia - A Sociological Interpretation of an African Response to Christian Missions,** (Madison - Drew Univ. 1980) p. 70. Unpublished Ph.D. Dissertation.
     Agwu a tutelary divinity, is not only seen as a patron deity of medicine-men but also as a capricious deity who can bring calamity as well as prosperity. It is difficult to placate and can possess someone and cause him to become his devotee.
21   E. Ikenga Metuh, **African Religions in Western Conceptual Schemes,** pp. 41-42. See also E.I. Metuh, **God and man in African Religion,** (London: Chapman 1981) pp. 64-68.
22   Ibid.
23   Ibid. pp. 78-79.
24   Ibid. pp. 82-86; cf. Edmund Ilogu. "The Problem of Christian Ethics Among The Igbo of Nigeria". **Ikenga** vol. 3 No. 1-2. 1975, pp. 40-41.
25   Awolalu et al., **West African Traditional Religion,** p. 213. See E.G. Parrinder, **West African Psychology,** (London: Lutherworth Press, London 1951) p. 223.
26   J.S. Mbiti, **African Religions and Philosophy,** p. 166-181; J.S. Mbiti, **Introduction to African Religion,** pp. 141-145.
27   John Beattie, **Other Cultures: Aims, Methods and Achievements in Social Anthropology,** (New York: Free Press 1964) p. 139

28 J.S. Mbiti, **Introduction to African Religion,** (Ibadan: Heine-
    mann 1975) p. 175-177.
    Jack Nobbs etal., **Sociology,** (London: Macmillan 1975) pp.
    5I-55.
29 O.U. Kalu, "Religion and Social Control in Cross-River Igbo
    land". Unpublished Seminar Paper at University of
    Nigeria, Nsukka 1987. Here Professor Kalu notes that
    there are broadly two types of secret societies - the
    anti-social and the social. It is the secret societies
    with social ends that this paper refers to. They func-
    tion more or less like Age-grade groups. They empha-
    sise the acquisition of skills in hunting, fishing, farm-
    ing, bravery in war and the like. Elechi Amadi, **Ethics
    in Nigerian Culture,** (Ibadan: Heinemann, 1982) pp. 52-53.
30 Akpenpun Dzurgba, **The Relevance of Christian Ethics ...,**
    pp. 136-139. See also E.I. Metuh, **God and Man in Afri-
    can Religion,** pp. 107-109.
31 J.O. Awolalu, "The African Traditional View of man," **ORITA,**
    vol. 1, 1972, p. 112.
32 J.S. Mbiti, **Introduction to African Religion,** pp. 180-181.
    cf. Elechi Amadi, **Ethics in Nigerian Culture,** (Ibadan:
    Heinemann Ed. Books, 1982) p. 15-20.
33 J.S. Mbiti, **African Religions and Philosophy,** p. 213.
34 Ibid. p. 214.
35 Edmund Ilogu, **Igbo Life and Thought,** (Onitsha: The varsity
    Limited Press, 1985) pp. 28-30.
36 Ibid; see also Metuh, **God and Man ...,** pp. 108-109. Metuh's
    qualifications for the element of utilitarianism in Afri-
    can (Igbo) morality should be taken seriously.

THE SALVIFIC VALUE OF AFRICAN RELIGIONS

by

Patrick Kalilombe

Are the African traditional religions authentic channels of God's saving activity? Christian thinkers have traditionally supported their answers primarily from the witness of scripture, notes this Roman Catholic bishop and biblical scholar from Malawi. But he also observes that usually these scholars were non-Africans. However "sympathetic and broadminded" they might be, they still look at the problem "from the point of view of an outsider who is not really personally involved in the religions at stake," and are conditioned by factors of which an African "can normally hope to be free." Bishop Kalilombe notices how foreign missionaries were most struck by those biblical texts that "have overtones of opposition against the 'gentiles' as enemies of God's people and practitioners of idolatry and abominations," and normally ignored those which displayed God's positive solicitous acts toward those who were not "special choices (that of Israel and that of the Church)." The African writer then offers "a contextualized Bible reading for Africa": what could happen if African traditional religions were to be assessed by Africans themselves. He concludes that "it is not fair to give a final judgment in such important matters only from a partial standpoint, be it Jewish or Christian, primitive or civilized, black or white." This is an extract from the paper delivered to the first Congress of African Biblists, held at Kinshasha, December 1978. It first appeared in the June 1979 African Ecclesial Review (AFER), published by the AMECEA Pastoral Institute, P.O. Box 908, Eldoret, Kenya.

Are the African traditional religions salvific? Or to be more precise, were these traditional religious systems and practices effective means whereby in the past, before the coming of Christianity, their adherents in Africa were able to "seek the deity and, by feeling their way toward him, succeed in finding him (who) is not far from any of us, since it is in him that we live, and move, and exist" (Acts 17:27-28)? And for those who even today live sincerely by them, are these religions still authentic channels of God's saving activity, so that we could unequivocally assert that the practitioners of these traditional religions are saved through them, and not in spite of them?

Individual Salvation and Salvific Value of Religions: Distinct Questions

We need to distinguish two questions: one is the possibility of salvation for any individual who is not a member of Christ's visible Church. The second concerns the providential role of other religions as historical, socially structured and outward expressions of human communities in their search for God.

As far as the first question is concerned, quite early in Church history the attempted answer took the form of the famous axiom: **Extra Ecclesiam nulla salus.** Such formulation, however, could never be taken in the absolute form that its wording suggests. As better, more comprehensive knowledge of human history and geography became available, it was necessary to start introducing more and more subtle distinctions, all amounting to the admssion that, after all, salvation was possible outside the visible institutional Christian Church. (1) We can consider the question finally settled at least in its basic elements now that Vatican II has said in so many words that, "those also can attain to everlasting salvation who through no fault of their own do not know the gospel of Christ or His Church, yet sincerely seek God and, moved by grace, strive by their deeds to do His will as it is known to them through the dictates of conscience." (2)

But the problem of religions as such is a more difficult one because it is not possible to bypass here far-reaching implications that touch the very center of the Church's self-understanding and the meaning and goal of its missionary outreach. What becomes of Christianity's uniqueness as God's final salvific self-revelation if it is conceded that other religions are also divinely ordained normal channels of God's salvific activity? Where is the urgency of the "Great Commission" (Matthew 28:19-20) if non-Christian communities can just as well find salvation in their own traditional religious systems? The Church has had to come to grips with these questions, for they are basic in determining what its own identity is in God's unfolding plan of salvation. They become all the more poignant as the historical Church becomes aware of the existence and dynamism of numerous civilizations, cultures and religious traditions that have developed outside the influence of Christianity. Given the divine command to go and make disciples of all the nations, what attitude should the Church have towards these social realities? Opposition or dialogue? Competition or cooperation? Respect or contempt? Fight or peaceful coexistence? Can these religions be seen positively and with respect, or should they be dismissed as of no theological importance. In other words, are these religions in some sort of lineal continuity with Christianity, or are they not?

Karl Rahner (3) asserted in 1961 that unfortunately it could not be said that Catholic theology, as practised in recent times, had really paid sufficient attention to the question posed in this precise way. Indeed, judging from the normal practice of Christian missionary activity, it has to be admitted that until rather recently it was customary to deal heavy-handedly with what were called "pagan practices". Although some respect was often paid to elements found in these religions, the systems themselves were seen in a rather negative way as essentially aberrations, and little effort was made to explore the possibility of their providential role in the history of the peoples concerned. The good elements in them which could be respected as positive were accepted as such mainly because they happened to resemble what were taken as authentic Christian values. This did not affect the negative judgment on the religions themselves. Only sporadically, and mainly in recent times, has a serious attempt been made to evaluate the religions themselves and to find out what role they might have in God's plan of salvation for their adherents. But even before Vatican II, theologians (4) finally started discussing the question. Vatican II's Declaration on Relationship of the Church to Non-Christian Religions (Nostra Aetate) seems to allude to it in some way. It says: "The Catholic Church rejects nothing which is true and holy in these religions. She looks with sincere respect upon those ways of conduct and of life, those rules and teachings which, though differing in many particulars from what she holds and sets forth, nevertheless often reflect a ray of that Truth which enlightens all men."

The Decree on the Church's Missionary Activity has more interesting reflections (n. i, 1, 7, 9, 11) which, though still rather timid and general, furnish avenues for a more hopeful treatment of it by theologians. One such pregnant reflection, and perhaps the most significant, is Vatican II's favourite portrayal of the Church as "Universal Sacrament of salvation" (Ad Gentes, 1) ...

In discussing the question of non-Christian religions all parties and opinions among Christian thinkers were starting from the witness of the scriptures and basing on it their evaluation and judgment. What questions were being asked? Were all the relevant elements of the evidence carefully taken into account; or was there a tendency to highlight only certain trends of thought appearing in the Scriptures while pushing into the background other important trends which might have modified the nature of the investigation? Were there certain prior working assumptions and attitudes that commanded the selection of the evidence and determined the relative weight given to apparently conflicting lines of thought?

The reading of the Bible is never a totally neutral exercise. The reader who takes up the Bible comes with all sorts of conditionings. Besides the more personal ones resulting from the individual's own psychological and spiritual history, he or she carries along also the effects of his/her belonging to a specific class, family, culture, community or interest group. The individual bears also the imprint of the epoch in history within which the investigation is being made. All this has an influence on how the Bible will be interrogated, what the expectations of the reader will be, what evidence will be readily selected and given importance, but also what "blind spots" will occur in the exercise.

I take as point of departure the fact that, as far as African traditional religions are concerned, the prevailing judgment and attitudes are the result of Bible study conducted mainly by non-Africans. These students, however sympathetic and broadminded, were still looking at the problem from the point of view of an outsider who is not really personally involved in the religions at stake. In a way, this was an advantage: it made for a type of objectivity and detachment that would however, they could not claim to be totally impartial since they were in their turn conditioned by other factors of which an African can normally hope to be free ...

The main aim of this essay is no show what could happen if the enquiry were initiated from the point of view of an African Christian reader of the Scriptures. The contention is that a fresh vision could ensure in that former problems which used to dominate might be found to take a secondary place, while newer preoccupations might become more important and relevant. A slightly different way of posing the question could also result, demanding a new assessment of the testimony of Scripture. We might even hope to touch on some aspects of the Bible message that have remained "blind spots" until now because they were not really needed from the point of view of former preoccupations.

Examining the Context of Past Attitudes

Within the Christian tradition the problem of the encounter with other religious systems and traditions has not been a purely intellectual one, engaging people's minds on a calm theoretical level. It has always been first and foremost a practical, existential challenge, involving strong sentiments of a sacred duty to be accomplished calling forth concrete tasks and programs and eliciting a lot of deep-seated emotions. It is necessary to start by examining the main aspects of the context that gave rise to the attitudes that people manifested in discussing this point.

One thing is sure. As far as African traditional religions are concerned, the discussions of professional theologians and biblists are only secondary. The main context within which the decisive attitudes towards these religions were formed is the missionary enterprise, especially in its more recent expressions starting with the mid-nineteenth century. Missionary work was seen as the Church's bounded duty to bring the true faith to pagans, or to save souls that were in darkness. The challenge attracted vigorous and enterprising people, ready for action and for suffering even up to death. It was like a military expedition: it thrived on an ethos of struggle and conquest. Understandably the enemy was Satan. But Satan was disguised and active through his network of false religions. He and his associates had to be encountered, unmasked in their perfidy, and then engaged in mortal battle. The missionary's encounter with the traditional African customs and religious practices was thus not a peaceful one. The missionary may have had sympathy and genuine love for the individual natives, for after all, they were the ones on behalf of whom the war was being waged. But towards their religious systems and practices, and towards those who were guardians and promoters of these practices, there could be no compromise.

And so when missionaries went to the Scriptures for guidance in their encounter with the traditional religions, the texts that struck them most were normally those that had overtones of opposition against the "gentiles" as enemies of God's People and practitioners of idolatry and abominations. It was so simple to see the Christian Church as the People of God, and the non-Christian religious systems as the expression of enmity against Yahweh and his plan of salvation.

The most natural selections were those passages where there are expressions of hostility towards the "pagans," for example, where there is abundant diatribe against the idols of the gentiles. Choice texts would be those in the ridicule style in which Deutero-Isaiah excels (Isaiah 44:9-20; 46:1-7), and those portions of the Old Testament which are tributary to this literary form (Psalm 115; Baruch 6; or even Daniel 14). These texts are a reinforcement of the affirmation of strict monotheism (rather than mere henotheism) so characteristic of exilic and post-exilic Judaism (cf. Isaiah 45:7-13, 18-25). It was a sort of apologetic style aiming at consoling and strengthening the chastened exiles or at restoring self-confidence to the struggling bands of the "Golah." This helped to develop the theme of the Holy People separated from all that is impure and profane, a people privileged to have the Law of their God and the only true worship. It was at this time that the great synthesis of the Priestly Tradition was framework of the Scriptures. But there was a dark side to this. From the notion of Holy People and the preoccupation to express this holiness and protect it, the tendency developed towards an exclusivist ghetto mentality. The Law ran the danger of legalism and intransigence as is witnessed by Ezra's fierce treatment of "mixed marriages" (Ezra 9-10). Later persecutions under the Seleucids and the Romans helped only to reinforce these tendencies. The Apocalyptic and allied literatures of these times do have admirable lessons. But they also betray a hardening of attitude towards the "gentiles." There is very little sympathy towards anything outside the "People of God."

These developments are to be seen mostly as prompted by a defensive spirit: the need of a socially and politically disadvantaged group to protect itself from corrosive outside forces and to compensate psychologically for its inferiority by exalting whatever redeeming aspects it believes it possesses. It is to be remembered that the New Testament dawned in the midst of this period. This will help us to put in proper context several texts which reflect attitudes of Christ's contemporaries (and those of the early Church) towards non-Jews. But here we must note that a current opposed to this narrow ghetto spirit and its negative attitude towards the gentiles had developed alongside the more intransigent one. We can only recall such obvious testimonies as the book of Ruth where we sense a subtle criticism of current "purist" ideas about who the "People of God" really are. The satirical novel of the Prophet Jonah is even more explicit in its castigation of Judaism's exclusive claim to God's favor. We have here a rather radical presentation of a theme which was dear to many prophets, as we shall see later on.

In the New Testament times, we have echoes of this more positive tradition. John the Baptist and Jesus himself are examples. The sayings about descent from Abraham are an important evidence. Both the Baptist (cf. Matthew 3:9-10; Luke 3:8) and Christ went out of their way to stigmatize the misplaced confidence in mere belonging to an ethnic group, albeit a divinely chosen one (cf. Matthew 3:11-12; John 8:37-41). The early Christian community, composed mainly of Jews, had the difficulty in ridding themselves of the ghetto mentality, as we can judge by the controversy about the requirements for the conversion of non-Jews (Acts 15). The book of Acts is quite clear in showing how hard it was even for Peter to widen his vision on this point (Acts 10). But the author of Romans feels the need to expound in a new way the theme about descent from Abraham (Romans 4, cf. also Galatians 3 and 4). These sayings of the Baptist, of Jesus, and of Paul are manifestly part of a tradition of protest against a hard-line attitude towards the "pagans."

There seems to have existed in the New Testament a current of thought which felt that the problem about those outside the visible membership of God's People was not as simple as the standard Jew might have wanted to make it. It was too simplistic to think that God loved his chosen people, but had no time for the others. In interpreting the message of the New Testament, this point is very crucial: it may help to give importance to some forgotten texts. Christian missionaries could have given more thought to this counter current in their assessment of the place of non-Christian religions in divine providence. It would seem strange, in fact, that missionaries would give relatively more importance to the contrary current, for they were interrogating the Scriptures in view of a commitment quite contrary to that of a ghetto community. Jewish religion, in spite of its late efforts at proselytism, remained basically a non-missionary community and tended to see its relation with outsiders mainly in terms of opposition and exclusion. The Christian Church, on the other hand, is institutionally outgoing: sent to go out to the whole world. There does not seem to be any necessary reason for the Christian Church to look at the encounter with non-Christian religions from a systematically negative viewpoint, and for thinking that the primary normative texts capable of guiding the Church in its missionary enterprise should be those that suggest an easy and blanket dismissal of other religions. The history of Christianity in Europe led to such a close link between the Christian faith and Western culture that it became difficult to distinguish between them, or between the expansion of religion and the expansion of Western civilization. This ambiguity becomes obvious especially starting with the Crusades. It will not have disappeared in the 16th and 17th centuries when the Christian nations of Spain and Portugal will be busy with their conquests in the New World. It certainly had not disappeared when colonial expansion came to its zenith in the second half of the 19th century and well into our own century. However much one hates to say this, it is not by pure coincidence that missionary work flourished most during the colonial period. In the atmosphere of the Western conquest, the meeting of Christianity with other religions was conceived of in the spirit typical of Christendom's crusading tradition. There is a streak of the Crusader in Western Christianity. It tends to identify its own interests and vision with those of God himself. We only have to think of the bitter sectarianism that has pitied Christian denominations against one another over the past generations. And yet they all claim to belong to one and the same Christ. It should not be surprising then that the same spirit of systematic opposition prevails whenever Christianity meets non-Christian traditions.

The source of this type of intransigence seems to be a tendency to simplify realities into an "either/or" pattern whether it is a question of truths and beliefs or of lifestyles and customs. It is as if anything that is different from what belief to be true or good is a threat to my feeling of security and must be dismissed as bad or inferior. Variations then become oppositions; and it becomes difficult to think of such variations rather as complementary aspects which might create a richer reality by being combined rather than by excluding one another. Seeing variations and differences as complementary aspects first rather than oppositions has an advantage. It helps to discover many things that are valid and good in a position different from my own. And this is salutary when we are dealing with human realities, for such human realities can never claim to have the monopoly of goodness. The tendency to opposition has another side to it, a side we would do well to remember when we are dealing with the encounter of religions. The crusading mentality is usually accompanied by a highly motivated proselytism. When other religions and systems have been proven wrong their adherents are not simply left in peace: they must be persuaded to abandon those false religions and to adopt the true religion as presented by the crusader. This persuasion may be peaceful, relying on respectful dialogue and the power of moral attraction. Often, however, the crusader becomes impatient when conversions are not being realized fast enough for his liking. He may then resort to other

202

methods of persuasion. It may not be outright physical force (although both Islam and Christianity have not always abstained from such methods), but it can be other ways that to a greater or lesser extent do not fully respect the religious freedom of the people. There have been instances where, for example, works of charity were used as mere instruments of proselytism. But in any case such an impulsive desire for converts can affect the modality of the encounter between the religions. It can push the crusader to falsify the picture in view of more immediate success: the Christian religion will be presented only in its idealized form, while only the weaker and repulsive aspects of the other religions are highlighted.

What I am trying to say is that in the encounter of Christianity with other religions, the spirit that motivated the missionary was not always of a type to facilitate a more positive assessment of these religions. This may have impeded a fruitful study of the salvific nature of those religions. It also explains in part the choice of scriptural evidence adduced to account for Christianity's attitude towards them. As we have seen, the texts by which most store was laid were those which form part of a definite trend in the Old Testament: Israel's and Judaism's opposition to the gentiles, and the exclusive claims of God's Chosen People to divine favor.

Christianity claims to be the new People of God. It inherits that feeling of being a privileged people which Israel has had because of the Covenant (Exodus 19:4-6). But by the same token, Christianity has inherited also the danger that stalked Israel throughout its history: the danger of misunderstanding the real nature and aim of this choice by God, and of drawing false conclusions from it concerning God's relations with other peoples and nations. The covenant then, as a fulfilment of the promises made to Abraham and the ancestors, ran the risk of losing its raison d'être as a nationalistic privilege, independent from, or even cancelling God's worldwide salvific interests. Israel's prophets were often obliged to rectify such misunderstandings. Amos (9:7-8) reminds the Israelites that the distant peoples are just as much objects of God's solicitude as they themselves. Yahweh is as concerned with what these foreign nations do to one another as with the way Israel and Judah are acting (Amos 1-2). The first chapters of Genesis (1-11) serve as the setting of the whole scene within which God's plan of salvation is to unfold: the whole of creation, the universe where the history of mankind takes place. Abraham's calling and the election of Israel would have no meaning except as part of this encompassing plan. So while he is dealing with the Chosen People, God's eyes are on the whole of mankind. The authentic traditions of Israel saw the covenant at Sinai as a covenant within a wider Covenant; for creation itself was the primordial Covenant; and God does not break his word. To him belong heaven and the heaven of heavens, the earth and all it contains, even when he makes special choice of Abraham's descendants. He is never partial or to be bribed (Deuteronomy 10:15-18). It is significant that the Wisdom literature which flourished especially among the Jews of the diaspora shows a broader view of God's active presence in the world. The reflections of the book of Wisdom on God's dealings with Israel's enemies are astounding in their insistence on divine forebearance. For indeed God "is merciful to all, because he can do all things and he overlooks men's sins so that they can repent ... he loves all that exists and holds nothing of what he has made in abhorrence, for had he hated anything, he would not have formed it" (cf. Wisdom 11:226). We can feel here the same spirit as the one that prompted the author of the book of Jonah, and which refused to imagine God as partial or narrow (Wisdom 6, 8).

The Historical Visible Church and the Non-Christian Religions

There is, as we mentioned earlier, a current in the New Testament which carried on this open vision of God's dealings with the universe. The early Church was conscious of its task of proclaiming the Good News of Jesus up to the ends of the earth, because the Christ was the final revelation of the true God. The apostles and the early Christians were convinced that only through faith in Christ could the world be saved, "for all the names in the world given to men, this is the only one by which we can be saved" (Acts 4:12). But this conviction does not seem to have become an easy explanation of God's dealings with those who as yet did not know Christ explicitly. For the early Christians the problem was doubly complex. Those who did not know Christ were not only the ones called "gentiles" by the Jews, but also the Jews themselves in so far as they had rejected the Messiah. The pressing question then was to determine where this Chosen People now stood before their God in this new situation in which God's election is now through Christ. The state of the gentiles was only a subsequent problem. Were the Jews at any real advantage as compared with the non-Jews as far as faith

204

in Christ was concerned? As we saw, this is basically the point at issue in the controversy about the condition for conversion to Christ (Acts 15; Romans and Galatians). Although the resolution of the question at Jerusalem was rather a compromise as far as practical tactics were concerned, on the theoretical level a great step had been taken. It was now accepted that "in Christ Jesus, whether you are circumcised or not makes no difference - what matters is faith that makes its power felt through love" (Galatians 5:6). Or as the letter to the Romans would say: "A man is justified by faith and not by doing something the Law tells him to do. Is God the god of the Jews alone and not of the pagans too? Of the pagans too, most certainly, since there is only one God" (Romans 3:28-30). This was a radical statement: it says clearly that through Christ God has shown that he has no favorites: "Pain and suffering will come to every human being who employs himself in evil - Jews first, but Greeks as well; renown, honor and peace will come to everyone who does good - Jews first, but Greeks as well. God has no favorites" (Romans 2:9-11). In this context Paul is able to turn to the "gentiles" and state that "pagans who never heard of the Law but are led by reason to do what he Law commands, may not actually 'possess' the Law, but they can be said to be' the Law. They can point to the substance of the law engraved on their hearts - they can call a witness, that is, their own conscience - they have accusation and defence, that is, their own inner mental dialogue" (Romans 2:14-16).

This statement of humanity's basic equality before God is where the study of the salvific nature of non-Christian religions should start. It shows God present within the whole of mankind, in different ways perhaps, but really present nevertheless, whether through the agency of the Law among the Jews or through the working of conscience for the others. All peoples are subject to sin and God's wrath; but just so are they all open to the saving faith in Christ. Another way of putting it is to affirm that "God wants everyone to be saved and reach full knowledge of the tuth. For there is only one God, and there is only one mediator between God and mankind, himself a man, Christ Jesus who sacrificed himself as a ransom for them all" (1 Timothy 2:4-6). It is possible to situate within proper context Paul's statement during his speech at Athens (Acts 17:26-28). It is a validation of the insights found in the first chapters of Genesis: there is a cosmic Covenant of love between God and mankind by the very fact of creation. Mankind may break this Covenant through sin and infidelity. But again and again God renews it and reaffirms his salvific intention. His special choices (that of Israel and that of the Church) are not an abolition of the cosmic Covenant. If anything, they are a hopeful sign or proof of what in less evident ways he is doing all along with the whole of mankind, and they are meant to serve this wider Covenant.

This does not answer all the question. But if we start with it, then the answers to those other problems will follow a particular line where we do not have to come back on this important basis. For example, it will be necessary to find out what is meant by the affirmation that only faith in Christ brings salvation. The easy way out would be to say that those who do not know Christ explicitly cannot have faith in him: and cannot be saved. But our starting point will oblige us to return to the Scriptures and ask whether and how Christ can be really present even if his face is not explicitly revealed. This might help us to give fuller consideration, for example, to John's statement: "The Word was the true light that enlightens all men ... He was in the world that had its being through him, and the world did not know him" (John 1:9). We would return to the Wisdom literature in the Old Testament and meditate on the fuller meaning of the theme of God's Wisdom. And then we might take up the Captivity Letters. We would see that the Christ of God's plan of salvation (cf. Ephesians 1 and Colossians 1) is a cosmic presence that is not contained within the limits of the historical visible Church only.

Another problem would be to assess the role of this visible Church. Is God's intention to introduce every human being into this historical Church under pain of not being saved? The history of Israel would furnish us with food for thought. God did not call every person and nation in that special way by which he had called Israel. But as we have seen, this special election did not mean that God was neglecting the other nations in favor of Israel alone. On the contrary, although Israel often forgot this, the special election of the Chosen People was a call for service. Deutero- (and Trito-) Isaiah makes this quite plain, especially in the Songs of the Suffering Servant of Yahweh (Isaiah 42:1-9; 49:1-6; 50:4-9; and esp. 52:13-53:12). In these texts the meaning of Israel's calling, history, suffering and final triumph is of world-wide validity. She lives, suffers, dies and rises again as an instrument of Yahweh's salvific designs for the whole world. Although the other nations are not racially or physically integrated into the Jewish nation, in a sense they are all brought into real association with her. In a way that is hard to explain in terms of experiential evidence, these nations can look up to Sion as to their "Mother, since each one of them was born in her, and all have their place in her" (Psalm 86:5-7). Not only are the explicit proselytes accepted (cf. Isaiah 56:1-8), but all the nations walk in her light (Isaiah 60) bringing in their riches into a worldwide commonwealth of the redeemed. Israel therefore is a sort of prototype, a light to enlighten the nations and make them realize their God-given destiny. The New Testament echoes this by comparing the New People of God to "Light," "Salt," "Leaven" of the earth, to a "City" up on the mountain whose presence assures the world that God is in the midst of his people (Matthew 5:13-16; also Philippians 2:14-16). This is the meaning of Vatican II's favorite description of the Church as "light of the nations" (Lumen Gentium, 1) and universal sacrament of salvation (Ad Gentes, 1).

It would seem therefore that the Church's destiny is to be inserted into the heart of the world as a sacrament, i.e. visible and effective sign, of the coming Kingdom of God, pointing towards this Kingdom, and proving its efficacious working by acting as a privileged champion of the tenets of the Kingdom. By looking at the Church and by hearing its prophetic utterances, the rest of the world is challenged by the judgment of God on them a judgment that, like light, reveals the dross and the good metal. If this is so, the Church's preoccupation should be less with mere recruitment of numbers, and more with authenticity and efficacy of its witness in the world. The other religions should be seen, not so much as an adversary or a threat, but as the field within which her witness makes the good grain grow and bear fruit a hundredfold, while the tares are being pulled out and burnt.

The Salvific Value of African Traditional Religions

What could happen if the problem of non-Christian religions were examined by people who are part of the societies among whom these religions have a validity? What would happen if African traditional religions were to be assessed by African Christians themselves? Perhaps the main lines of the enquiry would shift.

There would be a first basic change: it would be an enquiry from the inside rather than from the outside. I would have to return in spirit to where my people were. So we would not be talking anymore about the customs and beliefs of those "pagans" in the bush of Africa: I could not have the heart to speak of my own ancestors and religion in this contemptuous way. We are dealing with concrete people now: my father and mother, my uncles and aunts, my brothers and sisters, my relatives, friends and neighbours, a lot of people who mean a lot to me and whom I cannot handle as if they were mere objects of curiosity and detached study. And especially, I would remember that I am looking at a venerable and sacred tradition handed over by generations of ancestors. These beliefs and customs will command my respect and careful consideration, even when I may not share them. I cannot act as if these are childish superstitions or mere primitive mumbo-jumbo, for I feel with my whole person the seriousness of the problems, questionings, preoccupations, hopes, fears, desires and joys from which these religious attitudes spring. I have no right to look down on my father's culture or to offer simplistic solutions to questions I know to be very complex.

We can think here of Paul's case, when in the letter to the Romans)9-11) he had to meditate on the fact that the majority of his fellow Jews did not believe in Christ and were thus hostile to what was most precious in his own religious experience. His sorrow was so great, his mental anguish so endless, for these were his own flesh and blood. With them he shared a rich history of relations with God and the ancestors. So his questions take on a dramatic and deeply personal character. He sees difficulties and problems where perhaps a fellow Christian, but of a non-Jewish origin, might not have seen them. He finds himself unable to accept several easy answers that suggest themselves to his questioning mind. The problem of Jewish incredulity is not as simple to him as it might look to an outsider. It is not just a question of bad faith or blindness on the part of the Jews. The complicating factor is that God himself and his promises are all part of the question. And so Paul is forced to go back to the Scriptures and start a thorough-going midrash in order to find out the theological implications of the problem. In so doing he comes up with scriptural texts which take on a new meaning as approaches to the solution. We have an example of contextualized Bible investigation where the reading and interpretation are shaped by the personal involvement of the inquirer.

It is some such process that an African would have to initiate if he wanted to re-examine the problem of his ancestors' religious traditions. He would not start from a position of assumed righteousness and superiority as a member of an already Christianized culture might be tempted to do. He would therefore avoid selecting as guidance those texts of the Bible that represent

208

doubtful tendencies of a superiority complex vis-a-vis the other cultures, or of an exclusivist mentality which would want to restrict God's favor and interest to one's own group as if God can be partisan and a respecter of persons.

But above all, he would start from the conviction that God has been ever present among his own people, just as he has been in all peoples, cultures and religious tendencies of the world, not just as a condescension, but because this benevolent presence is in the logic of the cosmic Covenant of creation and re-creation. We must therefore assume that in all serious efforts of mankind to make sense of its own life and destiny, God has been in and with his peoples. The Spirit of God has indeed filled the whole world. There are enough serious trends of thought in the Scriptures to show that this feeling is not just sentimental, but is based on revelation. The African Bible reader will thus not fear to state that the religious systems of his ancestors were not just tolerated by God. They were the results of the efforts of our cultures wherein the Spirit of God was an active agent. And therefore, there would be no fear in me to assert that, as long as these religions were the serious searchings of our cultures for the deity, they are to be respected as the normal divinely-given means for salvation, put by God in his will for the salvation of all the peoples.

This will not mean that everything in those religions is good or to be retained. Scripture will remind us strongly that human nature and its strivings are under the shadow of sin, and therefore constantly subjected to God's judgment whereby the evil is always condemned by him and by mankind's deepest level of conscience. But because God's Spirit is nevertheless actively present, it will be necessary to assume that there are also a lot of good and valid elements in this "grouping"; and these positive elements must be worthy of respect and survival since they are the results of God's activity which is never ultimately defeated by sin and death.

But I shall remember that, according to Scripture, this judgment is not reserved only to those nations that have been favored with a special election by God. For according to the Bible, the whole world lies under the wrath of God: "Jews and Gentile alike, because all have sinned and have fallen short of God's glory. God's wrath and condemnation tend to begin with his own household." And so I shall not be bothered by tendencious readings of the Bible which give an easy superiority to any special historical group and is taken as authorization to despise, reject, or condemn off hand whatever is different from, or looks strange to such a historical group.

Let us admit that this caution in assessing African non-Christian religions, and the systematic favorable prejudice in their regard, will come easy to me because I feel personally involved in these religions. But that does not need an apology: it simply shows that it is not fair to give a final judgment in such important matters only from a partial standpoint, be it Jewish or Christian, primitive or civilized, black or white. The problem of the salvific value of non-Christian religions should be tackled from a holistic standpoint in which full account is taken of the special choices or elections of God, but also of all the other elements in God's relations with the whole of mankind. Only thus can full justice be given to the witness of the Scriptures. For indeed, "God has no favorites" (Romans 2:11).

Footnotes

1   For a summary treatment of the fortunes of this axiom, cf. H. Kung, **The Church** (Garden City, N.Y.: Doubleday Image Book, 1967), pp. 313-19.
2   Lumen Gentium, n. 16.
3   K. Rahner, **Theological Investigations** (London: Darton, Longman & Todd, 1966), vol. 5, Later Writings, p. 117.
4   Like Danielou, Congar, and others. For a brief evaluation of these essays, cf. Schlette, **Towards a Theology of Religions** (New York: Herder & Herder, 1966), pp. 28-33.

SOURCE: MISSION TRENDS NO. 5 Faith Meets Faith, (Edited by Gerald H. Anderson and Thomas F. Stransky, C.S. P. Paulist Press New York/Ramsey/Toronto and W.B. EERDMANS PUBLISHING CO. Grand Rapids.

PART FOUR

IMPACT ON:

THE IMPACT OF RELIGION IN A TRADITIONAL AFRICAN SOCIETY

by

E.M. Uka

Role of religion in traditional societies: General (1)

Traditional religion exerts great influence upon the thought patterns and life styles of traditional people like the pre-colonial Igbos of Nigeria. This religion evolved gradually without a founder. It has no sacred scriptures. Its beliefs and teachings are enshrined in ceremonies, rituals, symbols, myths, and proverbs. It has a wealth of beliefs aboutGod, spirits, man and the world of things (plants, animals and the physical universe). Religious leaders include village and family elders (recognized and respected due to their age and store of knowledge about tradition), priests (male and female) of the various local deities, diviners (interpreters of the will of the deities or means to consult deities), medicine-men and sacral rulers. These officials serve as interpreters of the religious tradition and as guardians of social solidarity. Since religion mingles with festivals, with work and the various incidents of life, Igbos hardly distinguish between the sacred and the secular or between what is spiritual and what is material. Their world is a single whole, which is constantly animated by religion. Religion is not merely a system, with a creed, a moral code and a liturgy, but it is an institution in which one has one's whole life. (2)

Religion permeates the social, economic, and political life of the Igbos. It also embodies and symbolizes their sense of community. It helps them to interpret their values, dreams, symbols and deep wishes. Igbo religious beliefs are not formulated in a systematic set of dogmas which a person is expected to memorize. Their beliefs and practices are transmitted and engraved in people's mind through the process of living. Everybody is a religious carrier and thus specialized missionaries and proselytisers are unnecessary in Igbo religion.

Among the Igbos, religion is not primarily for the individual but for the community of which he is a part. Indigenous Igbo society does not contain non-religious people because for the Igbos being human implies participating in the beliefs, ceremonies, rituals, and festivals of the community. A person cannot detach himself from his religion and still be considered human. Therefore, to be without religion is to be severed from one's roots, foundation, security, kinship and that group which makes a person aware of his own existence. The Igbos, therefore, do not know how to exist without religion. They are instinctively religious. Religion is one with their life. What Idowu says for all of Africa applies to the Igbos: "They are in all things ... religious." (3)

In sum, the principles of Igbo religion give custom, order, discipline and cohesion to the traditional society. These principles create in the people the concept of solidarity in life and of mutual and corporate responsibility in socio-economic matters. Religious practices express a deep spiritual dimension of culture which serves the traditional society in various ways. Igbo religion gives people an insight into the unknown; and it enables them to gain more knowledge of the mysteries about this life and about their relatonship to the invisible world. It equips them with spiritual power to deal with some of the baffling, socio-religious problems around them. Moreover, the practices of religion and its world-view give guidance to the people as to what to expect in the future. Therefore, their religion provides a basic cosmology wherein they live and carry on their cultural, economic, social and political activities. It is a religion of strong conservative tendencies that seeks to maintain the social order through its influence on the family and kinship system, and on the economic and political spheres. Let us now elaborate on these.

The Family

Family is the unit of society. The father in each family is regarded as the priest and leader of the family. He offers morning prayers to God and their patron deities on behalf of every member of his family. He offers sacrifices to their ancestors and other traditional gods such as the god of Yams - **Ifejioku.** during planting or harvesting seasons. He acts to ensure that the norms and values of society are observed by members of his family. He teaches them to revere the gods and respect the traditional customs.

The concept of family goes beyond the nuclear to the extended family system. (4) For example, the Igbo family and extended family system constitute a vast net work of relationships

214

which embrace everybody in a given local group. So an evil act by a member of a family, tarnishes not only the personality of the person but also that of his father, mother, brothers, sisters, uncles, cousins, aunts and even that of the entire community. By the same token the glory from the good act by a person extends outward from the person's nuclear family i.e. from father, mother, son, daughter, brother, sister to grand parents uncles, aunts, nephews and grand children. Consequently, everybody comes to be related to everybody else. For the Igbos, this relationship extends not only to the living people but also to the dead members of the family and to those who are yet to be born. (5) A family kingship system among the Igbos is either matrilineal when it traces its descent through females exclussively to a common ancestress. It is patrilineal when the same procedure applies to the male line of desent. In some societies, both groups exist, so that an individual is at once a member of his father's patrilineal group and his mother's matrilineal group. (7) For the Igbo, communities are either matrilineal like the Ohaffia people or patrilineal like the Awka-Onitsha communities. (8)

As a system, the kinship relationships imply a relationship of interdependence between the component parts, and the gods especially the ancestors who are constantly 'fed' with sacrifices offered to them and are venerated by being mentioned during family prayers, the breaking of **Kola** and during festivals. Members of the family are also mindful of the taboos associated with inheritance, marriage, extramarital sexual relations and the like, which they observe so as not to incur the wrath of the ancestors. (9)

Religion and Morality (10)

In African traditional society (e.g. the Igbos of Nigeria) morality and religion are inseparable. Laws, taboos, customs and set forms of behaviour all derive their power from religion. Morality flows out of religion. God is generally regarded as the source of morality. The divinities are seen as His agents who punish or reward those who violate or observe the moral norms of the society. The divinities also have their own taboos which their devotees are also expected to keep. The observance of these religion - social rules of conduct or taboos are aimed at ensuring the welfare and solidarity of the society.

For example, some of the practices that encourage the maintenance of social solidarity and harmony are enshrined in the prohibitions or mechanisms of social control. These operate at a subconscious level of socialization and consist of prohibitions designed to preserve domestic life, regulate sexual urges, protect economic life, preserve the normal rhythm of nature and ensure proper reverence for the ancestors and the community of the spirit world. Those designed to regulate domestic life and ensure harmony in the home include the prohibitions against adults deliberately inflicting harm on their parents, a wife throwing her husband to the ground in a fight, or a husband stripping his wife naked in a fight, and so forth. Prohibitions which regulate or control powerful sex urges in people include those against adultery (either by husband or by wife), homosexuality by menfolk, incest, and any form of sexual relation with an animal. Prohibitions designed to protect economic life include prohibitions against the theft of yams, domestic animals or any valuable belongings of another person; alteration of land boundaries in secret; arson and any act betraying the community's secrets to an enemy. Prohibitions which are designed to prevent the disturbance of the normal rhythm of nature include a woman climbing a palm tree, acts of deliberate or accidental homicide, a woman giving birth to more than one baby at time, and a baby coming out feet first at birth, or developing the upper teeth first before lower ones. Prohibitions instituted to ensure proper reverence of ancestors and the community of the spirit world are made against the killing and eating of totem animals, the disclosure of the identity of a masquerader or the breaking of mourning customs. (11) Essentially, therefore, the moral observances or prohibitions we have considered are concerned with relationships between man and his fellow man in society and between man and the gods, in the unseen world. So the taboos or prohibitions are observed because to contravene them would upset the moral tone and balance of the cosmos. In effect, therefore African (Igbo) traditional morality lays emphasis on what promotes social harmony, and enhances the survival of the individual and the community. Hence it condems all acts that threaten social harmony, such as: as theft, murder, adultery, incest, robbery, rape, covetousness, violence, greed, selfishness, falsehood, bypassing, wickedness, cheating, treachery, dishonesty, alteration of land boundaries, setting fire on another person's house or crops, disclosing secret or sacred information and violation of taboos etc.

Those who violate the canons of moral decency in society are punished by the gods with terrible and sometimes incurable diseases such as accidental deaths, bad luck in activities such as hunting, fishing, travelling, courtship, business transactions childlessness, bad dreams, suicide, snake bites and deformities. For serious violations such as murder or incest or patricide, punishment could come to the entire community in the form of famine, draught, flood, earthquake, thunder and lightening, epidemic, locust invasion or enemy attack. (12)

God, with the help of His agents the tutelary spirits not only punishes evil, but also rewards the virtuous and good life in both private and public affairs. The virtues approved of God include moral values such as love, honesty, truthfulness, justice, obedience, loyalty, compasion, chastity before marriage and faithfulness during marriage, friendliness, helpfulness, self-control, courage, bravery, hospitality, humility, patience, wisdom, kindness, forgiveness and the like. All these virtues are regarded as manifestations of the good character which are believed to be implanted by God in man.

Morality in traditional societies is not only enforced by God through his agents the earth-goddess, **Ala**, the god of thunder, **Amadioha**, the Ancestors, **Ndichie** and the rest, but also through social institutions such as the family, the age-grade, the secret societies and through informal methods of moral educations such as through stories, told in myths, fables, folktales, riddles and folksongs. (13)

Traditional Economy

The Igbo modes of economic production and distribution are the products and consequences of their religious beliefs and practices. They believe that it is the gods who supply their needs for food through fertility given to theland and to the domestic animals. Production is carried on in accordance with the religious rituals and for subsistence purposes not for capital accumulation. Concerning the traditional economy, Ilogu aptly states:

> Igbo traditional society knows only of subsistence economy and trade by barter. Self supportive family units do farm work on land sometimes commonly owned ... They alternate this farmwork with the making of crafts of household necessities ... land, food crops, communal work, pure craftsmanship and attention to

217

the gods of economic life are the main factors of such economy. (14)

In short, it is neither a money economy nor a wage-earning form of production system. The aim of agriculture is to provide food for the family and for festive occasions as required by their religious custom. Livestock (cows, chickens, goats, pigs) is reared to meet mainly domestic and ceremonial needs. Communal farmwork is practised to strengthen the existing extended family ties. In addition, this extended family structure provides for the care and maintenance of the aged, the infirm, or handicapped. Wealth, seen as God's favour is measured for the adult male in terms of the number of his wives and children, the type of titles he acquires and the number of yams he owns. Since yam production is more for prestige than for trade or consumption, the goal is to have a barn full of yams in order to earn a yam title. (15) These items of wealth are more or less perishable commodities, since there are no adequate storage facilities or preservation techniques for such farm products. Besides, they yield no "monetary interest" when they are stored as in a money economy. There is a distinction here which must be clearly understood. For the Igbo the importance of wealth lay in its social significance rather than in the wealth itself. Thus the person earning a yam title ("**igwa nnū**") with a thousand or more yams shares them with all the members of his community. He is expected to support the needy members of his family and extended family. By contrast a wealthy man in an industrial capitalist society would be more apt to use his wealth to create further wealth rather than spend it or share it. (16)

On the level of material culture, Igbo techniques are at the handicraft stage. Occupations are mainly manual and range from woodcarving pottery, cloth weaving, blacksmithing, fishing, hunting, farmwork and sculpture.

There are occupations which are not subsistence oriented, such as sculpturing. As Ilogu observes: "Almost all sculpture in Igbo land are devoted to religious uses and therefore are not regarded as economic activity at all." (17) Artists in general do not earn steady incomes but are frequently honoured for their work.

218

Traditional Government

No society can live without a governing body to make decisions, pass judgments, allocate power and resources and initiate courses of action calculated for the preservation of law and order within the society.

So in traditional, "primal, undifferentiated societies, like a traditional Igbo society, religious beliefs and political ideologies belong together in suplementary as well as complementary relationships. In these societies, it was unconceivable to think of politics and religion as separate entities as is done in modern, industrialized, differentiated and 'secular' societies. Indeed, classical politcal thinkers like Aristotle believed that religious homogeneity was crucial for political stability. And Fustel de Coulanges (1830-1889) who studied classical cities of Rome and Greece came to the conclusion that the social and political foundations of those cities were strictly and exclusively religious". (18) Basil Davidson a renowned African scholar, arrived at the same conclusion with respect to pre-colonial Africa and so did Harold W. Turner. (19)

Davidson stated that:

> ... religion and politics were inseparably bound together in traditional civilization. Like Europeans of the Middle Ages ... Africans lived in an 'age of faith'. They believed in short that political authority came not from man but from God and the spirits. Those who exercised authority on earth could do so ... only if they were accepted as speaking and acting with the goodwil of the departed ancestors who, in turn, were man's protectors and helpers in the world of the spirits. Rulers could rule only if they were spiritually appointed to do so, and their subjects obeyed them not simply from respect for the courts of law or for the kings power, but also for reasons of religion. (20)

Also, Harold W. Turner observed that:

> In most traditional societies of Africa the tribe itself and its rulers and institutions were set within a sacred cosmic order. The patterns and the sanctions for political organisation were derived from a religious cosmology and the mythology that expressed and sup-

ported it and the political leader or head was. The channel through which ultimate or cosmic forces operated for the welfare of the society. Sacred kingship has been widespread and separation between religious and political institutions and activities has been rare...(21)

The fact of the matter therefore is that traditional Africans believed in the divine origin of power and rulership.

In view of this, the political functionaries in Igbo traditional societies see themselves as instruments to enforce the overall will of the gods and ancestors and as guardians of public morality and welfare.

According to my interview with **Eze-Akpan,** the leader of the Age Grade group who weild political power in Akanu Ohafia, the role of our government is to protect and promote the welfare of every member of the village and to ensure the safety of strangers. The community feels their impact not only through the announcements they make to inform the people on what to do but mostly during the periods of crisis such as draught, famine, enemy attack and the committal of abominations like incest, murder, yam theft by any member of the community.

At such moments of crisis, the members of **Akpan** meet to deliberate on what to do to appease God and the gods in order to grant them rain or fertility. Usually they offer propitiatory sacrifice with a big goat to God at the public shrine of the earth deity, pleading for forgiveness if they have done anything wrong for which they were being punished with draught or famine. (22)

In matters of pollution, purificatory sacrifices are offered to cleanse the pollution arising from a breach of **Nso Ala** (a sacred prohibition of the Earth Deity). Here a fowl is used not a victim as big as a goat.

During traditional festivals most of which are agricultural festivals, traditional Africans have the gods participate directly in the natural, moral and spiritual life of the community. At such festivals it is the political leaders who decide and remind the people about the seasons for such festivals. (23)

So we find that those who bear political power in the community exercise their power both for the welfare of the community and in obedience to the will of the gods.

In sum, it could be said on the basis of the preceding account that religion permeated every facet of the traditional African life: social, economic and political. Indeed it is true to say that the traditional African is in all things religious.

Footnotes

1 This study examines the functions of religion in a traditional society. It is not a study of religion as a dimension of human life 'suigeneris'. So, the focus is on the milieu or the functions of religion not on religion per se.

2 R. Larocha, "Some Traditional African Religions and Christianity" in **Christianity in Tropical Africa** ed. C. Baëlà (Oxford: Oxford Univ. Press 1968) p. 295. In the same book see E.B. Welbourn "Some Problems of African Christianity: Guilt and Shame" p. 184.

3 E.B. Idowu, **Olodumare: God in Yoruba Belief** (New York: Frederick A. Praeger 1963) p. 1. Cf. A.O. Iwuagwu "Chukwu: Towards a definition of Igbo Traditional Religion" in **West African Religion** vol. 16 (1975). For works in traditional religion of other African societies see E.E. Evans Pritchard, **Nuer Religion** (Oxford: The Clarendon Press, 1961) S.F. Nadel, **Nupe Religion** (London: Routledge and Kegan Paul, 1954).

4 Edmund Ilogu, **Christianity and Igbo Culture.** E.J. Brill, (1974) p. 11. Cf. J.S. Mbiti, **African Religion and Philosophy** (London: Heinemann, 1969) pp. 104-109.

5 **Ibid.** Mbiti, p. 105. Mbiti's remarks are applicable to the Igbos of Nigeria.

6 Leslie A. White, "Kinship System" in **A Dictionary of Social Sciences,** ed., Julius Gould and Willsam L. Rolb. (New York: The Free press, 1964) pp. 366-368.

7 Philip Nsugbe, **Ohaffia: A Matrilineal Ibo People** (London: The Clarendon Press 1974).

8 Ilogu, p. 11.

9 Fred Eggan, "Kinship" in **International Encyclopedia of Social Sciences,** vol. 9, ed. David Sil's (New York: Free Press, 1968) pp. 355-390.

10 See the article on "Ethics in African Traditional Religion", in this volume for further details.

11 Michael Olisa, "Taboos in Igbo Religion and Society" **West African Religion** No. 11. (Jan. 1972) pp. 4-10. See also A.K. Opoku, **West African Traditional Religion** (Accra: FEP Ltd. 1978) pp. 152-163.
Cf. Zulu Sofola, **Wedluck of the Gods** (London: Evans Brothers 1972). E. Ikenga Metuh, **West African Religions**

221

    in **Western Conceptual schemes** (Ibadan: Claverianum Press, 1985) p. 73-93.

12 J.S. Mbiti, Introduction to African Religion p. 181. Cf. A.B. Jacobbs, **A Textbook on West African Traditional Religion** (London: Aromolaran Pub. Co. 1977) pp. 245-247.

13 Akpenpuun Dzurgba, **The Relevance of Christian Ethics in the Search for Political Values in Nigeria** unpublished Ph.D. Thesis - UNN. 1984, pp. 107-109.

14 Ilogu, p. 20.

15 Victor C. Uchendu, **The Igbo of South Eastern Nigeria** (New York: Holt Rinehart and Winston, 1965) p. 26.

16 E.M. Uka, "Elements of Protestant Ethics in African Traditional Culture" (Term paper Graduate School Drew University 1978).

17 Ilogu, p. 22.

18 Friday Mbon "Islam in West Africa: Some Sociological Reflections" in **Islam and the Modern Age.** (New Delhi, Nov. 1981) pp. 221-222.

19 I am indebted to Friday M. Mbon for the citations I have made here from his article "Islam in West Africa: Some Sociological Reflections" in **Islam and the Modern Age** A Quarterly Journal (Nov., 1981), pp. 221-223.

20 Basil Davidson, **The Growth of African Civilization: A History of West African 1000-1800** (London: Longmans 1965) p. 157.

21 H.W. Turner "The Place of Independent Religions Movements in the modernization of Africa" **Journal of Religion in Africa** II. Fasc. 1 1969 p. 49. It is to be noted that among the Igbos there are five sub-cultural ethnic groups and they have varieties of political systems representative of many African traditional political systems. According to Dr. Ikenna Nzimiro, each of these sub-cultural groups has given a clue to a proper scientific classification of Igbo political system. They include:
- Centralized State System
- Age-grade system
- Titled officials and elders
- Republican system

characterised by flexible democratic federated autonomous lineages organised through lineage heads. Cf. Ikenna Nzimiro, **NSUKKA: The Problems of Change and Continuity - Social Structure and Social Change** (Seminar paper presented at the Institute of African Studies, University of Nigeria, Nsukka 1972).

22 **Akpan** is the name of the Age grade in Akanu Ohaffia who
    weilds the political power in the community. According
    to their leader Nnana Ukpai aged 63 the **Akpan** rules
    in obedience to the gods and for the welfare of the
    people. Cf. Emefie I. Metuh, **African Religions in
    Western Conceptual Schemes** p. 63.
23 J.N. Amankulor, "Ekpe Festivals as Religious Rituals and
    Dance Drama" in **IKENGA** (July 72) pp. 35-47.

THE CONTRIBUTION OF AFRICAN TRADITIONAL RELIGION AND CULTURE TO MARRIAGE IN NIGERIA

by

Rev. Dr. J.O. Kayode

Social Scientists often refer to Marriage as a social phenomenon. Parrinder also observes that the religious element in marriage, at least, appears small and the wedding itself but a detail in a process of social arrangements. (1)

Admittedly, it is social because marriage involves two or more families which are involved in the exercise; but Traditional Africans do not dichotomise life into the religious and the secular; although there is a subtle line of demarcation between the two which applies on appropriate occasions. Thus, when we consider the subject of marriage, we are thinking of all that the Africans bring into it: of their spiritual, emotional and social heritage. Z.K. Matthews remarks that marriage is regarded as "One of the best ways of cementing a friendship between individuals or groups within the tribe or between tribes". (2)

It is a popular view among many African peoples that from the very beginning of human life, God commanded or taught people to get married and bear children. "Therefore marriage is looked upon as a sacred duty which every normal person must perform. Failure to do so means in effect, stopping the flow of life through the individual and hence the diminishing of mankind upon the earth ... Therefore anybody who, under normal conditions, refuses to get married, is committing a major offence in the eyes of society and people will be against him. In all African Societies, everything possible is done to prepare people for marriage and to make them think in terms of marriage". (3)

Marriage ceremony may be regarded for all human beings as a time in life when the couple can participate actively and share with friends and relatives the joy of mutual love and good will. At birth, the young babe would not be consciously alert at its ceremony of naming; so also at the funeral ceremony when the individual is not physically present. Marriage ceremony, therefore, constitutes the crown of personal rituals particularly among Africans. The new couple would see exchange of gifts and hear songs praising their ancestors. Congratulatory messages would pass among families with good will and cheers. The newly born babe or the corpse of the dead cannot appreciate in this way.

Care is, therefore, taken in choosing the partner since the relationship is a lifetime affair. The line of marriage consummation commonly follows given steps. They are:

1. Agreement between the intendants,
2. Sanctions of the Oracle,
3. Sanctions of Parents and Relatives,
4. Courtship rituals,
5. Marriage ceremony.

The five steps are integrated within social, religious and ethical network.

Agreement between the intendants

Basically, marriage is a close union between husband and wife and it is important that the two people should be in LOVE before the union can last long. They cannot start loving at marriage the love should have begun at courtship; but would be intensified at and from marriage henceforth. All Religions emphasise the importance of such a mutual love (4) between the two persons that come forward for marriage.

In African Traditional Societies, the initial approach between the young man and the young lady is gradual and each of them could have intermediaries that will bring messages across to him or her and give advice as the situation may demand. Such intermediaries could be Married housewives and/or trusted friends.

Married housewives in mutual relationship with the young lady or man in their traditional households consider it a helpful role to be associated with the courtship of the marriage intendants. Their suggestions are considered vital and they may assist in approaching young lady or man on behalf of their group.

Trusted friends also can assist in bringing the two intendants together and faithfully act on behalf of their colleagues particularly in their absence. They offer useful suggestions, protect the lovers from any contact other than the one for their friend and would be prepared to fight physically if need be, to secure and protect the lovers.

Apart from the assistance of married housewives and friends, courtship could also be initiated by the young man and lady secretly and usually in the evenings. It is customary for the lady to be shy when approached by the young man. The young man may start off showing love by special greetings or sending

226

gifts which, if accepted by the lady, would indicate her willingness to continue courtship. A good lady with no intention of marriage would return gifts and tell the young man or his friend or housewife (the intermediary) the reasons why she refuses; and would not want the young man to waste his materials. It is however, a different case for a lady who is a dupe. She disappoints in the end but may earn herself physical combat, hot exchange of words and serious quarrelling between the families or friends of the two factions.

The two lovers would put into consideration genuine love as existing between the young lady and man, good character of the families of both, non-hereditary disease, the sanction of the oracles and of their parents and relatives. If the courtship terminates, the youngman or lady can still look for his or her partner from elsewhere; but assuming mutual love, the sanction of the oracle would be sought.

Sanctions of the Oracles

In the proposal and consent between the youngman and the lady, the oracle comes in as a vital factor. This is through divination which "is a method of finding out the unknown by means of pebbles, numbers, water, animal entrails, reading the palms, throwing dice and many other methods". (5) Whether a family is contemplating offering a daughter to another family, or a family is asking for the hand of the daughter of another family for one of its own sons, or two young people have reported back to their families that they have agreed and would like to begin the process leading to marriage, the Oracle is almost invariably consulted. "This is to find out whether the undertaking will meet divine sanction or not; or whether there are any precautions to be taken in order to remove certain obstacles and ensure success in the undertaking". (6)

Normally, it is when the Africans ascertain the divine approval through the oracles that any further step can be taken in the arrangement leading to marriage. Also, whenever a marriage proposal is made from one family to another a period of "waiting" must intervene between 'proposal' and 'giving of the reply'.

From the consultation of the Oracle, it may be revealed that certain sacrifices should be performed and certain

227

medicines made and used. In Benin, it is still a condition for a prospective husband to establish an **Olokun** shrine for his would-be wife; but that is after divine and family approvals have been obtained.

However, opposition could come up if the two intendants are unmarriageable relatives, (7) or if the oracle says 'No' without prescribing any sacrifice, or there has been family quarrel for which the two families intend no settlement. In many cases, however, such marriage ties often help to settle family disputes and terminate long standing enmity.

Sanctions of Parents

The sanction of the oracle is closely tied up with the sanctions of the parents and relatives. If the Oracle approved the mutual love of the two young people, parents and relatives have to give their formal approval. The approval entails various forms of responsibility, the most common of which are:

1. That due respect is henceforth given to each other's group.
2. That co-operation towards the marriage should be maintained in the interest of all the groups.
3. That gifts would be exchanged periodically as indication of love and interest in each party.
4. That each member of the family constitutes and informant for the youngman or lady on the behaviour of his/her intendant in public and private.
5. That the parents of the Lady could assign any duty to the youngman such as hoeing the farm, thatching the roof, or any other form of work.

The parents of the lady would be happy if their intended son-in-law has a good job or possesses acres of farm land or numerous livestock. A lazy son-in-law, on the other hand, would earn himself poor commendation and courtship could even land on the rocks.

Betrothal signifies that there has been mutual consent on both sides and that the prospective marriage has the sanction of both families. More often than not, betrothal is as good as marriage, although usually, it is expected that the actual marriage ceremony should take place.

Courtship rituals

The parents of the intendants would commence courtship rituals only when they were satisfied that the two intendants are not blood relations, that no hereditary disease exists in either of the families, that there is no kleptomaniac tendencies in either of the intendants, and that neither of them had committed any crime. Age-mates may have to perform necessary rituals. Among the Arusha, for example, "when a girl undergoes clitoridectomy at her initiation the man to whom she is betrothed, together with his age-mates, not only assemble to witness the operation, but they aggressively prevent other men from approaching near. At such a time the girl is referred to as the 'wife' of the age-group". (8)

In Bendel State of Nigeria, the youngman, having given the betrothal fee, can take the girl off from the age of ten to stay with him; but there must be no sexual relations until the marriage ceremony is performed. In this way, both of them can live together at the man's place in order to understand each other fully before the actual marriage. Courtship in this pattern can last ten or more years.

Another pattern among the Yoruba is that the young girl, say from the age of two, three and so on will be given as wife to the youngman of seventeen years of age or more, but the girl would not move to the man's house. The man would occasionally bring gifts (palmwine, kolanuts, yams) to the parents-in-law and could be assigned any duty on the latter's farm or estate. Whenever the youngman is called upon by the parents-in-law to do such type of duty, he performs the task cheerfully. His colleagues may also assist him in performing the duty efficiently. Such duties may include making heaps or hoeing the farm, clearing cocoa plantation, thatching the leaking roof, etc.

Actual Marriage

Radcliffe Brown and Daryll Forde rightly observed that "the African does not think of marriage as a union based on romantic love although beauty as well as character and health are sought in the choice of a wife." (9) Emphasis is laid on good character which is very important in African culture.

We have so far looked at the steps taken in choosing a wife or husband. We must also indicate that various methods are followed in observing marriage ceremonies in the traditional communities in Africa. Assuming that the traditional injunctions of how and when to choose the partner (endogamous or exogamous) are completed, the families have to meet and share the joy of the union issuing from the love of the couple.

(II) Among the Yoruba of Nigeria, it is important that the couple should receive prayers and blessings from their parents (particularly the parents of the bride). Any marriage among the Yoruba which lacks this religious act is precarious and undesirable.

Prayers are offered for the couple with such similar elements which the Yoruba use at the Naming ceremony (the first personal ritual ceremony). The elements brought forward are symbolically meaningful.

Salt: That the new life into which the couple are entering may be pleasant and their lives, preserved. Salt is chosen because of its preservative character.

Honey: That their married life may be harmonious.

Alligator Pepper: That the marriage may be blessed with children, just as the alligator pepper fills its cell with seeds.

Kolanuts: That impediments to their happiness may be utterly removed.

Red Palm Oil: That their life's problems may receive amicable solutions.

Clothes: These symbolise the prayerful wish that the clothes will be used to welcome new born baby or babies into the family. In fact the bride keeps these materials for use when she has the first born. In Yorubaland, when a person puts on a new dress, the Yoruba pray "May your baby urinate on your new dress". This is considered a blessing when it happens.

Money: It symbolises the idea that the bride is entering a 'wealthy' family and that she too should strive to contribute to the wealth.

Usually, figure forty (10) is regarded as a marriage number in the presentation of elements as forty kolanuts

forty bitter kolanuts

forty alligator pepper

forty big yams, etc.

Figure forty in Yoruba numeration means **Ogoji** and the symbolism lies in the **ji** which means "to give out something to a person absolutely". In this idea therefore, the bride is heartily given to the bridegrooms' family absolutely. The bride is

230

given to the bridegroom just as the bridegroom is given to the bride; both are to share the joyful experience of togetherness.

There are certain symbolic traditions which must be observed by either the bride or the bridegroom or by both. We maynote the following:

a) That the bride should carry a pitcher of water which she will break into pieces at the threshold of the bridegroom's house. She should then try to reset the broken pieces and collect the water back into the pot. It is when she is able to do this that she could "leave" the husband's house. The implication of this tradition is that as it is impossible for the lady to collect the water back so also will it be symbolically impossible for her to abandon her bridegroom.

b) That the bride should not meet the bridegroom at home when she is being led to her groom's house admist singing and dancing. The popular story connected with this tradition is that one bridegroom who, in his impatience, watched the in-coming procession over a mud-wall, was crushed to death as the wall fell on him. The lesson is that the bridegroom should not be unnecessarily anxious throughout his new phase of life which commences at marriage.

c) **Washing of the bride's feet:** The bride's feet are usually washed with cold water directly at the entrance of the bridegroom's house. This symbolises that the bride enters her new home with clean and blissful feet which will usher good destiny into the home.

d) **Right foot:** After the washing by the most senior wife of the compound, the bride steps into the threshold of the house with the right foot first. 'Right' symbolises goodness and all virtuos principles. The most senior wife's part is symbolic of bestowing on the new bride, protection and quidance and the same blessings which she, as a wife in the household, had enjoyed; (her children would have become adults and possibly married) it is hoped that the new bride will be similarly blessed.

(III) In Benin, when a baby girl is born, suitors may begin to approach her parents for her hand, sending to them a log of wood and a bundle of yams; this is known as **ivu-omo** "asking for the child".

Ideally a man should obtain a first wife for each of his sons and it is common for men to have girls betrothed to themselves with the object of securing them for their sons who are still minors. When the father of the girl, with the approval of his own father or elder brother, has chosen a suitable man, he informs him of the date of the formal betrothal. The suitor prepares gifts which in some villages consist of a jar of palmwine, two trays of sliced coconut with two kola-nuts on each and 24 pence. These are taken to the altar of the girl's patrilineal ancestors to notify them of the betrothal. The suitor kneels before the girls' father who says "We give the child to you".

Henceforth the suitor should give service (11) to his prospective parents-in-law, giving presents of yams to the father and mother each year, helping the former on his farm, and providing the mother with firewood etc.

When the girl has passed puberty, the father informs the suitor that the time for him to claim her is approaching. When a date has been fixed, the latter prepares more gifts of wine, kola and coconut as further offerings to the ancestors of the girl to notify them that the marriage is about to take place and to ask their help in making it a fruitful and prosperous one. It is at this stage that the groom or his father makes the marriage payment of £12 (N24) to the girl's father, together with gifts for the mother and for the "people of the house".

A day is then fixed for the ceremony of "taking the bride to her husband". The latter's relatives and friends gather at his house to dance and sing. Meanwhile the girl is conducted by her brothers, sisters, and friends, carrying her property, to the husband's house. Her father and mother do not come, for, it is said, they are too sorrowful at "losing" a daughter, but it is a joyful occasion.

On arrival, the bride, feigning shyness, is placed on her husband's lap by her brother. The husband's senior wife, if he has one, or some other woman in the house, brings a bowl of water in which money or cowries have been placed and washes the bride's hands. This rite symbolises the acceptance of her into the household and the money expresses the hope that the marriage will be fruitful. She is then led away to be bathed and she eats a solitary meal. The husband then entertains the bride's party and makes gifts to them; some for themselves and some to take back to his parents-in-law. The bridal party leaves and the husband continues to entertain his own people with feasting and dancing.

About two days later, the husband goes to thank the parents of his bride and is entertained by them. A few days later, the father pays a return visit. On the seventh day after the bride's arrival, her mother comes to see her and to demand the cloth on which the pair slept on the first night. (12) If the girl proved to be a virgin, the cloth is given to the mother who receives presents in cash and is entertained by the husband; but

232

if otherwise, an empty kolanut pod is given to the mother who would not wait any longer because the message would have been understood that their daughter was a flirt before marriage. The same day the bride cleans the walls of the husband's ancestoral shrine and prayers are said for her. It is on this day too that she enters the kitchen and cooks for the first time.

At first, the girl is made to live with another of the husband's wives or with his mother or some other woman in the house, and may remain with them until she has given birth to her first child; then she is given a room of her own.

(IV) Among the Tivs, marriage takes any of the following forms:

Exchange Marriage: "Every man takes his immediate younger sister as his marriage ward, gives her to another man, who in return gives him his ward as wife. These two women, called exchange partners, (13) then bear children of the same number and sex. On the deaths of the wives the matter is finished. In practice, complications arose at every step.

Marriage by Capture: Closely associated with exchange marriage is this type called **Iye** - "a term applying to an arrangement between two lineages, generally adjoining **utar,** to allow the mutual capture of wives (i.e. marriage by elopement) without revenge". (14)

Where such a treaty existed between lineages A x B, a man of A might elope with a girl of B without fear of her kinsmen's vengeance. Generally, someone was sent to inform her kinsmen of her whereabouts and presents were made to the parents-in-law.

Marriage by Purchase: During the days of exchange marriage, a man might purchase a wife from the **Udam** and sometimes from very distant Tiv lineages. The purchase would be made with wealth in the form of cattle, cloths or brass rods. A man could be sure of keeping such a wife and her children, but after his death the children ran every risk of being considered slaves.

Marriage Ceremony: On the wedding night the groom must distribute tobacco to all the previously married men in the compound and must kill a chicken or two to be eaten by all the previously married men.

On the same night the mother-in-law or senior wife of the new wife kills a chicken for her; the feathers are plucked and placed in the thatch over the door of the hut in which she is placed.

Generally, on the second or third day, a goat is killed by the man's father or by his compound head for the bride;

all the people who "received the wife" receive pieces of this meat.

When the bride "comes out" she is made to dance to the hut in which she will live, and there she is smeared with camwood. The next morning, for the first time, she goes with her mother-in-law or senior wife to the stream to draw water.

Other marriage ceremony is called "staying the night": a wedding dance participated in by the husband's group, dances given by the husband's age-set in his compound and in the market, or if the groom "stole" or captured his wife, he may build a mud platform and give a very large dance and beer drink to mark his exploit.

(V) Among the Igbo people, partents of the richer class often select a wife (or wives) for a son (15) whilst he is still quite a boy, irrespective of his wishes or inclinations, he probably is not even told of the transaction until it is an accomplished fact, and the girl is presented to him as his wife. However, in the majority of cases the youngman makes his own choice.

If he happens to meet a girl who attracts his attention, he immediately institutes inquiries as to her parents and whether she has already been engaged or not. If she is free, he endeavours to elicit through her friends, information concerning her capabilities. The intermediaries, therefore, proceed to open up negotiations followed by the youngman visiting the girl in her home. Later, as evidence of love is being realised, the youngman presents a bottle of gin or a pot of palmwine offered as **oji** (kola); if the present is accepted, family relations are established but no mention should be made at that state of the contemplated marriage. (16)

In Aba, Imo State, after the initial courtship, the parents of the girl are contacted. And on a given date by the family of the bride, the two families will meet. The lady will be given a cup of wine by her father who will instruct her to drink some of it and give the rest to whomever she likes. If she drinks and gives the rest to the prospective youngman, their marriage starts from there.

After paying a bride-price of seven Naira the bride becomes his wife followed by a big feast for visitors, families and friends. Nowadays the bride-price depends on the status (educational standard) of the lady. It ranges from N120.00 to N800.00.

The African Traditional Home

The basis of the African home, as of every other home in the world, is the family. The word "family" however has been used here both in the limited sense of the Western world and in the more extended African sense in which even very distant relations are regarded as "brothers" and "sisters".

The nature of the family hierarchy reveals the way in which this extended family asserts its influence on the immediate family. The father of the home is regarded as the "Head" of the family and he has the last say in most matters. But instead of the wife or wives coming next in importance as one would expect, they come only after the father's kin, i.e. his immediate brothers and sisters. This, of course, is understandable in a polygynous society where to choose one of the many wives as a confidant is to expose her to the envy of her compeers. In most families, in fact, even the first son has greater authority in the house than any of the wives and sometimes than his mother.

Within the hierarchy so described, certain conventions and courtesies are observed. The father is the object of great respect, often verging towards reverence both by the children and even by wives.

The mother, however, should be thought of in the content of a polygynous home. Her children are her main gains from the marriage, and their achievements are her only happiness. This happiness has to be protected from the envy of the less fortunate mothers or wives of the same husband.

Love and respect are the most important things which keep the African traditional married life going. Whatever might be the pattern of marriage it is essential for everybody in the family circle to intensify togetherness. Towards attaining this objective, therefore, each member of the family or of the extended families has his or her roles to play; and to deviate from the norms is to pave way for divorce, and unpleasantness.

The family-head protects all members and their properties from external force. He keeps rigidly to the traditional norms of performing religious rituals, judging cases without fear or favour and teaching the young ones the virtuous ways of behaving.

The senior wife sees also to the welfare of members of the family and directs the younger wives and children in performing their house-hold roles. She teaches the younger wives by precept and always strives to nurture the young children in love and firmness.

Disputes among the young couples are settled by the family heads or by age mates (17) or by lineage heads or clan heads. Attempts would be made to settle matrimonial disputes especially since much had gone into courtship and marriage ceremonies.

With the nature of the long, fairly expensive and service-rendering courtship, both the wife and the husband are careful in managing their married life affairs. The wife knows her duties in the home and with due sense of responsibility, both comfort and happiness are achieved. The husband too has to demonstrate a high sense of responsibility for his family. He must realise that if he is the "Head", the wife is the "Neck"; without the neck, the head cannot stand. Indeed "divorce is said to have been unusual and forbidden in many towns" (18) but it may result from ill-treatment, witchcraft, adultery or any other vicious crime. Nowadays, regrettably, by the nature of the urgency in contracting marriages neither founded on deep love of the husband and wife nor upon the approval of the two families, such marriages quickly land on the rocks. Polygyny, being the popular traditional way of marriage in Africa, has proved more successful over the ages than our present monogamous system of marriage. There is nothing wrong with a rightly managed home in the polygynous system. The Church is considering very seriously the relaxing of the rigid rule of depriving its members of the polygynous class, the partaking of the Holy Eucharist. If their money are acceptable as Church dues, surely their eternal life must be catered for also.

Islam is clear on the two issues of polygyny and monogamy, and prescribes no pretence. It has commonly been held in Christendom that the distinctive feature of Islamic marriage is the permission to have four wives. The practice is based on a verse of the Holy Qur'an which says: "If ye fear that ye may not act with equity in regard to the orphans, marry such of the women as seem good to you: two or three or four - but if ye fear that ye may not be fair (to several wives), then one". (19)

Emphasis is placed here on love and being fair to the wives. Any form of marriage which lacks the fairness emphasised here is a faked marriage and cannot last long.

All religious bodies in Nigeria must continue to say it loud that the ingredients of a lasting marriage include the following - love, mutual understanding, helping each other, suffering for each other, absence of self centred materialistic values etc. Beauty is not the basis of a successful marriage, neither are egoistic propensities. The most important aspect of African marriage is simply "good character".

African culture gives much value to character. An Odu in Ifa emphasises character building which cuts across a common heritage in Africa. It says:

> It was divined for Orunmila,
> That he should take Good Character for wife.
> Orunmila replied saying: 'Good Character is the virtue of life;
> If a person has a wife who lacks character,
> He, indeed, possesses another's wife;
> If he has a child who lacks manners,
> It is another person's child'.

Every good thing in our culture should be preserved; but problems cannot but arise with our mixture of our traditional system with foreign system. Our moral values should also be upheld and respect paid to our extended family heads and relatives.

Our children should be well acquainted with members of our extended families, and indeed with the family history (including culture in its widest sense). Peace in the world starts with the individual who is morally brought up in a peaceful and happy home. Dr. Aggrey is often quoted as saying, "when you educate a man, you educate an individual; when you educate a woman, you educate a family". (29) We therefore owe a great deal to our women in assisting immensely in moulding the good character of children in order that our nation may produce virtuous and useful citizens.

Footnote

1 E.G. Parrinder: **African Traditional Religion** S.P.C.K., London, 1962, p. 96.
2 Z.K. Matthews: "Marriage Customs among the Barolong" **Africa,** Vol. XIII, January, 1940, No. 1. p. 7.
3 John S. Mbiti: **An Introduction to African Religion** Heinemann, London, 1975, p. 98.
4 Cf. Colossians 3 **Revised Standard Version of the Holy Bible.**
5 John S. Mbiti: **Op. Cit.** p. 156.

6 J.O. Kayode: **Symbology with particular reference to the religion of the Yoruba.** (Unpublished) Ph.D. Thesis, University of Ibadan, June 1975, p. 208.

7 Cf. **The Book of Common Prayer.** Oxford 1928. A Table of kindred and Affinity wherein whosoever are related are forbidden by the Church of England to marry together. p. 383.

8 P.H. Gulliver: **Social Control in an African Society. A study of the Arusha: Agricultural Masai of Northern Tangayika** Routledge & Kegan Paul, London, 1963. p. 35.

9 A.R. Radcliffe - Brown and Daryll Forde: **African Systems of Kinship and Marriage:** Oxford University Press, London, 1967, p. 46.

10 J.O. Kayode: **Op. Cit.** p. 210.

11 Daryll Forde (Ed.), **The Benin Kingdom and the Edospeaking peoples of South-Western Nigeria,** Ethnographic Survey of Africa, Western Africa, London International African Institute part XIII. 1970, p. 48.

12 To ascertain the bride (their daughter) has never had sexual intercourse before her first copulation. It is a pride to the bride's parents and the bride in particular: not only among the Benin but also among the Yoruba and indeed in many parts of Africa.

13 Laura and Paul Bohannan (Daryll Forde) Ed.: **The Tiv of Central Nigeria,** London, Sidney Press 1969, p. 69.

14 **Ibid.**

15 G.T. Basden: **Among the Ibos of Nigeria,** Frank Cass & Co. Ltd., 1966, p. 69.

16 **Ibid.** p. 70.

17 E.g. P.H. Gulliver: **Op. Cit.** plate 8.,

18 Daryll Forde: **Op. Cit.** p. 61.

19 **The Holy Qur'an** (4:3).

20 W.E. Ward: **Short History of Ghana,** Longmans, London, 1960, p. 255.

SOURCE: RELIGIOUS UNDERSTANDING AND CO-OPERATION IN NIGERIA. Proceedings of a Seminar Organized By the Department of Religions, University of Ilorin, Ilorin, Nigeria 7th-11th August, 1978 (Edited by I.A.B. Balogun, B.A., Ph.D. (London) Professor and Head of Department)

THE CONTRIBUTION OF AFRICAN TRADITIONAL RELIGION TO NATION BUILDING

by

S.N. Ezeanya

Introduction

O God of all creation
Grant this our one request
Help us to build a nation
Where no man is oppressed
And so with peace and plenty
Nigeria may be blessed. (1)

Nation building is a herculian task whose magnitude only very few realize. Some see the work as consisting mainly in technological development and the setting up of all kinds of modern structures; accumulating almost inexhaustible supply of the most sophisticated and deadly weapons, ability to defend the frontiers of a nation, high percentage of mass literacy, control of buoyant economy and in short, being in possession of all kinds of material goods which are calculated to make man's life happy here below and guarantee national security by force of arms.

But is that the type of goal that Nigeria envisages in her anthem? I do not think so. Rather, in this beautiful anthem, Nigeria prays to God, the Creator of all things, to help her build a nation in which no man is oppressed, namely, a nation in which everyone gets that which belongs to him by right. She prays too that Nigeria be blessed with peace. "Peace" the Second Vatican Council says:

> is not merely the absence of war. Nor can it be reduced solely to the maintenance of a balance of power between enemies. Nor is it brought about by dictatorship. Instead, it is rightly and appropriately called 'an enterprise of justice' (Is. 32:7). Peace results from that harmony built into human society by its divine Founder, and actualized by men as they thirst after ever greater justice. (2)

She prays also that Nigeria be blessed with plenty. "Plenty" in this context should not be interpreted solely in a material sense for a nation can have plenty of material wealth and yet within it we find many people languishing in penury and moral decadence. It should be taken to mean plenty of those things that man needs to live a decent livelihood in accordance with human dignity and God's design for man. Therefore, it should be understood to mean plenty ofmaterial blessings which come from God and plenty of spiritual gifts which are also bestowed by God, prominent among which is love for one another as children of the same heavenly Father. In short, Nigeria is praying to build a kingdom of justice, love and peace.

The building of a nation such as we envisage, cannot be achieved by the mere accumulation of material things or the procurement of a life of comfort and ease often to a limited few. This alone will not make man really happy for the simple reason that man is not mere matter. He has a spiritual part which matter is too base to satisfy. He is a composite of matter and he has his destiny far beyond the confines of this world. He has an eternal destiny.

Any project for the building of a nation which loses sight of, or ignores the spiritual and material well-being of man taken as a whole, cannot succeed in building a nation "in which no man is oppressed". Therefore, the work of nationbuilding has both the material and the spiritual aspects.

Aristotle, the great Greek philosopher was well aware of this and that was why he said that:

> ... the end of the state is not mere life; it is rather a good quality of life ... Similarly, it is not the end of the state to provide an alliance of mutual defence against all injury or to ease exchange and promote economic intercourse ... But it is the cardinal issue of goodness or badness in the life of the polis which always engages the attention of any state that concerns itself to secure a system of good laws well obeyed. The conclusion which clearly follows is that any polis which is truely so called, and is not merely one in name must devote itself to the end of encouraging goodness. Otherwise a political association sinks into mere alliance, which only differs in space (i.e. the contiguity of itsmembers) from other forms of alliance where the members live at a distance from one another. (3)

According to Aristotle, the work of nation-building must concern itself with more than mere temporal care of the individual. It is solidly hinged on the formation of man in such a way that the polis enjoys true goodness. The building of a nation is first and foremost the building of the people that make up the nation which in effect boils down to the building up of the individuals themselves. Justice, love and peace which are essential ingredients for nation-building, are products of the human heart. These qualities cannot be imposed by the force of arms. They cannot exist in the state if they do not first and foremost exist in human hearts and minds. Man must deliberately make efforts to do good and avoid evil. He must see himself as a creature who owes his existence to a higher power, from whom he came and to whom he must render account for his behaviour and who ultimately will reward him for his conduct.

This is where religion comes in. True religion teaches man that he is a creature of an all-powerful Father on whom he depends for his life and well-being and to whom he must render an account of his life. Man learns from religion that he has specific obligations to himself, to his fellow human beings and to the society to which he belongs and above all, to his Maker. Religion of its nature tends to unite individuals, communities, and nations under the divine umbrella of one and the same heavenly Father, God.

Remove this religious inclination from man, blot out of his mind the belief in his Maker who rewards the good and punishes the wicked - the fact that he has an eternal destiny, and what we have left is an animal who acts out of sheer material and egoistic motives and sheer convenience, one who obeys the law out of fear of punishment or hope of material gain or for pure intellectual satisfaction.

Religion, therefore has a vital role to play in the building of a nation. And in this paper, we shall consider what the African Traditional Religion has to offer specifically in the difficult task of nation-building. We shall look at the basic elements in the African Traditional Religion, the traditional religious attitude of the African towards life in general, in order to be able to see what this religion has to offer to Nigeria.

The African Traditional Religion Permeates Every Department of Life

Professor Mbiti, in the opening sentences of the very first chapter of his book, **African Religions and Philosophy.** summarised the traditional religious attitude of Africans when he said that:

> Africans are notoriously religious, and each people has its own religious system with a set of beliefs and practices. Religion permeates all departments of life so fully that it is not easy or possible always to isolate it. A study of these religious systems is therefore, ultimately a study of the peoples themselves in all complexities of both traditional and modern life ... Religion is the strongest element in traditional background and exerts probably the greatest influence upon the thinking and living of the people concerned. (4)

For the Africans, life is religion and religion is life. It is unimaginable for the Africans, following their traditional environment and culture, to think of human life divorced from religion. For the African, there is nothing like a person becoming converted to embrace a religion because life is impossible for anyone who is not religious from birth. (5) There cannot be existence, not to talk of a person making any head-way in life if he divorces himself from religion.

Man has an innate obligation to be religious. It is unnatural for the African that man should be otherwise than religious from the cradle or rather, conception to grave. The African lives, moves and has his being in a religious atmosphere, in an atmosphere controlled by countless invisible powers both good and evil that steer the course of human destiny. After observing how religion thoroughly permeated the life of every Igbo-man, Bishop Shanahan of immortal memory came to the conclusion,

> that the average native was admirably suited by environment and training, for an explanation of life in terms of the spirit rather than of the flesh. He was no materialist. Indeed nothing was farther from his mind than a materialistic philosophy of existence. It made no appeal to him. (7)

For the African it is not possible for an individual or society to survive and make anything out of life without religion put into practice. Pope Paul VI of blessed memory echoed the same truth when he said that:

> The constant and general foundation of African tradition is the spiritual view of life. Here we have more than the so-called animistic concept, in the sense given to this term in the history of religions at the end of the last century. We have a deeper, broader and more universal concept which considers all living beings and visible nature itself as linked with the world of the invisible and the spirit. In particular it has never considered man as mere matter limited to earthly life, but recognises in him the presence and power of another spiritual element, in virtue of which human life is always related to the after life. (8)

This point, namely, the absolute and unconditional dependence of man on God and the powers above man is fundamental in the traditional life of the African. Any other points we may make on the contribution of the African Traditional Religion to nation-building take their origin from it and are based on it. The saying of Jesus Christ that: "apart from me, you can do nothing", (9) is an axiom in the traditional African religion. It does not require any proof. The people are convinced they can do absolutely nothing cut off from God and the preternatural powers that sustain them. For the African,

> To be is to be religious in a religious universe. That is the philosophical understanding behind Africans myths, customs, traditions, beliefs, morals actions and social relationship. (10)

The Unique Place of the Supreme God

The Supreme God occupies an altogether unique place in the religious life of the African.

> All African peoples believe in God. They take this belief for granted. It is at the centre of African Religion and dominates all its other beliefs. (11)

243

It is to him alone that creation is attributed. He is the maker of all things, vsible and invisible.

> This belief is common everywhere in Africa. For that reason, there are many names which describe him as creator of all things, Moulder, Begetter, Bearer, Maker, Potter, Fashioner, Architect, Carpenter, Originator, Constructor, and so on. (12)

All other beings owe their origin to him. It was he who made the minor divinities through whom he governs the universe. Though direct cult to him is scarce in many parts of Africa, he nevertheless remains the supreme power that governs the world and sustains things in existence.

In the message referred to above, Pope Paul VI clearly outlines the special place of the Supreme God in the life of the African when he said:

> In this spiritual concept, the most important element generally found is the idea of God, as the first ultimate cause of all things. This concept ... is very different from culture to culture, but the fact remains that the presence of God permeates African life, as the presence of a higher being, personal and mysterious ... Nearly always fear of God's omnipotence is set aside and He is invoked as Father. Prayers made to him whether by individuals or groups, are spontaneous, at times moving, while among the forms of sacrifice the sacrfice of first fruits stands out because of what it plainly signifies. (13)

In his fatherly care for man, God made the minor divinities that take care of the various departments of life. For his overall wellbeing, progress, security, protection from his enemies, recovery from sickness, man must have constant recourse to them by prayers and sacrifices of different kinds. He must be constantly on good terms with them and when, knowingly or unknowingly he offends them, he must quickly offer prayers and sacrifices of atonement or purification, as the case may be to restore harmony in their relationship.

Belief in Life after Death

One central theme runs through the African concept
of man's destiny: namely, that at death, while the
carcass in buried in the earth, the essential person
passes on into another life, it is held responsible for
deeds or misdeeds, and it is rewarded or punished accordingly by the author of life ... Thus in Africa it
is strongly believed that death does not write FINISH
to human life. There is in man an element which is
immortal; and this sense of immortality gives comfort
in privation and misfortune and acts as a revenge to
death. (14)

This belief in life after death has obviously a far reaching effect
on the present life in so far as the kind of life an individual
lives hereafter is determined by his present life. Since all are
anxious to have a happy hereafter, everyone makes a strenuous
effort to live a morally blameless life; all the more so because
one likes to enjoy the company of one's ancestors who are waiting
to welcome their dear ones home.

The belief is therefore another great incentive for the
Africans to a life of a very high standard of morality at all levels,
but especially among those who play a leading role in society.
Village and clan heads who are often spiritual leaders as well,
are expected to play their leadership role by exemplary life.

The Dignity of the Human Person

Even a cursory glance at the traditional religious
practices of the African shows it is anthropocentric
in the sense that all the religious practices invariably
point to one objective, namely LIFE and its preservation. Prayers and sacrifices offered to the Supreme
God, the minor divinities, the ancestors have all one
end in view, namely, the welfare of man. Even when
offerings are made to evil spirits, the only reason for
doing so is to ward them off with some objects often
not good for human consumption or for a real sacrifice
to benevolent spirits or powers that help man. Divina-

245

tion, consultations of oracles, the use of charms and magic and so on, have only one end in view, namely, the preservation of life. (15)

It is right to hold that in the African thought, man sees himself as the centre of the universe. God has made him the focal point of the universe. Some scholars have interpreted African religious thought as a pyramid:

At the apex was God the Supreme Being, On the two sides were the great spiritual powers manifested in gods and ancestors, and at the base were the lower powers of magic. In the middle was man under the influence of many different kinds of power. (16)

GOD (The Maker and
General Overseer).

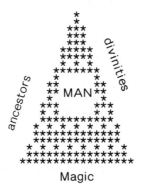

Magic

Animals, plants and other creatures, all subservient to man.

Man is therefore seen as the paragon of God's creative power. He is such a precarious gift of God that everything must be done to preserve him in existence. Human life is considered so sacred, that it cannot be taken awaywith impunity. Suicide is a most abominable crime against the human person. Among the Igbo for instance, any person guilty of suicide is denied formal burial. (17)

It must however, be admitted that in general, the African Traditional Society adopted a different attitude towards those who did not come from the same "town". The sacredness of life according to many African traditions, cannot be applied universally to include every human being in the same degree.

The killing of human beings for example, was common in the olden days either in the course of funeral rites as a means of providing attendant spirits to accompany a dead chief into the great beyond, or as a sacrifice to atone for sins. (18) In each case, the victim was usually someone procurred or bought from a distant town. Acts of injustice committed against a "non-native" belong to a different moral species from that committed against one who was a son of the soil. (19)

It appears therefore that most of the cases where the killing of human beings was done, were in fulfilment of convinced religious obligations:

> either to satisfy the demand of a divinity for a human victim so that a community might not perish or because it was necessary to give a departed chief some retinues to accompany him to the land of his fathers ... Where twins were killed, this was done because it was unnatural for a human being to imitate lower animals. Similarly, children who were born with feet foremost perished because such "abnormal" births were regarded as a crime against the mother earth. (20)

Apart from those aberration like the ones mentioned above which were characteristic of the primitive societies practically all over the world, the fact remains that in normal circumstances in which the people lived, life was sacred and the dignity of the human person was highly respected.

The Unifying Force of the African Traditional Religion

> God must have a place of honour in our ... National Life.

As we have already stated, the African Traditional Religion firmly holds that God is the creator of everything that exists. It believes that it is God, who, both directly and often indirectly through his agents, maintains man and the entire universe in existence.

The African Traditional Religion holds firmly that both the individual and the nation must believe in the Creator and pay due homage to him in order to survive and enjoy peace and prosperity. It believes that the evils that befall individuals and societies are a result of castigation from God and his agents because of man's failure to live up to his obligations as a creature of God.

Today, with so much feverish pursuit of wealth at all levels, the basic religious principles are being trampled under foot, but of course with disastrous consequences. Most of the immortal and precious spiritual legacies of our forefathers are completely ignored by many. Many politicians think they can build a nation without any recourse to God. In this childish endeavour the African Traditional Religion says to them in the words of the Psalmist that:

> Unless the Lord builds the house, those who build it labour in vain. (21)

In other words, the religion of our forefathers says to our country that Nigeria, in order to be a truly successful nation, must give God a place of honour in its national life. If ever there was a time when such an appeal must be heeded, it is more so now. Once the country has the love and fear of God strongly entrenched in its national life then the nation is on a safe road to progress in all respects.

In its closing messages to earthly rulers, the Second Vatican Council said, among other things that:

> We do honour to your authority and your sovereignty, we respect your office, we recognise your just laws, we esteem those who make them and those who apply them. But we have a sacrosanct word to speak to you and it is this: Only God is great. God alone is the beginning and the end. God alone is the Source of your authority and the Foundation of your laws. (22)

This is the appeal which the African Traditional Religion is making to the nation: to build Nigeria on the solid rock of a living faith in God.

Morality in Nation Building

Among the Africans, there was never a question of adherence to the faith handed down by the forefathers without a corresponding practice which showed itself in morality. Morality flows naturally from religious creed. Man, as we pointed out above has a hereafter whose condition is determined by his present life. To gain that hereafter as a place of enjoyment, man must behave in ways consonant with the endless demands of the divinities and ancestors. Above all, he must see to it that his behaviour does not precipitate calamity not only for himself and his family, but also for society at large.

What Placide Temples says about the Bantu equally applies to the Nigerian society, namely that:

> Every injustice is an attempt upon the life (so upon the vital force) of the person injured and the malice in it proceeds from the great respect due to human life, the supreme gift of God. In this sense, every injustice, every attempt against human life ... is a stupendous evil, an evil measured in terms of the worth of life and infinitely exceeding in every case all calculations in economic terms of the loss suffered, but the measure of the outrage on life endured, which will serve as the basis of assessment of compensation or damages. (23)

For the African, good and evil behaviour, but especially the latter, have their social dimensions. This is a logical consequence of the people's belief in the close relationship between man and the Supernatural powers that steer the course of his destiny and on whom man depends entirely for his life and progress. If God, the divinities and the ancestors are offended, the offence, if not quickly atoned for, has its unfailing repercussions on man.

Every individual who is acting, whether in private or in public, whether by day or by night, whether on his own behalf or on behalf of the community of which he forms a part is acting in full awareness that the eyes of God, the divinities, spirits and ancestors are on him, taking note of every moral act of his. Every act posited, has a corresponding reward or punishment recorded against it.

It is this awareness of the unfailing sanction from the divinities that was responsible for the prevalence of law and order in the traditional society where before there were no policemen or soldiers to enforce the laws of state. Today on the other hand, our nation is plagued with armed robbery; bribery and corruption, embezzlement of public funds, widespread sexual immorality at all levels of society, cases of murder for various material ends, indiscipline in schools, shameless desecration of holy places by stealing, and so on.

When the traditional society was strictly faithful to its religion, those crimes were very rare indeed. Professor Mbiti puts it very well when he said that:

> African religious beliefs, values and practices are directed towards strengthening the moral life of each society. Morals are the food and drink which keep society alive, healthy and happy. Once there is a moral breakdown, the whole integrity of society also breaks down and the end is tragic. ... Traditional African societies kept a close eye for any individual weeds in its moral life and often uprooted them before they twined human life into an immoral wasteland. In that exercise, the belief in God, the invisible world (with its spirits) pressing hard on our visible world and the continuation of life after death seam to have made a lasting contribution. Thus African Religion emphasizes the importance of morals in practice, and insists that they must extend into all areas of life for the welfare of the individual and society at large. (24)

Patriotism

Patriotism is defined as:

> love and loyal or zealous support of one's own country, especially in all matters involving other countries (25)

In the traditional African society, we know that patriotism was extremely high. In discussing patriotism here, I am not thinking of a Nigerian of the last century showing love for, and loyalty to the whole nation, for this was practically impossible as a result of many factors some of which were physical, which limited communication and social life on a wide basis. Some of those factors were the language, border disputes, ethnic differences, absence of roads, and so on.

However, the essential elements that make up patriotism were present in every town which constituted a homogenic entity. Men made great sacrifices for the welfare of their town. They defended their borders gallantly, to the points of paying the supreme sacrifice for their towns, they maintained peace and order in the town, offered prayers in common for the welfare of the citizens, honoured their heroes with coveted titles both in life and after death, worked zealously and free of charge for their towns, donated generously in cash and kind for the welfare of their town. The town or clan-head who often was a religious leader, enjoyed the esteem of the people and was a living symbol of the unity of the town. People so loved their fatherland and were so attached to it that even when death occurred outside the fatherland, every effort was made to bring the individual home and bury him with his fathers.

This devotion to the fatherland was essentially linked up with religion. The inhabitants of any given area are together under the special custody of the local divinities to whom each and every member must show love and loyalty and under whose guardianship they are all united. In fact, to do anything against the welfare of the town is to incur the anger of the town divinities and ancestors.

This patriotism, limited though it may be in scope, has nevertheless provided, a sound basis for patriotism in the present day Nigeria. Nigerians today should learn from the traditional set-up to love their country, respect its leaders and be ready to serve the nation and make veritable sacrifices for the welfare of the state. Everybody, from all works of life, should make his or her own contribution in order to build a nation where no man is oppressed.

Conclusion

Nigeria aspires after greatness. It strives to build a state in which all are united, a state free from tribal hatred and prejudices, a state in which everyone gets that to which he is entitled, a state free from the endemic vice of bribery and corruption, and where justice, love and peace reign supreme. The aspiration is noble and laudable but Nigeria must be ready to pay the price.

She cannot import these virtues from abroad with her oil money, neither can she impose them with force of arms. God, the Maker of man is the sole Source of all that is good. If Nigeria wants to enjoy peace, prosperity and internal cohesion, she must make room and a spacious one, for the author of peace and unity in her national life, namely God as her forebears did.

Etienne Gilson, the world renowned philosopher puts it very well when he said:

> Just now, States are beginning to realize that they are not equipped to provide themselves with the kind of citizens they need. They do not need citizens merely, but law abiding citizens; that is people who neither steal nor kill, even though they could get away with it; not judges but incorrupitble judges; not police-men but policemen who do not draw a salary from the very gangsters they are to catch; not soldiers but soldiers who are willing to lay down their lives for the defense of their country. (27)

The three major religions of Nigeria, the African traditional religion, Islam and Christianity are saying the same thing loud and clear, namely, that religion is an indispensable recipe for building a happy and stable nation. Each religion has its own specific contribution to make for a united and peaceful Nigeria.

The African traditional religion has provided the basic religious and moral structure for constructing a solid national edifice. Foremost among the constituent elements of that structrure is belief in one God, the Maker of all things, visible and invisible. To attempt to build a nation without God is to hope to construct a massive structure upon the foundation of sand. Such a building will collapse at the slightest gust of wind and the fall will be great.

By holding firmly to the belief that man is a composite of matter and spirit and that there is a hereafter, where each must get his due reward for his conduct, the African traditional religion provides a very efficacious incentive for doing good and avoiding evil. Man must try always to behave in a manner that is conducive to the welfare of the individual as well as society. Man, according to the African traditional religion is living his life in an environment that is eminently peopled with spiritual forces and he must live a life that will make him always acceptable to the supernatural powers on which he depends.

252

Nigeria as a nation, must learn from the traditional religon that the nation as such, no less than the individuals that make it up, needs prayers for its survival. Religion supplies the basic principles of morality which if faithfully adhered to, helps man to live well or reform himself should he have erred. The crisis of our society today are crisis borne out of sheer neglect of God or downright denial of him and our traditional religious and moral values. Fulton Sheen has said that:

> Man, by attempting to exist either apart from God or defiant of God, has made the world as delirious as his own mind is neurotic. The crisis today is so deep in its causes that all social and political attempts to deal with it are bound to be as ineffective as talcum powder in curing jaundice. It is man who has to be remade first; then society will be remade by the restored new man ... The constant refusal of man to allow a suprahistoric Divine Power to break into his closed mind is the pride which prepares catastrophe. (28)

Nigeria must consider herself fortunate to be blessed with such a basically sound, and enduring religious and moral tradition. We are however, aware that not every element of our religious traditional heritage is sound and beneficial to mankind. But we maintain nevertheless that the religion of our ancestors minus the harmful elements has still in its basic traditional beliefs and practices enough salutary elements with which it is ready to meet other religions in a fraternal spirit of fruitful dialogue to reconstruct this nation.

One of the saddest mistakes of our growing generation of intellectuals and neopagans is to despise our traditional religous and cultural heritage as downright evil and primitive. But we know that an objective appraisal has shown that Nigeria is blessed with a previous religious legacy. We must go back to recover the moral and spiritual foundations on which our traditional society was built. Let us get hold of them and make use of them in the sacred task of nation-building.

This is the traditional approach of the church as is clear from the official pronouncement of Pius XII in his encyclical letter On Promoting Catholic Missions. The Pope said, among other things:

> The Church from the beginning down to our own time has always followed this wise practice: let not the

Gospel on being introduced into any new land destroy or extinguish whatever its people possess that is naturally good, just or beautiful ... Whatever is not inseparably bound up with superstition and error will always receive kindly consideration and, when possible, will be preserved intact. (29)

I will conclude with the words of the learned historian Christopher Dawson which aptly apply to African Traditional Religion vis-a-vis its contribution to the work of nation-building:

What is vital is to recover the moral and spiritual foundations on which the lives of both the individual and the culture depends: to bring home to the average man that religion is not a pius fiction which has nothing to do with the facts of life, but that it is concerned with realities, that it is in fact the path way to reality and the law of life. (30)

Footnotes

1 First Nigerian National Anthem.
2 **The Documents of Vatican II**; The Church Today, N. 78.
3 **The Politics of Aristotle,** translated by Ernest Baker, Oxford, 1961, pp. 118-119.
4 John S. Mbiti, **African Religious and Philosophy,** Heinemann, London, 1970, p. 1.
5 "It is difficult to separate religion from the social groups. A person born in such a society, unless he requires a professional knowledge of being a priest or chief he needs not receive formal religious instructions such as those given by the christian churches. A member is born and grows up with the beliefs and practices of his religion. He acquires his religion by virtue of being a member of his society." Kwabena Ampinsah, Topics on Wet **African Traditional Religion, Vol. 1,** Adwinsa Publications Limited, Ghana, 1977, p. 7; cf. also John S. Mbiti, African Religions and Philosophy, o.c., p. 103.
6 Cf. Acts 17:28. "In him we live, move and have our being."

7 John P. Jordan, C.S.Sp., **Bishop Shanahan of Southern Nigeria,** Elo Press Ltd., Dublin, 1971, p. 115.

8 Pope Paul VI in **Message of His Holiness Pope Paul VI to all the Peoples of Africa for the Promotion of the Religious, Civil and Social Good of their Continent,** Vatican, City 1968, N. 8.

9 Jn. 15:5.

10 John S. Mbiti, **African Religions and Philosophy,** o.c. p. 262.

11 John S. Mbiti, **An Introduction to African Traditional Religion,** Heinemann, London, 1975, p. 40.

12 John S. Mbiti, An Introduction to African Traditional Religion, o.c., p. 44.

13 Pope Paul VI, l.c.

14 J.O. Awolalu, 'The African Traditional View of Man' in **Orita, Ibadan Journal of Religious Studies,** VI/2 (1972) 116.

15 S.N. Ezeanya, **The Dignity of Man in the Traditional Religion of Africa** (an unpublished article), Nsukka, 1976, p. 6. See also Basden, G.T., Among the Igbos of Nigeria, Frank Cass and Co. Ltd., London, 1966, p. 224.

16 E.G. Parrinder, "Monotheism and Pantheism in Africa" in **Journal of Religion in Africa,** Vol. III, 2 (1970) 85.

17 Cf. G.T. Basden, **Among the Ibos of Nigeria,** Frank Cass & Co. Ltd., London, 1966, pp. 58, 60, 270, 276. Formal burial with appropriate rituals is denied to any one who has met his death through the power of the devil. This, is what people call "Onwu Ekwensu". It is believed that people who die through the power of the devil have received fitting punishment for the offences, some of which are secret, which they have committed against human life in one form or another.
    "People dying as a result of accident; women dying in child birth, lunatics, suicides and those who have been murdered, drowned or burned are considered as having come to their untimely ends by "Onwu Ekwensu", that is, by the instrumentality of the devil. None of these may be rubbed with "ufie" and they must be disposed of without delay." (o.c. p. 276).

18 Cf. G.T. Basden, **Among the Ibos of Nigeria,** o.c., p. 122.

19 Cf. Placide Temples, **Bantu Philosophy,** Presence Africaine, Paris, 1959, o.c., p. 142: "Towards a foreigner of equivalent status, injustice has no longer the same character of "injustice" as against the elders or brothers of a clan." Also Basden, o.c., p. 127: "... it was forbidden to eat a member of one's own community."

20   S.N. Ezeanya, o.c., p. 9.

21   Ps. 126:1.

22   **The Coduments of Vat. II,** o.c. Closing Messages: To Rulers,
     p. 729.

23   Placide Temples, o.c., p. 143.

24   John S. Mbiti, **An Introduction to African Religion,** Heine-
     mann, London, 1975, p. 181. In a paper presented at
     the 38th Annual Conference of The Nigeria Union of
     Teachers held at Ilorin in 1971, Dr. J.A. Adegbite,
     first Vice President of the N.U.T. had said, among
     other things that "From the beginning of time, God
     - call Him Nature, the First Cause, or what you will,
     revealed Himself to man in many ways. The recognition
     of His existence and of His presence in the scheme
     of things is a stronger sanction for morality than
     atheistic humanism. To deny His existence is to cut
     our moral boat from its mooring without a rudder or
     a paddle in the midst of a stormy sea". **Education for
     Public Morality,** Nigerian Union of Teachers 38th An-
     nual Conference, Ilorin, 4-6 May 1971, p. 26.

25   **Webster's New Twentieth Century Dictionary,** Unabridged,
     Second Edition.

26   G.M.P. Okoye, C.S.SP., **The Christian and Sense of Respon-
     sibility,** Lenten Pastoral, 1977, p. 14.

27   Etienne Gilson, **The Breakdown of Morals and Christian Educa-
     tion,** Doubleday & Co., New York, 1960, p. 10.

28   Fulton J. Sheen, **Peace of Soul,** Image Books, New York, 1954,
     p. 244.

29   Pope Pius XII in Encyclical **On Promoting Catholic Missions,**
     Rome 1951, N.56, 59.

30   Christopher Dawson, **The Crisis of Western Education,** Image
     Books, New York, 1965, p. 140.

AFRICAN TRADITIONAL EDUCATION: ITS EMPHASIS ON RELIGION AND MORALITY

by

A.O. Iwuagwu

The task of this paper is to analyse Traditional Education and to examine its curriculum in order to find out what place it assigns to Religion and Morality. Such an analysis, it is hoped, will help us to understand the content, aims and objectives of traditional education and it compares with modern philosophy of education.

What is Education?

For our purpose here, we simply give the layman's definition: Education is the giving of intellectual and moral training to the child or to the learner for his development and well-being and for that of his society. It involves the training of the human faculties, or the acquisition of knowledge through observation, experiment, practice and through systematic instruction.

Education covers the whole range of man's experience and the whole range of waht can be learned. It includes both the learning and the understanding of self and other beings, of the essence of life, of the physical world and of its basic relationship with the supernatural plane of existence. In the scheme of education is included the learning of ways of solving the problems of life as in the study of the Arts and Sciences. It includes the learning of a trade or business for man's "bread and butter" needs and the learning of a vocation for the service of God and man. But the "business" of education is the search for knowledge and the quest for the Truth. And the basis of this quest is the conviction that" if you find the truth, the truth will set you free".

Traditional Aims of Education

Similarly, we can briefly sum up the traditional aims and objectives of education. It aims to develop the child or the learner physically, intellectually, spiritually and morally, so that he could be useful to himself and to the community which he belongs. In other words, education trains for healthy body, mature mind and for sound life. For education is the tool created by the society with which it can "re-create" itself. It moulds the individual in order that he may "re-create" his society. In order to achieve its goal, a sound philosophy of education holds together and as sacred the four cardinal aims of education as stated above.

What is "Traditional"?

Here also we need to define what we mean by the word "traditional" as applied to the subject of this paper. We may directly ask: What makes education traditional? Two concepts come out initially. First is the "handed-over" concept in education. That is the element that is basic and has been there from the inception of the institution called education, which had been trans- mitted or ought to be transmitted from one generation to another. Secondly, education is "traditional" when it is sound and good for all times, or when it preserves or conserves the principles, ideas and content of education which are valid for all times. The preservative and the conservative value of tradition is implicit in such a definition. It is important to note that in this context, we use the word "conservative" in its original and denotative sense, and not in its connotative meaning.

Traditional education is not opposed to change of scope, the widening of curriculum and the improvement of methodology of education. It rather insists that while we change with time, the essential ideas and values of education should be faithfully carried over from one generation to another. Traditional education emphasises the fact that all is not worthless "in the way we used to do it". For the traditional concept possesses the idea of the way "it is properly done for all times". The traditional concept in education relates to the way the ordinary man, whether in Nigeria or elsewhere in the world, looks at the philosophy, aims and objectives, practice, curriculum and method of education. The "traditional" represents what is basic, what must be preserved, what is transmitted, what it ought to be, and what in education is valied for all times.

Education - Old Way

The "old way" of education in Nigeria was informal. It was not an organised system of education. There were no public institutions. The home was the centre of learning. It was the right of parents to give their children the education that suited the people's way of life. The kindred, the village, or the town were centres of formal and informal instruction. But the parents saw to it that the children were taught all that they needed to know in order to be **ezigbo mmadu** or "proper person". The elder always saw himself as the immediate teacher, who had to guide the youth until he comes to maturity.

The "old way" of education was certainly limited. It provided for the training of the body, the mind, the spirit and for the formation of good character. But the modern trend in education concentrates on the training of the body and of the mind. It tends to pay lip service to spiritual and moral training. But the traditional education achieved this goal through proper balancing of its curriculum and philosophy of knowledge in order to emphasise the unique position which religion occupies in life and the need for moral identity in life.

Traditional Curriculum of Education

The traditional curriculum of education acquainted the child first with the culture of his people. And this was based on its philosophy that education begins at home. The curriculum started with the knowledge of the language of the child's parents. This was considered essential for self-expression, for social interaction, for proper belonging and for cultural identity. The traditional curriculum of education realised that the child should not only be taught all that is good in the way of life of his people, he should also respect that culture.

It was for this reason that the study of customs and etiquette was considered an important discipline in the traditional curriculum of education. The child for instance should learn to respect age, custom and tradition. He needs to know the culture and customs of his land for self-identity, for social integration, and in order to transmit his people's culture. As a matter of fact, the duty of education is not simply to criticise and despise culture, whether secular or religious, but to understand, modify, improve and to propagate it. Education is not simply the means of vilifying culture, but of upgrading it.

Acculturation has come to stay, at least as a necessary evil. But there is the need for a studied care in Nigerian education to preserve what is of value in the indigenous ways, in the face of an impact of a total culture.

What is lacking in Nigeria educational curriculum today is proper cultural emphasis. As a result our children have despised nearly everything in our culture as inferior, old-fashioned and mundane. We have got, for instance, to a stage where our children are more proud to speak and write foreign languages than to use their mother tongue. Some of them, as a matter of fact, cannot speak or write their native language. Traditional education sees it as a serious anomaly in a curriculum of education if it acquaints the learner with foreign cultures, while it allows him to remain an alien in his own culture.

Traditional curriculum of education in Nigeria did provide for the arts and sciences. In addition to Culture and Customs, the learner studied Pure Art in order to represent life, man and the divinities. Music, both secular and religious was also studied. It was then necessary for the child to know Civics and the History of his people, unlike what happens today when a learner knows much about foreign history, but nothing about the history of his own people. Pupils learnt philosophy through proverbs and parables; and direct instruction was given on what was considered as Common Sense. As we hope to show later, Religion and Morality were more than ordinary disciples in the Curriculum.

In the Sciences, Agriculture was the first subject. As a result, the child learnt the art of Agriculture for his daily bread. Every father made sure that he taught his child his own trade; because, according to the traditional philosophy of education the child should respect, learn, or participate in what parents are doing for a living. Elementary Mathematics was studied in the form of measurement, weighing, number work, and calculation. Economics was included as a necessary, general knowledge for both men and women.

But Home Economics or Domestic Science was compulsory for girls. Mothers taught their daughters Cookery, Home Management, Crafts, such as Weaving or Pottery, Mothercraft and Manners. Good manners or good behaviour was an essential quality for a girl. According to an Igbo saying, "**Agwa bu mma**". That is "Good character is the essence of beauty". Mothers look forward to their daughters getting happily married. They, therefore, taught their children how to become worthy, future wives and mothers, the love and respect for husband and the need to give him food promptly. They were not allowed to sing or whistle while cooking food for husband. They should not steal at home or in the market, or remove husband's property stealthily to their parent's home. Sexual immorality was a serious crime for a married woman. Faithfulness in marriage was emphasised and divorce condemned. It was an abomination for a daughter to produce an illegitimate child. And woman education condemned any woman who delivered a new baby after the first year of her husband's death. Rumour mongering among women was severely punished. The unmarried girls in their own groups, helped to prepare themselves for the future. They often fined some of their members to check immorality and to give themselves the moral training for their future roles.

In Social Science, parents educated their children on the principles of social life. The children were made to know their relations. They received instruction on their family responsibilities. The anti-social tendencies were curbed. The youths were educated on where and when not to marry. For family training stipulated and controlled social behaviour and social responsibilities. Through such a training, children learnt to belong to appropriate but various social groups in order to contribute to the moral tone of the village and to the social welfare of the community. Social and age groupings in this way provided forums for both formal and informal education, and for socio-cultural enlightenment.

For recreation and good health, Physical and Health Education was provided. Its programme included wrestling, fighting, shooting, swimming, throwing of weight, dancing and manual labour. Medicine was also an important discipline; and the student doctor studied under a medicine man, who was a professor in his own field. Medicine had other side-disciplines for its consultation. And they included Psychology, Psychiatry and Palmistry. The rules of good health, the use of herbs and the art of healing were the constituent courses of traditional Medicine. Local Geography was studied for economic enterprise, for movement in case of journeys or difficulties and for security reasons. What we learn as Botany and Biology today were studied as Nature Study.

By way of comparison, we can observe that while the traditional curriculum of education emphasised more of the Humanities and less of the Sciences, the modern curriculum of education emphasises the Sciences and regards the Humanities as containing less important disciplines. And this was brought about by a philosophy of education which contends that more of science will solve the world's ills. Such point of view so far has been proved wrong. In spite of thegreat achievements of Science for the good of man, it has not been able to give man peace and harmony. The spiritual needs of man are beyond its competence.

If traditional education did not study much of Science, it was not out of design. It was out of ignorance. For its knowledge of the extent of the sciences was limited. Traditional education did not venture into the unknown for similar reasons. But in spite of all its limitations, the earlier curriculum of education held the Arts and the Sciences together as of equal importance for the realization of the four cardinal aims of education.

Place of Religion in Education

In order to be true to itself, traditional education gave Religion an emphatic position in its curriculum both as one of the disciplines and as a guide in education. Religion had played this two roles in education ever since, until the "so called" modern outlook in education removed religion from its traditional position.

Both the colonial system of education and the church-sponsored education had emphasised the unique roles played by Religion and Morality in education. The colonial system of education prepared men for "white collar" jobs, but it agreed with the traditional education that Religion must be emphasised as the means of making the white man's employee an honest and responsible servant. That was why **onye olu bekee,** or the white man's employee, was much devoted to, and honest in his duty than the modern **onye olu obodo,** or the present day national servant. The later belongs to a philosophy of education which ignores religious and moral integrity. The church on its part in keeping with the traditional philosophy of education made Religion

262

the right base for educational take-off. It also taught such courses that could equip the learner for secular employment.

Religion in the traditional curriculum is first of all one of the academic disciplines. Before Christianity came, the teachers of Religion were the child's parents and the priests of the traditional religion. They possessed the religious outlook and qualities to teach Religion. They knew their aims in teaching Religion. They adopted whatever method could help drive their lessons home. Even during the colonial days, the teachers of Religion were committed men. They knew their facts. They had their scheme and were sure of their method of teaching.

Indeed Religion in our own time has its rightful place in the school curriculum and on the time-table. We have religious syllabuses in schools and colleges; and in the universities we have Departments of religious studies. There are school chapels; and students have their religious societies and they do cultivate religious loyalties and sympathies. But the problem of Religious Education in our time is that of getting the right persons to teach the subject. Most of the teachers of Religion in our schools, colleges and universities are not the right persons to teach the subject. Many are not sure of their facts, and some have no useful scheme of work. Such teachers hardly prepare their lessons or improve their teaching methods. They take Religion for granted, as an easy subject. As a result, Religion is the most incompetently taught subject in the school curriculum. The teaching or presentation of Religion does not mean a systematic and conscious effort to disparage it, to deny its claims, to explain away its truth or to compromise its principles. It does not consist of the doubting of every truth about it or of the rejection of ideas one does not understand and so cannot explain. Rather it calls for continued search and for open-mindedness in inquiry. It consists of an objective rather than subjective study of the subject with a view to understand and apply it. Moral instruction and Civics are no substitutes for religious instruction.

The other problem is the problem of uneven emphasis laid on subjects at school. We know that every child needs and has the right to religious education, and every parent would like his child to grow in his Religion. But his interest in Religion is often killed in the school. There has been a modern tendency to tell the learner that other subjects are more important than Religion, and that Religion is optional in education and in life. Some guides have even declared Religion "a useless discipline". But we know that apart from the study of religion as a discipline, the overall aim of the study of religion is the salvation of the human soul.

263

Secondly, Religion occupies a central position as guide in education and in life. The traditional curriculum of education saw Religion as more than a discipline in the curriculum. It had to play a guidance role in defining the principles, practice and methodology of education. The role of Religion in education is to advise, or to counsel both the teacher and the learner on his code of conduct in educational process and practice. Every subject should be studied in relation to Religion. For instance, the learner was made to see Religion as a higher culture.

Traditional education realized that both Art and Music have their origin in Religion. While the former paints life, the human and the divine in concrete forms, Music sacred and secular composes their splendour in joyful sounds. Even Physical Education had direct relationship with Religion. Religious festivals in the year were the occasions for public exhibition of man's best achievements in physical education. While the gymnastic and acrobatic displays express the height of festive joy in a religious festival, the rigorous **rumba** dance was the expression of self-enjoyment before the Maker and for the entertainment of his people. What is wrong in it if modern education maintained this fundamental and traditional connection between educational practice and religion?

The Sciences also were never divorced from Religion. The asgriculturists realised that their experiments will fail without God. They saw him as the patron divinity of the farmer. They asked him for help during the planting of seeds; and they thanked him when the harvest went well. There was no discipline in traditional education which man studied without reference to God. The problem of our time is how to make the scientist realise that what he calls nature is God himself. If the traditional principles are applied in education, both the chemist and the physicist, for instance, will respectively discover the relationship between the compounds and elements they analyse, the forces they calculate and measure, and God who is the great Causative Principle behind Chemistry and Physics. A basic philosophy of education should realise that religion as a way of life, dominates the whole of life. It ought to recognise the connection between classroom and the assembly. For "freedom of worship" is not the same thing as "option of worship". Moreover, it should be realised that education without religion is like a ship without rudder or like a moving engine without a cooling system.

If we define traditional education as the "standard education", "balanced education", the "content of education that is valid for all times", it can easily be seen that modern education has tended to depart from the traditional norm. A number of factors are responsible for the tenuous position which Religion holds in the curriculum today or why religion loses its central position as guide in education. First is rapid expansion and diversification of knowledge. There are too many things to learn. Greater importance is attached to "practical" and vocational disciplines. Learners often attach greater importance to what may be described as the "utility disciplines" or the "bread and butter" disciplines because of their market response. In consequence, Religion as one of the traditional and humanistic disciplines that belong to the philosophical basis of knowledge is pushed to the corner by other items in the curriculum as a peripheral course.

Secondly, there is over specialization in education. In a specialized study, the learner knows more and more of one thing and little or nothing about other disciplines. This is because the learner concentrates in a certain field and neglects its organic connections and larger settings. Specialization, is necessary for scientific advancement; it produces increased knowledge. But it stunts large mindedness which threatens the comprehension of the whole truth. Where there is an option, most students may not choose Religion at all. In some institutions, General Studies had been introduced in order to fill up the gap created by over specialization. But even at that, Religion had not regained its traditional role in education. The present situation is that modern education in Nigeria pays lip service to the study and practice of Religion. And that is grievous departure from the traditional norm of education.

Thirdly, there is progressive secularization or over secularization of life and education in this generation. Formerly religion was recognised as the key-note of education, the determining factor in educational theory and practice. The removal of religion from its central position in education result to a change in importance accorded to religion in people's life. When religion becomes an elective in school curriculum, it is bound to become an elective in the life of the educated man. When religion ceases to be principle and instrument of cohesion in education the national life is affected. We have not got to the stage of complete secularization which is atheism. But we have started to notice godlessness in the loss of interest in anything holy, transcendent and divine.

Fourthly, modern civilization is a materialistic civilization produced by a new philosophy of education, "untraditional", which has artificially disconnected the intricate link between Religion and other disciplines. Such a philosophy tries to destroy what is of value in the old ways of life. Modern civilization tries to destroy basic human values. Life is nowadays seen more and as superficial, as something without depth and without spiritual basis. But whenever the supernatural element in life is denied, and whenever conceptions of man and life seize to belong to religion, society goes to blazes. It is a fact of experience that Modern theory of education tries to establish a non-religious civilization or development without religion.

But Emil Brunner has emphasised the indispensable role which religion plays in edeucation and life when he declared,

> Religion - I am not speaking now exclusively of Christianity - is the depth of our existence, the root out of which the human character of life grows. Cut off from this root, all the finer forms of life, all sense of responsibility of sacredness, of obligation, of respect and of sacrifice, as well as all real creativity, must die. Life becomes in the ontological sense of the word "superficial", surface without depth, process without meaning. Man cannot understand himself any more as something different from mere nature. The absence of the Holy, of the Transcendent ... must leave life shallow, empty and soulless. *

Traditional education whether ancient or modern holds Religion and Morality together as more than core courses in education. It does not present morality as merely moral instructions but as the bye-product of religion. It realises that religion and morality are so closely knit together that an attempt to sever their traditional connection is to limit the practical expression of the fruits of religion and to deprive morality of its basic sanction and authority. Traditional concept in education realises that morality is the fruit of religion, and it rejects the subjective point of view that man invented morality to preserve his society or that man upgraded the code of conduct which he had invented, as divine command.

Traditional education taught the learner that morality originated in religion. It made man aware of the sacred and the profane, and put in man the idea of the holy and the respect for the sacred. Religion declared the taboos or "things of forbidden",

---

*Emil Brunner, Critic or Apologist of Civilization?', **Religion in Life**, Vol. XX, No. 3, New York, 1951, p. 324.

and stipulated the do's and the don'ts. It defined the laws of blood or covenant relationships, and of moral and social responsibility.

Experience has shown that the absence of religious awareness leads to inhumanity, to beastial behaviour, to social intolerance and to totalitarianism in government. Bribery and corruption, robbery, oppression and injustice become the order of life in any society whenever it turns its back to the ideals that are religious. Parents were very conscious of this in the traditional place of education; and so they carefully emphasised the **taboos** which the family, village, clan or the divinities frown at.

It is one thing to know what is right, but another to do what is right. What is needed for this is the moral compuction and the motive power. And both of these come from religion. Religion recognises the existence of law and order in life; but it believes that greater power to fulfil the demands of law originates from religious motivation more than it does from the application of the ordinary human force. We know, for instance, that the facing of the firing squards by armed robbers cannot stop armed robbery in a country without the help of the transforming power of religion and morality. This is why Religion emphasises the need for moral discipline in education. It believes that the learner who misbehaves should be disciplined. He should be made to realise the place of law and order and of authority in education and in real life. Traditional education realised the role of religion and morality as great forces of socialisation; and they are indispensable tools in the moral and spiritual training of the child.

Alongside with religion, the teaching of morale was emphasised in the curriculum of traditional education. In teaching, special emphasis was laid on example and practice and not on theory, as in the teaching of Ethics today. For it was realised that one of the aims of education is character-training. For a Nigerian in the traditional setting, good manners is an indispensaable qualification for a successful life. On account of this, the parents of the learner attached more importance to character-training than to mere acquisition of factual knowledge.

In conclusion, there is the need for us to recover the great principles and concepts which guided traditional education. The first is to affirm the organic unity of truth and of all knowledge. For truth is an organic unity and knowledge a coherent whole. Knowledge is not simply countless fragments of truth without pattern or unity. No fragment of truth or knowledge should be seen as distinct and as isolated but as related to the whole.

Education remains traditional, if it is always conscious of the inter-relatedness or inter-dependence in education and life.

Such an awareness reveals the need for a fundamental reorientation of every subject in the curriculum in order to restore the central position of religion in every human activity including learning. Traditional education emphasised and does emphasise Religion and Morality in other words, God and his demands. It considers as false learning any approach to the truth which does not confess or discover or acknowledge the reality of God.

Thus the centrality of God in the scheme of things including education should be discovered through education. For if education studies Reality, it should make Religion the keynote to that understanding. It does not mean that Religion will dictate procedure and methods for the Sciences. What it means is that in Traditional education the learner, irrespective of his discipline ought to discover in all things the presence and activity of God as the Ultmate Reality.

HEALING IN AFRICAN TRADITIONAL SOCIETY: AN ASPECT OF THE RELIGION

by

Udobata Onunwa

"Chi gboo mkpa, Onu Dibia adi ire" (Igbo Proverb)
"Whan God solves a person's problem, the words of
the medicine man become effective."

Introduction

The African world is said to be suffused with religion.
In other words, an African sees his world and interpretes it in
a 'religious perspective.' The whole structure of society is suffused in religion. The traditional religion is indeed **Society** itself
and there is no clear demarcation between the **Sacred** and **Profane.** Both the spiritual and the physical realms of the universe
are believed to work in a consistent harmony and are subject to
an order and systematic rythm. Any breach in the system by
man's misdemeanor or misconduct causes a disaster and the whole
system is disrupted. The whole essence of man's religious rituals
is to keep the whole system in constant harmony (to maintain
the balance).

Healing is a part of the whole complex religious attempt by man to bring the physical and spiritual aspects of the
universe as well as man who lives in it into that desired harmony.
The idea of "wholeness" is therefore, not alien to the African.
Healing thus becomes a cardinal religious practice because African
cosmology which is "world-affirming" demands that life in the
world must be kept free from problems, illhealth and obstacles
which may hinder the fulfilment of desired goals. Life here on
earth is believed by the Africans to be desirable and essential.
Elaborate protective measures and strict caution or ethical principles are among the several ways recommended for effective
and happy sojourn here on earth. Among the unfriendly agents
that threaten life here on earth, is illness. It is an enemy which
the African has tried to fight, avoid and eradicate. The other

enemy which the African hates as much is death itself. Aylward Shorter is therefore right when he observed that:

> sickness for the African is a diminution of life, a threat posed to life; and healing is an activity second only to that of giving life. Petition for healing is probably the most subject of prayers. (1)

This observation is true when seen against the background of the traditional African in worship, or any other ritual performance. Health and healing are connected just in the same way they are with the fundamental theme of life. They involve both rational and mystical procedures so much so that a substantial aspect is kept out of view of the ordinary human activity but shrouded in the mystery of the religion.

Concept of Health

Health as understood by Africans particularly the Igbo of Nigeria and in many other traditional societies, is far more social than biological. It does not entirely mean an absence of physical ailments. One tends to observe that there is a more unitary concept of psychosomatic interrelationship - that is an apparent reciprocity between mind and matter. Health is therefore not an isolated phenomenon but part of the entire magico-religious fabric - far more than an absence of diseases. (2) That is why when a person is not 'progressing' nor does not seem to 'prosper' in one's undertakings, the one is said to be 'sick'. One who does not act in conformity with the stipulated rules of the society or does not reason along the same logical line of thought with his people's established norms is said to be sick - **O. di ndu onwu ka nma:** (better dead than alive). Such a person is seen as a disgrace to his people. One who is 'haunted' by **Agwu** deity (the patron deity of traditional medicine) is said to be 'sick'. This deity is believed by the Igbo to strike people with such dehumanising sicknesses like insanity, epilepsy, extravagant living and joblessness. It may also strike a man who refuses to serve as a special devotee to him with similar diseases and experiences. The one would be cured only when he has accepted to serve the deity in the capacity he is 'called'. Treatment of such diseases may involve offering sacrifices and performance of some rituals. As already indicated, this comprehensive concept of health is not an exclusive reserve of the Igbo or any other non-industrialised societies. For instance, Bernard Haring, writing from his experience of orthodox medicine in the West, has clearly stated that:

> a comprehensive understanding of human health includes the greatest possible harmony of all man's forces and energies, the greatest possible spiritualization of man's bodily aspect and the finest embodiment of the spiritual. True health is revealed in the self actualization of the person who has attained that freedom which marshalls all available energies for the fulfilment of his total vocation. (3)

The subtle difference between Igbo concept of health and Haring's view lies in the isolation of the causes of disease which each view makes. The Igbo may emphasize the mystical while the Western-oriented scientific view may emphasize the physical causes. A man's mental instability, any sign of abnormal behaviour or physical disability are not necessarily a result of only the physical distortion of the physiological process but something far more than that.

A healthy man, therefore, is one who has not been uprooted from the context of his primary solidarities, one who is in harmony with his fellows and the deities, one who is not destabilized or incapacitated. He is the one who can obviously say that "I am because we are and because we are, I am." (4)

In a subtle way, a lazy man or one who does not participate actively in the affairs of his community is often described as "Ozu", (a corpse, implying a dead fellow) showing that his presence is not usually felt by his colleagues because of his passive attitude to life or because of his irresponsible living. He is not counted as a responsible member of his community. This is a travesty of Igbo concept of self because no Igbo man would like to be taken for granted or ignored in any matter that involves him to show that he is alive, he is active, healthy and sensible.

In Africa, particularly among the Igbo of Nigeria, what people understand as sickness would affect a person's worldview, ethical values, self-image and relationship with other neighbours, as we have already indicated. Healing therefore, is an elaborate ministry which does not seek to attend to a selected aspect of human life. The 'healer' is understood from such elaborate ministry as a "medicine man", a "teacher", a "restorer", a "pastor", and a "counsellor". His work combines the restoration of the greatest values and virtues in man for the services of the highest ideals in the society. The "healer" is a "medicine man" in the sense that he is an expert in handling what the Igbo call **OGWU** - medicine. The term is used for a number of medicines and charms and magic. When it is used for saving life, protecting life and for other profitable purposes in the interest of all concerned, it is called **Ogwu.** It is **NSHI** - poison - when it is used for selfish ends to harm another person. The medicine man who uses African herbs to restore 'health' of other human beings is also called the **Dibia** in view of his knowledge of the materials which can be used to restore health to a sick man. A medical doctor in modern hospitals is understood as **Dibia-onye-Ocha**(white man's doctor) in the sense that he is a form of medicine man who uses Western materials and methods to bring 'health' to his fellow men.

Methods of Healing Old and New

The African art of healing has been traditionally associated with a thorough knowledge of herbs, roots etc. through revelation, and inspiration by the powers of the spirit. The place of skill, learning and method of trial and error is prominent in the art of healing. The methods of healing vary from place to place in addition to the nature and type of disease in question.
Because healing is a part of religious ritual and an act of worship, the diviner is usually the first religious personnel that is consulted. His house is the first port of call before any serious thought is given to any application or administration of medicaments. The diviner's recommendations are taken seriously. He is consulted to ascertain the causes of the sickness and the doctor to consult.
Who is responsible for the sickness? Is it 'poison' by an enemy or as a result of evil machination of a foe? Could it be an attack by an unplacated ancestors? Natural causes are usually not thought of because misfortune is generally explained through the instrumentality of "agents" and this is the basis of sorcery found and believed in by a good number of people. When the illness is not considered a serious one, some form of physical treatment may commence with the administration of simple herbs and anti-dotes like oil, or other "charms". In some cases, the

diviner is not consulted before the commencement of the administration of medicines. Among the Mende, for instance, Harry
Sawyerr and W.T. Harris have jointly observed that the diviner
is consulted when the sickness refuses to respond to treatment.
The fact remains that the African world-view upholds the power
of the spirits over the medicines. It is believed that an unaided
effort of man is weak. Besides, some evil spirits and other unfriendly forces might be lurking at some secret places to destroy
the potency of genuine efforts of the 'doctor' to help his patients.
Religious rituals are therefore important to ward off such unfriendly spirits and enhance the powers of the friendly ones in order
to revitilise the efficacy of the medicines.

In the past, the **Nri** and itinerant ritual expert, served
as medicine men in the different subculture areas of Igboland,
particularly in the North and North-West Igboland. They later extended their influence to the more central areas of the South
and some part of the Cross River Igbo subculture areas. The
Nri hegemony lasted for long till the **Aros,** another group of Igbo
people, came into limelight and competed with them. Even as
late as the 1960's, the **Nri** ritual specialists were found in some
parts of the Central subunit of the South Igbo culture area (Isu-
Ama) where their influence was very high. The **Nri** people were
believed to be the first group of people to learn from **Chukwu**
the art of medicine and agriculture (Igbo Myth of creation) and
were asked by the Supreme Being to teach others the same art.

Medicines from a different town or community were
believed (even till today) to be more effective than the local
stuff. That is why in the past, a guild of itinerant medicine men
opened "mobile clinics" in many places and visited homes to
administer the medicine on their patient. As they moved about
in groups of three or more from one village to the other, the
Nri medicine men carried on themselves heavy bags full of their
instruments, herbs, roots and other 'medicaments' including food
stuff and other gifts in kind given as part of their fees. As the
'healers' moved about with their trainees, they collected the herbs
and roots from the bushes along their routes. Occasionally, a
medicine man could send one of his trainees to attend to a
patient in a patient's home. The **Nri** guild of itinerant 'healers'
used to sojourn in a town from about three to six months and
from there attend to other patients from the neighbouring communities. This group of 'itinerant medical team' has virtually disappeared and given way to new group of healers who stay in
their homes and attend to the patients who consult them there.
This is a recent development in the pattern of healing in the tradi-

tional setting. While in their homes, the traditional healers have the time to monitor the patients. Many have built what we may describe as 'clinics' in their compounds whre they admit patients whose casea are considered serious. They display very conspicuous advertisements describing all sorts of diseases they claim to cure. Those admitted to such 'clinics' are closely monitored and looked after.

This new development is a result of two principal factors. In the first place, illness as understood by Africans (particularly the Igbo) is believed to have got several causes. Some may be entirely physical while others may have both physical and mystical causes. To isolate a patient whose case is serious makes room for better management and the home of the 'native doctor' offers the best chance for that. Visitors would be restricted and in such a situation the 'doctor' would be able to check the visit of any unwanted person who may come in disguise to render impotent all the good medicines being administered to the patient. The Igbo believe that an enemy might visit a sick man with dangerous 'charms' to weaken the good and effective medicines which are being given to him by his doctor.

Secondly, the indigenous 'healer' is an accomplished psychologist who understands his people's background and their interests. He understands that the new 'clinic' pattern compares favourably with the pattern of Western-oriented hospitals springing up in many places today. There in modern hospitals, some sick people are treated as 'out-patients' while others are kept on admissions as cases that need close supervision. This new method devised by the traditional 'healers' has not only enhanced their status but has also afforded them opportunities to learn from the techniques of modern medicine in the area of maintaining clean environment that had been one of the problems of traditional healing methods all through the centuries.

Therapy for each sickness varies from one traditional healer to the other. Some of the methods are rational and scientific while others are crude, mystical and subjective. This is observed from the sample cases obtained from a number of traditional healers in their treatment of most common sicknesses. For instance, light headache, is treated in several ways. Some treat it by burning a certain type of plant and giving it to the patient to inhale its smoke. Others pour in some fluids extracted from some undisclosed leaves into the eyes, nostrils and on the forehead of the patient. Sometimes, some ointment are applied on the forehead and on the eyes of patient as a therapy for severe headache. In some cases, a number of incisions are made

274

at the ends of the two eyes of a patient who complains of constant headache. The aim of the incision is to allow some quantity of blood to rush out and release the tension in the nerves which are believed to be pumping much blood to the brain cells thereby causing the ache. Yet there are others who tie a small band of cloth (like a ribbon) round the head to hold the skull from splitting or breaking into pieces.

Traditional therapy is not only curative. There are some "prophylactic" treatments which are applied when an epidemic strikes a town. For instance, a heavy padlock may be hung on the neck of a child when there is an outbreak of whooping cough in the community to protect a child from being attacked. The essense of "locking the neck" of a child is to prevent it from being attacked by the disease. This practice is based on Igbo theory of **Imitative Magic**. However, this is one of those mystical and irrational devices in traditional healing method which look absurd and do not avail much.

Some elderly people eat a type of brownish paste called **ARUBUNSI** (meaning, body rejects poison) as a prophylactic against any disease or physical poison either in food or drinks. Often men take it before going out in the morning or attending a public meeting where they suspect that some enemies might make attempts on their lives.

There is no disease that is not subject to the treatment which the traditional healers give. In other words, the traditional medicine men claim to heal all diseases. Usually, rubbing, massaging and squeezing of some parts of the body of the patient are considered helpful methods of treatment of diseases. Ointments, lotions and balms are applied on the skin, face or other parts of the body where the patient may complain of pains. Concoctions of unspecified dosage are given to the patient because the medicine man would want the disease to have an instant cure. This is also in line with the expectations of the patient who does not want to stay too long in bed. Sometimes liquid extract of leaves, roots, barks etc. are poured into the eyes, mouth or ears of a patient as a therapy for such minor complaints like conjuctival-allergy, tooth-ache or ear-ache. People suffering from such diseases like dropsy or rheumatic pains often have some incisions made on their backs, joints, muscles to allow some impure blood to gush out. Snake bites and such bites from human beings, and dangerous reptiles are treated with different types of herbal extractions and pastes which are rubbed on the skin.

In the South Igbo culture area, lunacy of non-violent type may be treated by means of inhalations repeated several times a day. Usually schizophrenics and other mental patients are given all sorts of 'mystical' and scientific therapeutic treatments on herbs and roots. Violent lunatic patients are confined and are often in chains. They are given some concoctions that would make them drowsy and sleepy so that they would not be strong enough to harm any body around or destroy any valuable property. In some cases, they are compelled to do strong physical exercises and hard work or flogged mercilessly to weaken them. Besides, a lunatic is not expected to add weight. So he is given some laxatives regularly to make him have constant soft bowels. In addition, some liquid irritants and emetics are given to such a patient to induce vomiting. It is believed that through constant vomiting, a lunatic patient could "throw off" the very elements in him that intoxicate and make him behave abnormally.

The traditional healers and herbalists are not only knowledgeable in the variety of roots and herbs that have therapeutic values, but also understand the psychology of their people very well. Healers in simple dress or plain clothes are not believed to have got potent medicines. Consequently, most of them dress in curious and aweful attire in which they look either ludicrous, fearful or both. In such exotic fashion, they strike fear in the minds of their clients and establish some credibility. This notwithstanding, the knowledge of many of the traditional healers of the chemical properties of different herbs and roots is amazing. Some claim that such knowledge is at times revealed to them in dreams by the gods. Others also acquire the skill through long years of apprenticeship and disciplined personal research in their 'clinics.' By the method of trial and error, some have discovered the potency in different leaves for curing different types of diseases. This knowledge of the chemical properties in some leaves has not only challenged Africans themselves but also such honest and serious European scholars of African Traditional Religion like Professor E.G. Parrinder. He has rightly observed that:

> West African doctors have a wide knowledge of the properties of many roots, barks, leaves and herbs. They are called 'observers' of plants in Fon and workers in roots in Furi. (5)

This remark is true of many traditional medicinemen in Traditional African societies. For instance, some have the ability to discover the therapeutic properties in the horns of the buffalo (**Mpi atu**). The traditional healers at Enugu-Ezike in Nsukka, (North Igbo subculture area), give cold water in a horn of buffalo as a therapy for all stomach problems. Women in protracted labour are also given water in such horns to hasten delivery of the baby. The discovery of the 'therapeutic power' in the horns of the buffalo is a convincing evidence that African traditional medicinemen have the ability to probe into the secrets and mysteries of nature.

In recent times, most of the practitioners of the traditional medicine have started to improve on their techniques. For instance, in some of the 'clinics' the liquid extracted from leaves and barks of trees are stored in clean bottles, decently labelled and displayed on the shelf.

Many traditional bone-setters are making use of splints, bandages plasters and clutches in their practice. They have been credited with success in treating very bad cases which were initially mismanaged in some orthopedic hospitals. They are cases where orthopedic surgeons wanted to cut off the broken limb as hopeless but when the relatives of the patients transfered them to the traditional bone-setters, they were properly treated without amputation. Some physiotherapists have confirmed such cases as properly healed. The traditional bone-setters at Obollo-Ugiri Mbano (Isu-Ama subunit of the South Igbo subcultural area) and Enugu-Ezike in Nsukka, (North Igbo subculture area) have been particularly popular in handling a number of such cases which were said to have been mismanaged initially in some orthopedic hospitals.

A lot of new things are now happening in traditional healing practices in recent times. A recent breakthrough was made by Njoku Nwigwe, a middle-aged 'native doctor' from Ehime Mbano in the South Igbo area, who discovered how African herbs and roots could be used to cure stomach ulcers, pile and parasites in the human body without the patients undergoing any surgical operation. Nwigwe also claims to have made the discoveries known to the Chief Pharmacist in the Imo State Ministry of Health, Owerri. The Ministry is yet to confirm whether the discovery is a valid scientific feat or not. (6)

Problems of Traditional Healing Method

Inspite of the recent breakthrough and successful healings registered by traditional medical practitioners, the system is still fraught with problems. The traditional medical practice either as a professional or religious skill is shrouded in secrecy. The practitioners of this ancient art still keep their therapeutic techniques and discoveries out of reach of any other person. They rarely allow their work to be subjected to further research either

277

by their colleagues or the western trained scientists and doctors. Some "apprentice medicine men" might qualify from their masters' clinics without getting enough information from them. They develop more skill and acquire wider knowledge and experience when they practise on their own. The intention to keep the secrets of any discovery away from others has led to a very slow rate of development and progress in the practice of traditional medicine. On the death of many skilful medicine men, their wisdom and knowledge are lost because they did not disclose them to others and could not write them down in any documentary reference. The concept of secrecy has been the bane of traditional medicine and healing method. It has made the traditional healing ministry a "secret cult" where some dupes could hide to cheat some needy citizens. Many genuine enquiries who would have probed deep into the dynamics of the practice of traditional healing are kept away from knowing much about what goes on within. Consequently, traditional medicine men are called all sorts of derogatory names. Even in recent times when the call for the integration of traditional medicine and Western-oriented medicine has been consistent, the traditional medicine men are still suspicious of the intentions of the practitioners of western medicine.

Attitudes to Modern Medicine and Healing Methods

There is an ambivalent attitude towards modern medical healing methods and practices in many traditional societies. The scope of modern western medicine and therapeutic techniques is obviously enlarging. Many conservative Igbo traditionalists in the rural communitieshave obviously seen the mysteries of the western science. The surprises and wonder of surgical operations are immense because they are entirely unknown in the traditional healing methods. (7)

The hospital is believed to be a good place for the treatment of some diseases which must, however, be validated by a traditional healing ritual. To the Igbo, the basic worldview holds that every sickness has got its own spiritual and physical causes. In spite of the immense contributions of modern medicine, the traditional Igbo man still believes that his healing is incomplete if he has not performed the necessary traditional rituals. He therefore, in a way cherishes his own traditional healing methods. He does not completely deride the achievements and benefits of modern western science yet he believes that there are some ailments which the hospital cannot cure. Even when a man is physically cured, he still believes that there are some aspects which are beyond the scope of western medical science. He may perform some rituals on his return from the hospital; a ritual may be going on at home while he is in hospital, being performed by his relatives. This shows the interest and regards which the Africans still have in the traditional healing methods of their ancestors. The interest in western medicine does not completely destroy that which the people show in their traditional medicine and healing methods. Three major deductions have been made from discussion we had with many traditionalists on this issue:

a) There are some diseases which the 'hospitals cannot cure' because their causes are beyond the knowledge of western science. The hospital does not touch the fundamentals of African religious and cultural life.

b) The practice of modern medicine is at present too impersonal for a traditional African to appreciate its contributions without reservations. The medical team rarely meets his longing for a 'personal touch'. Often the difficulty in obtaining a card, seeing the doctor in his consulting room and obtaining the prescribed drugs from the pharmacy (if it is in stock), may take a whole day. Some times the patient goes home without success. The experience is such that a votary of the traditional religion who had for long enjoyed the services of the traditional medicine man will not have any strong attraction to the new to make him abandon the 'old faithful' practice he had enjoyed. He sees the hospital as at best, a supplement to what he gets from the traditional medicine man but not a better substitute in all its entirety.

c) Thirdly, the village is a "healing community" where the patient is not only cared for but also made to believe that both his recovery and reintegration are important.

Meanwhile we have confined our concepts of healing and medicine to the curative and prophylactic elements which are primarily manufactured by man. We have, however, mentioned in passing, the belief and discovery in the traditional religion that power resides in certain material substances which may be either vegetable, animal flesh, human flesh or blood which can be manipulated for both good and evil purposes. The miraculous substances are spoken of as "medicines" or "fetishes" but the translation is obviously not appropriate because the underlying concepts do not have parallel views in contemporary western society. (8) "Medicines" in Africa are meant to secure "power", health, fertility, "personality" or moral reform. They may be used to heal, save life or destroy it. Medicines are not as at now 'traditional', new substances are sought and in the changing societies "medicines" are put to new uses, such as success in examinations, sports and competitive concerts, (9) in attracting customers in the markets, in securing employment, escaping police arrest, etc.

There are people who claim that they could consciously harness and manipulate the forces in nature to cause harm on others - through "casting spells" from a distance, either causing a big tree to fall on someone or cause an animal to strike him down to death. This is the basis of sorcery which is practised in many parts of Africa. John Middleton and E.H. Winter have in a joint study made a clear distinction between sorcery and witchcraft as conceived of and understood in Africa. In their view:

> witchraft is part of an individual's being, a part of his innermost self, while sorcery is merely a technique which a person utilises. Thus in some societies a person's witchcraft can operate at times without his being consciously aware ... This can never be the case of sorcery. Recourse to it must be on a deliberate conscious voluntary basis. (10)

While the witch is believed to be an agent of evil spirit which is unconsciously manipulating him, the sorcerer manipulates some elements and harnesses some "natural" powers to harm others. In this case there is a deliberate and voluntary desire to be one (that is a sorcerer). E.E. Evans-Pritchard had earlier discovered among the Azande that:

> the witch performs no rites, utters no spells ... and possesses no medicine ... art of witchcraft is a psychic one. (11)

Furthermore, E.G. Parrinder, in the same vein, makes a clear distinction between sorcery and witchcraft as he observed it in Africa. To him,

> witchcraft is best reserved for those people ... have no magical apparatus but work harm on others by devouring their soul ... while the sorcerer prepares harmful medicine for a price ... which may be spells

against him ... or plain poison to be dropped in his food. (12)

The practice of witchcraft and sorcery have been going on in Africa for quite a long time. Both may be included in the broad genre of medicines which may be seen from various perspectives. In terms of healing, the chief personnel in the whole complex ministry is called the **Dibia,** the medicine man. From the point of view of Igbo traditional religious spirituality, the **moral attitude** of the dibia, his people's impression of his personality are among his weapons which he could use to effect a healing on a patient. The religious dimensions of African traditional medicine and healing are essentially a fundamental issue of African ethics.

Conclusion

Thus far we have observed that although there is an increasing influence of many external change-agents, the belief of many Africans irrespective of their religious affiliation, educational attainment and economic status is still deeply rooted in magico-religious principles.

Besides, the traditional healer's charge being cheap, he is more easily accessible to his patient than the westerntrained medical practitioner in a modern hospital. His patient sees him as a complete man: a healer, a friend, a counsellor, a priest and a pastor whose reassuring touch adds to his recovery. Una Maclean, after several years of intensive research on traditional medicine in the city of Ibadan, Nigeria concluded that the enduring value of the traditional healing practice lies not necessarily in the material but in the methods and concepts which underlie them and the continuing power is a tribute to the practitioners of this ancient art. (13)

The traditional healer understands the psychological background of his patients. It is obvious that some of the rituals involved in the healing may be removed and yet a patient benefits from the efficacy of the herbs that have some natural therapeutic powers in them. It is now being realized more than ever before that a substantial number of sick people in contemporary society still seek primary help from assorted native healers partly because the patients and their relatives have more confidence in the native healers than in doctors of orthodox medicine. One of the foremost Nigerian psychiatrists Professor T.A. Lambo who realized this fact several years ago has been consistent in his call for inclusion of African cultural values and therapeutic techniques into western medical care of the sick in order to provide efficient health services to the Africans. He has consistently and strongly suggested that:

> western psychiatry must learn to make more creative use of the native culture if it is to increase its effectiveness in dealing with mental illness and to hasten the acceptance of modern medicine among the primitive peoples. (14)

Footnotes

1 Aylward Shorter, **Prayers in Religious Traditions of Africa** (Nairobi: Oxford University Press, 1975) p. 60.
2 T. Adeoye Lambo, "Patterns of Psychiatric Care in Developing African Countries" in Ari Kiev, (ed.) **Magic, Faith and healing** (New York: The Free Press, 1964) 445-446.
3 Bernard Haring, **Medical Ethics** (England: St. Paul's Publications, 1972) 154.
4 J.S. Mbiti, **African Traditional Religious and Philosophy** (London: Heinemann, 1969) pp. 2 & aO.
5 E.G. Parriner, **West African Religion** (London: Epworth Press, 1949, Reprinted, 1969) 156.
6 See **Nigerian Statesman** (A Government owned Newspaper, Owerri, Nigeria, 27th September, 1980) 1.
7 See S.F. Nadel, **Nupe Religion** (London: Routledge and Kegan Paul, Ltd., 1954) p. 141.
8 Monica Wilson, **Religion and Transformation of Society** (London: Pengui Books, 1971) 34.
9 Monica Wilson, **Ibid.**, 34.
10 John Middleton and E.H. Winter (eds.) **Witchcraft and Society in Africa** (London: O.U.P. 1969) p. 12.
11 E.E. Evans-Pritchard, **Witchcraft, Oracles and Magic among the Azande** (London: O.U.P. 1937)21.
12 E.G. Parrinder, **Africa's Three Religions** (London: Sehledon Press, 1969) 65.
   Cf. Dominique Zahan, **The Religion, Spirituality, and Thought of Traditional Africa** (Chicago: and London: The Uni-

versity of Chicago Press, 1970: English Translation 1979) 93.

Adrian Hastings, **African Christianity** (London: Geoffrey Chapman, 1976) 67ff.

13   Una   Maclean, **Magical Medicine: A Nigerian Case Study** (London: Penguin, 1971, Reprinted 1977) 146.

14   T.A.   Lambo, "Patterns of Psychiatric Care in Developing African Countries". **Ibid.**, p. 441.

PART FIVE

ENCOUNTER WITH MODERN WORD

CHRISTIANITY MEETS TRADITIONAL AFRICAN CULTURES

by

Peter K. Sarpong

Abstract

In the judgment of the Roman Catholic Bishop of Kumasi, Ghana, "the Church has not become 'African' enough," and he hopes that the religious "symbols, imagery, signs, etc. that are clearly remnants of other cultures will be replaced by those comprehensible to the African." The African traditional cultures are deeply religious, even though they contain some objectionable elements which the Ashanti bishop lists. But areas of convergence are many and profound: godliness, fatherhood and religious authority; veneration of ancestors; extolled virtues of respect, hospitality, purity, truth, and hard work; and liturgical sensitivity about the "life cycle" or rites of passage. Sensitive in dialogue with these traditions, the evangelist discovers that one need not preach "a new God" but "an old God who has been revealed to us positively by his Son." Indeed, "there is a vast Christian theological potential in Africa, not simply in spite of contemporary change, but because of it." Peter K. Sarpong is a pastor, prolific writer and scholar, who holds degrees in theology from Rome's Angelicum and in literature and anthropology from Oxford University. The article from which these extracts are taken appeared in Worldmission (vol.30, no.2, Summer 1979), a publication of the U.S. office of the Society for the Propagation of the Faith (366 5th Ave., New York, NY 10001).

Introduction

The ordinary African is not "logical" in the Western sense. By and large he has no interest in cause and effect but in actual happenings. Neither does he reason along strict syllogistic lines. This does not mean that he is not a thinker or that he is unintelligent. In fact, he is a philosopher in his own right. But he philosophizes in the concrete, not in the abstract.

The African can pursue a particular cause or act in a definite pattern for, say, 20 years and when the Westerner has concluded that he will continue to do so for the rest of his life, he suddenly goes off at a tangent. To the non-African this is illogical, but not to the African who on the whole does not accept absolutes. To his way of thinking, behavior must be related to his needs, to what he considers good. So it is not wrong to tell a "lie" for a good purpose. Baptism is a good thing; then should be permissible to have a person unfit for Baptism receive the Sacrament by concealing the truth about him ...

I am not by any means suggesting that the African has no appreciation of what is true and what is a lie. I am only trying to explain that his understanding of these concepts is more pragmatic ... The Catholic Church is the true Church founded by Christ, but if my petition is unanswered when I go to Mass then there is nothing wrong in praying in a Spiritual Church or falling back on the traditional magico-religious ritual for help. After all, religion is worthwhile only inasmuch as it helps man to get rid of the many inevitable hazards of life - childlessness, illness, poverty, death, disgrace, hunger, etc. In some African languages there are no abstract terms and one has to seek a concrete image to convey the thought.

The African believes in God and spirits, but he is not interested in defining these realities, and most of the theological terms used in such an exercise mean nothing to him. His interest stops with how God and the spirits influence his life and what good or evil they mete out.

Much has to be accomplished in studying the culture and institutions of different African societies and endeavoring to harmonize the authentic teaching of Christ with the everyday lives of people.

To my mind, the Church has not become "African" enough. By "African" I am not referring to the skin or origin of people; I am not preaching racism. I am only expressing a concern that the Church truly become incarnated in the African soil, hoping that the symbols, imagery, signs, etc. that are clearly remnants of other cultures will be replaced by those comprehensible to the African.

The problem then is comprehending the unacknowledged and unanalysed standpoints from which the African's views are taken.

The Vatican Propagation of the Faith in 1659 issued to missionaries in China and Indo-China the directives:

> Put no obstacles in their way; and for no reason what-
> ever should you persuade these people to change their
> rites, customs and ways of life unless these are ob-
> viously opposed to religion and good morals. For what
> is more absurd than to bring France or Spain or Italy
> or any other part of Europe into China. It is not these
> that you should bring but the faith which does not
> spurn or reject any people's rites and customs, unless
> they are depraved, but, on the contrary, tries to keep
> them ... admire and praise what deserves to be respect-
> ed.

My contention is that like all other cultures, African traditional
cultures contain several objectionable elements. This is not to
say that they do not or did not fulfill a social function now or
in the past. A careful examination of many an African custom,
no matter how repulsive it may be to modern man, will reveal
that it once played or even now plays a role in the social life
of the people.

In the light of the Christian message one can hardly
justify the reign of terror of some chiefs in Africa. The tests
of endurance that young boys and girls have to undergo during
their initiation ceremonies, and widows during the funeral celebration of their husbands, amount to objective cruelty. Those being
initiated are sometimes subjected to circumcision and clitoridectomy, deep cuts on the forehead and other parts of the body, and
forcible extraction of teeth - all with very crude instruments.
Some bleed to death or die through infection of their wounds.
Widows are sometimes placed in solitary confinement for days
on end, made to sleep for weeks with stones as their pillow, or
have pepper thrown into their eyes.

In the past, the atrocities committed through traditional
secret societies were so horrifying that, as far back as the
beginning of this century, the Colonial Powers had to proscribe
societies, such as the **Ogboni** in Nigeria, from the purely human-
itarian point of view.

Traditional cultures' estimation of women, even in
strictly matrilineal societies, has always been very low. Often
the woman is considered only a second-class citizen, the mother
of theman's children. The Christian teaching of the equality of
all human beings would have taken many African cultures a very
long time to appreciate.

Christianity insists on our loving everyone, even our
enemies. Traditional cultures regard the downfall of the enemy

a desirable thing to be sought vigorously. Love is the cornerstone of Christian religion. Traditional cultures emphasize fear as sufficient motivation for going good and for avoiding evil. Traditionally, religion is useful because, and insofar as, it helps man to solve the many problems that beset him in life. A religion that prepares man mainly for a reward after death is, at best, of dubious utility.

In the context of traditional cultures, the African could never rise to the lofty heights of revelation attained by Christianity. The Trinity, the Incarnation, the Eucharist and the Resurrection are theologically beyond the reach of "primitive revelations." Christianity gives meaning to suffering. Suffering has no place in traditional cultures except as the sign of the spirits' anger, the reward of man's inequity. Neither can traditional cultures understand the meaning of the virtue of humility. Traditionally, the African is by nature a proud person. He always feels more important than anyone else.

One could go on enumerating points of divergence between Christianity and traditional African cultures. Nevertheless, the areas of convergence appear to be many and profound. In fact, it looks as if the good Lord from all eternity has prepared the African soil for the reception of the Christian seed.

Godliness has always been part of the African tradition. Indeed the attributes of the African God are so "Christian" that many 19th-century ethnographers doubted their originality. It is true that besides the Supreme Being, Africans venerate or even worship other spirits, human and non-human, and have belief in totems, witches, magic and taboos. But these are considered as manifestations of God, his functionaries who do his will. The preacher in Africa is therefore not preaching a new God; he is preaching an old God who has been revealed to us positively by his Son. If he studies and makes use of the belief of the Africans, then he is giving a new dimension to, rather than correcting, their religious conception. This belief is in fact basic to what is going to follow. As a matter of fact, in African traditional cultures there appears to be not distinction made between a person's religious practices and his other spheres of activity. Religion is a way of life, not a fashion. It permeates every aspect of a man's life, from cradle to grave. For the African, religion is not a subject to learn. Nor is it a subject for debate. Being part of ordinary life, it is accepted and absorbed in the normal cause of events. As an integral part of culture, is shares culture's compulsory, impersonal, objective and universal nature. Religion is part of African Society ...

The structure of African societies may and sometimes does have effects which may be inconsistent with Christian aspirations. For example, Christianity would insist that marriage is primarily an institution of love between a man and a woman for their mutual happiness and the well-being of their children. In many African cultures, however, marriage may be regarded as a social affair between two lineages which agree to hand over their people in marriage primarily for the benefit of the group. If an uncle or father can say: "I have arranged a marriage for my nephew or son," then there should be no wonder that they sometimes control the marriage, interfere with it, help it to last or cause its disruption ...

The education of children may provide a serious point of conflict in African lineal cultures. Matrilineal fatherhood approaches the idea of the fatherhood of God more than the patrilineal fatherhood. For the matrilineal father has no juridical rights over his children and exercises authority over them only by virtue of a mystical bond that is supposed to exist between him and them. The patrilineal mother is in the same situation. Both love the children for the sake of the children. Here is love which does not ask for or expect something in return. It is love which is reminiscent of the words of the hymn: "My Lord, I love thee not because I hope for heaven thereby." But friction arises when Christianity advises that the education of the child is the responsibility of both parents. In African lineal cultures the responsibility falls on the lineage.

The patrilineal father and the matrilineal mother are the parents with authority over their children. They are not likely to neglect the training of their children. They guard and protect the children from harm. The children, in turn, develop the virtue of reverential fear towards them. However, parental or filial love of the kind expected between a Christian and God is strained. The son, especially the eldest son, is a sort of rival to his father for his property. In some African societies, the threat posed by an eldest son against his father is so feared that it is counterbalanced by a strict regulation making it illegal for a king's or chief's eldest son to succeed him. The absence of specialization of work which in Euro-American societies helps the child to become easily independent, coupled with the group sense which makes the child regard his father's possessions as his by right, makes him the potential "usurper" of his father. He is therefore, looked upon askance by the father.

However, even here the concept of fatherhood is pregnant with "Christian" ideas. God indeed is our master, he possesses power and authority over us. He is provident, looking after us, guarding and protecting us from bodily as well as spiritual harm. He is jealous for our service and undivided loyalty. But his intolerance of man's infidelity is always altruistic, rather than egoistic. There can be no question of a strained relationship between us and God. His love for us increases precisely when we try to "inherit" his Kingdom.

Consequently, the very comparison and contrast between the two types of "African" fatherhood could be extremely useful in instructing catechumens. They project God's personality better on the catechetical screen.

Among other by-products of African social systems is the tendency to unfair play. Social structure alone cannot adequately explain the high incidence of bribery and corruption, nepotism and favoritism everywhere in Africa. However, in any society it should be difficult for a person conducting an interview not to give first consideration to ten candidates for whose education he feels responsible in some way. I would not like to be a judge in Ghana. The number of clansmen appearing before me expecting to be treated leniently, the number of the friends of these relatives in the same situation, not to count those on my wife's side, would leave very few people upon whom I could test my integrity!

But to be a little charitable to African social structures, let me explain that they do not always obstruct the practice of the Christian religion. On the contrary, they are capable of being used to promote the Christian cause. For one thing, the idea of authority in the lineage to whom lineage members look for direction and whom they willingly obey is a good example of the hierarchy in the Church. The communal spirit that ideally should reign supreme in a lineage and the mutual assistance given by and to members of the same lineage remind us of the early Christian communities described for us in the Acts of the Apostles, the spirit of which unfortunately appears to be found nowadays only among the Religious in their communities. Theoretically, no single person should die of hunger, nakedness or lack of shelter. What belongs to one clansman belongs to another.

In African societies, terms like "father," "mother," "Brother", and "sister", which elsewhere, are employed to refer to strictly biological relations, have much wider practical and sociological connotation and application. At a time when so much is being said and recommended about "basic communities," a fresh look at African traditional cultures could point the way to the true salvation of mankind ...

The veneration of lineage tutelary gods and ancestors may be compared with our Christian cult of angels and saints. Here again we are strongly reminded of the doctrine of the Communion of Saints. African social structures well-utilized could afford us traditional ways of securing good relationships among members of our Christian communities. Their effects on marriage could be commendable, for loyalty to the lineage exercises a restraining influence on its married members.

African traditional cultures extol the values of respect, honor, hospitality, magnanimity, purity, truth and hard work. Traditional cultures demand that all citizens have character, and life in conformity with their conscience. Without these, a person is not a human being. He is clothed only in the skin of a human being. If people in practice do not live up to the expectations of culture, this is because, as St. Paul tells us, they cannot understand their own behavior. They find themselves doing the very things they know they should not do. Moreover, African traditional religions lack the concept of grace, enabling weak and trail man to act in accordance with his nature and convictions, to do what is right.

The need to utilize the African's culture for the benefit of Christianity cannot be over-emphasized, especially in the area of the Liturgy. Africans want to enjoy a liturgical situation. They want to play an active and meaningful role in what is happening. Singing and dancing have always formed a constitutive part of their religious celebrations. What takes place must be relevant to their life. They seek room for spontaneous expressions of filial sentiments towards God. They desire the minister to be persoanlly interested in them. To treat the individual as only one in a crowd, and as an impersonal, unnoticed, unacknowledged and unaided spectator is to refuse to fulfill the innermost craving of his heart.

In reflecting on African cultures in relation to Christianity, one must mention the "life cycle" or rites of passage. These rites, which are very much religious in character, are found everywhere in Africa. Because of their varying complexity, my comments are based mainly on my Ashanti experience.

Until these rites of passage have been carefully analyzed and all their implications truly ascertained, we would do well to refrain from equating them with the Sacraments. The thought is tantalizing because the rites contain elements which on the surface are similar to features in the Sacraments. For instance, the rites are performed at crucial turning-points in a man's life - in particular at birth, puberty and death. The same seems to be true for at least some of the Sacraments. Rites of passage are meant to produce what they symbolize. So also are the Sacraments. Each of the rites may be performed only once for any one person. Baptism, Confirmation and the Priesthood too are received but once by any one individual. In the performance of the rites, material objects accompanied by words are employed, and the Sacraments, in scholastic terminology, are constituted of matter and form, and so on.

The two sets of ceremonies contain somewhat similar ideas indeed, but they are not therefore identical - the rites should not be regarded as some sort of primitive Sacraments, since the discrepancies between them are notable. Baptism, for Christians, is a new birth, which renders one a child of God, and an heir of his Kingdom. It produces its effects on the recipient alone. It is not necessarily received in babyhood - a 100-year old man may be baptized just as validly as a one-day old baby. Baptism, therefore appears to be different from child-naming or outdooring ceremonies. The latter are not regarded as a new birth, but a "ratification" of the old. They are not thought to benefit the child alone, but its mother, father and the whole community; and they cannot be postponed until adulthood.

The same view may be expressed on puberty or initiation rites. Their effects are not intended only for the novices. True, a girl neophyte is prayed for in order that she may be pleasing to the ancestors, have a happy and especially fruitful life, and grow old. But it would appear that the main motive behind her initiation is to change an alarming condition from a calm but unproductive girlhood to potentially dangerous but fertile adulthood. The adults in the community do not want to associate with an "unclean" girl at their level and thereby suffer from famine, plagues, child-death, etc. They cleanse her from her "impurity" before admitting her into their company. The rites are as important to them as to her. I therefore do not see which of the Sacraments can be favorably compared with initiation rites.

Funeral rites are probably the best example of ceremonies performed for the sake of community, and not those for whom ostensibly they are meant - the dead. In the first place they are rites of passage performed after the person has given up his soul. They are cautiously gone through lest the deceased become annoyed and visit the living with various calamities. Even when references are made to the dead, they are not necessarily meant to benefit them. The living are sorry that they no longer enjoy the good services of the dead; they petition them for things, ask them to protect them and so on. Therefore, one cannot by the wildest stretch of imagination, claim that funeral obsequies are comparable to the Sacrament of the Sick, which is advantageous to the dying, not the dead. A close study of widowhood and other funeral rites will confirm this opinion.

So the Sacraments differ from rites of passage, but here again my intention is not to give the impression that they are so opposed that they cannot be reconciled. I want only to guard against the hasty and probably false hope that we have in Africa specimens of the Sacraments.

I am all for purifying the rites and then preserving them if only because of the good pragmatic effects they produce. They engender the spirit of solidarity in a community; funerals are attended by all and sundry and while in progress, disagreements and hatreds are buried. Puberty or nubility were once the mainstay of juvenile or premarital purity, not to say virginity. Even now it is the painful truth that the morally good girl or boy is more difficult to find among literate Christian children than among pagan children who still hold fast to their traditional beliefs. The same rites focussed attention on the girl, and gave her the publicity through which she hoped to attract a husband. They further served as an instrument of instruction in the qualities of a wife, in motherhood and in maternal attributes. Educators of children used them to maintain the accepted standards of morality and good behavior. They also acted as sanctions against bad husbands.

Another "African" theme of importance to Christianity is that of fecundity. Because of their fundamental humanity, Africans place a great value on physical generation, on life and the sharing of life. In the Western world, the "good life" is equated with proficiency in science and technology. It is a dehumanizing equation. Africa might assist in the process of revaluation.

Closely linked with the theme of fecundity is that of "man-in-community." Pope Paul VI, in his letter to Africa of 1967, pointed out that this has three characteristics: the spiritual view of life, the sense of the family and the sense of community.

Finally, Africa has the potential to place a much-needed priority on a theology of relationships between human and spiritual beings, particularly between the living and the dead. As Aylward Shorter points out, this is a strong preoccupation of traditional religious systems in Africa and it could well provide an enrichment for the Christian idea of the Communion of Saints.

It is evident that there is a vast Christian Theological potential in Africa, not simply in spite of contemporary change, but because of it. That is why it behooves Christianity in Africa to heed the exhortation:

> Prudently and lovingly through dialogue and collaboration with the followers of other religions, and in witness of Christian faith and life, acknowledge, preserve, and promote the spiritual and moral good found among these men, as well as the values in their society and culture (Vatican Council II, Nostra Aetate, 2).

ISLAM: ITS ENCOUNTER WITH AFRICAN TRADITIONAL RELIGION IN NIGERIA: A REVIEW

by

E.M. Uka

Introduction

This paper will consider the religion of Islam firstly and by way of an introduction, its founder, its main teachings, its role in pre-Islamic Arabia and its spread into West Africa. Secondly and finally, it will examine its encounter with the indigenous religions of some traditional societies in Nigeria such as the people of Nupe, Yoruba and Benin. Islam did not spread mightly towards the southern part of Nigeria. Its spread was checked by the British colonial presence in Nigeria in the 19th century. So its presence in the South-Eastern part of Nigeria is minimal but tends to be gathering some momentum. (1)

Islam is a missionary religion. It seeks to convert people from whatever religion and socio-political organisation they had to that provided by Islam. In Arabia, its place of origin, it transformed the socio-political as well as the religious life of the people. In Nigeria, it made its debut in Bornu in North-eastern Nigeria in the eleventh century and in the Hausa States between 14th and 15th centuries. Until the 19th century, Islam in Nigeria was mainly the religion of the city dwellers, notably the upper classes. The mass of the people in the rural areas retained their traditional religion. (2) The Jihad, holy war, initiated by Usman Dan Fodio to revive and reform the syncretist Islam of the Hausa States, marked a new era in the Islamic missionary strategy in Nigeria. In this paper therefore, we shall look at the overall Islamic missionary strategy in Nigeria, its pattern of penetration into new areas which is first of all by peaceful infiltration and contact with the upper class, secondly by means of force, the Jihad, holy war, and finally by peaceful co-existence. (3)

Islam: Its Founder, Its Teaching and Impact in Arabia (4)

Islam is the religion which Mohammed preached in Arabia in six century AD. Those who belong to this religion are called muslims. Islam means 'to surrender or to submit oneself in obedience to God. So a moslem is one who surrenders or submits himself to obey God, **Allah.**

Mohammed spread his religion in Arabia between 610-632 AD. He taught the Arabs to believe in the one living God and live as the servants of God. After the death of Mohammed, the Prophet, his followers carried his religion into Asia and Africa. Today, this religion has spread to many parts of the world.

All muslims honour Mohammed as a prophet of God. They accept his book, the Koran as the scripture which God delivered to them through His prophet - Mohammed. Their creed is summed up in the statement: "There is no God but Allah, Mohammed is the Prophet"! According to David A. Brown, (5) muslims express their belief about God thus: He is

- The One, the Real, the Living, the Secure, the First, the last.
- The Wise, the Knower, the One who comprehends everything.
- The Great, the Powerful, the Strong, the Mighty.
- The Agent, the Creator, the King, the Sovereign.
- The Hearer, the Answerer of prayer.
- The Giver, the Merciful, the Compasionate, the Forgiver, the Loving.

Muslims believe that God appointed human beings to be His agents on earth and gave them the earth with all its resources. A human being can have no higher dignity than to be servant of God.

Muslims believe that God gave man guidance through the natural world so that men may learn about Him from it. In the Koran, the good things of the natural world are called signs of God's bounty and mercy (30:46-50). They also learn about God through His Angels who are His messengers. He sends them to carry out His will. His angels are sexless, they neither eat nor drink. One of the most important is angel Gabriel who brought the Koran to Mohammed and taught him the prayer-act. Muslims believe that God caused the contents of the Heavenly Book, the Scriptures to be revealed to other prophets before Mohammed. For example, the Torah (Law) or **Tawrah** was revealed to Moses.

298

The Psalms **Zabur** to David, the Gospel **Injil** to Jesus and finally the **Koran** to Mohammed.

Concerning destiny, the muslims believe that God will judge the world. On that day, the angels will bring everyone for judgment. Those who pass the test will be admitted to Paradise, those who fail will be sent to Hell (18:49; 17:13-15). Islam teaches that every person is responsible for his own action and his own punishment. Those who commit great sins and die unrepentant will go to Hell. They also believe the prophet will intercede for them and they will eventually pass into Paradise.

The Pillars of Islam (6)

Muslims, as servants of God, perform or owe certain duties to God. The duties are called:

The Pillars of Islam. They are:

Declaration of Islamic creed - the Shahada

The Prayer-act: The Salat

Almsgiving: The Zaket

Fasting during the month of Ramadan - The Sawon

Pilgrimage to Mecca - The Hajj.

Muslims are expected to declare their faith thus: "I testify that there is no god except Allah and Mohammed is His Prophet." To say this with sincerity makes a person a muslim.

Impact of Islam on Pre-Islamic Arabia (7)

When Mohammed made his debut on the socio-religious scene in Arabia, he brought about many reforms. For example, Mohammed abolished tribalism, i.e. membership of the **Shaikh** which was by adoption or by blood relation. In its place, he created the **Ummah** which was based on membership of the Islamic community. By this token, the head of Islamic community was Allah not the Shaikh.

Homicide

Formally, murder cases led to civil wars, but the prophet laid the policy of "an eye for an eye and a tooth for a tooth" for murderers. However, provision was made for blood money or outright forgiveness where the killing wasnot premediated.

Infanticide

The Arabs of pre-Islamic times buried their daughters alive. The poor buried for fear of poverty while the rich buried because their daughters did not contribute to the glory of the tribe with special reference to wars. But the Qur'an (6:52 and 17:30ff) stipulates that one should not kill one's children for fear of poverty for it is Allah who provided for the children and their parents. Furthermore the Qur'an says that those who bury their daughters alive would be brought to judgement on the judgement day.

War

During the pre-Islamic period minor and trivial cases resulted into war. But the new law removes war except in extreme cases. The case must first be taken to the prophet or his representative for trial. Furthermore there was the ruling that a Muslim must not fight a fellow Muslim.

Wine

Before then, the Arabians took pride in being drunk. But the reform emphasised outright rejection of alcoholism. The prophet claimed that wine was of the devil and as such must be abhored.

Polygamy

At first there was no limit to the number of wives to be married by the men. Women also practised polyandry. The reform completely rejected polyandry. There was provision for the man to marry up to a limit of four wives simultaneously on

300

condition that the man would love and treat them equally. Muslim scholars doubt a man's ability to be impartial in such a case. They strongly recommend one wife.

Divorce

Divorce jamboree was replaced by restricted grant of divorce conditions which protected the interest of the down-trodden women were stipulated. Enough provision was made for reconciliation. It was however granted where a couple could not live peacefully together.

Inheritance

Formerly, inheritance was the exclusive preserve of the male issues. Islamic reforms allows the women folk the right to inherit. The women were to share the deceased's property with the men in the ratio of 1:2. It further stipulates that a person's heir are not only one's spouse and children but also one's parents and grand-parents if they are living, as well as one's grand children and their children without regard to their sexes.

Will

At first one could will out almost all his belongings to the detriment of the family. But Islam imposed restriction to this. No one was allowed to will more than one-third of one's property. Furthermore Islam lays out specific ratio of property to be given to each heir.

Usury

Commercial dishonesty was in vogue during the pre-Islamic period. But Islam completely rejects this. Even conservative Muslims frown at the rate of interest charged by banks in respect of loans and overdraft. Islam of course makes allowance for **'maslaha'** - where the greatest advantage is given to the greatest number of people.

Islam: Its spread into West Africa and to Nigeria (8)

Islam penetrated into West Africa through The Senegal Region and the empires of Ghana, Mali, Songhay, Kanem-Bornu and the Hausa States. We shall consider its spread only in the Hausa States. When the Berber people migrated into the Northern states of Nigeria, they lived with the indigenous tribes, intermarried with them and in time became dominant over them. Out of this development arose the original Hausa States known as **Hausa Bakwai**: Daura, Kano, Zaria, Gobir, Katsina, Rano and Biran. Still another group developed in the south which came to be known as **Banza Bakwai**: They include Zamfara, Kebbi, Nupe, Gwari, Yauri, Yomba and Ilorin.

The Hausa people are not a tribe. The unifying element among them is a common language, and after the introduction of Islam, a common religion, Islam was introduced into Hausaland between 1350-1400. It entered from the West and was propagated by missionaries from Mali. The religion was first adopted by the chiefs and spread to the masses from there, inspite of opposition from them.

Although Islam was accepted, it had to co-exist with the indigenous religious beliefs and practices. The emergence of Shehu Usman Dan Fodio with his concern to spread and purify Islam in the Hausa states, marked the rise of the Holy War, (Jihad) and the ascendency of the Fulani empire among the Hausa states between 1804-1810. Usman Dan Fodio began his crusade in his home town of Gobir by defeating and displacing Yunfa, the King of Gobir. After this initial success many of the Hausas followed him. He selected fourteen of his best warriors and gave them authority to lead the jihad in various parts of the Northern Nigeria. Under their leadership, the Hausa states were conquered and the fourteen warriors began the line of Emirs that have governed the state of the Fulani Empire with Sokoto as their administrative headquarters. Later, the religious fervour that had characterised the Jihad abated and the Emirs gradually became more independent of the Sultan of Sokoto. As the political power of the Sultan waned, his authority as the spiritual leader of the Islamic community waxed stronger.

Spread of Islam among the Nupe of Northern Nigeria (9)

Islam came to the Nupe people as a religion of conquerors, and what mattered to the conquerors was the assimilation of the upper class culture and only secondarily their deliverance from unbelief. This is the reason why Islamic religion reached only a section of the population and remained superficial. It provided the people with new religious ceremonies in addition to, but not in place of their traditional religious practices.

In the early stages of Islamization of the people they were attracted to the religion by reasons of its prestige since the ruling class were muslims. The promise of protection from slavery and patronage of the ruling class for the peasants and craftsmen also drew these classes of people to the faith.

As Nadel (9) observed, Nupe Muslims did not follow strict Islamic traditions. For example, they observed only two of the five pillars of islam - i.e. the daily prayers and fasting. They omitted the giving of alms, going on pilgrimage to Mecca and confessing of faith in God. They did not consider the confession of faith in Allah as important since like all Africans, they already were acknowledging one supreme God before the coming of the muslims. Even though they recite Islamic prescribed prayers in Arabic, yet they say their own personal prayers in Nupe language. They observe three of the seven muslem festivals namely the **Mutarran** i.e. the New Year festival. The **Idel-Fitr** which marks the end of the Ramadan fasting, and **Id–el-Kibir** i.e. the great feast in the pilgrimage month which ends the year.

Muslim women in Nupe do not put on the veil and they are not allowed into the mosque. There are Nupe religious and customary practices which agree with that of the Islamic tradition. These are in the areas of marriage gifts and easy divorce, circumcision, divination, kinship rites and the prohibition in eating pigs. In matters of inheritance however, the Nupe custom takes precedence over the Islamic practice.

In sum, Nadel considers Nupe's conversion to Islam as social rather than religious.

Islam and Yoruba in Religious Contact (10)

Dada Adelowo has written an incisive paper on this subject and we shall depend largely on his insight in our attempt to examine how much of Yoruba land is truly Islamic and how much of her is still unIslamic despite the imprint of Islam in Yoruba land over the centuries.

Before the advent of Islam in Yoruba land, the people already believed in a supreme God whom they called **Olodumare, Oluwa, Olorun, Olofin orun.** These were synonymous with the Muslim Allah. So in their ritual prayers, the Yoruba-muslems or non-muslims use the vernacular in invoking God, Allah. This is because, the vernacular names for God are more meaningful to the muslim and nonmuslim Yorubas.

Whereas the crucial question in issues of religious change is to determine to what extent whatever was worshipped before had validity for authorising sanctions of conduct, has been rejected, one would then like to know what the Yoruba Muslims have done with their traditional beliefs in the local divinities who were believed to be God's messengers, His servants.

According to Adelowo, (11) the situation is one of a mixture of some elements of adaptation and ambivalence. The question of the latter is much more noticeable in the reaction of Yoruba muslims to their erstwhile belief in divination and ancestral spirits. In Islam, Allah, and only He is to be worshipped not the divinities nor the ancestral spirits. But as has been revealed from the history of Islam in Africa, this cardinal principle of radical monotheism has not been strictly adhered to. The grip of the traditional religion is still so strong that even some Yoruba muslims still consult the oracle, the divinity and some still feel inclined to participate in the annual traditional festivals in honour of the tutelary divinities. For these Yoruba muslims, they feel that family solidarity comes first before religious affiliation. However, the muslims feel seriously guilty of ambivalence with regard to their intercourse with their dead ancestors. A good number of Yoruba muslims do not feel any qualms about this since they rank family solidarity higher than religious solidarity. So for the village muslims, the supernatural world is comprehended and apprehended as a synthesis of both Islamic and traditional Yoruba beliefs. Although Islam provides a radically new departure, with the stress upon the uniqueness of God, yet it does not deny the existence of other spiritual deities.

304

The Yoruba muslim like other non-muslim Yoruba believe in witches who possess powers lodged within them which may be used for good or for evil purposes. (12) The Yoruba Muslims believe that witches are mostly women flying about at night through a bird, familiar particularly with the night jar.

The Yorubas have diviners and traditional healers who are trained to check and counter the nefasous activities of socerers who use their occultic powers for anti-social ends. Though the British and the Europeans call them witch-doctors, the fact is that they exist both in the traditional Yoruba quarters and in the Yoruba Islamic quarters. They both exist to effect peace and tranquility as well as socio-religious peaceful existence. They labour together to exterminate the sources of evil perpetrated by the witches and socerers.

Among the Yoruba-Muslims, divination plays an important role in their daily life just as in the life of a non-muslim-Yoruba. The main difference in their art of divination is that the Yoruba muslim diviners use sand brought from Mecca while the traditional priest uses the traditional sand. (13) The Yoruba Muslim use the **tasbih,** the rosary a good deal. Some muslims use the Koran for divinatory purposes too. Sometimes it is believed that certain kinds of divination **"Alutas"** came to Yoruba land from muslim resources of the North where similar systems are practised. But the Yorubas have made Ifa divination fully their own. The Yoruba muslims and non muslims consult either of the muslim or non muslim diviners in times of crises. The attitude of the Yoruba muslims in this regard can be explained in terms of the fact that divination in general results from man's urge to obtain the best out of life and to penetrate the future and to plan adequately. The Yorubas practise divination due to their anxiety to know the intention of God and the gods with regard to their future and their immediate relations. Hence, the Yoruba-muslims regard Islamic and local amulets and the two systems of divination as both effective and efficacious. This attitude toward divination is eating deep into Yoruba christians who join "spiritual churches" where dreams and visions, and speaking in tongues and prophesies are practised in place of the traditional and Islamic forms of divination.

The adaptation of Islam to the traditional religious setting of the Yorubas implies a radical transfer of values from the Yoruba moral awareness, formed under the influence of the spirit world, to a legalistic morality introduced by Islam. (13) The great change which Islam brought lies in its exclusive claim for the supremacy of its system of moral conduct, their privileges and taboos. Though Islam has displaced some of the traditional sanctions, yet those sanctions that are connected with social inter-course and conventional taboos remain.

With respect to marriages, (14) Islam allows polygamy, but limits the number of free women - legal wives at any one time to four. It also tolerates an unlimited acquisition of second-ary wives of slave origin. In this practice, only men who are wealthy and belong to the higher status group can benefit from this practice. Since this practice tallies with the traditional Yoruba position on marriage, it gives a boost to the spread of Islam in Yoruba land as against christianity which insists on one man one wife.

The Episode of Islam in the Ancient City of Benin (15)

Benin received Islam from Yoruba land. This came about through the Yoruba muslims who settled in Benin City around the end of the 19th century as artisans and traders. Most of them came from Lagos, Abeokuta, Ibadan, Oshogbo, Ilorin etc. They came to Benin City because at that time, Benin was a great commercial and diplomatic center which possessed an advanced culture and a traditional religion. Along with trading, some of these muslim-Yoruba traders practised healing with herbs and the verses of the Koran. This feat attracted some Binis to Islam, but not to the extent of converting them to the new faith since their attachment to their traditional religion was too strong for any possible conversion at those early stages.

Some Binis however became moslems, through their contact with Yoruba muslim traders in places like Lagos, Akure, Owo, Ilorin. When those Binis finally returned home to Benin, they joined the group of Yoruba moslems whom they met in Benin City and all of them worshipped and practised Islam together.

According to Balogun (16) the name of the person who actually established Islam in Benin is one Olojo Kosoko who came from Lagos. He was a trader and the chief of the Yorubas in Benin City. He later married the daughter of a prominent and philanthropic Bini muslim named Lawani Borokini. Consequently Olojo Kosoko, a decendant of King Kosoko of Lagos, built the Central Mosque which today is situated at No. 1 Lagos Street Benin City. (17)

Some of the ways by which the Binis were converted to Islam was through Bini muslim merchants who encouraged their townsmen attached to them as business partners to accept Islam. Some of the Bini Muslim merchants also attracted a lot of people to the muslem faith through their generosity. In order to retain converts within their fold, some of the merchants married the duaghters of their trading partners or vice-versa. The jealous ones among them like Ibrahim Elaiho Guobadia is reported to have engaged in burning idols of converts before initiating them into Islam. Guobadia incidently became the first Bini man to become an Imam. (18)

One important feature in the spread of Islam in Bendel State was the involvement of influential personalities in the Islamic evangelistic strategy. For example, royal princes who embraced Islam in Agbede and Auchi; the wealthy merchant who wielded great influence in the traditional court of Eweka II, in the case of Bini - all of them were influential in converting their communities to the Islamic faith. (19)

In sum, it could be said that the Yoruba-muslim attitude to their traditional religious beliefs and attitudes are largely similar to that of the Binis whom they won to the Islamic faith.

Conclusion

This paper has tried to review the pattern of penetration and relationship between Islam, an external change agent and traditional indigenous non-missionary religions of the Nupe people, the Yoruba and the Binis. According to O.U. Kalu, (20) no one could categorically claim that international religions or new religious change agents (like Islam, Christianity and Buddhism) overtly destroyed or displaced traditional, indigenous religious beliefs and practices such as the traditional religions of Nupe, Yorubas, Binis, or of the Dinka of Sudan or the religion of Ga in Ghana, or the Maori religion of the Polynesians. (21) Kalu observed that apart from overt rejection or resistance to overt erosion, middle positions which characterise the situation in Nupe, Yoruba and Bini exist. They are:

- continuities at the points of contact or correlation;
- transvaluation of native symbols, where traditional symbols acquire new meaning;

- substitution, where the new faith absorbs ingredients of the traditional
- and a transformation, where completely new symbols and values are created in the confrontation of the old and the new. (22)

In the patterns of interaction we have reviewed, we observed that the traditional religious forms like in Nupe have persisted inspite of the 'invasion' of Islam. This is due to the nature and function of religion in traditional societies, where religion is integrative, and unifies and centralises all the individual's values to that of the group. It is important to observe also that Islam recorded a very rapid spread and growth among the Yorubas and the Benin people because it was more accommodating to certain traditional practices and its propagators were mainly Binis and Yoruba themselves.

Footnotes

1   Ikenga-Metuh, "Muslim Resistance to Christian Missionary Penetration of Northern Nigeria 1857-1960" in **The God's in Retreat: Continuity and Change in African Religions** (Enugu: Fourth Dimension 1986) pp. 85-103, edited by I. Metuh. See also J.S. Trimingham, **History of Islam in West Africa,** (London: OUP, 1962) pp. 230-231.

2   Ibid., Mucizz Goriawala, "Maguzawa: Influence of Islam on Traditional Religion in Hausaland" in **God In Retreat ...** edited by Ikenga-Metuh, pp. 45-55.

3   J.S. Mbiti, **African Religions and Philosophy,** (London: Heinemann 1965), pp. 242-254.

4   David A. Brown, **A Guide to Religions,** (London: SPCK 1975) pp. 182-197.

5   Ibid., pp. 2o7-210.

6   Ibid., pp. 214-216.

7   Trevor Ling, **A History of Religion East and West,** (London: Macmillan Press 1968), pp. 209-232.

8   J.S. Trimingham, **History of Islam in West Africa,** (London: OUP, 1962).

9   S.F. Nadel, **Nupe Religion,** (London, 1954), pp. 230-258. Note that the people of Maguzawa did not accept Islam inspite of the Jihad, see article by M. Goriawala.

10 E. Dada Adelowo, "Islam and Yoruba in Religious Contact: An Episode of Acculturation" in **Nigerian Association for the Study of Religions,** (NASR), pp. 66-72, 6th Annual Conference, Univ. of Jos, Sept. 1-6, 1980.

11 Ibid., pp. 66-67.

12 Ibid., p. 68, see also M. Warwicks ed. **Witchcraft and Socery,** Penguine 1970 et-passim. J.A. Omoyajowo, **Witches,** Ibadan 1974 et passim. By the same author, **A Study of the Belief in Witchcraft and Its Future in Modern Africa,** (Ibadan, 1965), p. 11. See also E.B. Idowu, "The Challenge of Witchcraft", **Orita,** vol.IV, No.1, June 1970.

13 Ibid. See details on taboos in Idowu, **Olodumare** ... (London: 1962), pp. 83, 99, 108, 118, 146.

14 Ibid., Adelowo, p. 70. See also Ade Dopamu, "Trad. Religion, Islam & Xtianity in Yoruba ..." in **Gods In Retreat,** ed. by Ikenga-Metuh, pp. 107-129.

15 I.A.B. Balogun, "The Episode of Islam in the Ancient City of Benin", in **Nigerian Journal of the Humanities,** (vol.1 No.1, Sept. 1977, Univ. of Benin), pp. 18-27.

16 Ibid., pp. 18-19.

17 Ibid., p. 19.

18 Ibid., p. 20.

19 Ibid. See Koran 21:51-70.

20 O.U. Kalu, "Gods in Retreat: Models of Religious Change in Africa" in **Nig. Journal of the Humanities,** pp. 42-50.

21 David A. Brown, **A Guide to Religions,** (pp. 14-44).

22 O.U. Kalu, Gods in Retreat ... in **The Gods in Retreat: Continuity and Change in African Religions,** ed. E. Ikenga-Metuh (Enugu: Fourth Dimension 1986), p. 15. In the same book see also Y.A. Quadri, "Some Attempts At Reforming Muslim Practices in Nigeria", (pp. 219-140).

GODS IN RETREAT:
MODELS OF RELIGIOUS CHANGE IN AFRICA

by

Ogbu Kalu

Locating the Problem

World religions, especially Christianity and Islam, in-
vaded Africa many centuries ago. These external religious forces
have made great impacts and contributed to vast changes in African cultural, political and economic life. However, the study of
their impacts on African traditional religion and society is remarkable for the absence of viable models or conceptual schemes to
organize the increasing data.

This paper sets out to highlight the poverty of conceptual schemes in the study of African traditional religion by
appraising the current techniques.

The retreat of the African gods is rather obvious, however difficult nationalists may find the fact. Three crucial issues
in the study of religious change are, therefore, the cause of conversion from traditional to world religions, the pattern of the
impact of these external religious change-agents on African cosmology, and an explanation for the persistance of traditional religion.

Missionary hagiography and accounts by travellers and
colonial administrators left the impression that the defeat was
a rout. Waves of nationalist resurgence at various points in time
appeared to accept the verdict and romantically sought to replant
the gods firmly in the African's firmament.

Models of Religious Change

The model of change which puts it most blandly is the
dualistic typology utilised in the study of the colonial era. It assumes the existence of dominant colonial and dependent indigenous
structures, the former introducing the dynamic element into the
situation and deriving their objectives from the metropolitan

centre, and the latter serving the former and exercising an independent authority derived from earlier social forms only within the limits set by the demands of the metropolitan centre. (1) The implicit assumption in most nationalistic cultural renaissance and the danger in the dominant/dependent model would be that the impact of the external factors was an overt displacement of the traditional. (2)

Empirical studies have shown that change does not occur in this fashion; that within a spectrum ranging from overt rejection to overt displacement are middle positions which tally with the complexity of real life situations. Beneath the apparent harmony of the dominant/dependent model of the colonial period was a deep-seated contradiction; the forces released by this contradiction later created the protests of the nationalists. The persistence of traditional religious forms and values has called attention to the need of a new model for understanding the pattern of religious change in Africa, Perceptive missionaries, even at the height of their triumph, were always more sober than the colonial regimes in appraising the degree of their success over traditional religions. As late as 1967, T.A. Beetham, the Secretary to one of the most successful missionary bodies, still wondered whether christianity has sunk deep roots in Africa and delivered a death-blow to African traditional religion. (3) The degree and depth of christianization and islamization are not settled questions.

The irony is that sociologists and political scientists have shown greater interest in the dynamics of change. The field of African traditional religion has been dominated especially by social anthropologists and this has left an indelible imprint. Studies of African traditional religion have tended to be descriptive. The roots lie in the origin of the discipline. Colonial anthropologists either utilised the assumptions of nineteenth-century European theorists of primitive religion or merely described the structures of "primitive" societies for policy-making purposes. (4) "Various colonial governments", observed M. Fortes, "encouraged and assisted important anthropological researches which could not otherwise have been possible." He referred to the degree of such aid as "the flood of government largesse". (5) Naturally, such researches subserved the practical needs of the colonial system. They bore the mark or stripes of the dominant racist intellectual milieu. (6) No one thought in terms of models of change but rather described the various primitive religious practices which must be wiped off. G.M. Haliburton commented that before Prophet Harris appeared on the Ivory Coast scene, the French colonial government had mounted an unsuccessful campaign to rid the people of fetishes and other aspects of traditional religious practices. (7) An anthropologist in such a setting would catalogue and describe such practices for eradication. The subtleties in native perceptions of the change-agents were easily ignored.

Yet these colonial anthropologists and their progenitors (Evans-Pritchard, Godfrey Lienhardt, Placide Tempels, Victor Turner, Fortes, Daryll Forde, Monica Wilson and Aidan Southall) rendered some useful service. They initiated a systematic study of African religions through field work. This differed from the works of the nineteenth-century arm-chair theorists, Tylor, Spencer, Marrett, Frazer, Durkheim and their disciples. Besides, these early theorists were not concerned with sympathetic understanding of "primitive religions" but rather with the origin of religions and the differences between primitive mentality and European scientific mind. They were agnostics who assumed that christianity in Europe could be attacked by appeal to origins of elementary forms. (8) Evolutionary and racist theories also characterized their attitudes.

An implicit model of religious change in the unilinear evolutionary theory undergirding Frazer's work is that as the small-scale, primitive societies evolve towards the higher position occupied by nineteenth-century Europe, their religious mentality and organization would become more complex. This could only occur by the displacement of the traditional by an external change-agent, western civilization. Durkheim might sneer at British psychological interpreters of the origin of religion, but a point of contact existed. Both parties utilized an organic conception of society. Religion is a social fact, claimed Durkheim, therefore religious change is a function of social evolution. As a society evolves, her clan cults change because "religion is a unified system of beliefs and practices by which individuals represent to themselves the society to which they belong and their relation to it." (9)

Durkheim's social analysis became the presupposition of two schools of functionalist theorists who attempted to explain cultural and social phenomena on the basis of the functional prerequisites they satisfy. They studied the dynamics of a social process in terms of interaction of institutions and groups. Resources in language structures and religious symbols (10) were utilized to underscore the relationship between religious and social structures. The flaw in the functionalist approach for the African is firstly ideological. It pursues harmony and equilibrum and ignores the disfunctional dimension or what Chairman Mao calls "contradictions" in the society. A functionalist approach would direct religious change in African towards harmonious adaptation of the traditional and the new. An emphasis on social contradictions would seek the pattern of change in the confrontation of the religious forces. Furthermore, the functionalists do not adequately explain conversion and the rate of religious change precisely because the inner experience of the individual eluded them.

Durkheim's insights must not; however, be ignored. He demonstrated that though religion starts as a dependent variable, a creation of the society, it evolves to become an independent variable capable of catalysing change. Building on this, his disciples emphasized the functions of religion as a store-house of values, an integrative force and legitimizer of social foundations. Religious structures and values are, therefore, not static but evolve with the society, changing other ingredients of the culture and being changed in the process. The days are gone when African traditional religion was considered áhistorical and studied as static in a narrative and descriptive form as Geoffrey Parrinder did. (11) On the contrary, African traditional religion must be studied historically as a changing form concomitant with the changing patterns of an evolving culture. Frantz Fanon could, therefore, sneer at the romanticist confusion among the cultural Negritude movement.

There is a remarkable agreement among social theorists of various hues (e.g. symbolists who start with an assumption that African spirits are symbolic representations of reality, and intellectualists who regard the spirits and the whole cosmology as a theoretical framework) that conversion from African traditional religion to "Word religions" occurred in response to changes in social organization. As Robin Horton, the major current advocate of the intellectualist approach, put it, conversion became pronounced when a period of rapid social change obliterated many of the fields of experience with which the traditional cults concerned themselves. He observed:

> If thousands of people find themselves outside the microcosms, and if even those left inside see the boundaries weakening if not actually dissolving, they can only interpret these changes by assuming that the lesser spirits (underpinners of the microcosms) are in retreat. (12)

314

He goes on to explain the process of the change as achieved by an exploitation of a latent ingredient in the African cosmology, the deus remotus. Under the new dispensation or enlarged scale, the Supreme God came down to be the underpinner of morality in the macrocosm. Horton's is a bold hypothesis which, among other flaws, fails to explain the pattern of change in those African communities where God was not hiding somewhere paring his fingernails. (13)

Two factors must be noted in Robin Horton's approach. Firstly, his revamped intellectualist model assumes that there is a degree of rationality in African traditional cosmology comparable to western scientific thinking. (14) He dispenses with Levi-Strauss's distinction between mythical thinking among primitive and rational thinking in science. This is a remarkable shift from the racialist notion that African beliefs are a mere aggregation of irrational reactions to natural phenomena and environment. To Horton, African thinking is not scientific but both Africans and westerners start from a theoretical framework which they then correlate with empirical situations.

Secondly, Horton does not explain change by a mono-causal reference to external change-agent. He virtually argues that change was caused by the internal factors, for instance, the potential within the traditional cosmology for a Surpeme Being to cater for the macrocosm. Also, it must be added, conversion from traditional beliefs and practices was related to internal strains within the socio-religious system (15) However, Horton moves towards an economic explanation - that changes in conception of God and morality are merely functions of changes in the socio-economic structures. Here we must turn to Karl Marx.

A prominent nineteenth-century figure whose reputation has obscured the fact that he did not carry out any field work among the so-called primitive peoples is Karl Marx. Unlike the other arm-chair theorists (as far as African traditional religion is concerned), Marx was concerned more specifically with the problem of change. However, he bothered to comment on religion only as an example of one of the obstructions to change. "The abolition of religion as the illusory happiness of the people is required for their real happiness." (16) Man created his gods and therefore religion is a product of consciousness; consciousness is determined by man's social existence and the real dynamic of change is man's action in shaping his world. "The mode of production in material life determines the general character of the social, political and spiritual processes of life." Marx denied that religion could be an independent catalyst of social change. On the contrary,

> Morality, religion, metaphysics, all the rest of ideology and corresponding forms of consciousness, thus no longer retain any semblance of independence. They have no history, no development, but men, developing their material production and their material intercourse, alter, along with this, their real existence, their thinking, and the products of their thinking. Life is not determined by consciousness but consciousness by life.

This is the heart of the Marxist materialist critique, repeated in various forms in many of his writings. It points to a model for studying religious change which simply states that the degree and rate of such change is a function of the mode of production. By this perspective, African traditional religion would be displaced in inverse proportion to the rate of change in economic mode.

If Marx were to argue that the pattern of religious expression is a function of the mode of production, he would be making eminent good sense. Agricultural, pastoral/nomadic and industrial communities worship differently. As the Israelites moved from a nomadic existence, wandering through Palestinian wilderness to a sedentary agricultural mode of existence, their religious practices changed. They worshipped the same God in different ways reflecting differing styles of existence. Nieburh's Social Basis of Denominations in America makes the same point.

Evans-Pritchard's study of the Nuer (1956) and Lienhardt's study of the Dinka demonstrated that their religious, legal and political structures reflect the dominant bovine culture. John Mbiti's observations on the African's conception of the other world provides a fodder for the Marxist view that existence determines religious consciousness "The world of the spirits", says Mbiti:

> wherever it might be situated, is very much like a carbon copy of the countries where they lived in this life. It has rivers, valleys, mountains, forests and deserts. The activities of the spirits are similar to those of human life here ... (17)

In short, concludes Evans-Pritchard, "in all societies religious thought bears the impress of the social order." Religious change must therefore be a function of social change. (18)

The distinction must, however, be drawn between religious experience and religious expression, between belief and practices. Admittedly, the pattern of practices could give an insight into the intensity and character of religious belief, but the former does not comprehend the fullness of the latter. Marx assumed that religion was illusory and therefore ignored the force of religious experience and made religion a mere epiphenomenon of society. Even Emile Durkheim did not go so far; religion could develop from a dependent to an independent variable. Max Weber agrees too.

There is no doubt about Marxist contributions to analysis of social change. Firstly, Marx grasped the force of the economic factor in the political, social and cultural processes. The innumerable economic interpretations of national histories are a legacy. Sir Lewis Namier later reinterpreted the history of England in the Eighteenth Century by insisting that the pursuit of material interest constituted the dynamic of change rather than the ideas which leaders espoused. There is no doubt that the penetration of both Islamism and Christianity could be partially explained by the material benefits they offered: wealth, status, protection. But could we conclude that African traditional religion was a mere illusory creation of peasant societies, to be discarded under the new dispensation heralded by western scientific methods? If this were so, then, any cultural renaissance including the reconstruction of African traditional religion is a romantic enterprise. African traditional religion has no future in a continent whose economic mode is becoming increasingly technological.

Secondly, Marxist "this-wordly" humanism and his espousal of the conflict theory (emphasis on the contradiction in social institutions) have contributed immensely to an understanding of change. The conflict theory demonstrates how change could occur in response to internal contradictions, strains or disfunctional elements as well as in confrontation with intruding external change-agents. A new mode is fashioned in the crucible of conflict rather than by mere adaptation or grafting the old to the new.

This is crucial in considering religious change in Africa because the much-vaunted indigenization process has been bedevilled with confusion in conception as well as practice. Yet, the conflict theory does not deny that change occurs more easily when there are lines of continuities between the traditional and the new. That is, Ruth Benedict's concept of continuity, extended to a situation or religious change, explains how "modern" religious behaviour can have the same meaning as a traditional act and can be used to reinforce traditional values. (19)

Marxist monocausal or economic determinist theory of change limitshis usefulness. Besides, most theories which claim that social change catalyses religious change or vice-versa run into the problem of establishing direct causality amidst many variables. For instance, in the following diagram of causal connection

```
A          E
B          F
C          G
D          H
```

the effect of A is unambiguously E; similarly the effects of B F, C G, D H are direct. Suppose, on the other hand, a theory recognises a wider range of variable, e.g. the following connection,

```
A
B
C          E
D
```

E cannot be unambiguously ascribed to A, B, C, or D. The fate of Weber's attempt to link the development of capitalist ethic with protestantism is a case in point. First, the shift in Calvin's ethic on usuary from the Thomistic was too slight and conservative to catalyse substantial change. Secondly, the financial organisation (banking, exchange and accounting method) which oiled the capitalist entrepeneurial system as well as the factory system developed in the Roman Catholic enclave of Italy before Calvin came to the scene. Other variables and contradictions could be enumerated. Weber was, of course, dealing with an ideal type who breathed nowhere at no point in time.

The pattern of the retreat of the gods could further be probed with theories which provided overviews. Firstly, systems analysis provides an over-view since it emphasizes institutional changes. A close relation exists between the systems theory, in the strict sense, and the structural functional theory. It is primarily a conceptual framework focussing on three notions: the in-put or demands which groups make on a particular structure, the output or ability of the system to fulfil those demands and the feedback or the degree of loyalty which the system could harness.

Applied to the traditional African religious structure, the communities demanded that religion should fulfil certain functions: explanation, prediction and control of space-time events. These ensured order, security and prosperity. Did christianity, for

318

instance, yield a greater out-put than the traditional system in meeting the demands and, therefore, was able to harness greater feed-back or loyalty? How capable was traditional religion in the face of the change-agent?

A basic problem of the system-function analysis is that it does not primarily employ dynamic elements like the rate, forms and sources of change. Surely, there were ambiguities in the feed-back christianity harnessed. Some missionaries complained that communities flocked to them not out of true conviction but because of the material benefits. Some products of christian indoctrination turned from traditional religion to secularist positions. Besides, the impact must be studied historically because various generations reacted differently to the changing impacts of external religious forms. (20)

A second option which focusses more clearly on the sources of change is the social-process approach. The social-process approach does not start with concepts of social system but rather with a focus on social processes such as industrialization, urbanization, commercialization, literacy expansion, occupational mobility, which are presumed to be part of modernization and, therefore, have implications for religious change. (21) The approach is more behaviorally and empirically oriented than the system-function approach and it typically leads to the accumulation of substantial amounts of data, often quantitative in nature, about these social processes which it then tries to relate to religious changes. It attempts to correlate processes rather than impute functions. The practitioner may attempt to move beyond correlation to causation and shed light on the latter through various techniques of causal or path a analysis. It endeavours to establish relationship between variables and particularly between changes in one set of variables and changes in another. For instance, urbanization, which is supposed to lie at the heart of social change in Africa, as a dependent variable is triggered by mobility and industrialization. In turn, urbanization by its habitat structure breeds anomie, forces changes on moral values, reference scale and cosmology of the community (and therefore, the religious structure). The major difficulty in this approach is the casual link between the usually social, economic and demographic independent variables and the religious dependent ones. As mentioned, the nature of religious phenomenon raises difficulties for many empirical approaches. The chief proponents of this model are Burridge, Cohen and Fernandez. Recently, Carolin Ifeka-Moller had to hold the fort against resurgent intellectualist marauders. (22)

Finally, it has been noted that in spite of the vast changes, there has been a persistence of traditional religious beliefs and practices. S.N. Ezeanya called it "the endurance of conviction". (23) Years ago, the American sociologist, W.F. Ogburn, built one the organic conception of society enunciated by the classical sociologists to explain the process of change. He drew a distinction between material (objective artefacts) and non-material (ideas, beliefs, behaviour, etc.) parts of culture. His culture lag theory proposed that material culture changes more rapidly than non-material culture, so that a lag is created between the two realms. This differential rate of change explains the persistence of traditional values in a changing culture. Eventually, Ogburn contends, a more harmonious adjustment of the invention and its related cultural parts will occur. The theory has come under criticism but its basic contention is usually accepted and makes sense in explaining the schizoid religious mentality among African converts, (24) the ability to combine traditional values with western christain culture.

Ogburn's overview does not adequately explain the persistence of traditional religious values in Africa. Moreover, it does not adequately explain regional differentiations in absorbing new relgious forms. Some societies keeled over while others clung tightly. The incidence of radical, sectarian (jihadist or spiritualist) vorms appears more in some areas than in others. Persistence, regional differentiation and conversion to radical sectarian forms still need to explained. We shall return to these issues.

Sheep from Goats

Bryce F. Ryan has pointed out that "the very diversity of sociological orientation to problems of change practically precludes the adoption of any particular theoretical premise". (25) Perhaps, the poverty of models of religious change in Africa is embodied in the complex problems of the discipline.

From the various models of change certain insights emerge as an aggregate of variables which caused conversion from traditional to world religions. No society is static; the organic parts evolve with the process of social evolution. Religious values and institutions evolve in the process either catalysed by internal strains or by external change-agent. Eventually religion moves from being a dependent variable and catalyses change in the other

320

part of the society. The direction of the change could be that of exploiting adaptive potentials within the cosmology. The balancing emphasis for Africans must be the contribution of internal factors in understanding religious change or any other form of change. Robin Horton put it aptly:

> it is surely a cardinal principle of modern historiography that one does not treat any human group as a tabula rasa automatically registering the imprint of external cultural influences. (26)

However, non-evolutionary factors like colonial expeditions, christian missionary enterprise and islamic military raids brought new cultures, ideas and religious values. In response, new social organizations emerged supporting the new religious forms. The enlargement of social scale and military defeat of the traditional order softened the soil for the encounter between the old and new gods.

In Africa, one could hardly ignore the contribution of economic factors. Change in economic mode of production could affect the reception of alien religions and the mode of religious expression. The pursuit of material benefits - wealth, health, education, social status, security, protection - could cause switches in allegiance. The rivalry among communities and families for these benefits intensify the rate of conversion. The process of islamization in the families for these benefits intensify the rate of conversion. The process of islamization in the Sudanic Empires occurred through trade contacts. Moslem Arab traders brought Mediterranean goods, a cosmopolitan culture and a new religion. They set up separate communities and infiltrated the courts and the rest of the "pagan" communities.

The revelatory dimension of religious consciousness would posit inner vision or spiritual conviction as a cause of religious change. Such conviction could capture the super-ego of the converts making them reorder or rationalize their reality and lifestyle in terms of their new belief system. Religious faith is a vision according to which an individual is linked to those basic resources of life, both within and without, which give a sense of worth and meaning. It is implicity assumed that the outward expressions of religious experience - its language, cultic acts, and cultural and sociological expressions - are the symbolic codes which point beyond themselves to the religious reality they at the same time at least partially embody. But the dynamic force of religious experience must never be neglected in the pursuit of scientic theories of objective expressions. (27) This has been the flaw in Marxist and Freudian reductionisms. (28)

The rate of permeation of new religious forms may depend on the strength of this covenant and the socio-political structure which maintains it. Here, geographical position becomes important: communities on sea-coasts or trade routes tend to face persistent and full onslaught of traders, missionaries and imperialists, and tend to collapse more overtly to new cultural and religious forms. However, it often happens that such areas attract competing religions and are so allured with material goods that their religion becomes characterized by materialism and absence of spiritualist sectarianism. Hinterlands which are slowly but steadily nurtured by only one missionary organization tend to yield a higher incidence of spiritualist sectarian religiosity.

In the final analysis, the spread of both Islam and Christianity in Africa was achieved by the overwhelming military power and the cultural baggage the agents carried with them. Arms, new ideas, new material goods, dedication of the agents and the clear signs of their God won the day.

Footnotes

1 G. Balandier, "The Colonial Situation" in Social Change, ed. I. Wallerstein (New York, 1966).

2 Impassioned as Okot P'bitek was in his criticism of writing on African Religions, he does not deal with the problem of a conceptual scheme or model for understanding the pattern of the encounter. See **African Religions in Western Scholarship** (Nairobi: East Afr. Lt. Bureau, 1971).

3 T.A. Beetham, **Christianity and the New Africa** (London: Pall Mall Press, 1967), pp. 5-7.

4 For a criticism of the nineteenth-century anthropologists, See, E.E. Evans-Pritchard, **Theories of Primitivie Religion** (London: Oxf. Univ. Press, 1965). See also, A. Edwards, "The Study of Religion in West Africa, 1959-69", **Religion (Journ. of Relig. and Religions),** 2 pt. I, (Spring 1972), 42-5; G.I. Jones, "Social Anthropology in Nigeria During the Colonial Period" **Africa,** XLIV, 3 (July 1974), 280-89.

5 M. Fortes, **Social Anthropology at Cambridge since 1900** (Cambridge University Press, 1953), p. 4.

6 P.D. Curtin, **The Image of Africa: British Ideas and Action,** 1780-1850 (Madison: The University of Wisconsin Press, 1964); "Scientific Racism and the British Theory of Empire", **Journal of the Historical Society of Nigeria** (Dec. 1960).

7 Gordon M. Haliburton, **The Prophet Harris** (New York: Oxford University Press, 1973).

8 It was Frazer who intoned that "The sceptic, on the other hand, with equal confidence, will reduce Jesus of Nazareth to the level of a multitude of other victims of barbarous superstition, and will see in him no more than a moral teacher". Frazer was such a sceptic and this conclusion was the motive for studying the origins of primitive religions. **The Golden Bough,** 3rd edition, 1919, pp. 422-3. Evans-Pritchard, **Theories of Primitive-Religion** (Oxford Univ. Press, 1965) has analysed the characteristics of the British Anthropologists and the French School. I have attempted to argue the dominance of the French School in the study of African traditional religion in an unpublished paper "Snake Skins?! Marxist Materialist Critique and African Traditional Religion", Paper read at Oha-na-Eze (Faculty of Social Sciences, University of Nigeria), Seminar, 1974.

9 Emile Durkheim, **The Elementary Forms of Religious Life** (London: George Unwin & Co., 1916).

10 Victor W. Turner, **The Forest of Symbols** (Ithaca: Univ. of Wisconsin Press, 1967); John Beattle, "Ritual and Social Change", Man, ns. I (1966), Iff.

11 Geoffrey Parrinder, **West African Religion** (London, 1949).

12 Robin Horton, "African Conversion", **Africa,** XLI (Ap. 1971) 102.

13 In reply to H. Fisher, "Conversion Reconsidered", **Africa** 43 (1973), Iff Horton (a) groups african societies along positions ranging from those ˏwho report having no concept of Supreme Being, through those whose religious lives center on the lesser spirits with varying degrees of concern with the Supreme Being to those who worship the Supreme Being directly; (b) acknowledges the increased activity of the Supreme Being need not be the only effect of the weakening of the microcosmic boundary. See "On the Rationality of Conversion", Africa, 45, 3 (1975), 219-235.

14   Robin Horton, "African Traditional Thought and Western Science", in M.F.D. Young (ed), **Knowledge and Control** (London: Callier-Macmillan Publ. 1971), pp. 208-2 . The old intellectualist approach of Tylor and Frazer runs contrary to Horton's in its conception of the African mentality.

15   C.Y. Glock and R. Stark, **Religion and Society in Tension** (Chicago, 1965).

16   T.B. Bottomore (ed), **Karl Marx: Early Writings** (London, 19 3), 1 7.

17   John S. Mbiti, **African Religions and Philosophy** (New York: Praeger, 1969), 80.

18   B.I. Chukwukere sees a close resemblance between the Nuer and Igbo social structures and accepts Evans-Pritchard's conclusions. See, "Individualism: An Aspect of Igbo Religion", CONCH, 2/3 (Sept. 1971), 111.

19   Ruth Benedict, "Continuities and Discontinuities in Cultural Conditioning", **Psychiatry,** I (1938), 161-167; Frank A. Salamone, "Continuity of Igbo Values After Conversion: A Study in Purity and Prestige", **Missiology: An International Review,** 3" I, (Jan. 1975), 33-34.

20   Elizebeth Isichei, "Seven Varieties of ambiguity: Some patterns of Igbo response to Christian Missions", **Journal of Religion in Africa,** 3/3 (1970), 209-227.

21   Robin Horton observed that the acceptance of Islam and Christianity is due as much to development of the traditional cosmology in response to other features of missionaries. **Africa,** 41 (1971).

22   K. Burridge, **New Heaven, New Earth** (Oxford: Blackwell, 1969); A. Cohen, ("Political Anthropology: The Analysis of the Symbolism of Power Relations", **Man,** 4/2 (1969), 1 1-182; J.W. Fernandez "African Religious Movements", **Journal of Modern African Studies,** 2/4 (1964), 531-549; C. Ifeka-Moller, "white Power: Social Structural Factors in Conversion to Christianity, Eastern Nigeria, 1921-1966, **Canadian Journal of African Studies,** 8/1 (1974), 55-72.

23   S.N. Ezeanya, "Endurance of Conviction in the Converts: The Force of the Traditional Religion of Africa", **West African Religion,** 8 (July 1970), 20-24.

24   William F. Ogburn, **Social Change** (Chicago, 1922); for criticism see, R.M. MacIver and C.H. Page, **Society: An Introductory Analysis** (New York: Rinehart & Co., Inc, 1949).

25 B.F. Ryan, **Social and Cultural Change** (New York: The Ronald Press Co., 1969), V.

26 Horton, R., "On the Rationality of Conversion", **Africa,** 45/3 (1975), 22.

27 See, P.O. Ingram's cutting critique, "Method in the History of Religions", **Theology Today,** 32, No. 4 (Jan. 1976), 382-394.

28 See R. Bellah, "Transcendence in Contemporary Society", in **Beyond Belief** (New York. Harper & Row, 1970), pp. 196-207.

29 Allan R. Tippett observed the same factor in his **Solomon Islands Christianity** (London: Lutherworth Press, 1967), pp. 3-19.

30 Haliburton, **The Prophet Harris** (New York: O.U.P., 1973), p. 89, Okot p'Bitek observed that "most of the religious activities in African religions seem to be part of the ways and means of dealing with existing or threatening dangers". **African Religions in Western Scholarship** (Nairobi: East Afric. Publ. House, 1973), p. 108.

EPILOGUE

THE FUTURE OF AFRICAN TRADITIONAL RELIGION

by

E.M. Uka

In view of the fact that some ancient religions like the religions of ancient Egypt, Greece and Rome have come and gone for good, and whereas the impact of Western civilization and culture on Africa has been so great and overwhelming, one begins to wonder about "to be or not to be" of African Traditional Religion.

According to Idowu, (1) a Nigerian Professor of African Traditional Religion, Africa has undergone radical changes as a result of her encounter with the Western world. One of the aspects of the African culture that has suffered severely as a result of this unequal clash of cultures is the African traditional religion.

For the 19th century European missionaries, Africa was inhabited by heathens. According to their conception of a heathen, he was one whose temporal condition was marked by dire poverty, wretched homes, unremitting toil, gross intellectual ignorance, all in mute and pathetic appeal for help. The moral condition of the heathen was described as reeking with filth and degrading habits, abominable practices, unmentionable cruelties and crimes. (2) In all, the traditional missionary as portrayed by Glover saw the heathen as spiritually lost, wicked, a wilful sinner, without Christ, having no hope and without God in the world.

With this kind of opinion about Africans, the Western missionary came to Africa with the aim of converting the heathen from his traditional beliefs and practices to Christianity, and to Western culture. A classic example of this fusion of Western civilization with Christianity perhaps is best illustrated in an article entitled "Influence of Missions on the Temporal Conditions of the Heathen." (3) The author of the article said

> ... the office of the gospel is to bring the heathen na-
> tions to be like christian nations, because a true
> civilization cannot exist apart from christianity. And
> the proof of this is attested by the fact that the
> heathen possesses 'no chamber of commerce, no in-
> surance companies, no banks, no joint stock associa-
> tions' because the complete development of the tender

affections and the institutions of these associations by which men express their interest in one another and aid one another depends almost entirely upon the diffusion of Christianity. (4)

In the light of this type of thinking, the missionaries and their supporters believed that both the African institutions and African "character" had to be transformed. To achieve these goals of character transformation and the introduction of civilized institutions, the heathen had to be instructed. The missionaries were to persuade the Africans by every rational motive to the practice of civilization. And civilization in this respect meant that Christianity and protestantism were seen as embracing the highest evolution of morals. It was Reginald Heber who put this whole idea of missionary mentality and motive into a song, part of which reads thus:

> From Greenland's icy mountains
> From India's coral Island ...
> From many and ancient river
> They call us to deliver
> Their land from errors chain
>
> Can we whose souls are lighted
> With wisdom from on high
> Can we to men benighted
> The camp of life deny? (5)

This missionary motive was supported to the hilt by social anthropologists who upheld the unilinear evolutionary concept of society. In their conception, the non-European societies were seen as occupying the zero point on the scale of social human evolution with the Europeans at the apex. With this opinion, the social anthropologist and the missionaries reasoned that there was to be a displacement of the traditional religions and social practices by Christianity and Western civilization in order to aid the heathen societies evolve towards the higher position occupied by nineteenth century Europe. In view of these assumptions, they reasoned that the lost heathen had nothing of value in his primitive system and that his religious mind was totally void of insight. So they saw the African, not only as a heathen but also as "tabula rasa", an inert and passive field, a clean slate on which Western religion was to be engraved.

So, as far as the missionaries were concerned and given their motive and the support they enjoyed by being part and parcel of the colonial power, the African traditional religion was doomed to die. As Timothy Njoya put it the missionary conversion practice in Africa achieved this:

> They separated converts from pagans. They wanted to save Africans from being Africans, as if to be themselves was the greatest sin. In their scheme of salvation, no distinction was made between sin and African custom. Sin and evil constituted such things as African homes, art, ethics, history, skills, play and beliefs. African Christians had to be saved from such imagined evils as their dress, diet, ritual, tools, market, government. It was pagan to kill with spear and christian to kill with a gun. (6)

Another potential threat to the survival of African traditional religion was the colonial policy of Assimilation of French acquaintance. As a colonial power in parts of Africa, the French tended to give the Africans under their control the impression that he was a European in all but the colour of his skin, which he should 'never mind'. He was given the impression that he could become the President of France if elected. (7) With this type of bait, the tendency to live up to the dignity of the whiteman became an absorbing concern. Consequently his own native traditions, including his religion became atrophied.

Apart from these external attempts to displace and destroy African traditional religion, the internal logic, the make up of the religion itself also militated against its survival. For example the absence of written records posed a serious threat to its future preservation particularly with the death of the old men, the cultural and religious traditions of the people come to be remembered in less detailed forms and naturally dislocations, distortions, and gaps begin to occur. Moreover, without written records, the principles, creed and dogma began to die or become distorted with the passage of time, especially in the face of formidable challenges like Christianity and Islam. (8)

Another weakness that threatens the survival of traditional religion is that it has neither founders nor reformers, that is, there has been no prophets to awaken and keep alive in the people the primitive purity of the religion as was the case with the religion of the Hebrews in the Old Testament.

It must also be noted that African traditional religious objectslike shrines, altars, magical and medical objects, sacred stools religious garments from which some historical study could be made, are constructed with high perishable objects like wood and rafia which do not last long on account of the weather conditions in Africa. Here we are left only with primary oral sources in the form of languages, concepts, myths, beliefs, songs and music from which we may gather something about the history of the religion. (9)

Schools and Churches and other Missionary Agencies

The missionary agencies for socialization were the schools, hospitals, and churches. They spared no efforts in condemning everything African as worthless, pagan, primitive and poor. Consequently young educated Africans, through Western indoctrination not only lost interest in African beliefs but despised them as if they themselves were whitemen. In this way the vitality of the African traditional religion suffered a severe set back as the Africans themselves began to lose confidence in anything African. Through mission schools and churches most of the Africans believed that anything that whiteman possessed and provided was superior to that of the African. Hence the Africans treated things African with contempt and felt no qualms in changing his name from African to English names; he had to change his religion and even his language in order to sound civilized, saved and educated. (10)

Because of the activities of the missionaries many of the traditional African gods have gone into a retreat. What need is there for shrines and centers of traditional worship when they are abandoned and discredited? For example, where the priesthood is hereditary, heirs who have received western education refuse to wear the mantle of priestly office. So when the priests of these shrines die away there are hardly any replacements. In this way most of the shrines and cults disappear or fall into disuse.

Science and Technology

The achievements of science and technology have radically altered the balance of traditional religious beliefs and practices. In most cases fear and awe usually associated with supernatural phenomena have been banished. The achievements in the field of medical science have put a number of traditional medicine men out of job and eliminated dependence on superstitious beliefs and magical rites. The increasing use of hospitals, health centers, maternity homes, cholera and small pox innoculations, attention to rules of hygiene and environmental sanitation, all have combined to reduce the effectiveness of diviners who were traditionally consulted to prevent health hazards. (11)

Agriculture

Most Africans are an Agricultural people. They have agricultural gods and fertility cults. These gods are worshipped at the appropriate season (planting or harvesting season) to ensure safety and good harvest. In this age of science and technology, medicine men and diviners have discovered that their magic powers over the fertility of the soil and crop yield have been over taken by the use of fertilizers, insecticides and herbicides. The practice of mystic rites to appease the gods or to drive away evil spirits believed to cause plant disease and poor yields has tremendously reduced and with it the traditional religion has suffered another death blow. (12)

Urbanization

The increasing march of African societies towards industrialization and consequent urbanization has tended to change the character of traditional societies. With Western education, mercantile industrialization and improved means of communication, most Africans have become alienated from their own traditional culture and have become ignorant of their folklores, myths, proverbs, songs and religious rites and rituals. So when a people

333

who should uphold the religion of their fore-fathers begin to despise, neglect and forget them, certainly the future of such a religion is bleak. (13)

Emergence of African Christian Ministers and Priests

With their control of schools and churches the missionaries albeit with good intentions, trained a corps of African medical doctors, teachers, engineers and priests to sustain the African heritage of Western civilization and culture. The net result of this development has been the introduction of many new roles - engineers, accountants, civil servants, managers, priests and ministers of the gospel. These new roles to a great extent disorganised and in most cases displaced certain traditional roles and also altered the status symbols of the traditional society. Therefore, rather than accord respect and authority to age, to traditional offices, like the priestly office, to high lineage, the industrial hierarchy built on technical skills and Western education accorded respect to university degree holders, to doctors and engineers and church ministers and priests irrespective of their age, tribal history or lineage. (14) With this shift in mental climate and occupational orientation, some of the young African men and women who joined priesthood and sisterhood, knowingly or unknowingly took up cudges to destroy and desecrate African traditional shrines, symbols and functionaries. The impact of this whole development was devastating for the religion and culture of the African.

Persistence of African Traditional Religion

It is intriguing to observe that inspite of all the pressure mounted by the missionaries and other agents of Western civilization and culture, certain vital aspects of African traditional religion still persist. Some of them are ancestor veneration, traditional oath taking, funeral rites, traditional family rites, title takings and the like. Also, beliefs in magic and in the operations of rain-makers, diviners and medicine men still persist. This is proven by the fact that at moments of crises, even Christians

334

educated men and women resort to traditional methods of controlling time-space events. (15)

One wonders why some of these traditional beliefs and practices have survived till today. W.F. Ogburn (16) an American sociologist proposed the culture lag theory. With it he drew attention to the distinction between material, (i.e. objective artefacts) and non-material aspects of culture - (i.e. ideas, beliefs and practices). He argued that material culture changes more rapidly than non-material culture. In other words, ideas, beliefs and ritual practices last longer than objective artefacts like clothes, houses and icons. This is why even though many shrines have fallen into disuse and groves have been cleared, these do not mean that the peoples' beliefs have been destroyed as well. Also the triumphal mentality of Western missions in evangelising non-European world within a century led to the use of false evangelical strategies in calculating successes in the mission fields. For example, gifts were sometimes used to entice converts into the Christian faith. Such converts never experienced any genuine conversion experience. Hence their old beliefs still held sway. This is why some of the traditional religious beliefs still persist.

Measures taken to recognise and revamp African Traditional Religion

Nationalist sentiments had taken roots in the mission churches even before the movement found expression at the political scene. The concept of **Ethiopianism** was employed in describing nationalistic feelings expressed through the mission churches. The concept took its origin from Psalm 68:31. It reads: "Princes shall come out of Egypt; Ethiopia shall stretch out her hands unto God".

The concept therefore represented attempts by Africans (Ethiopians) to stretch out their hands unto God independently of any foreign missionary agency. This movement brought in its wake, attempts to indigenise the Christian church, the founding of churches by charismatic African Christian leaders and the growth of Independent churches free from foreign or missionary interference. Most of these African Independent churches incorporated African traditional religious beliefs and practices such as polygamy, the use of African names at baptism, singing of African hyms in the church, the use of African traditional instruments of music during worship, and the recognition of spiritual power for service in the church not academic degree certificate from a theological school.

With the resurgence of vigorous nationalism as already championed by 'Ethiopianism', a political 'God of Africa' was born as an opponent of 'the God of the Europeans'. This church in its Nigerian variant crystallised into 'Godianism', (17) which according to K.O.K. Onyioha, the founder and chief priest of the church, is the universal traditional name for African religion. There is also the Arousa church of Benin City: the aim of this church is to make the Edo people of Benin worship God in the language of the people. The religion was founded by the Oba of Benin. Its set principle was to purify and restore the traditional religion to its place in the life of the people. The independent church of the Cherubim and Seraphim is an indigenous African variant of the Christian church. This church has an irresistible attraction for Nigerians largely because it appeals to their native spiritual temperament. It has a system of 'prophecy' which performs acceptably the function as the old system of divination (18) Also some of them employ certain elements from the traditional religion in meeting the needs of their adherents.

Other attempts to recognise and revive African religious beliefs and practices include attempts by African Christians to indigenise christianity in order to render its teachings and beliefs both practical and meaningful. Some of the independent churches in their bid to indigenise christianity, practise acts of exorcism, interpretation of dreams, divination, spirit possession, and gifts of prophecy. Some of the "main Line" churches like the Roman Catholic church in Igboland have begun to incorporate traditional religious beliefs and practices such as belief in ancestor worship which finds expression in their form of memorial service. Also the ancestral festival of **'Igbu Onwu'** is now practised by the church as 'Iwa-ji' festival i.e. New Yam festival. Both Christians and non-Christians participate in its celebration. The **'Iyo Chi'** festival, which was connected with women's 'chi' has been adopted by the Roman Catholic Church as **"Uka Nne"** - i.e. Mothering Sunday. This is now being celebrated by both Christian and non-Christian women. "Ozo Title" for men has also been incorporated into the Church and priests now bless the regalia of the title holders. (20)

In addition to all these, there has been increasing interest in the study of African traditional religion not only at the University level but even at the secondary School level. These studies have led to a joyful discovery of a host of indigenous

336

spiritual and cultural treasures which have been found to be of great moral value. The interest has not only been academic, but also cultural in that the religion has been discovered to have satisfying spiritual values to offer. Besides, there is evidence that African diaspora still practise elements of African traditional religion (Idowu, p. 203-208).

Conclusion

Now what is the present state of African traditional religion in the light of the preceding discourse? According to this paper, the opponents of African traditional religion believe the religion is old and tired and about to die. They argue that the religion in its conservative form is entirely a priestly affair. And since the priests are illiterates and depend entirely upon oral traditions and upon memory, the religion is bound to be impermanent as there is nothing set down in writing for its preservation. Also as the priests die with no successors, the cults die out as well.

Apart from these inherent weaknesses, the opponents also argue that having been assailed by two world religions and their cultures, together with colonial policies that aimed at depriving Africans of their beliefs and practices, the traditional religion stands a very little chance of survival.

Contrary to the views of the opponents, the proposers argue that the religion is still surviving and spreading. This is due to the increasing appreciation of the African personality by Africans themselves. This has directly led to the appreciation of the vital elements in African traditional religion and culture. These vital elements are now being adapted by some "main line" christian churches. Besides, the activities of the African independent churches to indigenise christianity adds greatly to the survival potential of the religion. Moreso, the inclusion of the religion as a subject in the school curriculum at all levels tends to immortalise the religion. All in all, as long as there are Africans in this world, so long will the vital elements of their religion remain. In other words, the future of African traditional religion is very much tied to the future of the Africans as a distinct people.

Footnoses

1   E.B. Idowu, **African Traditional Religion: A Defination,** (New York. Orbis Bks. 1975) pp. 203-208.
2   Robert H. Glover, **The Progress of World Wide Mission,** rev. and enl. H. Herbert Kane (New York: Harper and Brothers, 1960) pp. 4-5.
3   "Influence of Missions on the Temporal Conditions of the Heathen" **Baptist Missionary Magazine,** (April 1849): cited by Robert E. Berkhofer, **Salvation and the Savage,** (Univ. of Kentucky Press, 1965) pp. 1-15.
4   Ibid.
5   Culled from the Methodist Hymn Book.
6   Timothy Njoya, "Dynamics of change in African Christianity" (Ph.D. dissertation, Princeton Theological Seminary, 1976) p. 28.
7   E.B. Idowu, pp. 80-81.
8   Ibid.
9   Angela M. Nnaka, "Future of African Traditional Religion with special reference to Igboland", (unpublished B.A. Thesis Univ. of Nigeria, Nsukka 1982) pp. 34-35. This piece of work has been very helpful. It deals with the topic in some considerable details.
10 Ibid. p. 35.
11 Ibid. pp. 37-38.
12 Ibid. p. 41.
13 Ibid. p. 41.
14 E.M. Uka, "Ideology or Utopia - A Sociological interpretation of an African Response to Christian Mission" (unpublished Ph.D. Thesis Madison, Drew University 1980) pp. 207-213.
15 H.N. Nwosu and O.U. Kalu, "The Study of African Culture" in O.U. Kalu ed. **Readings In African Humanities,** (Enugu: Fourth Dimension Publishers 1978) pp. 3-7.
16 W.F. Ogburn, **Social Change** (Chicago, 1922).
17 K.O.K. Onyioha, **Godianism,** (Published as Paper presented to the Conference of Traditional Religions of Nigeria May 22, 1975).
18 E. Bolaji Idowu, **God in Nigerian Belief,** (Lagos: Federal Ministry of Information Press, 1963), p. 37.
19 Angela M. Nnaka, p. 63.
20 Ibid. p. 64.

THE WAY FORWARD IN THE RELIGIOUS STUDY OF AFRICAN PRIMAL RELIGIONS

by

Harold W. Turner

The International Study of African Primal Religions as Religions

Before making a closer study of the methods that have been used it is necessary to place this study firmly within the various disciplines as they are practised internationally, and thus to reject both overt attempts to impose racial or cultural limitations upon those who may study African primal religions and upon their methods. There has been a widespread tendency, often appearing at conferences, for African scholars to reject all studies of African primal religions made by non-African and using what are labelled 'merely Western' categories and methods. This rejection has been supported by some Western anxious to atone for attitudes which have depreciated, despised or distorted African religions in the past. It is implied that African phenomena are unique, that only Africans can develop a study of African religions that will do them justice, and that this study has no need for Western religions studies and methods which can only hinder true understanding.

In spite of the undoubted mistakes of the past this attitude must be firmly rejected when applied to the international resources available today for the study of religions. A similar attitude applied to anthropological studies in Africa has been dealth with by Professor Mayer Fortes. Speaking of African scholars he asserts that:

> those among them who are engaged in the same academic enterprises and enquiries as their Western counterparts have been concerned with in the past thirty years, come out, broadly, with the same observations and conclusions ... And this holds out not only for anthropology but also for musicology ... for historical research, for economic and demographic studies, and of course for all the national sciences. And this is typical of the whole of modern Africa. (3)

The same possibility is open to religious studies, and for a number of reasons. There is nothing new in the endeavour to study a religious tradition set within a culture quite different from one's own; it is going on all the time and all over the world. Further, one of the basic principles is that these studies should, in the end, be acceptable to at least some of the people involved, and even in spite of their being presented, perhaps, with another way of looking at their own religion. And again, the onlooker does see more of the game; all cultures and religions are parochial and need to see themselves as others see them; this is part of the critique of religions that leads to their development and refinement and is unavoidable in this shrinking world. More importantly still, men resemble one another more than their cultures do; when all has been said about the unique features of African cultures and religions and their own identity has been fully recognized, it remains true that Africans share a common humanity with the rest of us, and their religions are authentically religious in the same basic senses as anywhere else in the world. Dr. J.O. Awolalu, for instance, to quote the publisher's blurb for his recent book, sees Yoruba religion "as a specific variant of the universal response to the Divine." (4)

African religions, through all their varying forms and degrees, still show men worshipping, praying, sacrificing, building altars and shrines, making pilgrimages to holy places and exhibiting so much of what is recognized as religious belief and practice across the whole world. Granted there are hosts of African ways of being religious, these distinctives when examined only show how firmly the great common patterns and forms of religion are embedded in African peoples. For the sake of Africans themselves, and of their religions, we must continue to insist that they are human beings first and Africans second.

As an older example of the results of an approach confined to Africa there is Dr. J.O. Lucas' study (1948) relating the religion of the Yoruba people to a source in the religion of the ancient Egyptians. (5) Some of the similarities on which he based his argument were not merely Yoruba-Egyptian forms but religious forms found also in many other parts of the world; the failure to discover this produces a quite false thesis. In my own experience it was the discovery of the remarkable similarity between the origins of the **aladura** religious movement in Nigeria and the beginnings of the Ratana Church among the Maori people of New Zealand, at exactly the same time, that encouraged me to see Africa's new religious movements as African forms of a worldwide phenomenon among primal peoples in interaction with more powerful and sophisticated societies. (6)

Historical Study of African Religions - In Two Senses

There will be little need here to point out the break-through in the historical study of the primal religions of Africa that has occurred in the last fifteen years, especially for Central and East Africa. Western-trained historians have shown a respect for these religions as authentic systems in their own right, with their own dynamics and development that cannot be treated as merely an epi-phenomenon of economic, social and political changes, however much all these factors are interwoven with the religious. Without abandoning their Western-developed equipment they have pushed out beyond the more familiar reliance upon archaeological and archival evidence to use the oral tradition, the interpretation of myths, and historical linguistics in the course of discovering and testing new methods required by the African situation. Nor has this historical concern been confined to profes-sional historians; from a social science base Professors Schoffeleers and Van Binsbergen have been doing the same for Malawiland adjacent areas and for Zambia, just as a missiologist-theologian, Dr. Daneel, has for the Mwari cult in Zimbabwe. One of the land-marks in this historical work is a volume with contributions from archaeology, the social sciences, and professional history, and edited by two scholars who have done as much as any to assist this advance, Professors T.O. Ranger and I.N. Kimambo. (7) We now see something of the dynamics of African religions, their capacity for change and innovation, and their influence upon the other forces at work in history.

It is no depreciation of this achievement to say that there is also another kind of historical study which overlaps with it but cannot be simply identified with it. The need for this will appear if we consider historical enquiry into other fields such as philosophy or economics. Any historian may deal with these sub-jects, but their full historical exploration requires a specialist with two kinds of equipment, in history on the one hand and in philoso-phy or economics on the other. The historian who is not also a philosopher may make very useful contributions, and partly because he is not a philosopher, but a full account of the development and interactions of philosophic systems requires specialist equipment of a philosophic kind. By the same token the specialist who is a history of religions scholar will provide a 'history of religions' history of African religions. The conventional name for the discipline to which we refer is rather confusing, especially in the context of this discussion; we refer to someone trained in the study of religions in their own distinctive forms and especially in their historical developments, with concentration upon the religious dimension itself rather than upon all the ramifications of interaction with the milieu.

Such a 'history of religions' scholar will bring a specialist knowledge of the characteristic dynamics and internal processes of religions, with their forms of decay and revival, degeneration and reformation, fresh revelation, transposition and conservation. He will be able to recognize these processes and show how African religious history exemplifies them and presents perhaps new variations upon the forms found elsewhere. He will also be familiar with the various types of religious leader - priest, prophet, mystic, saint, diviner, teacher or guru, founder, reformer, proselytizer, mediator, saviour, messiah, or sacral ruler. He will use these terms with some exactness and according to international usage, something that is badly needed in the study of African religions, as witness the varied and uncertain use of the term 'prophet'. Under the general rubric of 'history of religions' there exists a notable body of twentieth century religious scholarship that has as yet made hardly any connection with the study of African, or indeed of most other primal religions. I can indicate this by listing the most notable names and observing their absence from most works on African religions and indeed from most courses on this subject in African or other universities. In the Netherlands there is the notable succession from Chantepie de Saussaye through W.B. Kristensen, G. van der Leeuw, Jan de Vries, C.J. Bleeker, and K.A.H. Hidding to Jacques Waardenburg; in Germany the great Otto and Heiler followed by others, such as Goldhammer and now Hans Greschat; in Sweden, Soderblom and now the notable work of Ake Hultkrantz; in Italy, Pettazoni and Ugo Bianchi; in Britain, E.O. James, Ninian Smart and others; in the U.S.A., Joachim Wach from Marburg, then Eliade, Kitagawa, Charles Long, Cantwell Smith and now J.Z. Smith; and others in Asia and especially Japan Of all these only Charles Long, (8) an American Black, and Hans Greschat (9) who has taught and researched in Africa, have begun to bring the resources of this body of scholarship to bear upon enquiry into African religions, although a recent work by Benjamin Ray (10) also makes some move towards use of these rich resources. Of the others, their concern has been with the Semitic religions or the great religions of antiquity or of Asia, apart from Hultkrantz and his outstanding work on North American Indian and Arctic religions. We can therefore apply to African religions the remarks Eliade has made about the study of the cargo cults of Melanesia:

> Numerous works have explained the socio-political context of the "cargo-cults". But the historico-religious interpretation of these millenarist minor religions has hardly begun. Now all these prophetic phenomena become completely intelligible only in the history of religions. (11)

In other words, while the work of Professor T.O. Ranger, and those associated with him, and many others, "demonstrates what can be achieved if historical questions are asked about African religious ideas and institutions" (12) still further achievements wait upon the asking of the relevant religious questions about these same African religions.

Phenomenological Study of African Religions

The history of religions in its specialist sense passes over into and interacts with the phenomenology of religions as this has already been identified, and it is here that we see most sharply the equipment that is lacking in the study of African religions. Two examples will serve to illustrate the relevance of phenomenological study.

The analysis of individual religious experience

One of the twentieth century's three or four most influential books on religion is Rudolf Otto's Das Heilige (1917), or as it is rather unfortunately entitled in its English version, **The Idea of the Holy** (13) This has been as everything from psychology to philosophy but is best taken as a profound and complex phenomenological analysis of individual religious experience of the encounter with the Numinous, based on intimate acquaintance with a great range of religious traditions. Otto, however, had the same limitations as all the other scholars we have

343

listed, with the exception of Greschat - he had never lived and worked in Africa and indeed had no real contact with any other primal religions. In this field he was dependent upon such anthropology as there was in 1917, before most of the great studies of African cultures and religions had appeared; in fact, his sections on primal religions and magic are better omitted by students. This important analysis of religious experience has therefore not been extensively tested upon African materials, nor the latter provided with the illumination this work might provide. Otto's analysis would seem to be especially important in examination of the High God feature to see if the ambivalence between deus remotus and the intimacy of direct prayer can be understood in terms of Otto's system; or again, rites which seek to remove the dangerous aspects of spirit power and restore its protective presence suggest analysis in terms of Otto's mysterium tremendum et fascinans. Apart from the most passing of references to Otto I can find only one more sustained attempt to use his contribution, by Charles Nyamiti, (14) although in various papers Dr. Christian Gaba of Ghana acknowledges his indebtedness to Otto for his concept of the Holy. It is equally important to test the universality of Otto's work by seeing if it does apply to the primal, and especially to the African, religions. If it does then we have discovered a very important common language of discourse between African and other religions, and African and other peoples.

The analysis of sacred places

Most phenomenology of religion deals less with the elusive inner experience of the believer and more with the overt manifestations of religion; of these manifestations places of worship are perhaps the most widespread and most accessible to study. Examination of the essays by social scientists, an archaeologist, and historians in the volume by Ranger and Kimambo reveals a number of references to shrines both in the titles of essays and in the text. When these references are examined in detail it soon becomes clear that a limited number of physical features are being referred to time and again: caves or rock shelters, sacred stones or stone circles, hills and mountains, sacred groves, trees and poles, and graves. The overarching and commonest term is the 'shrine', with or without a hut or house as part of its strucure. One is grateful to those who have recorded this much detail, however incidentally mentioned, for all these terms are familiar in the phenomenological analysis of the structure and functions of places of worship. Indeed we would like to know much more in detail about their forms and uses, for often we are told merely that there was a shrine at a certain place and something of its history. The various disciplines involved would profit from a general knowledge of the objects that have been significant and characteristic in the history of shrines or places of worship across all the religions, and of the spatial and structural patterns that these places have tended to exhibit; to a certain extent one sees and records only what one is looking for. When supplied with fuller and more relevant information by all the other disciplines, the phenomenology of religion can then press the enquiry further into the religious functions and meanings of shrines in Africa in the light of what is known about these matters elsewhere.

My own eyes were first opened to the possibilities of this combination of disciplines when a graduate student of mine in the U.S.A. took an intensive course on the phenomenology of places of worship and then applied this in a study of such places among the Native American peoples. From historians and social scientists he found a superabundance of ethnographic information in great detal, about hogans, kivas, Big Houses, sacred mountains, stone circles, caves, altars, ceremonial chambers, sundance grounds, prayer enclosures and temples. These were then discovered to possess in remarkably exact fashion the very functions and patterns described in the phenomenology of religion in general. The ethnographic data was, as it were, crying out for this further analysis by specialist religious equipment. (15) I have every reason to expect that similar discoveries await us in African religions, although I have been able to suggest this only through briefer studies of Igbo Alosi shrines, the Igbo Iba house in the Onitsha area, and the Ashanti shrines of Ghana in my recent phenomenological study of places of worship. (16)

It is interesting to note the comments on this subject from an archaeologist, Professor Posnansky of Ghana, in the volume of essays already mentioned. Speaking of both Stone Age and Iron Age shrines he laments that "little attention has been given to many of these sites by the archaeologist since they very often provide very little evidence of occupation." (17) Other features than the signs left from human occupation can of course be of the greatest value for the phenomenology of religion. Professor Posnansky continues by declaring that: "of the utmost importance and priority for new research in Africa is an accurate description of modern shrines." He then details reasons for this and some of the things to look for, (18) and continues by declar-

ing that "this is clearly a field for co-operation between historians, anthropologists, archaeologists and linguists." (19) The
disciplines missing from this team are clearly the phenomenology
and history of religions; this becomes plain when he goes on to
assert the value of elucidating the spatial arrangements that the
religious disciplines may find much of their most valuable
evidence. The same obtains for other human structures governed,
at least in part, by religious or cosmological beliefs; as notable
examples we may mention the well-known land use and residential
patterns of the Dogon people so fully described by French ethnographers.

Example of a Search for Method

We take two books published in the seventies by Dr. Aylward
Shorter for an example of a search for a methodology for the
study of African religions that begins with some reference to the
body of religious scholarship we refer to, but ends without any
reference to the disciplines we are commending. In his very useful
book on **Prayer in the religious traditions of Africa** Shorter
chooses an admirable point of departure, the classic study **Prayer:
a study in the history and psychology of religion** by the great
Fredrich Heiler already mentioned. (20) This is most encouraging
from one who is known as a social anthropologist, and he makes
good use of Heiler to emphasize that prayer is essentially a religious activity of communion and communication "that transcends
and reinterprets every social relationship and social experience." (21) Heiler's sixty-page chapter on 'Primitive prayer'
provides little formal assistance to Shorter, and when we remember that Heiler published in 1918 and that the few anthropological
sources he used are anything from seventy to over a hundred
years old, this is not surprising. Shorter proceeds in his own way
with some interesting suggestions for various classifications of
his prayer materials in terms of the addressee of the prayer, the
prayer, the literary forms, the 'life-situations' and the 'dominant
purposes'.

      Then follow four pages on 'The problem of methodology
in the study of African traditional religions'. This question is
taken up in his other work which, although called **African Christian theology - adaptation or incarnation?** is mainly prolegomena
devoted to the problem of method and expanding his other brief

treatment. In ch. 3 Shorter canvasses eight different 'approaches': the particularist, the enumerative, the hypothesis of unity approach, the historical, the limited comparative, the categorical (e.g. theistic/deistic, or sociological), the thematic, and finally the multi-dimensional approach which he himself commends. This is to be confined to the last four methods - the historical, limited comparative, categorical and thematic methods. What is patently absent is any reference to the specialist religious disciplines, and so we have a combination of methods not so very different from those commended by Posnansky. Towards the end of the book, however, even this limited company recedes from view and the author reverts to:

> the importance of ... social anthropology ... not only in providing a correct understanding of African traditional religious ideas, but also in placing these ideas in their total life context. It also demands respect for the characteristic African forms of communication, symbolism and ritual, and provides the methodology for their analysis. (22)

Shorter never intends to reject the other methods but this method is clearly where his heart lies and his confidence rests. And the total absence from the index of all the names that indicate the main body of twentieth century study of religions confirms that this had not been considered as a source of methods for the study of African religions.

Shorter's discussion of the thematic method might have led him towards this neglected scholarly resource. Values which are expressed as a regularity of pattern in a culture are what he calls 'themes', and those not confined to the particularities of a culture but relating to universal human experience are called 'life-themes'. Some of these "refer to explicit religious experience, for example: human inadequacy and sin, the experience of God, creation and creativity, judgment, salvation ..." (23) It should not be difficult to move from these remarks into a consideration of the characteristic themes, patterns or forms that represent the common coin of the history and phenomenology of religion. Instead of this there is a chapter on the following themes in African religion: "memorial, co-creativity, judgment, the whole community". There is much interesting and valuable material here, but the selection and the terminology are so idiosyncratic that the study does not tie in with the categories of the phenomenology and history of religions. No advantage is therefore taken

347

of the body of religious scholarship already available, and this is not tested further against the African materials and so subjected to possible criticism, modification or extension. Although the author asserts that "the study must be scientific and systematic" (24) in this failure to discover an adequate range of scientific methods there is loss both to African religions and to the world of scholarship.

Existing Religious Studies: Limitations and Further Development

Part of Shorter's problem is that he sees the limitations of the existing religious studies of African religions, to which we have so far made no reference. These would include the various works of E.G. Parrinder that have done so much to arouse interest in the subject, together with those of E. Dammann, Bolaji Idowu, J.S. Mbiti (whose works are widely used as textbooks), H.A.E. Sawyerr, J.V. Taylor, N.Q. King, J. van Wing and the succession of Francophone scholars associated with the valuable journal **Cahiers des Religions Africaines** from Zaire. Shorter places these within what he calls the 'enumerative' or the 'hypothesis of unity' approaches, which have no permanent place in his team, and are alleged to be pessimistic about the possibility of any history of African religions of the kind seen in the Ranger and Kimambo volume. This, however, is a more recent and specialized development which I am sure all the scholars named would now warmly welcome, while sharing perhaps some of my comments on its own limitations even as history.

These other religious studies also have widely recognized limitations which have been summarized by Benjamin Ray:

> They try to be exhaustive, covering too many societies and too many types of religious phenomena. Consequently they present little more than supperficial catalogs of examples extracted, Frazerian fashion, from concrete, socioreligious contexts. They tend towards abstraction, lacking both any "feel" for African religious ideas and behaviour and any interpretative depth. They also rely heavily upon outdated anthropological theories and ethnographic data, and, at times, reveal a noticeably Western theological orientation. (25)

348

My own judgments would be somewhat more generous. There is a place in first level studies for faithful description, enumeration or cataloguing, and all studies, especially in their earlier stages, involve a degree of abstraction from the whole context, for such abstraction and concentration upon distinguishable aspects of reality lie behind the very existence of the different disciplines. There is also a place for theologically orientated studies (Western or any other) of all aspects of reality and Frican religious can claim no exemption from this. Such study, however, must be preceded by work of 'interpretative depth' in the religious dimensions, and here we return to the need for the specialist contributions of the phenomenology and history of religions without which we do tend towards the 'superficial catalogs' of which Ray complains. These contributions will include indications of what to look for as significant data, the categories that are likely to prove both scientific and helpful in classifying the data, the religious forms and structures that may be expected, and what interpretations and meanings are potentially present in these forms and structures.

There is no major work which uses such equipment in the study of an African primal religion, nor indeed of Christianity or Islam in Africa, for these traditions like all others need the same application of phenomenological and history of religion methods. It is surprising that no work of this kind has appeared in South Africa in spite of the long association of its many scholars with the great schools of religious scholarship in the Netherlands and Germany. From the latter one small monograph should be mentioned as a pioneering achievement. Professor Hans has applied the phenomenological method to the study of West African prophets as religious specialists, and in so doing has developed current phenomenological categories still further in response to the demands of the African data. Greschat at Marburg stands in the great tradition of Otto, Heiler, and Joachim Wach and this is plain in his work. Attention should also be drawn to the work of Professor Christian Gaba in Ghana which shows considerable understanding of phenomenological methods and of the body of scholarship behind them. The writings of some of the Francophone scholars in Central Africa should also be watched for the development of a more professional and scientific religious methodology.

Conclusions

It is plain that behind our particular methodological recommendations there lies a more general concern for the use of the right model in the study of African or any other religions. Cultural, anthropological, psychological, sociological, political and other models have proved their value in the elucidation of the interaction between religions and their milieux. Religion, however, cannot be equated with culture, society, morality, psychic processes or political systems and the distinctive features of religion escape us if we reduce it to any or all of these other categories, no mater how intimately it is also interwoven with these aspects of the total reality. We need therefore a religious model for the study of the 'religion' of African religions, and this model will depend upon what we mean by religion itself. Since this cannot be captured in a universally acceptable definition there will always be some variety in the models employed for the understanding of religions. It is important, however, that a religious model of some kind be used. My own preference is for a conception of religion as existing in the interplay between revelation of the transcendent and the response of the human, both set always, of course, in a particular milieu; it is this model which I have endeavoured to employ in my elementary attempt at a school textbook for primal religions. (26) I would appreciate any application of this to a particular African religious tradition.

To relate African religions to revelations of the transcendent is to place them as firmly in the category of the authentically religious as any of the great or universal religions. To relate them also to the response of the human is to recognize that they share in some of the major human universals such as the basic archetypal religious structures of the human psyche and the human sense of a distorted existence and a lost destiny. African religions will then be discovered with all the values of their spirituality, their communality and integration with earthly and daily existence, and with the characteristic forms they share with the religions of other continents. By the same token it will become apparent where they stray from the authentically religious, pass over into the mirror-image world of magic or reveal various degenerations or distortions, in part resembling those of other peoples and in part perhaps distinctively their own. Against the wider backdrop of the religions of the world it will be possible to identify any lack of correlation with morality, any limitation to the anthropocentric, the rarity of ascetic traditions, or the

350

submergence of the disinterested contemplation and adoration of the Holy by overly pragmatic concerns.

To recognize less than this, and extol only the merits, would reduce African peoples to the innocence of childhood or of the mentally retarded or defective, and so deprive them of mature human responsibility. To focus only on the demerits would be to fall back into those earlier Western ethnocentric superiorities we all now lament, and exaggerate defects in African religions as if Westerners had none in their own. To confine methods of study to those of the social and behavioural sciences is not to avoid these problems, for, as Dr. Gaba has pointed out, restriction to these studies may unwittingly create the impression that African religions are no more than social and psychological phenomena rather than essentially religious and worthy to be professed as the faiths of persons. (27)

The contribution of the specialist religious disciplines is to reveal both the religious forms and the ambivalence of African religions, with achievements and failures that reflect, like all other religions, the human condition in its shame but also in its glory. In this way African primal religions form part of the common spiritual heritage of mankind.

Footnotes

1 Originally presented to the International Conference on Recent African Religious Studies, Afrika-Studiecentrum, Leiden, December 1979.
2 H.W. Turner, 'A model for the structure of religion in relation to the secular' **Cahiers des Religions Africaines** 3, 1969, 173-197; reprinted in **Journal of Theology for Southern Africa** 27, 1979, 42-64.
3 M. Fortes, 'African cultural values and the situation of the intellectual', unpublished paper, African Studies Association (UK) Conference, Liverpool 1974.
4 J.O. Awolalu, **Yoruba beliefs and sacrificial rites,** London: Longman 1979.
5 J.O. Lucas, **The religion of the Yorubas,** Lagos: CMS Bookshop, 1948.
6 H.W. Turner, 'The primal religions of the world and their study', in V.C. Hayes (ed.), **Australian essays in world religions,** Adelaide: Australian Association for the Study of Religions 1977, 27-37.

351

7   T.O. Ranger and I.N. Kimambo (eds.), **The historical study of African religion,** London: Heinemann 1972.

8   C.H. Long, 'The West African High God: history and religious experience', **History of Religions** 3, 1964, 328-342.

9   H.J. Greschat, **Westafrikanische Propheten. Morphologie einer religiösen Spezialisierung,** Marburg/Lahn: im Selbstverlag 1974.

10 B.C. Ray, **African religions,** Englewood Cliffs, N.J.: Prentice Hall 1976.

11 M. Eliade, **The two and the one,** London: Harvill Press 1965, 132.

12 Ranger and Klimambo, op.cit., cover 4.

13 London: Oxford University Press 1923. See also H.W. Turner, **Rudolf Otto: The idea of the holy - a guide for students,** Aberdeen: The author 1974.

14 C. Nyamiti, **African religion and the Christian God,** (Spearhead 49), Eldoret, Kenya: Gaba Publications 1977.

15 J.R. Cabbage, **Functions of sacred places in North American Indian religion,** unpublished research paper, Candler School of Theology Emory University, Atlanta, Georgia, 1971.

16 H.W. Turner, **From temple to meeting house,** The Hague, Mouton 1979, 44-46.

17 Ranger and Kimambo, op.cit., 40.

18 Ibid., 41.

19 Ibid., 42.

20 Translated as Prayer. **A study in the history and psychology of religion,** London: Oxford University Press 1932.

21 A Shorter, **Prayer in the religious traditions of Africa,** Nairobi: Oxford University Press 1975, 4.

22 A. Shorter, **African Christian theology-adaptation or incarnation?** London: G. Chapman 1975, 159.

23 Ibid., 112.

24 Ibid., 160.

25 B.C. Ray, 'Recent studies of African religions', **History of Religions** 12, 1972, 75-89.

26 H.W. Turner, **Living tribal religions,** London: Ward Lock Educational 1971.

27 C.R. Gaba, 'The study of "other religions" in pluralistic societies: the case of the seminaries in West Africa', **Ghana Bulletin of Theology,** December 1976.

Sources of Articles

A. **Mission Trends No. 5:** FAITH meets FAITH
  1. The Salvific Value of African Religions by Patrick Kalilonbe pp. 55-68.
  2. Christianity meets Traditional African Cultures by Peter K. Sarpong pp. 238-248.
B. **Journal of Religion in Africa:** Vol. XII No. I LAIDEN 1981
  3. The Way forward in the Religious Study of African Primal Religions by Harold W. Turner.
C. 4. Sources of African Traditional Religion by J.S. Mbiti in **Introduction to African Religion** by J.S. Mbiti.
D. **Nigerian Journal of Humanities:**
  Vol. 1 No. 1 Sept. 1977 University of Benin, Benin Nigeria
  5. Gods in Retreat: Models of Religious Change in Africa.
E. **Nigerian Dialogue: A Journal of Interfaith Studies on the Relation between Christianity and Non-Christian Religions:**
  Vol. 3 No. 3 Edited at UNN 1979.
  6. The Contribution of African Traditional Religion to Nation Building by Msgr. S.N. Ezeanya.
  7. **Religions** 2 No. 2 1977. African Traditional Religion As an Academic Discipline by T.O. Awolalu.
  8. Towards Understanding of African Traditional Religion by P.A. Dopamu in **Religious Understanding and Co-operation in Nigeria** ed. by I.A.B. Balogun Nigeria.
  9. The Concept of Man in African Traditional Religion with particular reference to the Igbo of Nigeria from Emefie Ikenga Metuh, **African Religions in Western Conceptual Schemes.** (Ibadan: Claverianum Press, 1985).

THE STUDY OF AFRICAN TRADITIONAL RELIGION
A SELECT BIBLIOGRAPHY OF UP-TO-DATE MATERIALS ON THE SUBJECT

by

O.U. Kalu

Table of Contents

Abbreviation

1.	A.W.S.	-	African Writers' Series
2.	BULLSACH	-	Bulletin of South African Church History
3.	I.A.I	-	International African Institute
4.	I.R.M.	-	International Review of Mission
5.	J.A.H.	-	Journal of African History
6.	J.A.S.	-	Journal of African Studies
7.	J.H.S.N.	-	Journal of Nistorical Society of Nigeria
8.	J.R.A.	-	Journal of Religion in Africa
9.	N.A.E.	-	National Archieves Enugu
10.	W.A.R.	-	West African Religion (Journal of the Department of Religion, University of Nigeria, Nsukka.)

Study of the Origins of Religions (including exotic and
curious reports of explorers, Missionaries, Travellers, etc.

Books

1. Bowen, T.J., **Adventures and Missionary Labours,** 1857. (reprinted, London: Frank Cass Ltd., 1968.
2. Burton, Richard F., **A Mission to Gelele, King of Dahomey,**
(2nd Ed.) 2 Vols. London: Tinsley Brothers, 1864.
3. Eliade, Mircea, **Patterns of Comparative Religion,** (English
Translation), London: 1958.
4. Eliade, Mircea, **The Sacred and Profane: The Nature of Religion,** New York: Harvest Brok-Harcourt Bruce and
World Inc., 1959.
5. Eliade, Mircea, **Cosmos and History,** New York: Harper and
Row Publishers, 1959.
6. Evans-Pritchard, E.E., **Theories of Primitive Religion,** Oxford:
The Clarendon Press, 1965.
7. Frazer, J.G., **The Golden Bough,** (3rd ed.) 1922, 2 vols.
8. Frobenius, Leo, **The Voice of Africa. Vol I,** London: Oxford
University Press, 1913.
9. Hopins, E. Washburn, **Origin and Evolution of Religion,** New
York: Cooper Square Publishers Inc., 1961.
10. James, E.O., **Primitive Ritual and Belief,** Oxford: Oxford
University Press, 1917.
11. James, E.O., **The Beginnings of Religion,** London: (n.d.).
12. King, Noel, **Religions of Africa,** New York: Harper and
Brothers Publishers, 1970.
13. Lang, Andrew, **The Making of Religion,** London, 1898.
14. Leuba, James H., **A Psychological Study of Religion, its
Origin, Function and Future,** 1912.
15. Livingstone, D., **Missionary Travels and Researches in South
Africa,** New York: harper and Brothers Publishers, 1858.
16. Marrett, R.R., **The Threshhold of Religion,** (2nd Ed.).
17. Pittazoni, Raffle, **Essays on the History of Religions,** (English
Translations) London: 1954.
18. Radcliffe-Brown, A.R., **Structure and Function in Primitive
Society,** New York: The Free Press, 1965.
19. Ranger, T.O. & I.N. Kimambo, **The Historical Study of African Religion,** Berkely: University of California Press,
1972.
20. Schmidt, Wilhelm, **The Origin and Growth of Religion,** London: Metheun and Co. Ltd., 1931.

21. Smart, Ninan, **The Science of Religion and the Sociology of Knowledge,** Princeton: Princeton University Press, 1973.
22. Stone, R.H., **In Africa's Forest and Jungle,** New York: 1899.
23. Thouless, Robert H., **The Psychology of Religion,** Cambridge: Cambridge University Press, 1923.
24. Vries, Jan de, **The Study of Religion: a Histrocal Approach,** (translated, K.W. Bolk, 1972).

Articles

25. AWOLALU, J.O., "African Traditional Religion as an academic discipline" **RELIGIONS: Journal of Nigerian Association of the Study of Religion,** 1,1 (1976), 21-36.
26. Barker Samuel, "The Races of the Nile Basin", **Transactions of the Phonological Society of London:** 5 (1867).
27. Baudin, P., (Revd.), "Fetishism and Fetish Worshippers in P. Baudin (Ed.), **Missionary on the Slave Coast of Africa,** (translated by M. Macmmahon, New York: 1885.
28. Edwards, A., 'The Study of Religion in West Africa 1959-1969', **Religion (Journal of Religion and Religions),** 2,1 (Spring 1972) 42-56.
29. Erivwo, S.U., 'The Study of Religion as an academic discipline', **RELIGIONS,** 1,1 (1976) 7-20.
30. Fatunde, A.K., 'An introduction To the study of Religion', Ife Mimeo, 1968.
31. Horton, Robin, "A definition of Religion and its uses" **Journal of Royal Anthropological Institute,** 90,2 (1960) 211-212.
32. Kishimato, H., "An operational Definition of Religion" **NUMEN,** DEC., 1961.
33. Warner, W. LLoyd, "Methology and field Research in Africa" **AFRICA,** 6,1 (1933) 51ff.
34. Welbourn, F.B., "Mary Douglas and the study of Religion" **J.R.A.,** 3;2 (1970) 89-95.

II. Ethnographic Survey of Africa

Books

35. Barth, Fredrick, **Models of Social Organization,** London: Royal Antropological Institute of Great Britain and Ireland, 1966.
36. Bindloss, Harold, **In the Niger Country,** London: 1898, (Reprint; London: Frank Cass, 1968).
37. Ellis, Alfred B., **The Ewe-speaking peoples,** Chicago: Benin Press, Repring 1965.
38. Ellis, Alfred B., 'The **Yoruba-speaking People of the Slave Coast of West Africa: Their Religion; Nature, cutoms** etc. London: Curson Press, 1974.
39. Evans-Pritchard, E.E., 'The **Divine Kingship of the Shilluk of the Nilotic Sudan',** Cambridge: C.U.P., 1948.
40. Evans-Pritchard, E.E., **Witchcraft, oracles and magic among Azande,** Oxford: The Clarendon Press, 1937) (Reprinted 1958).
41. Forde, Daryll and G.I. Jones, **The Ibo and Ibibio-speaking Peoples of South-eastern Nigeria,** London: IAI, 1950.
42. Gluckman M., (Ed.), **Closed systems and Open Minds,** Edinbourgh, 1964.
43. Green, Margaret M., **Igbo Village Affairs,** London: 1947 (2nd Edition; Frank Cass, 1964).
44. Leith-Ross, Sylvia, **African Women: A study of the Ibo of Nigeria,** London: Routledge and Paul Kegan Ltd., 1939, The Reissued 1965.
45. Mair, Lucy, **African Societies,** Cambridge: C.U.P., 1974.
46. Meek, C.K., **A Sudanese Kingdom: An Ethnographical Study of the Jukun-speaking peoples of Nigeria,** London, 1931.
47. Meek, C.K., **Law and Authority in a Nigerian Tribe,** London: Oxford University Press, 1937.
48. Ottenberg, Simon, **Leadership and Authority in an African Society: The Afikpo Village Group,** Seattle & London: University of Washington Press, 1971.
49. Roscco, John, **The Baganda: an account of their native customs and Beliefs,** London: Macmillian & Sons, 1911.
50. Smith, Edwin W. and A.M. Dale, **The Ila-speaking People of Northern Rhodesia,** Vol. I. London: Macmillian, 1920.

Articles

51. Basden, G.T., "The Ibo Country of Southern Nigeria", **Geographical Journal,** 55 (1925) 32-41.
52. Evans-Pritchard, E.E., "Heredity and Gestation as the Azande see them" 1932, Reprinted in his Essays in **Social Anthropology,** London: Faber & Faber, 1937.
53. Meek, C.K., "An Ethnographical Reports on the Peoples of Nsukka Division", Lagos: **Governments Printer,** 1931.
54. Onwuejeogwu, M.A., "The Ethno-Historical Survey of Igbo East and West of Lower Niger Basin", Unpub. Mass., 1969.

III. Scientific Studies and Anthropological Writings

Books

55. Dennett, R.E., **The Religious and Political Systems of the Yoruba,** London: Macmillian, 1910.
55a Douglas, Mary, **Purity and Danger,** London: Routledge and Kegan Paul, 1966.
56. Durkheim, Emile, **The Elementary forms of the Religious Life,** (2nd Edition translated by Joseph W. Swain) New York: The free Prin, 1947.
57. Eliade, Mircea and Joseph Kitagawa, (Ed.) **The History of Religions: Essays in Methodology,** Chicago: The University of Chicago Press.
58. Field, M.J., **Search for Security,** London: O.U.P., 1960, Evanston: Northwestern University Press, 1962.
59. Jevons, F.B., **Introduction to the History of Religion,** London: 1921.
60. Lewis, I.M., **Ecstatic Religion,** Penguin Books, 1971.
61. Malinowski, B., **Magic, Science and Religion and other Essays,** New York: Garden City, Ancher Books, 1954.
62. Melland, F.H., **In Witch-Bound Africa,** London: Seekey Service and Co., 1923.
63. Middleton, John, (Ed.) **Gods and Rituals,** Garden City, New York: The Natural History Press, 1967.
64. Passons, Robert, **Religion in an African Society,** Leiden:
65. Pittazoni, Raffaele, **Essays on the History of Religion,** (English Translation), London: 1954.

66. Radcliffe-Brown, A.R., **Structure and Function in Primitive Society,** London: 1954.
67. Ranger T.O. and Kimambo, Isaacian (Ed.), **The Historical Studies of African Religion,** (London: Hiennemen, 1972.
68. Schneider, L., **Religion, Culture and Society (A reader in Sociology of Religion),** New York: 1964.
69. Tylor, E.B., **Primitive Culture,** London: John Murray Publishers Ltd., 1871.
70. Tylor, E.B., **Religion in Primitive Culture,** New York: Harper Publishers, Vol. I & II, Reprinted, 195 .
71. Wach, Joachim, **The Sociology of Religion,** Chicago: 1944.
72. Wach, Joachim, **The Comparative Study of Religion,** London & New York: Columbia University Press, 1958.
73. Westermark, E.A., **Early Beliefs and their Social Influence,** London: Macmillian, 1932.
74. Yang, C.K., **Religion in Chinese Society,** Berkeley: University of California Press, 1967.
75. Yinger, J.M., **Sociology Looks at Religion,** New York: Macmillian, 1966.
76. Yinger, J.M., **The Scientific Study of Religion,** New York: The Macmillian Company, 1970.

Articles

77. Davis, Walter, "The Hidden and the Revealed: Contributions of Social Sciences to the Study and Practice of Religion", **ORITA,** 12, 2 (Dec. 1978) 142-157.
78. Geertz, C., "Religion as a Cultural System" in M. Banton (Ed.) **Anthropological Approaches to the Study of Religion,** London: 1966.

IV. Colonial Era (Data for Governance)

79. Allen, J.G.C., Intelligence Report on the Izzi Clan (Unpub. Government Report, 1932).
80. Allen, J.G.C., Intelligence Report on the Ngwa Clan, Aba Division, Upub. Government Report, 1933.
81. Basden, G.T., **Among the Igbos of Nigeria,** London: 1921, Reissued Frank Cass, 1966.

82. Basden, G.T., **Niger Igbos**, London: 1938, Reprinted; Frank Cass, Co. Ltd., 1966.

83. Chapman, G.B.C., Intelligence Report on the Ezza Clan of Abakiliki Division (Unpubs Govt. Report, 1932).

84. Chapman, G.B.C., Notes on the Ofunbonga Clan, Owerri Province, Unpub. Govt., Report, 1934.

85. Jeffreys, M.D.W., 'Report on the Ibo-speaking peoples of Awka Division', (Unpublished Govt. Report, 1930).

86. Meek, C.K., Various Ethnographical Reports on Various Divisions (Igboland) N.A.E., 1930-1931.

87. Meek, C.K., Intelligence Reports on Various Division in Iboland E.P., 1160-1180, NAE.

88. Meek, C.K., 'The Tribal Studies of Northern Nigeria', I.A.I., 1931.

89. 'Report on the Social and Political Organization in the Owerri, 1933.

90. Meek, C.K., **Law and Authority in a Nigerian Tribe: A Study in Indirect Rule,** (2nd impression 1950), London: O.U.P. 1937.

91. Meek, C.K., **'Intelligence Report on Awgu'**, Unpub. Govt. Report; 1931.

92. Meek, C.K., 'The Religions of Nigeria', **Africa,** 3 (1943).

93. Rattray, R.S., **Religion and Art in Ashanti,** London: Oxford University Press, 1927.

94. Talbot, P.A., 'A Report on the Pagan Creed', CSA 1/2/18., N.A.E. 1922.

95. Talbot, P.A., 'A Report on Local Jujus' SCE 5/2/19 NAE 1922.

96. Talbot, P.A., A Report on Various Superstititions, CSE 1/2.20 NAE.

97. Thomas, Northcote, N., **Anthropological Report on the Ibo-Speaking Peoples,** London: Harrison, 1913-1914 (6 Vols.) Reissued 1973.

V. African Nationalist Era

Books

98. Danqua, J.B., **Akan Doctrine of God,** (2nd Ed.), London: Frank Cass and Co. Ltd., 1968.
99. Gaba, C.R., **Scriptures of an African People: The Sacred Utterances of the Anlo,** New York: Nok Publishers, 1973.
100. Idowu, E.B., **African Traditional Religion: A Definition,** London: S.C.M. Press Ltd., 1973.
101. Kenyatta, Jomo, **Facing Mount Kenya,** New York: Vintage Books of Random House, 1962.
102. Mbiti, J.S., **African Religions and Philosophy,** London: Heinemann, 1969.
103. P'Bitek, Okot, **African Religions in Western Scholarship,** Nairobi, East African Publishing Bureau, 1971.

Articles

104. Abimbola, 'Wande., 'The place of Ifa in Yoruba Traditional Religion', African Notes, 2,2 (1965).
105. Adewale, S.A., 'The Role of Ifa in the Work of the 19th Century missionaries', **ORITA,** 12,1 (June 1978 23-32).
106. Ajayi, J.F.A., & E.A. Ayandele, "Emerging Themes in Nigerian and West African Religious History", **Journal of African Studies,** 1,1 (1974) 1-39.
107. Bamgbose, Ayo, Yoruba Studies Today' **ODU: A Journal of West African Studies,** New Series, No. 1, 1969.
108. Echeruo, M.J.C., "Literature, Religion and Cultural Renewal" **ORITA,** 9,2 (Dec. 1975).
109. Gaba, C.R., "African Traditional Conception of Freedom and Responsibility", **ORITA,** 11,1 (June 1977) 41--55.
110. Kalu, O.U., "Missionaries, Colonial Government and Secret Societies in South-Eastern Igboland 1920-1950" **JHSN,** 9,1 (Dec. 1977).
111. Thompson, P.E.S., "Reflections upon West African Ideas of God", The Sierra Leone Bulletin of Religion, 7,2 (Dec.,) 1965.

VI. New Anthropological Approach: Localized and Fragmented Monographs

A Geographical and Regional

112. Abraham, Roy C., **The Tiv People,** Farnborough, England: Greg Press, 1968 (Reprinted).
113. Coutlander, Harold, **Tales of Yoruba Gods and Heroes,** New York: Crown Publishers, Inc, 1973.
114. Downes, R.M., **Tiv Religion,** Ibadan: Ibadan University Press, 1971.
115. Farrow, S.S., **Faith, Fancies and Fetch,** London, 1926.
116. Field, M.J., **Religion and Medicine of the Ga People,** London: Oxford University Press, 1937, Reprinted, 1961.
117. Horton, Robin, 'The God's as Guests', **Nigeria Magazine,** special publication, No. 3 (1960).
118. Idowu, E.B., **Olodumare, God in Yoruba Belief,** London: Longman Group Ltd., 1982.
119. Lienhardt, Godfrey, **Divinity and Experience: The Religion of the Dinka,** London: Clarendon Press, 1961.
120. Little, Kenneth L., **The Mende of Sierra Leone,** London: Routledge and Kegan Paul, 1951, reissued 1957.
121. Mair, Lucy, P., **An African People in the Twentieth Century,** London: Routledge and Kegan Paul, 1934, New York: Russell & Russell, 1965.
122. Middleton, John, **Lugbara Religion,** London: Oxford University Press (for 1A1), 1960.
123. Nadel S.F., **A Black Byzantium: The kingdom of Nupe in Nigeria,** London: O.U.P. (For I.A.I.) 1942, Reprinted, 1969.
124. Nadel, S.F., **Nupe Religion,** London: Routledge and Kegan Paul, Ltd., 1954.
125. Ogbalu, F.C., **Igbo Institutions and Customs,** Onitsha Nigeria: University Publishing Co. Ltd., (n.d.).
126. Ojo, G.J. Afolabi, **Yoruba Culture: A Geographical Analysis,** London: University of London Press and Univerity of Ife Press, 1966.
127. Rattray, R.S., **Ashanti,** Oxford: Clarendon Press, 1923, Reprinted 1969.
128. Talbot, P.A., **Life in Southern Nigeria: The Magic Beliefs and customs of the Ibibio Tribe,** London: 1923.
129. Talbot, P.A., **Some Nigeria Fertility Cults,** London: 1927.

130. Talbot, P.A., **Tribes of the Niger Dalta: Their Religions and Customs,** London: 1932.

B   Ideas and Values

131. Abimbola, Wande, **Ifa: An Exposition of Ifa Literary Corpus,** Ibadan Nigeria: O.U.P., 1976.
132. Awolalu, J.O., "The Concept of Death and Hereafter in Yoruba Traditional Religion" **WAR,** 18, 2/3 (1979) 57-69.
133. Awolalu, J.O., "The African Traditional View of Man", **ORITA,** 6,2 (Dec., 1972) 108ff.
134. Beir, Ulli, **African Mud Sculpture,** (1963).
135. Breidenbach, Paul S., "Colour Symbolism and Ideology in a Ghananian healing movement", **Africa,** 46 (1976) 37ff.
136. Caroll, K., **Yoruba Religious Carving,** 1967.
137. Chegwe, A.O., "Reincarnation: A Socio-religious Phenomenon among the Ibo-speaking riverines of the lower Niger", **Cahier Religiones Africainea,** 7,13 (1973).
138. Douglas, Mary, **Purity and Danger,** London: Routledge and Kegan Paul, 1966, reprinted, 1979.
139. Douglas, Mary (Ed.), **Witchcraft Confessions and Accusations,** London: Tavistock Publications, 1970.
140. Egbo, E.O., "A Reassessment of the concept of Igbo Traditional Religion", **Numen,** 19,1 (April 1972).
141. Ekejiuba, F.I., "Aro World View: An Analysis of the Cosmological ideas of Arochukwu People of Eastern Nigeria", **WAR,** 8 (1970) 1-12.
142. Ekejiuba, F.I., "Igba Ndu: An Igbo Mechanism of Social Control and Adjustment", **African Notes,** 7,1 (1971-72) 9-24.
143. Evans-Pritchard, E.E., **Witchard, Oracles and Magic Among the Azande,** Oxford: The Clarendon Press, 1937.
144. Ezeanya, S.N., "Igbo Religious Proverbs as a Means of interpreting the Traditional religions of the Igbo people", **WAR,** 15 (1974) 3-18.
145. Fortes, Meyer, **Oedipus and Job in West African Religion,** Cambridge: C.U.P., 1959.
146. Fortes, Meyer, "Ritual Festivals and Social Cohesion in the hinterland of the Gold Coast", **American Anthropologist,** 38, 4 (1936) 590-604.
147. Genep, Van A., **The Rites of Passage,** Chicago: University Press, 1960.
148. Green, M.M., "The Sayings of the Okonko Society of the Igbo-speaking People", **BULLSACH,** 21 (1958) 157-173.

149. Horton, W.R.G., "The Ohu System of Slavery in Northern Ibo Village Group", **AFRICA**, 24 (1954).
150. Horton, W.R.G., "God Man and the Land in a Northern Ibo Village Group", **AFRICA,** 26 (1956).
151. Horton, R., "Destiny and the Unconscious in West Africa", **AFRICA,** 31 (1961) 110-116.
152. Horton, R., "African Traditional Thought and Western Science" in M.F.D. Young (Ed.), **Knowledge and Control: New Directions for Sociology,** London: Collier-Macmillian Publishers, 1971, 208-266.
153. Horton, R., "Conference on the High God in Africa", **ODU,** 2,2 (Jan. 1966).
154. Horton, R., "Kalabari World-view: an outline in interpretation", **AFRICA,** 32,3 (1962).
155. Horton, R., "Kalabari Diviners and Oracles", **ODU,** 1,1 (July 1962).
156. Huntington, W.R., "Death and Social Order", **African Studies,** 32 (1973).
157. Ibuoba, V.O.I., "A traditional ceremony: the Burial of an Ibo King", Nigerian Field, 40,3 (Sept. 1975) 132-133.
158. Ikenga-Metuh, Emefie, Religion and morality in Traditional African Beliefs: Assessment of View Point, **WAR,** 18,2/3 (1979) 92-102.
159. Ilogu, E.C., 'Ofo', **Nigeria Magazine,** 82, (1964) 234-5.
160. Jeffreys, M.D.W., 'The Divine Umundiri King', **AFRICA,** 8,3 (1935).
161. Jeffreys, M.D.W., 'The degeneration of the Ofo Anam', **Nigerian Field,** 21,4 (1956) 173-177.
162. Jeffreys, M.D.W., "Ikenga': The Ibo ram-head god", **African Studies,** 13,1 (1954) 25-40.
163. Jones, G.I., 'Mbari Houses', **Nigerian Field,** 6,2 (1937) 77-79.
164. Kalu, O.U., 'Precarious Vision: The African's Perception of His World' in O.U. Kalu (Ed.), **Readings in African Humanities: African Cultural Development,** ENUGU: Fourth Dimension Publishers, 1978, 37-44.
165. Kenneth, Little, "The Political Function of the Poro", Part I, **Africa,** 35,4 (Oct. 1965) 349-365.
166. Leith-Ross, S., "Notes on the Osu-System among the Ibo of Owerri Province Nigeria", **Africa,** 10 (1937) 206-230.
167. Mandosa, Eugene, "The Journey of the Soul in Sisala Cosmology", **J.R.A.,** 7 (1975) 62-73.
168. Mbiti, J.S., **The Prayers of African Religion,** London: S.P.C.K., 1975.

169. Metuh, E.E., "The Religious Dimension of African Cosmogonies: A Case Study of the Igbo of Nigeria" **W.A.R.**, 17,2 (1978) 9-21.
170. Middleton, John (Ed.) **Myth and Cosmos,** Garden City, New York: The Natural History Press, 1967.
171. Middleton John (Ed.) Magic, Witchcraft and Curing. Garden City, New York: The Natural history Press 1967.
172. Njoku, O., "The Dibia Secret Society in Iboland", **Review Ethnology,** Vienna: 4,7/9 (1974) 66-70.
173. Noon, J., "A Preliminary Examination of theDeath Concepts of the Igbo", **American Anthropologists,** 44 (1942) 638-654.
174. Ottenberg, S., 'Oracles and Inter-group Relations' **South Western Jorunal of Anthropology,** XIV (1958).
175. Onibere, I.S., 'Otatha': Probings into Isoko concept of Predesting, **ORITA,** 12,2 (Dec. 1978) 87-95.
176. Olisa, M.S.O., "Taboos in Ibo Religion and Society" **WAR,** 11 (1972) 1-18.
177. Parrinder, E.G., **Witchcraft: European and African,** London: Faber and Faber, 1958. Reprinted: London: Pengiun 1963, New York: Barnes and Boble, 1963.
178. Parrinder, E.G., "Monotheism and Pantheism in Africa", **JRA,** 3,2 (1970).
179. Peter, M. Weil, "The masked Figure and Social Conrol", **AFRICA,** 41,4 (1971) 279-293.
180. Salamone, Frank, "Religion as Play: Bori, a friendly Witchdoor" **JRA,** 17/3 (1975) 201-211.
181. Shorter, Aylward, **Prayers of African Religion,** Nairobi, O.U.R., 1975.
182. Smith, Edwin W. (Ed.), **African Ideas of God,** London: Edinburgh House, Pren, 1950.
183. Spondili, J., 'Marriage customs among the Ibos', **Anthropos,** 37-40, 1-3 (1942-45) 113-114.
184. Tamuno, T.N. and W.R.G., Horton, "The Changing Role of Secret Societies and cults in modern Nigeria" **African Notes,** 5,2 (Jan. 1969) 36-56.
185. Temples, Placide, **Bantu Philosophy,** Paris: Presence Africaine, 1959.
186. Thomas, N.N., "Secret Societies (African), **Encyclopaedia of Religion and Ethics,** Vol. XI.
187. Turner, Victor M., "Colour Classification in Ndembu Ritual" in Michael Barton (Ed.) **Anthropological Approaches to the Study of Religion,** Edinburgh: Tavistock Publications, 1966, 47ff.

188. Turner, W., **The forest of Symbols,** Ithaca: Cornell University Press, 1967.
189. Turner, V., **The Ritual Process,** Chicago: University of Chicago Press, 1969.
190. Udechukwu, Obiora, "Concept Into form": Religion and Aesthetics in African Arts" in O.U. Kalu, (Ed.), **Readings in African Humanities,** 86-94.
191. Uzoho, V.N., "The Sacred and the Profane in the Traditional Religion of Africa", **W.A.R.,** 15 (1974) 36-43.

VII. Christian Missionary Strategists: Indigenization

Books

192. Arinze, F.A., **Sacrifice in Ibo Religion,** Ibadan: Ibadan University Press, 1970.
193. Dickson, Kwesi and Paul Elingworth, (Eds.), **Biblical Revelation and African Beliefs,** London: Lutherworth Press, 1969.
194. Harris, W.T. and Harry Sawyerr, **The Springs of Mende Belief and Conducts,** Freetown: Sierra Leone University Press, 1968.
195. Hastings, Adrian, **African Christianity,** London: London & Dublin: Geoffrey Chapman, 1976.
196. Idowu, E.B., **Towards an Indigenous Church,** London: Oxford University Press, 1965.
197. Ilogu, E.C.O., **Christianity and Igbo Culture,** New York: NOK Publishers, 1974.
198. Kato, Byan H., **Theological Pitfalls in Africa,** Kenya: Evangel Publishing House, 1975.
199. Mbiti, J.S., **New Testament Eschatology in an African Background,** London. Oxford University Press, 1971.
200. Sawyerr, Harry, **Creature Evangelism: Towards a new Christian Encounter with Africa,** London: Lutherworth Press, 1968.
201. Sawyerr, Harry, **God: Ancestor or Creator?** London: Longman, 1970.
202. Shorter, Aylward, **African Culture and The Christian Church,** London: Geoffrey Chapman, 1973.
203. Shorter, Aylward, **African Christian Theology,** London: Geoffrey Chapman, 1975.

204. Williamson, S.G., **Akan Religion and the Christian Faith,** Accra: Ghana University press, 1965.

Articles

205. Adewale, S.A., "The Role of Ifa in the work of the 19th Century Missionaries", ORITA, 12,1 (June 1978) 23-32.
206. Berger, Renato, "Is Traditional Religion Still Relevant?", **ORITA,** 3,1 (June 1969) 15-26.
207. Ezeanya, S.N., "A view of Christian and Pagan Morality", **WAR,** Nsukka, 2 (1964) 4-5.
208. Ezeanya, S.N., "The Use of Igbo Names", **WAR,** 3 (1964) 2-8.
209. Ezeanya, S.N., "Endurnace of conviction in the Converts: The force of the traditional religion of Africa", **WAR,** 8 (1970) 20-24.
210. Ezeanya, S.N., "The place of the Supreme God in the Traditional Religion of the Igbo", **WAR,** 1 (1963) 1-4.
211. Ezeanya, S.N., "The Sacred place in the Traditional Religion of the Igbo People", **WAR,** 6 (1966) 1-9.
212. Ezeanya, S.N., "God, Spirits and the spirit-world", in Kweai, Didckson and Paul Elingworth (Eds.), **Biblical Revelation and African Beliefs,** London: Lutherworth Press, 1969 35-43.
213. Ezeanya, S.N., "Christianity and African Traditional Religion", **WAR,** 13/14 (Sept-Oct. 1972) 29-38.
214. Ezeanya, S.N., "The Osu (Cult Slave) System in Igboland", **JRA,** 1,1 (1967) 36-45.
215. Gaba, C.R., "African Traditional Concept of Freedom and Responsibility", **ORITA,** 11,1 (June 1977) 41-55.
216. Ilogu, E.C.O., "Christianity and Igbo Traditional Religion", **Nigeria Magazine** 83, (1964) 304-308.
217. Ilogu, E.C.O. "Worship in Ibo Traditional Religion", **NUMEN,** 20,3 (1973) 230ff.
218. Ilogu, E.C.O., "Christianity and Ibo Traditional Religion", **IRM,** 54 (1965).
219. Ilogu, E.C.O., 'The Indigenization of "Imported religions"', **Journal of Asian and African Studies,** XIV, 1-2, 121-128.
220. Metuh, E.E., "Igbo World view: A Premise for Christian/Traditional Religion dialogue", **WAR,** 13/14 (Sept-Oct., 1972) 51-58.
221. Oduyoye, Mercy A., "The Value of African Religious Beliefs and practices for Christian Theology", Conference paper: Accra, Ghana (17th-24th Dec. 1977).

222. Sawyerr, Harry, "Traditional Sacrificial Rituals and Christian Worship", **Sierra Leone Bulletin of Religion** 2,1 (June 1960) 18-26.

VIII. Overviews. (Common Denominator Approach)

Books

223. Abraham, W.E., **The Mind of Africa,** Chicago: University of Chicago Press, 1962.
224. Adeyemo, Tokunbo, **Salvation in African Traditional Religion,** Nairobi Kenya: Evangelical Publishing House, 1979.
225. Awolalu, J.O., **Yoruba Beliefs and Sacrificial Rites,** London: Longman, 1979.
226. Bascom, William, **Ifa Divination,** Bloomington: Indiana University Press, 1969.
227. Lucas, J.O., **Religion of the Yorubas,** Lagos: C.M.S. Bookshops, 1948.
228. Mbiti, J.S., **Concepts of God in Africa,** New York: Praeger 1970.
229. Mbiti, J.S., **African Religions and Philosophy,** New York: Praeger, 1969, London: Henneman, 1969.
230. Mendelsohn, Jack, **God, Allah, and Juju: Religion in Africa Today,** New York: Nelson, 1962; Reprinted, Boston: Beacan Press, 1965.
231. Oduyoye, M., **The Vocabulary of Yoruba Religious Discourse,** Ibadan: Daystar Press, 1971.
232. Onibere Osovo, "Akpo-Eri Contiuum: A Critical Investigation into Isoko Eschatological Beliefs", **WAR** 18, 2/3 (1979) 3-12.
233. Parrinder, E.G., **West African Religion,** London: Epworth Press, 1949, re-edited, 1969.
234. Parrinder, E.G., **Africa's Three Religions,** London: Sheldon Press, 1969.
235. Parrinder, E.G., **African Traditional Religion,** London: Sheldon Press, (3rd Edition, 1962).
236. Parrinder, E.G., **West African Psychology: A Comparative Study of Psychological and Religious Thought,** London: Lutherworth Press, 1951.
237. Ray, Benjamin C., **African Religions: Symbol, Rituals and Community,** New Jersey: Prentice Hall, 1976.

238. Taylor, J.V., **Primal Vision,** London: S.C.M. Press, 1963; Philadelphia: Fortress Press, 1964.

Articles

239. Awolalu, J.O., "Sin and its removal in African Traditional Religion", **ORITA,** 10, 1 (June 1976) 3-23.
240. Chikwendu, V.E., "Evidence of Supernational Belief in a Belistoric Igbo Community", **WAR,** 18,2/3 (1979) 42-56.
241. Ezeanya, S.N., "Women in African Traditional Religion", **ORITA,** 10, 2 (Dec. 1976) 105-121.
242. Gaba, C.R., "The Idea of a Supreme Being Among the Anlo People of Ghana", **JRA,** 2,1 (1969) 64-78.
243. Gaba, C.R., "Man's Salvation: its nature and meaning in African Traditional Religion" in Gray, Fashiole-Luhe and Tasie (Eds.) **Christianity in Independent Africa,** London: Rex Collins, 1978.
244. Horton, Robin, "The High God. A comment on Father O'Connell's Paper", **MAN,** 42, 219 (1962).
245. Idowu, E.B., 'God' in Dickson & Elingworth (Eds.), **Biblical Revelation and African Beliefs,** London: 1969.
246. Iwuagwu, A.O., "Chukwu; Towards a Definition of Igbo Traditional Religion", **WAR,** 16,1 (1975) 26-34.
247. O'Connell, Fr., James, "The Withdrawal of the High God in West African Religion: An Essay in Interpretation", **MAN,** 108/109 (May 1962) 67-69.
248. Shelton, Austin, J., "On recent Interpretations of Leus Otiosus: The Withdrawn God in West African Psychology", **MAN,** (March-April, 1964).
249. Shelton, Austin J., "The Presence of the Withdrawn High God in North-Igbo Religious Beliefs and worship", **MAN,** (Jan-Feb., 1965) 15-19.

IX. New Approaches: Culture Areas, Pulls & Heartland

Books

250. Abimbola, "Wande", **Ifa: An Exposition of Ifa Literary Corpus,** Ibadan Nigeria: O.U.P., 1976.
251. Afigbo, A.E., **Ropes of Land: Studies in Igbo History and Culture,** Ibadan: University Press Ltd., 1981.

252. Buxton, Jean, **Religion and Healing in Mandari**, Oxford: Clarendon Press, 1973.
252a Ifemesia, Chieka, **Traditional Human Living among the Igbos, An Historical Perspective**, Enugu: Fourth Dimension Publishers, 1978.
253. Kiev, Ari (Ed.), **Magic, Faith and Healing**, New York: Collier Macmillian Publisher, 1974.
254. Maclean, Una, **Magical Medicine**, London: Pengiun Books 1971.
255. Uchendu, V.C., **The Igbo of South-Eastern Nigeria**, New York Holt, Rinehardt and Winston, 1965.

Articles

256. Achebe, Chinua, 'Chi' in Igbo Cosmology: in Morning **Yet on Creation Day**, New York: Anchar Press, 1975.
257. Afigbo, A.E. "Traditions of Igbo Origin: An Analysis", **Workshop Paper on Traditions of Origin of Nigerian Peoples**, Ibadan: (8-10 Feb., 1979).
258. Afigbo, A.E., "The Igbo and their Neighbours in Precolonial times", **Ahianjoku Lecturers**, Owerri: Nigerian **Statesman**: Owerri; Dec, 7, 8, 9, 10, 11, pg. 4 of each volume.
259. Afigbo, A.E., "The Indigenous Political systems of the Igbo", **TARIK**, 4,3 (1977) 13-23.
260. Amankulor, J.N., "Ekpe Festivals as Religious Ritual and Dance Drama", **Ikenga**, 1,2 (July, 1972).
261. Beir, Ulli, "Osezi Festival in Agbor", **Nigeria Magazine**, 78 (1963) 184-195.
262. Boston, J., "Medicine and Fetisher in Igala", **AFRICA** 41, (1971) 200-207.
263. Chukwukere, I., 'CHI', A Fundamental Interpretative Concept of Traditional Igbo religious Thought" Workshop paper an: **The Foundations of Igbo Civilization**, Institute of African Studies, University of Nigeria, (20-22nd May, 1980).
264. Forde, Daryll, "The Governmental Roles of Associations among the Yako", **AFRICA**, 31 (1961) 309-323.
265. Horton, Robin, "The Kalabari Ekine Society: A borderline of Religion and Art", **AFRICA**, 33,2 (1963) 94-114.
266. Horton, Robin, "Ritual Man in Africa", **AFRICA**, 34,2 (April 1964) 85-104.
267. Jeffrey, M.C., "Medicine, Fetish and Secret Society in West African Culture", **AFRICA**, 46 (1976) 247.

268. Latham, A.J.H., "Witchcraft accusations and economic tension in precolonial old Calabar" **JAH,** 23,3 (July 1972) 249-260ff.

269. LLyod, Peter, "Craft Organization in Yoruba town", **AFRICA,** 23,3 (July 1953) 34.

270. Nwanunobi, C.O., "The Deus Otiosus Concept in Traditional Igbo Religion: An Examination through Transactional Analysis" Workshop Paper on The Foundations of Igbo Civilization; Institute of African Studies, University of Nigeria, (20-22nd May, 1980).

271. Nzekwu, Onucra, 'Omo-Ckwu Temple', **Nigeria Magazine** 81, June, 1964, pp. 1971.

272. Nzewi, Meki, "Some Structural Features of the Igbo Festival", (n.d.) Private Mss.

273. Shelton, J.A., "The Worship of the Supreme Being in Northern Igboland", **MAN,** 1965, 65ff.

274. Uchendu, V.C., "The Social and Moral Character of African Ancestors: a Review of the Evidence in Igbo Society" Seminar Paper, Dept. of Religion UNN, 1978.

275. Verger, P., 'The Yoruba High God', **ODU,** 2,2 (Jan. 1966).

276. Weil, Peter M., "The Masked Figure and Social Control: The Mandinka Case", **AFRICA,** 41,4 (1971) 279ff.

277. William, Peter-Morton, "An Outline of the Cosmology and Cult Organization of the Oyo Yoruba", **AFRICA,** 34,3 (July 1964) 243ff.

X. Religious Change

Books

278. Achebe, C., **Things Fall Apart,** London: Heinemann, 1958. (A.W.S.).

279. Achebe, C., **Arrow of God,** N.Y.; John Day, 1964; Anchor Books, 1962, A.W.S.

280. Baeta, C.G., **Christianity in Tropical Africa,** London: 1968.

281. Bascom, W.R. & M.J., Hersevits (Eds.), **Continuity and Change of African Cultures,** Chicago and London: University of Chicago Press, 1959.

282. Ndiokwere, N.I., **Prophecy and Revolution: The Role of prophet in the Independent African Churches and in Biblical Tradition,** London: SPCK, 1981.

283. Ngugi James, **The River Between**, London: Hieneman, 1965) (AWS).
284. Oosthuizen, C.G., **Post-Christianity in Africa**, London: 1968.
285. Parrinder, E.G., **Religion in an African City**, London: University Press, 1953.
286. Parsons, R.T., **Religion in an African Society**, Leiden: E.J. Brill, 1964.
287. Peel, J.D.Y., **Syncretism and Religious Change: Comparative Studies in Society and History**, (1968).
288. SundKler, B., **Bantu Prophets in South Africa**, London: 1948.
289. Williamson, S.G., **Akan Religion and the Christian Faith**, Accra: Ghana University press, 1965.
290. Wilson, Monica, **Religion and the Transformation of Society**, Cambridge, C.U.P. 1971.

Articles

291. Abdul, M.O.A., "Yoruba Divination and Islam", **ORITA**, 4,1 (June 1970) 17-26.
292. Abdul, M.O.A., "Syncretism in Islam among the Yoruba", **WAR**, 15 (March 1974) 44-56.
293. Armstrong, R.C., "African Religion and Cultural Renewal", **ORITA**, 9,2 (Dec. 1975) 109-132.
294. Akpunonu, P., "The Religion of the Ibos, Yesterday and Today", **LUX**, 2,1 (1965) 85-94.
295. Berger, Renato, "Is Traditional Religion still relevant?", **ORITA**, 3,1 (June 1969) 15-26.
296. Comstock, Gray Lynn, "The Yoruba and Religious Change", **JRA**, 10,1 (1979) 1-12.
297. Egbo, E.O., "Conflict between Traditional Religion and Christianity in Iboland, South-Eastern Nigeria", WAR, 10 (1971) 7-17.
298. Egbo, E.O., "The beginning of the end of Traditional Religion in Iboland", **CIVILIZATIONS**, 21, 2/3 (1971) 269-279; WAR, 9 (1971) 1-12.
299. Ekechi, F.K., "African Polygamy and Western Christian Ethnocentrism", JAS, 3,3 (1976) 329-349.
300. Fisher, H.J., "Conversion Reconsidered: some historical aspect of Religious Conversion in Black Africa", AFRICA, 18,1 (1973) 27-40.
301. Fortes, Doris and Meyer, "Psychosis and Social Change Among the Tallensi, of Northern Ghana", **Cahiers d'Etudes Africaines**, 21,6 (1966).

374

302. Holiness, Lawell D., "Cults, Cargo and Christianity: Samoan Response to western Religion", **Missiology,** 8,4 (1980) 471-488.
303. Horton, R., "African Conversion", **AFRICA,** XLI,2 (April 1971).
304. Horton, R., "A Hundred Years of Change in Kalabari Religion" in John Middleton, **Black Africa,** New York: 1970, 193-211.
305. Horton, R., "On the Rationality of Conversion Part I", **AFRICA** 45,4 (1975) 373-399.
306. Ifeka-Moller, C., "White-Power: Social Structural factors in conversion to Christianity in Eastern Nigeria, 1921-1966", **Canadian Journal of African Studies,** 8,1 (1974) 55-72.
307. Isichie, Elizabeth, "Ibo and Christian Beliefs: Some Aspects of a theological Encounter", **AFRICAN Affairs,** 68, 271 (1969) 121-134.
308. Jeffreys, M.D.W., "A triad of gods in Africa", **Anthropos,** 67,5/6 (1972) 723-35.
309. Kalu, O.U., "Gods in Retreat, Models of Religious change in Africa", **Nigerian Journal of Humanities,** 1,1 (Sept. 1977) 42-53.
310. Katfelt, Niels, "African Prophetism and Christian Missionaries in North East Nigeria", **JRA,** 8,3 (1976) 175-188.
311. Michael, Pye, "Syncretism and Ambiguity", **Numen,** XVIII, 2 (1971) 83-93.
312. Mckenzie, P.R., "Samuel Crowther's Attitude to Other Faiths during the Early period", **ORITA,** 5,1 (June 1971) 3-17.
313. Noel, S. Booth Jr., "Time and Change in African Traditional Thought", **JRA,** 7,2 (1975) 81-91.
314. Noel, S. Booth Jr., "Civil Religion in Traditional Africa", **Africa Today,** 23/24 (Oct.-Dec., 1976) 59-66.
315. Wabara, S.N., "Christian Encounter with Indigenous religion at Onitsha, 1857-1885", **Cahiers d'Etudes Africaines,** 44,4 (1971) 589-601.
316. Odita, E.O., "Universal Cults and Intra-diffusion: Igbo Ikenga in Cultural Retrospection", **African Studies Review,** 16,1 (April 1973) 73-82.
317. Parratt, J.K., "Religious Change in Yoruba Society: AS Test Case, **JRA,** 2 (1969) 113ff.
318. Peel, J.D.Y. & Robin Horton, "Conversion and Confusion: A Rejoinder on Christianity in Eastern Nigeria", **Canadian Journal of African Studies,** 10,3 (1976) 481-498.

319. Peel, J.D.Y., "Religious Change in Yorubaland", **AFRICA,** 37,1 (1967) 292-306.
320. Peel, J.D.Y., "Understanding Alien Belief Systems", **British Journal of Soc.,** 20,1 (1969) 69-84.
321. Salomon, F.A., "Continuity of Igbo Values after Conversions: a study in purity and prestige", **Missiology,** 3,1 (1975) 33-43.
322. Welborn, F.B., "Some Problems of African Christianity: Guilt and shame", in C.G. Baeta (Ed.), **Christianity in Tropical Africa,** London: O.U.P., 1968, 182-199.
323. Williamson, Kay, "Change in the marriage system of the Okrika Ijo", **AFRICA,** 32 (1962) 58ff.

XI. Doctoral Theses

324. Achebe, P.O., "The Socio-religious Significance of Igbo Prenatal, natal and puberty rites" Ph.D. Thesis, University of Innsbruck, 1972.
325. Ahanotu, A.M., "The Economics and Politics of Religion: a study of the development of the Igbo spirit of Enterprise 1810-1955" Ph.D Thesis, University of California, 1971.
326. Ahunanya, Theodore, "Igbo Pagan Funeral studies in the light of Catholic Christian Funerals. Ph.D. Universities Urbaniane, Rome.
327. Ajoma, J., "Missionary Behaviour to Nigerian Cultural concepts and practices" Ph.D. University of Rome, 1968.
328. Anozia, P.I., "The Religious Import of Igbo Name" Ph.D. Universities Urbaniana, Rome, 1968.
329. Ezeanya, S.N., "The Method of Adaptation in the Evangelization of the Igbo-speaking People", Ph.D. Propaganda Urban University Lib, Rome, 1956.
330. Gbuji, Anthony, "The Problem of title society among the Ibo of Nigeria in the light of the Canonical Legislation" Ph.D. Propaganda University, Rome, 1963.
331. Iwuagwu, A.O., "The Spiritual Churches in the Eastern States of Nigeria", Ph.D. Thesis, University of Ibadan, 1971.
332. Nwokocha, C.C., "The Kola; Igbo symbol of Love and Unity, a valuable starting point for the study of the Eucharist" Ph.D. Thesis, Universities Urbaniana, Rome, 1969.

333. Obiefuna, A., "The Christian Education of Igbo Moral Con-
science" Ph.D. Thesis, Alfonsia, Rome, 1966.
334. Obiego, C.O., "Igbo Idea of Life and death in relation to
Chukwa, God" Ph.D. Thesis Universities Urbanianae,
Rome, 1971.
335. Ogunla, O., "Ritual Drama of the Ijebu People" Ph.D. Thesis,
University of Ibadan, 1967.
336. Okeke, Simon, "Priest Lord among the Igbo of Nigeria,
Studied in the Light of Catholic Priesthood", Ph.D.
Thesis, University of Innsbruck, 1967.
337. Ugboko, P., "The Betrothal Contract among the Ibos" Thesis,
Ponti Biblioteca, Missionum, Rome, 1958.

XII. Unpublished Long Essays

338. Adebanjo, O.F., "Oshun Festival and its Sociological effect
on the Yoruba Peoples of Nigeria" (B.A. Dept., of
Religion, UNN, 1977).
339. Adebayo, G.F., "Owe of Ibo-Oluji: New Yam Festival in Ondo
Province", (B.A. Dept of Religion, UNN, 1975).
340. Agwu, Adimoha A., "Confession in Igbo Traditional Religion
of Umuahia People", (B.A. 1980).
341. Ahirika, E.A., "The Cult of the Supreme Being in Maaise
Local Government Areas of Imo State" (B.A., 1978).
342. Akpuokwe, Esther, N., "The Role of Women in the Traditional Religion of Nimo, Njikoka Divison", (B.A. UNN,
1976).
343. Alade, O.F., "The Olofin Festival as an Instrument of Social
Organization amongst the Ilawe People of Ekiti South
West Local Government in Ondo State, Nigeria", (B.A.
UNN, 1981).
344. Ali, C.A., "Major Traditional Festivals in Enugu-Ezike, Igbo-
Eze Local Government Area", (B.A. UNN, 1981).
345. Aloka, B.S., "Ozo title-taking in Mbanasa Clan of Imo State"
(B.A. UNN, 1981).
346. Alaoma, H.U., "The belief in the Supreme Being among the
Igbo-speaking people of Nigeria as seen from the personal names with special reference to Mbaise Division
of Imo State" (B.A. UNN, 1977).
347. Amaechi, I.C., "Nso Ani-Abomination among the Udi people"
(B.A. Thesis, UNN, 1973).

348. Amayo, N.O., "Olokun: A minor deity in Benin, Bendel State of Nigeria" (B.A. UNN, 1976).
349. Anyika, F., "Shrines dedicated to minor divinites commonly worshipped in the East Central State of Nigeria" (B.A. UNN, 1974).
350. Arungwa, P.O., "The Ofo in the Traditional Religion of the Igbo people with special reference to Ngwaland" (B.A. UNN, 1972).
351. Asomba, O., "Priestland, in the Traditional religion of Nnewi and Ihiala Divisons (B.A. 1975).
352. Atemie-Obuoforibo, B., "Secret Societies among the Okrika of the Niger Delta", (B.A. UNN, 1976).
353. Bardi, J.N., "Totemism in the Traditional Religion of Asaba Division" (B.A. UNN, 1974).
354. Chuta, S.C., "Religion: A factor for socio-economic differention in Post-missionary South Eastern Nigeria: - The Akwete Case" (B.A. 1976).
355. Diakpomrere, T.O., "Initiation Rites among the Urhobo people in the Midwestern State of Nigeria" (B.A. 1973).
356. Dimoji, N., "The Supreme God in the Traditional Religion of African with particular reference to Igbo-speaking people, B.A. (U.N.N.) 1972.
357. Dzurgba, Akpenpuum, "The minor Divinites commonly worshipped among the Tiv people of Benue-Plateu, States of Nigeria" (B.A., 1974).
358. Edewor, E.E. (Mrs.), "Eya-Erii Wives of Divinities among the Owhe people of Isoko Local Government Area of Bendel State, (B.A. UNN, 1979).
359. Egbuna, C.C., "A Comparative Study of the concept and practice of priesthood in the Traditional Religion of Idemili Local Government Area and in the contemporary Anglican and Roman Catholic Churches" (B.A. June 1979).
360. Eke, Francis, "The place of Enwezocha in the life of Enugu Ezike people of Igbo-Eze Local Government Area of Anambra State" (B.A. UNN 1981).
361. Elenwa, S.O., "Prominent Shrines in Traditional Religion of Ahoada (Ehuda) Division (B.A. UNN, 1972).
362. Eze, Udochukwu, "The Worship of the Supreme God among the Igbo people of East Central State" (B.A. UNN 1975).
363. Eze, Udochukwu, "Shrines dedicated to the minor Divinities among the Igbos of the Anambra State of Nigeria" (M.A. Thesis, UNN 1979).

364. Eze, M.O., "Conflict Between Traditional Religion and Christianity in Isi-Uzo Local Government Areas" (B.A. UNN, 1978).

365. Ezea, S.O.K., "The belief in the Supreme Being among the Igbo-speaking people of the East Central State of Nigeria as seen from personal names with special reference to Udi Division and Old Nsukka Province" (B.A. UNN, 1974).

366. Ezeaku, I.D., "Haaba The Goddes of the Agulu People" (B.A. UNN, 1976).

367. Ezegbolu, B.C., "Divinities in African Traditional Religion with reference to Idemili Local Government Area, (B.A. 1979).

368. Ezeokonkwo, J.C., "Rainmaking in Igbo-Ukwu" (B.A. June, 1977).

369. Ibeji, S., "Minor Divinities in Mbaise Division, East Central State of Nigeria" (B.A. June 1974).

370. Ilogu, E.C., "Ozo Title-taking in Ihiala Division, East Central State of Nigeria" (B.A. June 1975).

371. Iwuagwu, J.N., "Traditional Burial-rites in Mbaitoli-Ikeduru Division, E.C.S. Nigeria" (B.A. June 1974).

372. Izobo, A.H., "The Ohworu Festival in Iyede Clan, Isoko Division, Bendel State", (B.A. 1977).

373. Metuh, John, Br., "Taboos in Nnewi Local Government Area" (B.A. 1979).

374. Mokwe, J.C., "Principal Cult Objects used in Igbo Traditional Religion" (B.A. 1972).

375. Molokwu, C.C., "Sacred Animals and Trees in Idemili Local Government Area" (B.A. UNN, 1979).

376. Morenikeji, J.A., "Priesthood in the Traditional Religion of the Old Oyo province" (B.A. UNN, 1975).

377. Nwokedi, J.I., "Burial Rites in Mbaitoli/Ikeduru Division, (B.A. 1974).

378. Ngoladi, D.N., "The New Yam Festival in Igboland" (B.A. 1974).

379. Nnadiekwe, D.C., "Rainmaking in Nkwere Division of Imo State" (B.A. Thesis, UNN, 1977).

380. Nworie, B.C., "Biblical prophecy and Oracles in Igbo Traditional Religion" (B.A. Thesis, 1976).

381. Obasi, B.A., "Ancestral Cult among the Igbos of Etiti Local Government Area of Imo State" (B.A. Thesis, 1980).

382. Obi, J.U. (Mrs.), "Title-taking by women in Nnewi Local Government Area; Ekwe and Ezenwayi Titles" (B.A. 1977).

383. Odume, A.D.C., "Reinceration and its critical evaluation in Aniocha Local Government Area of Bendel State Nigeria" (B.A. June 1980).
384. Ofor, P.C.M., "Agwazi: the mother Divinity of Akpulu in Ideato Local Government Area of Imo State" (B.A. Thesis, 1981).
385. Oju, S.O., "Taboos in Isoko Traditional Religion (Eware Na Regho Eva Isoko)" (B.A. 1975).
386. Okechukwu, A.A., "The Cult of the Supreme Being in Uzo-Uwani Local Government Area of Anambra State" (B.A. 1978).
387. Okoh, R.O., "Confession in the Traditional Religion of Akwumazi Clan" (B.A. Thesis, 1977).
388. Okolo, E.O., "Cult of Ancestor in Asaba Division" (B.A. 1974).
389. Okolo, E.O.C., "Mgbafor Ezira: The priestess of Oyilora (Oyilioha) Oracle" (B.A. 1973).
390. Okoro, J.B., "Nnemiri: A minor Divinity among the Igbo people of Etche Division" (B.A. 1977.
391. Okpala, O.U., "The influence of environment in the traditional Religion of Africa" (B.A. Thesis, June 1971).
392. Okoye, J.C., "Puberty Rites in Njikoka Local Government Area of Anambra State" (B.A. 1981).
393. Okunfunwere, O., "Taboos (Eewo) in the Traditional Religion of the Ondo Yoruba" (B.A. Thesis, June 1975).
394. Okwuo, Patricia, Sr., "Sacrifice among the Traditional Igbos of Orlu in Imo State" (B.A. Thesis, 1976).
395. Okpoli, U.G., "Contributions of Traditional Religion and Christianity to the Social and Political Ethics of Aniocha Division Bendel State Nigeria (B.A. Thesis 1977).
396. Olupona, J.K., "The influence of environment (physical features and natural phenomena) on Traditional Yoruba Religion" (B.A. Thesis, 1975).
397. Omopariola, E.O., "Witchcraft in Traditional Religion of the Yorubas" (B.A. Thesis, June, 1973).
398. Onunwa, U.R., "The influence of contemporary social changes on the traditional religious concepts and organizations: The case of Ezihe, Mbano, Imo State" (B.A. Thesis, 1978).
399. Onyeidu, S.O., "Cult objects in the traditional religion of the people of Ika Division of the Midwest State" (B.A. Thesis, 1973).
400. Opurum, J.C., "Nneudo and Iyiafo among the Mbieri people of Mbaitoli/Ikeduru Local Government Area, of Imo State" (B.A. Thesis, 1981).

401. Orji, H.J., "Agwu among the Ikedurus of Mbaitoli/Ikeduru Local Government Area" (B.A. June 1979).
402. Riesa, James, "Funeral Customs in Urhoboland; Midwest Nigeria" (B.A. Thesis, 1974).
403. Sotunde, V.O. (Revd), "Minor Deities as agents of the Supreme God in African Religion (with special reference to the Yoruba)" (B.A. Thesis, 1971).
404. Ufomba, J.U., "Divination in Ngwaland" (B.A. Thesis 1973).
405. Ugochukwu, O.J., "The Religious Rites in Ozo title-taking" (B.A. Thesis, UNN, 1978).

Healing, 269-272: methods, 272-8
heathens, 329
heathenism, 41, 69
Hinduism, 168
Historical study of African religion, 82
historiography: archeology, 85; legends, 87; linguistics, 85; interdisciplinary, 85; oral tradition, 82-83
history of religions, 144-5
The Holy War **see** Jihad
Hobesian thesis, 180
Horton, Robin, 80, 314-315
human dignity, 245-247
humanists, 114-116
Hutchinson, J.J., 97
Ibn Battuta, 93-94
    commentary on African religion, 94
Ibrahim Elacho Guobadia, 307
Ichu Aja (sacrifice), 175
Id-el-Kibir, 303
Idel-Fitr, 303
idolatry, 41, 69, 94
Idowu, E. Bolaji, 22, 24, 39, 42 117, 128
Ifenesia, C.C., 91
Igbo: health concept, 271-2 marriage traditions, 234; myth of origin, 12; ritual experts **see** nri
Igbo peoples: The family life, 214-215; morality, 215; sub-cultures, 84-85; religion, 85-86
Igbo religious thoughts: 53-67; man, 54-66; **chi,** 55-60
Igo Mmuo (sacrifice) 67, 175
Ikpu Alu (sacrifice) 175
Indigenization of Christianity: 335-336 **see also** African Independent churches
"Indirect Rule", 99

indigenous scholars, 110-121
indigenous christian scholars, 116-119
Impressions of West Africa, 97
International Association for the History of Religion, 130
Iron Age shrines, 345
Isichei, Elizabeth **see Ekwensu**
Islam, 21, 34, 35, 87, 168, 297-308
Islam in West Africa, 302
Islamic missionary strategy, 297
Israel **see** Jews
Iuu-omo, 231
Jeffreys, M.D.W., 98, 99
Jews, 40, 200, 203, 204-5, 206
Jihad, 297,302
Job (Bible study) 61
John the Baptist, 201
Jones, G.I., 99
Joshua, 12
Judaism,201, 203
juju, 69, 161
Kalunga, 25
The Kano Chronicle: 94
Kant, 13
Kimambo, 82, 141, 145
Kingsley, Mary H., 97
Kinship, 16: hierachial structure, 59; ontologico-spiritual, 58-59; socio biological, 58-59
"Kola", 46
Koran, 298 **see also** Quoran
Kuper, Adam, 97
Kwoth, 25
Lang, Andrew, 39
Lawani Borokini, 306
Leith-Ross, Sylvia, 98
Leonard, A.G., 98
Life after death, 245
Life-force: interdependency, 57-59 **Obi,** 57-59
"Living-dead", 61, 162 **see also** ancestors

CONTRIBUTORS

1. Prof. Ogbu U. Kalu — Professor of Church History, University of Nigeria, Nsukka Nigeria.

2. Dr. Emefie Ikenga-Metuh — Associate Professor of African Traditional Religion, University of Jos, Jos Nigeria.

3. Prof. J. S. Mbiti — Professor of New Testament Studies, Bosse, Geneva.

4. Prof. J. O. Awolalu — Professor of African Traditional Religion, University of Ibadan, Nigeria.

5. Dr. U. R. Onunwa — Lecturer in African Traditional Religion, University of Calabar, Nigeria.

6. Dr. Peter K. Sarpong — Bishop of the Catholic Diocese of Kumasi, Ghana.

7. Dr. P. A. Dopamu — Senior Lecturer, University of Ilorin, Nigeria.

8. Prof. A. O. Iwuagwu — Bishop of the Anglican Diocese of Aba - Nigeria.

9. Dr. E. M. Uka — Senior Lecturer, University of Calabar, Nigeria.

10. Dr. J. A. Kayode — Senior Lecturer, University of Ibadan, Nigeria.

11. Prof. S. N. Ezeanya — Archbishop, Onitsha Ecclesiastical Province, Onitsha, Nigeria. Formerly Professor of African Traditional Religion, University of Nigeria, Nsukka.

12. Prof. H. W. Turner — University of Birmingham, U.K.

13. Dr. P. Kalilombe — Professor of Religions, Selly Oak College, University of Birmingham, U.K.